NAZIS AND THE CINEMA

Nazis and the Cinema

Susan Tegel

hambledon
continuum

Hambledon Continuum is an imprint of Continuum Books
Continuum UK, The Tower Building, 11 York Road, London SE1 7NX
Continuum US, 80 Maiden Lane, Suite 704, New York, NY 10038

www.continuumbooks.com

First published 2007

British Library Cataloguing-in-Publication Data
A catalogue record for this book is available from the British Library.

ISBN 978 1 84725 000 1

Typeset by Egan Reid, Auckland, New Zealand
Printed and bound by MPG Books Ltd, Cornwall, Great Britain

Contents

Illustrations

For Peter

Preface

From the end of the First World War to the end of the Second World War, Germany had the largest film industry outside Hollywood. It is the second half of this period, when the Nazis were in power, which is the subject of this book. The approach is historical. Though individual films are discussed, they are always related to context. Film is a product of an industry. In the Third Reich, considerable control was exerted over that industry, though there was still some room for manoeuvre. Production histories are often revealing; the response to individual films by no means uniform.

Historians who write on film have often been criticized for concentrating too much on the so-called propaganda films. The boundaries, however, are blurred between propaganda films, often commissioned by the state, and other films, which were the majority, and which were not commissioned by the state but were nevertheless of use to the state. Such films were not devoid of political significance, even those which today might appear apolitical. Goebbels himself was clear that films which were less obviously political, but which pleased audiences, also achieved an important goal. In a variety of ways, all these films aided the Nazi cause. This, I hope, will be made clear.

Much work has already been done on cinema during the Third Reich, from which I have greatly benefited. This includes work by both historians and non-historians. My debts, I hope, will be clear from the notes.

Many of the films selected for close examination include Jewish characters, the best known being the villain of the oft-discussed, notorious *Jud Süss* (1940). But there were other films with Jewish characters, in the early years of the regime and during the war, though not after 1943. Such characters are villains, but their villainy is by no means uniform.

Almost forty years ago Dorothea Hollstein examined many of these films. Her thorough study was significant for uncovering these films, though her readings were not always nuanced; rarely did she consider the possibility that the particular film might not necessarily deliver the message. The list of films she compiled and then analysed is close to mine, though not identical, since included were one or two films in which, I would argue, the character though a villain was not actually a Jew. Régine-Mihal Friedman has also written on the image of the Jew in film during the Third Reich, though from a different perspective from mine, while the historian David Welch has also discussed the topic within his broader examination of propaganda and cinema during the Third Reich.

Aside from considering the treatment of Jews in Third Reich cinema, this study, I hope, will shed light on the contentious issue of how one might relate film to state policy, with particular regard to the Jews. Some of the difficulties inherent in the medium and in controlling and delivering the message, I would argue, make film slightly less useful to the state than has hitherto been believed. Not that the intention was not there; merely that delivery was not always possible.

Unfortunately, film reception – how films were received at the time rather than how they are perceived today – is more difficult to assess. Film criticism had been abolished; box office success, at a time when distribution was carefully controlled, can only tell us so much. The monitoring of audience response by the Security Services during the war is not an untainted source. Members of the audience could not be too free with their criticism, while the monitors themselves were hardly unbiased.

What is far easier to assess is what Joseph Goebbels as Minister of Propaganda wanted: he is free with his views in his diary, speeches and directives. We also discover from these sources when those in the film industry displeased him, though this was not always for political reasons. Conversely, it is also possible to work out, to some extent, what those involved in the industry wanted or did not want, bearing in mind that statements made only after 1945 should be treated with caution. Despite such caveats, it is still possible to learn more about cinema during the years 1933–45 and in particular its relation to politics.

Acknowledgements

I am grateful to the staff of a number of institutions, in particular the Wiener Library; the BFI National Library, the BFI National Archive; the British Library; the British Newspaper Library; the Imperial War Museum, Film and Video Archive; the Bundesarchiv; the Bundesarchiv-Filmarchiv; the Stiftung Deutsche Kinemathek; the Friedrich Wilhelm Murnau Stiftung; the Deutsches Institut für Filmkunde; the Bayerische Staatsarchiv; the Bayerische Staatsbibliothek; the Staatsanwaltschaft bei dem Landgericht Hamburg; Staatsarchiv Hamburg; Filmarchiv Austria; the United States Holocaust Memorial Museum; the Library of Congress, Moving Image Section; and the Yivo Institute for Jewish Research, US National Archives at College Park.

I have also greatly benefited from discussing films and film-making during the Third Reich with David Culbert, Jo Fox, Isa Van Eeghen and Roel Vande Winkel, as well as film propaganda in general with Nicholas Reeves and Weimar cinema with Cornelie Usborne. Barbara Rogers alerted me to material in the British press concerning German cinema and Susan Szczetnikowicz drew my attention to British newsreel coverage of the Third Reich as well as helping me to access material online. I would also like to thank Martin Sheppard for his editorial advice, patience and interest in this project from the outset, and finally my husband, Peter, for listening to me for so long and for reading and commenting on more than one draft.

1

Hitler: Image-Building

The First World War made Hitler. It created the conditions of defeat and upheaval in which a poorly educated drop-out and failed artist with extremist leanings could emerge as a serious contender for the German Chancellorship and then be appointed Chancellor. With a poor grasp of economics, a subject that bored him, but with a good grasp of propaganda, he had a sure political instinct. In the troubled Weimar Republic he found it easy to broaden his appeal, while defeat, hyper-inflation, the Depression, all weakened support for the republic.

Hitler believed in the power of propaganda, not only in words but also in images. In *Mein Kampf* he wrote:

> The picture in all its forms up to the film has greater possibilities. Here a man needs to use his brains even less; it suffices to look, or at most to read extremely brief texts, and thus many will more readily accept a pictorial presentation than read an article of any length. The picture brings them in a much briefer time, I might almost say at one stroke, the enlightenment which they obtain from written matter only after arduous reading.[1]

This idea seems to have come from the French psychologist, Gustav Le Bon, whom he probably never read, though Goebbels did.[2] Goebbels and other Nazis were fond of quoting him.[3] In *The Crowd, A Study of the Popular Mind* (1895), Le Bon contended that 'the masses think only in pictures.' Images, rather than texts, were a means of reaching large audiences, though this did not deter Hitler from giving lengthy speeches.

Photography and film have left us with the dominant images of the Third Reich. Hitler was filmed and photographed, his image appeared everywhere in Germany, becoming synonymous with the Third Reich, both at the time and subsequently. After 1933 his name was on everyone's lips; his image appeared in posters and photographs in all public places, on stamps, in film (newsreels), in newspapers and schoolbooks. His voice could also be heard on radio as well as in the newsreel. *Mein Kampf* was widely for sale. Modern means of mass communication were employed to the fullest to promote Hitler. By 1936 there was a fully-fledged Hitler cult in the media.[4]

Hitler was obsessed with visual symbols: swastikas, flags, posters, lavish public displays, spectacular rallies, which Albert Speer or Goebbels would orchestrate. Mass participation he believed superior to the mere ballot box. This of course did not stop him from fighting elections, even after he was made Chancellor, but he desired more than mere electoral success and certainly more than what could be allowed under the Weimar constitution. It was not a multiplicity of parties but one party, *his*, which would save Germany.

Despite his contempt for parliamentary democracy, once he was appointed Chancellor he insisted on holding another election in March 1933. Well aware of the political benefits of a semblance of legality, he campaigned with his ally the right-wing DNVP (*Deutschnationale Volkspartei* or German National People's Party). After the two parties obtained a majority, he set about dismantling the Weimar constitution. In the following year, after the death of Field Marshal Hindenburg, President of the Republic since 1925, he took over the post of President as well, claiming that the office had been bound up with the deceased.

The plebiscitary nature of that election suited Hitler. He would later hold several plebiscites and revelled in plebiscitary acclamations. After Hindenburg's death in 1934, he no longer shared power. This was affirmed by plebiscite, as the previous year had been the withdrawal from the League of Nations. In 1936, rearmament would be affirmed by plebiscite and in 1938 *Anschluss* with Austria. Both legality *and* mass approval had great propaganda value. Hitler had both an ear for and a flair for propaganda.

In *Mein Kampf* Hitler wrote about the importance of the flag, the Nazi flag, a white circle containing the swastika against a red background.[5] The red symbolized the social (the red flag having been stolen from the Socialists),[6] the white circle the nation, while the black swastika according to Hitler symbolized the triumph of the 'Aryan' and with it 'the idea of creative work, which as such has always been and always will be antisemitic'.[7] Apparently Hitler had already designed this flag in 1919 and the party standard in 1921. But the swastika flag was not adopted as the German national flag until one year after the death of Hindenburg in 1935. In March 1933 Hindenburg had agreed that the swastika flag could fly alongside the black–white–red imperial flag which had replaced the black–red–gold Weimar flag, the colours of 1848. Such colour changes reflected a disputed legacy. The swastika flag became fetishized in film, especially in Leni Riefenstahl's, with its forests of flags.

Elaborate flag ceremonies were introduced, the best known being the blood flag (*Blutfahne*) ceremony, which also appeared in the first two Riefenstahl documentaries. Incorporating an older important blood symbol associated with public law and the Burgundians who, according to the Song of the Nibelungs, set out from the Rhine under a 'blood banner',[8] this Nazi ceremony involved a swastika flag that had been drenched in the blood of Nazi martyrs, in particular, one who had died in the failed 1923 Munich putsch. In 1926 Hitler bestowed this bloody flag on the then head of the SS. Thereafter, in the presence of a witness to the 1923 putsch, new flags would be touched with this original blood flag. Such rituals had been established well before the Nazis took power.[9]

Before 1922 Hitler was occasionally known as the Führer; after Mussolini's March on Rome the title came into more frequent use. After the Munich putsch and his time in prison, during which his demoralized acolytes paid him frequent visits, the title stuck.[10] Without much of a movement, they were in need of a leader. The term began to take on more heroic overtones.

The fascist salute with right arm raised, and the words 'Heil Hitler!', the so-called 'German greeting' or 'Hitler salute', had been in use since 1923. In July 1933 it became compulsory for all public employees, replacing other forms of greeting as well as being used in correspondence. Whenever the national anthem was played, the right arm was raised. All soldiers and civil servants were required to swear an oath to Hitler.[11]

Hitler was a consummate actor.[12] The photographs from the 1920s are revealing. Heinrich Hoffmann, his personal photographer, first portrayed him in September 1923 shortly before the Beer Hall putsch. During the 1920s Hitler adopted a variety of striking poses in a variety of costumes, the most ludicrous and least flattering being in lederhosen, dating from 1926 and 1927 and issued as postcards after 1933.[13] One from 1925, never published, shows him seated in an armchair with an Alsatian dog.[14] In a set of six postcards from 1927, he appears in suit and tie in various poses, demonstrating his histrionic gifts, suggesting an actor delivering a melodramatic speech.[15] Another, also from 1927, is dramatically lit; Hitler again in a suit adopts a histrionic pose with one hand raised in a fist while the other clutches his breast.[16] Others show him in SA uniform.[17]

As Hitler approached power he usually appeared more formally dressed, in suit or in trench coat, or in both. He always wore a tie.[18] By February 1933 he appears statesmanlike, standing behind a desk.[19] One month later standing in military uniform he gazed straight at the camera. His trench coat is open, his Iron Cross clearly displayed on his chest; one hand is on hip, while the other is clenched. This postcard is entitled 'Reich Chancellor, Adolf Hitler'.[20] A few months later a three-quarters portrait shows him, again standing, this time wearing uniform, one hand on hip, his face well lit – the light illuminating his eyes, suggesting a leader with a vision.[21] By 1933 we have the more familiar and dominant Hitler image. In early 1936, wearing a smart double-breasted suit, he is seated on the edge of his very large desk (as befits a leader), clearly a prop since its surface is completely clear. His hands are folded across his chest, as he stares hard at the camera.[22] Other photographs, with children, reveal his softer side which he could well afford to display given his evident success as a strong leader: he autographs books for the Hitler Youth, talks to small children, is kissed by a little girl on his birthday and so on.[23] But a fierce one appeared as a postcard, entitled 'The Chancellor at Obersee near Berchtesgaden' (1933). With the snow-capped mountain peaks in the distance Hitler, wearing uniform, is seated – almost slumped – on a rock covered by his trench coat; glowering, he looks away from the camera; his hat is on his lap, a stick is in his hand, and his swastika armband is brightly displayed.[24] These photographs tell us that this tough, fierce, far-seeing leader can be gentle, but only with children, who are the nation's future.

The heroic image of Hitler formed part of the 'Hitler myth', which helped unite the Nazi movement. It made Hitler popular with a large majority of Germans but was often at odds with reality, protecting him while the party bore the brunt, especially when during the war things were not going well. Its most eloquent exponent was Goebbels, for whom the personality cult had great propaganda value. Towards the end of 1941, Goebbels claimed that his greatest propaganda achievement had been the creation of the Hitler myth.[25] Hitler's own popularity, however, never led to his party's popularity: often his popularity was even at the expense of the party.[26] Local Nazi leaders could be known as 'little Hitlers', which was not praise.[27]

The coming of war did not diminish Hitler's popularity; that happened only after conditions deteriorated. The first winter of the Russian campaign marked the end of the 'sunny Hitler weather'.[28] The failure to capture Moscow in December 1941 coincided with US entry into the war.[29] Stalingrad, the psychological and military turning point in the war, came as a shock for the ill-prepared Germans. The separation between party and Führer began to blur. Even with Allied air supremacy, the bombing of German cities, the failure of the African campaign, Allied landings in Italy, the fall of Mussolini, a minority still believed all was not lost.[30] The July 1944 attempt on his life provided a brief rally in support for Hitler.[31] But rhetoric alone proved insufficient.

Goebbels, a film buff, was keen that propaganda should come in a palatable form, in the guise of entertainment. Hitler liked film but, in common with Lenin, preferred his propaganda straight. However, he gave Goebbels a free hand while Goebbels, in turn, always sought approval from his hero, or the 'boss' as he often referred to him in the diaries he wrote for publication.[32] During the war, Hitler forswore films, associating them with a frivolity incompatible with the seriousness of war. Careful of his image, he also avoided being seen in public at premières, even of a major propaganda feature film such as the antisemitic *Jud Süss*, though members of the SS responsible for having located some of the Jewish extras were clamouring for tickets.[33] This reveals a different response to cinema. For Goebbels entertainment was important as propaganda, especially later in the war when he recognized the value of giving an impression of business as usual. For Hitler, as the supreme commander leading the war, cinema was frivolous and attending a première a dereliction of duty, while for Goebbels there was no conflict between propaganda, entertainment and the war effort.

Hitler did like to relax by watching film. A favourite after coming to power was *King Kong*, which he often viewed just before bed.[34] Dinner guests were also invited to watch with him late in the evening. During dinner, one of his servants, drawn from his bodyguard, the *Leibstandarte*, would present him with a list of films provided by Goebbels. They would include both non-German films and German films yet to be released. After dinner everyone, guests and servants, would watch the film of Hitler's choice.[35] In 1937 Goebbels's Christmas present to Hitler was thirty-two film classics from the previous four years, plus twelve Mickey Mouse cartoons.[36] During the Sudeten crisis, Hitler watched films with his regular entourage and favoured guests such as Albert Speer.[37] When Ribbentrop was in Moscow the following year negotiating the pact with Molotov, Hitler was at his Alpine retreat, the Berghof, watching a film with Goebbels, though, on this occasion given the tense international situation, as he waited to learn whether he could proceed against Poland without interference from the East, he was apparently, only 'half-watching'.[38]

Hitler had no desire to be heard on the radio; he did not like the sound of his voice in that medium, further evidence of the care with which he guarded and cultivated his image. The Nazis' first disappointment after they took power was to discover that Hitler, confined in the studio without an audience, was an ineffective speaker who shouted at the microphone.[39] During his first broadcast, his 'Call to the German people' (1 February 1933), delivered in a monotone, he sweated profusely.[40] It produced so many complaints of unintelligibility that it had to be re-recorded.[41] Hitler did not speak from a studio again until the very end of the war, by which time he was helped by improved recording methods.[42] He was heard live on radio, but only when addressing public meetings; sometimes they were scheduled specifically for that purpose. Approximately fifty were transmitted during his first year in office.[43] He was stimulated by his rapport with audiences,[44] which earlier he had touched on in *Mein Kampf*:

> the speaker gets a continuous correction of his speech from the crowd he is addressing, since he can always see in the faces of his listeners to what extent they can follow his arguments with understanding and whether the impression and the effect of his words lead to the desired goal.[45]

During the war Hitler had some speeches recorded especially for radio, but Goebbels read out some of his addresses to the German people. Extracts from most of his speeches were read by announcers once he had delivered them.[46] Hitler was more in his element haranguing large crowds, or addressing his acolytes, or charming women at his evening or lunchtime gatherings though on occasion he also lost control. This was witnessed, though never captured on film.

The first appearance of the Nazis on film was in 1922, when a Nazi demonstration was shown in a newsreel; but the first Nazi Party film, that is one for which they themselves were responsible, was a recording of the 1927 party rally.[47] After that every rally was filmed. They were undistinguished until Leni Riefenstahl began to direct them, though even her first effort in 1933 was not especially remarkable.

In the newsreels prior to 1933, Hitler appears both less important but also different. Such newsreels are purely reportorial, without fanfare, and of course were not controlled by the Nazi Party, though the two main newsreels were controlled by the right-wing media magnate Alfred Hugenberg who, once he became Hitler's electoral ally, gave Hitler more coverage. Hitler does not appear particularly different from other politicians, for example, when emerging from a vehicle. The cinematography is not especially good and no great care is taken with the camera angle. The function is to report rather than to enhance. After 1933 this changed. And with Riefenstahl, especially with her second attempt, *Triumph of the Will*, Hitler was endowed with a godlike transcendence thanks to the low-angle shot absent from the pre-1933 newsreel. That is how Hitler has come to be memorialized in celluloid.

Aside from newsreels and the Riefenstahl documentaries, Hitler appeared in only one feature film, *Wunschkonzert (Request Concert)* (1940), where he put in a fleeting appearance in an early sequence taken from footage from the opening of the Berlin Olympics. Unlike Stalin, no actor could play him on film. And no film was made about his life or which alluded to his life story.[48] His image did appear in feature films but only in portraits: paintings or photographs hanging on walls.

During the war Hitler wore uniform. He appointed one of Riefenstahl's excellent cameramen, Walter Frentz, whose work he considered sublime, to act as his personal cameraman at his wartime headquarters. Frentz knew the best angle and lighting to suit his subject, and Hitler refused to allow anyone else to film him. Hitler was against the use of additional lighting, which led Frentz to modify a French camera to enable adequate filming, though this did not work every time – some of Hitler's newsreel appearances were dimly lit.[49]

Hitler also did not want to be filmed with original sound.[50] Indeed, as the war progressed he showed reluctance to appear in any newsreels. Prior to the war he appeared in almost every third newsreel, on a variety of occasions: receptions, state ceremonies, party rituals and so on.[51] Once the war began, and to Goebbels's great irritation, his newsreel appearances became less frequent:

> It is a pity that the Führer is loath to have himself seen in the newsreel. We find ourselves in a real dilemma with regard to this wish. On the one hand, the Führer does not want to appear in the picture, on the other hand, countless letters from the public ask us not only to show the Führer but to show him as much as possible. I can find no way out of these opposing wishes.[52]

On a later occasion, Goebbels complained:

Again the Führer cut out all shots of himself, which is very damaging for the newsreel. But the Führer, as is known, is extremely frugal in showing himself. I am in a fix, the people want to see him but the Führer does not want to be shown in the newsreel. What shall I do?[53]

As early as 1940 Hitler stubbornly refused to have the original soundtrack of his speeches included in the newsreels. Goebbels tried to get him to change his mind, given public complaints, but to no avail. Only in 1944 did he occasionally relent and allow the original soundtrack to be heard, but then only sparingly.[54]

After Stalingrad, Hitler became a virtual recluse. He delivered only two more speeches in public, and no more than five broadcasts, while the Munich anniversary celebrations of February 1943, 1944 and 1945 as well as November 1944 were read for him in his absence.[55] In poor health, he had a tremor to hide, possibly the onset of Parkinson's.[56] After the 20 July attempt on his life, he reappeared to reassure the German people, and was seen welcoming the deposed Mussolini shortly afterwards.[57] One of his last photographs, which also appeared in a newsreel, is dated 20 March 1945, six weeks before his suicide. In it he is seen shaking hands with a twelve-year-old Hitler Youth, one of a group assembled in the courtyard of the Reich Chancellery where his bunker was located. The boy has been awarded the Iron Cross for bravery.[58]

2

Nazi Propaganda

Military defeat was difficult for many Germans to accept. The stab-in-the back legend, which surfaced in the early 1920s, blamed civilian politicians – the Social Democrats, left Catholics (in the Catholic Centre Party) and left-wing Liberals – who, infected with pacifism and internationalism, had sued for peace on 9 November 1918, two days before the Armistice. Though already active politically, Hitler was not responsible for the legend, which was created by others on the extreme right. But within a short time the civilian politicians became for him the 'November Criminals', and the 'Ninth November' a sacred day in the Nazi calendar. Five years later, on 9 November 1923, the Munich putsch took place; fifteen years after that, on 9 November 1938, *Kristallnacht* was unleashed.

It was actually the High Command of the German General Staff which had decided in the autumn of 1918 that the war could not be won, though this was not made public. A key figure in this decision was General Erich Ludendorff.[1] Later he and another member of the General Staff, Paul von Hindenburg, blamed the defeat on the effectiveness of British propaganda which, in their view, had demoralized German troops.[2] 'We were hypnotized by the enemy's propaganda as a rabbit by a snake,' Ludendorff wrote.[3] (German propaganda had in fact been made the army's responsibility.) The British were not averse to taking credit, though not at the expense of downplaying their victory on the battlefield. At least a victory in the war of words provided proof that right as well as might was on their side.

To what extent propaganda actually changed the course of the war cannot be known. At the time, however, many believed that it had. Allied propaganda played a role in the collapse of German morale – whether civilian or military or a combination of both – but the unwillingness of the Kaiser and the conservative elites to concede democratic reform was probably of greater significance.[4] For the losers, however, namely the Germans, blaming the defeat on propaganda suggested at the very least that they had fought honourably, since propaganda already implied dirty tricks.[5] Germany had lost the propaganda war – that was never in dispute, only whether it had cost them the war.

The Nazis soon became the loudest post-war critics of Germany's wartime propaganda. Once in power, Joseph Goebbels's deputy in the Propaganda

Ministry, Eugen Hadamovsky, claimed in *Propaganda and National Power*:

> The German people lost the war against the entire world not through the weakness of
> arms or soldiers, but through the bureaucratic barrenness of her leading state officials.
> They were defeated and her spirit was broken not on the battlefield but in the battle of
> words. They were not even given a slogan they could use while the enemy had 'against
> the Hun', 'for world peace', 'for the League of Nations'.[6]

Hitler described Lord Northcliffe's anti-German campaign as 'an inspired work
of genius' and in *Mein Kampf* devoted two chapters to the subject of propaganda.
The more important chapter, 'War Propaganda', appears in the first volume
published in June 1925 under the title, *Eine Abrechnung* (*A Reckoning*). The second
volume, *Die Nationalsozialistische Bewegung* (*The National Socialist Movement*),
which appeared in December 1926, also contains a chapter 'Propaganda and
Organization'. (The two volumes were brought together in 1930.) The latter is
mainly concerned with disorganization after the Munich putsch, and a settling
of scores for its failure, but there Hitler also draws a distinction between an
organizer, who primarily must be a psychologist, take people as they are, know
them and not underestimate them in the mass, and a great theoretician who
rarely is an organizer, and even more rarely a great leader. An agitator can be
one: he has the ability to transmit an idea to the broad masses, must always be
a psychologist and, even if only a demagogue, is still more suited for leadership
than the 'unworldly theoretician who is ignorant of people'. '*Leading means: being
able to move the masses*' (Hitler's emphasis).[7]

It is, however, in the earlier volume that Hitler writes extensively on propaganda,
which occasionally accounts for the mistaken view that he wrote one rather than
two chapters on the subject. Here one gleans his views, which in true Hitler
style might best be described as ramblings. Drawing little distinction between
agitation and propaganda, he concedes that it was his enemies (the British) who
were the successful propagandists. Prior to the war, however, another enemy,
the Austrian Social Democrats, were also 'masters' of propaganda, as was the
antisemitic Christian-Social Mayor of Vienna from 1897 to 1910, Karl Lueger, for
whom Hitler had a grudging admiration despite his hostility to Pan Germanism
which made him a political enemy.[8]

According to Hitler, the failure of wartime German propaganda stared
'every soldier in the face'. It had 'spurred' him on 'to take up the question of
propaganda':

> what we failed to do, the enemy did, with amazing skill and really brilliant calculation. I
> myself learned enormously from this enemy war propaganda. But time passed and left
> no trace in the minds of all those who should have benefited ...[9]

While the British regarded propaganda 'as a weapon of the first order', the Germans considered it 'the last resort of unemployed politicians and a comfortable haven for slackers'.[10] British 'atrocity propaganda' revealed a 'brilliant knowledge of the primitive sentiments of the broad masses'.

'Ruthless' as well as 'brilliant, it created the preconditions for moral steadfastness at the front, even in the face of the greatest actual defeats, and just as strikingly it pilloried the German enemy as the sole guilty party for the outbreak of the war'. He went on to say that 'the rabid, impudent bias and persistence with which this lie was expressed' understood 'the emotional, always extreme attitude of the great masses and for this reason was believed'.[11]

Hitler criticized Austrian and German propaganda for presenting the enemy as ridiculous, patently not the case when they finally met up. Allied propaganda, in contrast, depicted the Germans as barbarians and Huns. That prepared their soldiers for the terrors of war, preserved them from disappointments and at the same time increased their rage against the enemy. As a result, he concluded (revealing a psychological astuteness), the British soldier unlike the German never felt misinformed.[12]

Propaganda, Hitler claimed, was akin to a form of advertising, 'whether in the field of business or politics'.[13] It should not be addressed to the intelligentsia but 'always and exclusively to the less educated masses'.[14] It 'must be popular and its intellectual level ... adjusted to the most limited intelligence ... the greater the mass it is intended to reach, the lower its purely intellectual level'. 'The over-whelming majority' he characterized as 'so feminine by nature and attitude' that their thoughts and actions are determined less by 'sober reasoning' and more by 'emotion and feeling'. As in their atrocity propaganda, the 'English propagandists understood ... most brilliantly ... the primitive sentiments of the broad masses'.[15] Propaganda 'must confine itself to a few points and repeat them over and over ... persistence is the first and most important requirement for success'.[16] That was a rule Hitler never forgot. The masses, he concluded, are 'slow-moving'. 'Only after the simplest ideas are repeated thousands of times will [they] finally remember them.' Initially, the claims of enemy propaganda were so 'impudent' that people thought them 'insane' but later they were believed. The German revolutionary slogans of 1918 originated in the enemy's war propaganda.[17] Telling a lie often enough until it was believed to be the truth, it seems, came via the British.

Though propaganda was highly important for Hitler, he nevertheless proved incapable of realizing that its effectiveness relied on a favourable context. Loath to accept German military failure, he was also loath to accept the justness of the British cause, for after all it was Germany which had overrun Europe. That made it possible to depict Germans as the dreaded 'Hun' or 'Boche'. Since Hitler was bent on a similar path, whether a *Drang nach Osten* or *Westen*, it is not surprising that he overlooked this aspect.

Propaganda has a long history. The word, derived from the Latin *propagare*, to propagate or spread the word, was first used explicitly during the Counter-Reformation in 1622 when the Catholic Church set up a new papal department, a committee of cardinals or sacred congregation, charged with the propagation of the faith (*Sacra Congregatio de Propaganda Fide*). This proselytizing group was entrusted with the task of winning back the faithful (those attracted to Protestantism). By 1718 the word propaganda had come into use in English where it meant the advancement of sincerely held beliefs. During the nineteenth century, political visionaries in France also used the term propaganda, by which they meant persuading others through reason to see the rightness of their cause.[18] Nevertheless, in 1911 the *Encyclopædia Britannica* still associated propaganda with religion.[19]

During the First World War the British set up an office for enemy propaganda, headed by the Germanophobe Lord Northcliffe who was closely associated with the popular press – in 1896 he had founded the tabloid *Daily Mail*. Lord Beaverbrook, another press magnate, was made Minister of Information for the home front. 'Propaganda' was reserved for the enemy; the home front received 'information', while heavy censorship (negative propaganda) suppressed unpleasant truths – propaganda and censorship went hand in hand. Both offices were quickly dismantled after the war, by which time propaganda had become associated with lies and atrocity stories and had begun to acquire its negative meaning as persuasion by underhand methods. By the Second World War the British had learned that for propaganda to be effective it must not deviate too far from the truth.

Propaganda the phenomenon, however, antedated the coining of the word and can be traced to the ancient world when it was not enough to win the battle. Divine support had to be demonstrated to consolidate the royal position and elicit appropriate behaviour from the people. Religion played its role in warfare and had a psychological significance. Deception and disinformation also played a role, and morale had to be boosted, using not only words but also statues, buildings, coins, etc. War propaganda has been described as 'coming of 'age' under the Greeks. Rhetoric, the study of the language of persuasion, also comes via the Greeks.[20]

Forms of persuasion therefore are not new, though the means for persuasion were greatly extended in the first half of the twentieth century (popular press, then film and later radio). It is, however, easier to describe the organization and aims of propaganda than its reception, given the problem of assessing public opinion.

What was new was the setting up of a ministry of propaganda in peacetime – additional evidence, were that needed, of the Nazi commitment to persuading Germans of the rightness of their cause. Through its close association with the

Nazis, propaganda has acquired its most negative associations. So successful was Nazi propaganda perceived to be – based on the impressive German output of films, posters, mass rallies and speeches as well as Goebbels's own claims – that it has been argued that German propaganda was as successful as the Nazis believed it to be, and that this was 'the war that Hitler won', which also kept Germans fighting to the bitter end.[21] That view has not gone unchallenged: propaganda has its limits and in the German context worked best when reinforcing commonly held positions such as anti-Bolshevism, or a belief in the iniquity of the Versailles Treaty or the failure of Weimar.[22] Propaganda cannot work miracles; it flourishes in the right context and builds on existing sentiments. For Aldous Huxley: 'The propagandist … canalises an already existing stream … where there is no water, he digs in vain.'[23] It proved more difficult to persuade Germans of the benefits of a *Volksgemeinschaft* – though it is now thought there was more success in this than previously acknowledged. While old loyalties such as class or religion were not abandoned, the notion of a 'national community' was in itself still considered desirable.[24]

Even if Nazi propaganda was less effective than hitherto believed, what cannot be disputed is its importance for the Nazi leadership, and the brilliance of its Minister of Propaganda. Goebbels's reputation remains intact. On 12 March 1933, only days after the elections, the Reich Ministry for Popular Enlightenment and Propaganda was established by presidential decree. Nine days later the first concentration camps were set up to house the regime's opponents. For in the Third Reich, propaganda also went hand in hand with coercion and terror. Suppression of anti-Nazi opinion made the task of propaganda easier.

Appointed to head the new ministry was the thirty-six-year-old Goebbels who had been head of party propaganda since late 1928 and who was closely involved in its creation. The decision to set up the ministry had been taken earlier, but it was deemed advisable not to make this public until after the Reichstag elections in early March.[25] In many respects Goebbels was not a typical Nazi. Dark-haired, dark-eyed, small of stature with a deformed foot due to a childhood illness, he was hardly an ideal Nordic type, about which his enemies did not keep silent. His physical handicap, which had prevented him from fighting during the First World War, proved a political handicap in his relations with leading Nazis. He studied literature at several universities, but failed in his attempt to secure Friedrich Gundolf, the Goethe expert and professor of literature at Heidelberg, to act as his thesis supervisor. Gundolf was Jewish; the professor who eventually took on the task was half-Jewish. Goebbels was not yet antisemitic.[26] After discovering in 1922 that his fiancée was half-Jewish, he still maintained the relationship until 1926, shortly before leaving for Berlin.[27] During this time he wrote an expressionist novel, *Michael: ein deutsches Schicksal in Tagebuchblättern* (*Michael, a German Fate in the Leaves of a Diary*), which took five years to find a publisher, the National Socialist publishing house, Eher Verlag, and which only began to sell well once the Nazis were in power, reaching its fourteenth printing by the eve of the war.[28] Goebbels even sought work on liberal papers as well as with the Jewish publishing house, Mosse. Initially a conservative, he became involved with the *völkisch* parties but was quickly disenchanted. Only after reading Houston Stewart Chamberlain's *Foundations of the Nineteenth Century* (1899) did he become antisemitic; later, in 1926 at Bayreuth, he met the author, whom he described as the 'pathbreaker'. Another influence was Oswald Spengler who had predicted the 'decline of the West'. This could be averted, Goebbels now believed, through the 'elimination' of the Jewish element.[29] In early 1924 after reading the press coverage of Hitler's trial for the Beer Hall putsch, he began to sing Hitler's praises in the *völkisch* press. This was well before he had had the opportunity to read anything by him or to hear him speak.

After Hitler's release from prison, the Nazi Party was relaunched. The reorganization in the northwest was entrusted to Gregor Strasser, who came from the party's revolutionary wing, a fact for which he paid with his life in the 1934 purge. The Rhineland was more industrial than Bavaria, which partly explains the existence of this left wing. In early 1925 Goebbels joined the party and worked closely with Strasser. By that time he had become aware of his own gifts as a public speaker and threw himself into agitation and propaganda. The combination of being a Rhinelander and having previously led a somewhat bohemian life, which made him anti-bourgeois, put him on the party's revolutionary left, more drawn to socialism than nationalism. His then nickname was 'Robespierre'.[30]

Goebbels's first meeting with Hitler took place in the summer of 1925. By 1926 he had begun to see reason, or rather Hitler's way of seeing things, in the ideological conflict then raging within the party. Those on the right (mainly in Bavaria) held private property sacred – even that belonging to the despised aristocracy – in contrast to those on the left like Goebbels and Strasser. But Goebbels chose to side with Hitler because his belief in Hitler's mission overcame his commitment to 'socialism'.[31] The Strasser wing lost out and soon became sidelined.

In late 1926 Goebbels was sent to Berlin as Gauleiter for the Berlin-Brandenburg region; someone from outside the region was needed to sort out internal conflicts. He and the SA took to the streets, especially in areas which were mainly Communist or Social Democratic strongholds. For Goebbels, activism was inseparable from propaganda. As he later observed: 'he who can conquer the streets can conquer the masses; and he who conquers the masses conquers the state.'[32] The following year (1927) he founded his own National Socialist paper for the Berlin area, *Der Angriff* (*The Attack*), which by late 1930 began appearing weekly. In 1928, he was elected to the Reichstag, one of twelve deputies in the Nazi breakthrough. In 1929 Hitler made him the party's director of propaganda

(*Reichspropagandaleiter*), with Heinrich Himmler, serving as his deputy, but the latter soon left to take over the command of the SS.

In December 1930 Goebbels and other Berlin Nazis disrupted the showing of *All Quiet on the Western Front*, using white mice, stink bombs and sneeze powder in the Berlin cinema, and added insult to injury by demanding a refund on their tickets.[33] Symptomatic of the nationalist right's preoccupation with propaganda was the role of Alfred Hugenberg, who soon became a Hitler ally, having already built a media empire which included newspapers as well as Ufa.[34] The right-wing press had opposed the novel by Erich Maria Remarque, an international best-seller when published less than two years previously. That this novel was now being turned into a film by the American military victor further upset right-wing radicals. Not only was it a form of cultural imperialism which undermined Germany as well as weakened her film industry but Hollywood also stood accused of producing an inflammatory war film which propagated the war guilt lie. Nevertheless, despite the hostility of the Minister of Defence, Wilhelm Groener, *All Quiet on the Western Front* had passed the censor subject to a few cuts. Another element in the disruption was Goebbels's ongoing battle with the Berlin police commissioner, whose deputy commissioner was Jewish. A recent attack on the deputy had resulted in the suspension of *Der Angriff*, causing the party considerable financial loss.[35]

The cinema disruption and Nazi protests led to the film's withdrawal on the grounds of endangering public order.[36] Eventually, Universal Studios made some judicious cuts designed for a German audience. The film was re-released in September 1931, again accompanied by disruptions though this time confined to the provinces.[37] It is, however, worth noting that for a twelve-month period covering 1931–32 the film ranked sixth at the German box office, the only American film in the top ten.[38]

Goebbels believed his campaign against the antiwar film had the backing of the German public. Aside from the right-wing press, it also had support from several state governments. The German Federation of Cinema Owners called for a boycott against films which provoked public disturbances.[39] Moreover, it had an impact on film production since certain kinds of films were now seen as unlikely to pass the censor.[40]

The evening following the disruption, Goebbels claimed forty thousand people demonstrated; in reality it was only six thousand, though street battles did rage.[41] 'Fantastic! Berlin West has never seen anything like it,' he recorded in his diary. 'What a thrill! Onward! Onwards!'[42] Shortly after the Nazis came to power, the film was banned; Remarque's book was burned in the Berlin Opernplatz inferno on 10 May 1933. Nazi opposition to the film was but one of many incidents revealing Goebbels's flair for attracting attention and influencing public opinion.

His success in staging parades, battles and demonstrations on the streets of the German capital, combined with his journalistic talents – he always spoke and wrote with great precision and clarity – made Goebbels the obvious candidate to head the new Propaganda Ministry, though Hitler's right-wing allies, in particular Vice-Chancellor Franz von Papen and his Minister for Economics and Nutrition, Hugenberg, who had often been in Goebbels's sights, were not keen to see him appointed. Goebbels himself had never been reconciled to the party's alliance with the right-wing DNVP, a legacy of his earlier association with the party's left wing.[43]

Officially the ministry was set up to promote 'enlightenment and propaganda among the populace as to the policies of the Reich government and the national reconstruction of the German fatherland'. Unofficially, it was to be 'a mental mobilization of the masses', so that ultimately, as Goebbels told a government press conference on 16 March, they would offer no resistance to the Nazis: the people were to begin 'to think uniformly, to react uniformly, and to place themselves body and soul at the disposal of the government'.[44] There were to be no competing messages. It was not enough for the government to have 52 per cent of the people behind it (the combined electoral support for the Nazis and the Nationalists) and then terrorize the other 48 per cent. The first task was to win over that 48 per cent.[45] Terror, however, was not abandoned.

One of Goebbels's earliest actions was a call to party organizations to boycott Jewish businesses. This was to begin on 1 April 1933, the day that the Propaganda Ministry first began to function, and was intended as revenge for the negative response to the new government in the British and American press. That response was described as a plot fomented by 'world Jewry'. A few days later the Reichstag passed a law excluding non-Aryans from the civil service. Jews were arrested, Jewish shops smashed and synagogues raided, but Goebbels was disappointed that the action failed to elicit the desired response from the population as a whole.[46] Obviously, more work needed to be done.

The creation of the ministry was also a significant step in merging the party and the state, as Goebbels continued to act as head of party propaganda at the *Reichspropagandaamt* (Central Propaganda Office), a parallel bureaucracy. By heading the ministry, he was able to strengthen his own position within the party as well as be in a position which allowed him to determine the scope of propaganda. Part of his remit also included responsibility for organizing public celebrations.

Goebbels, however, was never popular with other leading Nazis. He could count amongst his enemies the former Luftwaffe ace, Hermann Goering, who as Minister of Prussia often came into conflict with him, since there was an overlap in cultural matters pertaining to Prussia, the largest region, especially over the control of the theatres and appointments. Another enemy was Himmler, his former deputy at the party's propaganda office; another was Alfred Rosenberg, who supervised the ideological education of party members; another was Dr Otto Dietrich who was Vice President of the Press Chamber and Deputy Chairman of the German news service (*Deutsche Nachrichtendienst*) and later government press chief. To Goebbels's disappointment, at the outset of the war the Foreign Minister, Joachim von Ribbentrop, was given control of propaganda relating to foreign affairs and foreign countries, with the Propaganda Ministry being forced to put its resources at the disposal of the Foreign Ministry.[47]

Never part of the inner circle, Goebbels was also not always in favour with Hitler, especially between 1936 and 1938 when he was conducting an affair with the Czech actress Lida Baarova which came to an end on the eve of the Munich agreement, after Magda Goebbels asked Hitler to intervene. Goebbels's enthusiasm for cinema extended to film actresses, which was held against him by fellow ministers. But if diplomacy was once considered war by other means, for Goebbels propaganda was war by other means. Once war commenced he came into his own, given the importance which Hitler attached to propaganda and his regard for Goebbels's talents.

In 1933 Goebbels quickly established an elaborate bureaucracy to control the arts: cinema, theatre, music, fine arts. He also established a third institution in autumn 1933, the *Reichskulturkammer* (Reich Chamber of Culture) or RKK, to exert additional control over and define the new German culture. He appointed himself its president. Thus propaganda was controlled through three different institutions: the ministry, the RKK and the party's central propaganda office with Goebbels acting as minister, president and director (in that order) of those institutions.

The ministry was divided into seven departments (expanded to fourteen during the war): legislation and legal; coordination of popular enlightenment and propaganda, race and travel; radio; national and foreign press, journalism; film and film censorship, newsreel; theatre; music, fine arts, people's culture. The staff were eager young Nazis, who were not only better educated – more than half had been to university and many had doctorates – than those who had joined the SA, but were also younger, often too young to have served in the war. They were usually of bourgeois or petty bourgeois background like Goebbels himself. Hitler also gave Goebbels his economic adviser, Walther Funk, to act as his manager until 1937, which enabled Goebbels to concentrate on propaganda rather than administration. Conflict with the Interior Ministry or other ministries was, however, not avoided. Goebbels did not get everything he wanted, though he was given control of 'all areas involving intellectual influence on the nation'.[48]

Radio was a medium the Nazis promoted. Nationalized prior to the Nazi takeover (in 1932), it now came under strict state control. In May 1933, German manufacturers agreed to produce a cheap mass-produced radio, the

Volksempfänger (people's receiver like the people's car, the Volkswagen), nick-named the 'Goebbels Blaster'.[49] Within a few months 100,000 had reached the market. Nearly three and a half million would be sold. By 1934 the power of transmitters was increased by 30 per cent. By 1936 half of all German households owned a radio.[50] By the outbreak of war, 3,500,000 had been produced and 70 per cent of households had radios, some of which were now technically superior.[51] Sales also helped the ministry financially: between 1933 and 1943 almost 90 per cent of the ministry's current expenditure was covered by the sale of radio licences after the Post Office took its cut.[52] Public ceremonies were broadcast and Hitler's speeches were heard on the radio in their entirety, as opposed to the fleeting exposure in newsreels. 'All Germany Listens to the Führer on the People's Radio' was the title of one 1936 poster. Loudspeakers were also introduced into factories, but plans to install loudspeakers in the streets were cut short by the war.[53]

Radio could also be listened to in the privacy of the home. Once ownership of radios became widespread, daily or evening entertainment could be enjoyed within the family, which strengthened the private sphere.[54] On the other hand, one might claim the public intruded on the private sphere. There was, however, safety in listening from home: listening to foreign broadcasts was banned but it has been estimated that roughly half of radio owners, which in 1941 was two-thirds of households, were doing this.[55]

Film, in contrast, was a mass entertainment, watched by a mass audience which, to quote Goebbels, was 'a medium of communication that appeals to an audience that is at the same time a mass'.[56] It was this medium, though not necessarily for the above reason, which was most dear to Goebbels's heart. A week after the Nazis came to power he described it as 'one of the most modern and far-reaching media that there is for influencing the masses today'.[57] Many twentieth-century dictators were devotees of film: Josef Stalin, for example, often viewed the same film over and over; Hitler and Mussolini were also fans of film, though not in quite the same category as Stalin. Goebbels was in a class of his own: as obsessive about film as Stalin, but occupying a different position since he was not running the country but serving the dictator who was. Passionate about film, he believed it eminently suitable to serve the state as a vehicle for propaganda and took an active and controlling interest in the German film industry. He was responsible for feature films, newsreels and documentaries (including shorts), though not for the pioneering Leni Riefenstahl documentaries of the first three Nuremberg rallies after the Nazi takeover which gave extended coverage to the rallies and to Hitler. These had been directly commissioned by Hitler and were not under Goebbels's direct control. And with *Olympia*, her film on the Olympics, he was also kept at a distance.

Goebbels's role was that of overseer, intervening as and when it seemed necessary, comparable to the head of a Hollywood studio or, to be precise, head of *all* Hollywood studios, with the added advantage that he had been appointed by a head of state who did not face re-election. Though the view that he was an all-powerful 'Nazi film dictator' has long been out of date, he was nevertheless (in his own words) in charge of the 'greatest cultural business in the world'.[58]

Two weeks after the creation of the Propaganda Ministry, Goebbels addressed radio and film personnel, calling on them to produce a film comparable to Eisenstein's *Battleship Potemkin*: 'If a nationalist sees the film *Battleship Potemkin* today he is in danger of becoming a Communist, because the film is so well made.'[59] This expressed his profound belief in the power of film propaganda. However, despite the arts generally serving as vehicles for propaganda, and feature film in particular, Goebbels still preferred the message to be covert rather than overt: 'Propaganda becomes ineffective the moment we are aware of it,' he declared.[60]

For the next twelve years Goebbels was responsible for determining German culture: overseeing radio, music, theatre and cinema, as well as ultimately the press. Organizing public celebrations, he also orchestrated *Kristallnacht*, created the Hitler myth and rallied Germans to the cause of war, which after Stalingrad became 'total war'. In the summer of 1944 Hitler made him responsible for waging total war, granting him far-reaching powers in civil and military areas. In late April 1945 after Hitler learned of Himmler's betrayal, he designated Goebbels as his successor. By then the Third Reich's cheerleader was confined to the bunker, and decided instead to commit suicide shortly after his Führer, taking his wife and children with him. Soviet soldiers who later searched the bunker discovered loose diary pages recording his final entries. They had been hidden under some film scripts, evidence that (even in adversity) he had not lost his enthusiasm for new film projects.[61]

3

The German Film Industry to 1918

Almost overnight, cinema became the most popular leisure time activity in the first half of the twentieth century, its technology a product of the second industrial revolution. Developing at the same time as the popular press, it coincided with rapid urbanization and appealed to an ever-growing mass urban population. Cinema, however, unlike the press, was intended as entertainment, mass entertainment.

The beginnings of cinema are usually dated to 28 December 1895, when the Lumière brothers, Louis and Auguste, whose family were the largest European manufacturers of photographic plate, first showed films in a Paris basement using 35 mm film. They filmed at sixteen frames a second, which became the standard film speed for the next twenty-five years. But almost two months before this screening, on 1 November, the Skladowsky brothers (Max, Emil and Eugen) offered a fifteen-minute programme of 'living photography' at the Berlin Wintergarten, an upmarket variety theatre.[1] Their system of projection differed from that of the Lumières; what they offered was also aesthetically and technically inferior.[2] Their Bioscope system proved cumbersome. Two years later they toured Europe but never established a stable production company. Even earlier, in 1891, the American inventor, Thomas Edison, after a visit to Paris, had developed a system to complement his phonograph, using Eastman-Kodak film; he even built a studio on the grounds of his New Jersey laboratory, the first film studio, but his films lasted a mere twenty seconds.

Beginning with two-reelers, films soon became longer. The camera could go virtually anywhere and did so, providing footage from remote parts of the world in short travelogues, able to show everyday scenes from specific locales as well as catastrophes such as earthquakes. Some events, such as the Dreyfus case, were reconstructed for the camera. Royalty also took an interest, both in front of the camera and behind; Tsar Nicholas II, amongst others, was an enthusiast.

By the early twentieth century, feature film, or to be precise fiction film, which became the main feature, began to dominate programmes. Fictional plots – shot outdoors or, if indoors, often against a painted background – were cheaper and easier to produce. Most were done in a continuous take. They proved popular. Programmes became longer and changed more frequently. Music was added: piano, or even a house orchestra, as in the American vaudeville theatres catering for the middle class – unlike the nickelodeon, which as its name implies, was a theatre (odeon) with a nickel or five-cent entry ticket.

Initially, in German urban areas films were part of variety theatre, one item in a programme; in the countryside the *Wanderkinos* were part of roving tent shows at local fairs and carnivals. By 1904, urban areas had the *Ladenkino*, shop spaces used exclusively for film, or the *Vorstadtkino*, a suburban space – both comparable to the nickelodeon.[3] By 1910 the *Lichtspieltheater*, the purpose-built theatre, was more centrally located. Keen to attract the affluent and move out of the fairground, the penny arcade or the nickelodeon, filmmakers hoped that longer and better-quality films would draw in the middle classes. Subject matter changed, imitating middle-class forms of the novel and the legitimate theatre.[4] Stage actors were persuaded to appear on screen, their gestures often histrionic; later a more natural and less theatrical cinema acting style emerged. By 1907 Germany had its first trade journal *Der Kinematograph*, published by press magnate August Scherl. A second, *Die Lichtbildbühne*, began publishing the following year.

By the eve of the First World War the middle classes had been won over. Cinemas were built with luxury in mind: the so-called 'picture palace'. At the opening of Berlin's Marmorhaus (Marble House, the name itself is revealing) on 1 May 1913, the theatre was even sprayed with French perfume.[5] After the war, theatre owners continued to aim for the middle-class market; this allowed them to charge more for tickets. Despite some appeals to art, commerce remained dominant.

Cinema had become popular, but in Germany the majority of films screened were not German-made. Germany's fledgling film industry – for which Berlin became the centre – arrived relatively late on the scene in about 1910. For the first half of January 1913 just under a third of new films came from the USA, followed by Italy with a quarter, France with under a fifth, then Britain with 15 per cent and Germany with only 11.7 per cent.[6] There were, however, approximately 2,500 cinemas, with three in Berlin seating more than a thousand.[7] Moreover, by 1913, according to a contemporary study, almost one-third of the German population visited the cinema at least once a week, attracted not only by what was on screen but also by the low price of the tickets, which, unlike theatre tickets, were not booked in advance.[8]

Cinema had its critics. Violent or sexually suggestive films, it was thought, might lower moral standards or encourage crime and delinquency, especially since initially audiences came from lower down the social scale.[9] Censorship was introduced in a number of countries. The state was concerned not only with what was being screened but also with the conditions of screening, especially given makeshift premises and the dangers of fire. A Cinematographic Act was introduced in Britain in 1909, ostensibly to make the premises safe, but it also enabled local authorities to control film content by withholding licences to theatres. This alarmed producers, distributors and exhibitors, who proposed that the industry rather than the state be allowed to operate censorship; the industry-run British Board of Film Censors came into existence in 1912.[10] Similarly, in the US, but much later, the film industry took on the role of censor when setting up the Motion Picture Producers and Distributors Association, otherwise known as the Hays Office, though individual states still retained the right to control what was screened.

As early as 1905 Germany had a cinema reform movement (*Kinoreformbewegung*). Associations of teachers, religious groups and cultural organizations demanded tighter censorship and greater control over the kinds of films being produced and distributed. They preferred cultural and educational films as opposed to *Schundfilme* (trashy films). The large Social Democratic Party (the SPD), for which one in three German male voters voted in 1912, was also worried. Its leaders, concerned with educating and politicizing the masses, found cinema a distraction which prevented the enlightenment of the working class. Later came calls from another quarter for censorship to protect the legitimate theatre, then considered the superior art form; this resulted in heated debates about the artistic value of cinema, the so-called *Kinodebatte*. By 1908 theatre directors were alarmed.[11] In 1912 Berlin theatre owners even tried to prevent their actors from working in the newly constructed film studios in Berlin Tempelhof and Babelsberg.[12]

German film censorship operated on a local basis, with variations in practice. In 1906 the Berlin police imposed the same controls on cinema that had existed for theatres since 1851: films prior to exhibition had to obtain approval from the police chief who had the power to ban. Despite the absence of a national law, strict controls were in place on a local level, stricter than in any other European country.[13] In 1914 the outbreak of war prevented the passage of a national law. Resubmitted three years later, it again failed to pass due to wartime political divisions.

The first proper newsreel was made in France in 1908. News stories had been a staple of cinema from the very beginning, though often they were reconstructions of events. *Pathé Journal*, as it was eventually named, brought newsreel to Britain in 1910, then to the US and also to Germany. During the First World War the French were the first to create an official newsreel, followed by the British. Germany had been importing newsreels from France but shortly before the war got its own newsreel, *Eiko-Woche*, intended to supplement the Scherl-owned newspaper, the *Berliner Lokal-Anzeiger*. With the outbreak of war, French newsreels were banned. Filmmaker and cinematographer Oskar Messter, who had been making films since 1897, offered his services to the government.[14] *Messter-Woche*, the first officially approved newsreel, began appearing two months after war began and attracted the middle class, keen for news of the war.[15]

A ban on films produced in enemy countries was introduced and not lifted until 31 December 1920. Initially films from France, Britain and Russia were affected, later Italy (in 1915) and the USA (1917). Aside from Russia, these countries had had a sizeable share of the German market. The ban proved a boon to German film production. Actors, directors and writers from the world of theatre overcame their disdain. Their belated contribution resulted in two film classics, *Der Golem* (1915) and *Homunculus* (1916), forerunners of the Expressionist films of the Weimar period.[16]

Germany was not the only country during the war to recognize cinema's importance, but it was in Germany that the military played an important role. They had become aware of the power of visual images (in addition to posters and photographs), and encouraged film production, finding it a useful medium for education and propaganda, putting the German case to neutral audiences and raising morale at home.[17] The more desperate the military situation became, the greater the need to consider non-military means.

In November 1916 Alfred Hugenberg, the Krupp chairman (he later bought out Scherl), founded Deutsche Lichtbild Gesellschaft (Deulig for short). Backed by heavy industry and supporting their expansionist aims, its purpose was to produce and distribute films publicizing German industry and culture. Two months later, in January 1917, the German General Staff created a military institution, Bufa, for the purpose of controlling filmmaking and countering enemy propaganda. *Feldkinos* (field cinemas) were set up in the reserve lines.[18] In July 1917, shortly after US entry into the war, General Erich Ludendorff wrote to the War Ministry, emphasizing the overwhelming power of images and film as a means of influence and pointing out the need to unify the film industry so that it could 'influence the masses in the interests of the state'.[19] The rivalry between the two organizations led in December 1917 to the founding of Ufa (Universum-Film Aktiengesellschaft) to produce and distribute patriotic feature films. Its arrival on the scene, however, came too late in the war to make a significant difference to film production. Vertically integrated, it was privatized after the war in 1921 when the Reich sold its shares to Deutsche Bank. It remained Germany's largest film company by far, with a reputation for providing nationalistic propaganda through mass entertainment.[20]

Despite the decline in Germany's military fortunes, its cinema flourished. Between 1914 and 1918 the number of theatres rose by 28 per cent – from 2,446 in 1914 to 3,130 in 1917[21] – and the number of film production companies from 25 in 1914 to 130 in 1918.[22] Annual film production also increased, reaching 376 films in 1918 which was 50 per cent up on the previous year.[23] Before the war, the majority of films screened in Germany had been foreign-made.[24] By the time the war ended, German cinema was on a firm financial footing. As a direct consequence of the war, and with help from the military, its film industry emerged strengthened.

4

Weimar Cinema

The First World War cost Germany some two million dead and four million wounded.[1] It also severely damaged the economy and destroyed the old political order. Germany's film industry, however, expanded during the war. After 1918 it indeed overtook the industries of the victorious nations, France, Italy and Britain, to become the dominant industry in interwar Europe, second only to Hollywood, though in the immediate post-war period it had to contend with the reluctance of the victorious nations to screen German films, which they considered an invasion in commercial form.[2]

The republican and democratic constitution adopted in 1919 in Weimar, the city of Goethe, which lent its name to the republic, granted liberties to German citizens hitherto unheard of. But the republic had been created in defeat: its constitution was adopted shortly after Germany had accepted the conditions laid down at Versailles, or *Diktat* as it was dubbed by Hitler and others on the extreme right. Germany lost territory as well as the population, the latter reduced to ethnic minority status in other countries. Its armed forces were reduced in size, reparations were imposed as well as a war guilt clause which blamed Germany for the outbreak of the war.

War and defeat brought in its wake economic dislocation. In the early 1920s Germany experienced hyperinflation, which added to political instability. Most people suffered terribly, but not the film industry. Cinema attendances boomed since a rapidly devaluing currency encouraged consumption. New theatres were indeed built. Inflation encouraged exports while discouraging imports, so that it was possible, for example, for Germany to undercut Hollywood in Latin America, since inflation brought down the price of German films.[3]

Once hyperinflation was cured and the German currency stabilized, the German film industry fared less well. The Dawes Plan (1924), which bailed out Germany, opened its markets, including cinema, to new investors, especially from the USA. In 1925 the German government decided to restrict imports: for every imported film a German film had to be exported. Lavish productions were no longer financially possible. Ufa, nearly bankrupted by Fritz Lang's grandiose *Metropolis* (1927), was forced to strike a deal with two Hollywood studios, the so-called Parufamet agreement, whereby in exchange for a two-million dollar ten-year loan Ufa gave distribution rights and access to first-run German cinemas.

Smaller studios entered similar agreements with other Hollywood studios.

In 1927 Alfred Hugenberg bought out the American interests in Ufa. One of the founders of the extreme nationalist Pan-German League in 1890, he had since 1920 been a member of the Reichstag for the right-wing DNVP (*Deutschnationale Volkspartei*) or German National People's Party, becoming its chairman the year after he acquired Ufa. During the 1920s the former Krupp director had bought up newspapers, magazines and the large Berlin publishing house of Scherl. This made him a press magnate and, with Ufa, a media magnate. Already the owner of Deulig, his plan was to add Ufa's newsreels to Deulig's to make Germany's two most widely shown newsreels a weapon in his fight against the republic.[4] Two years later he joined Hitler in a campaign to reject the Young Plan, an American-led plan of rescue. He was later rewarded with a post in the 1933 Hitler-led coalition government, though the honeymoon with Hitler was short-lived; by June 1933 he was out of government, eventually losing control of his media empire.

The second major economic crisis was a consequence of the Wall Street Crash. The film industry was badly hit, as it had been bailed out by foreign loans, especially American. The impact of the crash extended well beyond the film industry, since it was now difficult for Germany to pay reparations. Unemployment soared, benefits were reduced, governments changed, and political instability provided favourable conditions for a Nazi breakthrough.

The unemployed, though now enjoying free time, could not afford tickets. Productions proved difficult to finance since loans were no longer forthcoming, bankers having lost interest in risky investments. Production declined; work became scarce; audiences shrank. The recent introduction of sound, which involved the purchase of costly new equipment and the adaptation of studios, as well as legal battles relating to sound patents, was an added financial burden. It now coincided with the decline in audience numbers and the withdrawal of loans. The boom years were over.

The Weimar Republic is remembered as a political failure insofar as it provided a breeding ground for Nazism. Whether it was destroyed by Hitler, or had been destroyed *before* Hitler, is debatable. During the republic's early years German citizens had voted to support centre and left governments, but once the economy failed, that support was withdrawn in the July and November 1932 elections, the Nazis became the largest party in the Reichstag. In the multi-party system, they never secured an absolute majority of the votes, even in the March 1933 election held after the Reichstag fire.

Though military defeat and economic problems fuelled extremism on both left and right, there was an opportunity in 1918 (in theory at least) for the slate to be wiped clean and modernity embraced. Weimar culture is closely associated with modernity in the arts: in theatre, film, music, architecture, design, painting, sculpture, literature. One immediately thinks of movements such as the Bauhaus, Expressionism, the New Objectivity, of the theatre of Brecht and the music of Hindemith and Weill. The political capital, Berlin, was also the cultural capital: the centre for post-war modernity noted for sexual freedom as well as artistic innovation. Weimar has been described as the high point of 'classical modernity', where in just fourteen years all the possibilities of modern existence were played out.[5] In the myth of the 'Golden Twenties' it is still a synonym for modernity.[6] At the same time it was entering a crisis after which modernity would be revoked.

Having lost the war, Germany, in a sense, had won the battle for modernity. That victory was temporary; the Nazis, taking up views initially espoused by cultural conservatives, were harsh critics. For Nazis, as well as others on the right, Weimar, and in particular Berlin, signified cultural degeneration, even depravity. And, especially for the Nazis, it was the Jews who were held responsible.

Embracing the modern also meant embracing the most modern of the arts. Longer feature films, more sophisticated and extended programmes as well as grander theatres – though some had been built before 1919 – brought in middle-class audiences. In Germany there was an artistic conception of cinema linked to a literary and philosophical tradition.[7] German producers and directors (in contrast to their Hollywood counterparts) were often highly educated: Robert Wiene, who directed *Caligari*, had a doctorate; Fritz Lang had trained as an architect; Friedrich Wilhelm Murnau had studied art history and literature at Heidelberg.

An interest in art did not exclude business or profit since art could attract money, which is why the industry supported this development.[8] Though often subsequently categorized as 'art' films, Weimar films, including *Das Cabinet des Dr Caligari* (*The Cabinet of Dr Caligari*) (1920), were not at the time considered 'art films', that is intended to cater for a minority taste.[9] Nor were they considered unprofitable.[10]

When German directors and actors were invited to Hollywood, it was, ostensibly, to bring art. Another aim was to 'eliminate unwanted competition' since German films had been successful at the box office.[11] Thus began an exodus to Hollywood including directors, producers, actors, and cameramen such as Karl Freund, noted for his roving camera.[12] The producer for *Caligari*, Erich Pommer, went to Ufa in 1921 but left after Lang's *Metropolis* almost bankrupted Ufa (Lang had a penchant for very long films, apparent from his earlier two-part *Die Nibelungen* (*The Nibelungs*) (1924)). Pommer spent time in Hollywood. After making successful historical spectacles such as *Madame Dubarry* (*Passion* was its English title) (1919) and *Anna Boleyn* (1920), Ernst Lubitsch also left for Hollywood in 1923, the first director to be invited. There he produced sophisticated 'European' comedies. Murnau, a master of the *Kammerspiel* (chamber drama), after making *Der letzte Mann* (*The Last Laugh*) (1924) with Emil

Jannings, was invited to Hollywood. There he directed *Sunrise: A Song of Two Humans* (1927), based on a German novella, later remade by Veit Harlan as *Die Reise nach Tilsit* (*The Journey to Tilsit*) (1939). Jannings also went to Hollywood and won the first Oscar awarded to best actor, though he returned to Germany where during the Third Reich he played leads in many films as well as directing and producing. This exodus was helped by *Amerikanismus*, a German catchword for the admiration of all things American (especially technology, efficiency, commercial endeavour), and began well before sound or before any political need, though economic need was never absent.

Filmmakers felt challenged by Hollywood; none was immune to American influence.[13] 'The American film is the new world militarism,' according to film critic Herbert Ihering writing in 1926, 'more dangerous than Prussian militarism.'[14] The popularity of American films in Germany, however, has been exaggerated since there is good evidence that between the years 1925 and 1932 (for which there are records) German audiences still preferred German feature films to American imports.[15] There were always more American films than German on the German market (since Hollywood produced far more), but it was German films that led the way at the German box office. On the rare occasions that a Hollywood film made it to the top ten, it was usually one with a European theme.[16] Later in the decade, German film was also challenged from a completely different direction, though it was artistic rather than economic. Sergei Eisenstein's *Battleship Potemkin* (1925) got its German public release in 1926 after a battle with the censors and with cuts. (In Britain *Battleship Potemkin* had to wait until 1954 for a public screening.)[17] Once sound was introduced, a development that coincided with the Wall Street Crash, German films, as well as the industry, changed considerably.

With the largest film industry in Europe, Germany attracted German-speakers from Austria, Hungary, where German was the second language, as well as Soviet exiles like the director Victor Tourjansky and actress Olga Chechova. Alfred Hitchcock trained and then worked in Berlin and Munich for several years. As the centre of the German film industry, Berlin proved a magnet to those seeking work, especially from countries with weak or non-existent film industries. The German reputation for innovation meant that its technicians, designers, cameramen, directors and actors were greatly admired, though they were not always welcomed when later forced to seek work outside Germany.[18] Writing anonymously in 1936, John Grierson worried that the 'alien' could develop an 'unhealthy inferiority complex in the rest of the technical staff'.[19]

Language had not been a problem with silent film. Actors mimed and developed a visual language while inter-titles easily translated into many languages at almost no cost. Prior to the First World War, cinema was truly international. After the war it began to lose its international character, and with the advent of sound in 1927 it lost it completely. Careers in Hollywood for non-English speakers became precarious, that is for those in front of the camera rather than for those behind. This partly explains why some German actors, unlike the directors and technicians, returned to Germany, while travelling in the opposite direction were English-speaking stars of German films, such as the American Louise Brooks. The British-born Lilian Harvey was more fortunate; with excellent German she was the exception.

Ufa quickly converted its theatres to sound, since it was uneconomical to produce both silent and sound films when the former would no longer find an American market. Potential foreign audiences had also shrunk, given that language was now a factor. European companies, accustomed to an international audience, initially tried to make some films in three languages, retaining the set while employing different actors and directors. This practice, later replaced by dubbing or subtitles, was costly and by the early thirties had ended for English, German and French co-productions, though German and French co-productions continued for a few more years.

Siegfried Kracauer's *From Caligari to Hitler*, subtitled *A Psychological History of German Film*, was written during the war in American exile and published in 1947. A member of the editorial staff of the liberal *Frankfurter Zeitung* until 1933 and closely associated with the Frankfurt School, Kracauer was known not only for film criticism but also for reviews on social philosophy. It is therefore not surprising that he turned to film to explain the rise of Hitler. He was not the only exile to think in sweeping terms with Germany in mind. So too the exiled Berlin Neo-Freudian psychoanalyst Erich Fromm in *Fear of Freedom* (American title, *Escape from Freedom*) (1941).

Kracauer has been criticized for an over-deterministic thesis that the rise of Hitler was inevitable, given the German psychology and predilection for authoritarianism. That tendency, he argued, was already apparent in the early expressionist film, *The Cabinet of Dr Caligari*, hence the book's title. 'Behind the overt history of economic shifts, social exigencies, and political machinations', he wrote, 'runs a secret history involving the inner dispositions of the German people' which could be found on the German screen and could 'help in the understanding of Hitler's ascent and ascendancy'.[20] Psychoanalysis was in the air, and though Kracauer never mentioned Freud,[21] he probably took his Freudian categories from Fromm.[22] Fromm was also interested in cinema, having conducted a survey of factory and clerical workers about their cultural preferences, including their response to Soviet films.[23]

Kracauer's study has become a classic because of its detailed examination of so many Weimar films. Selective in his choice of films, he wanted – dare one say even had a psychological need, due to the trauma of exile and war – to prove a

German predisposition to accept authority. He made much – some would argue too much – of the ending of *The Cabinet of Dr Caligari*, where the director of the insane asylum, Dr Caligari, played by Werner Krauss, is confirmed as insane and bundled off in a straitjacket. A framing device, however, subsequently added, subverts the story so that instead of the liberated inmates taking over the asylum, the story becomes a tale told by one of the inmates, who becomes the narrator. Thus the inmates are revealed to be suffering delusions who require control. At the time of writing, Kracauer was unaware that the scriptwriters had in fact suggested a framing device – though one which did not subvert the story and which ended happily.[24] What this reveals is the element of choice, even arbitrariness, in the process of making a film, and that it is possible to attribute too much significance to one film.

One can argue against Kracauer with an alternative list: sound films such as the anti-war *Niemandsland* (*No Man's Land*) (1931) or *Westfront 1918* (1930) or the internationalist Franco-German co-production *Kameradschaft* (*Comradeship*) (1931) or the Communist-funded Brecht-scripted *Kuhle Wampe* (1932) and the low-budget *Menschen am Sonntag* (*People on Sunday*) (1930) co-scripted and co-directed by several who would soon go to Hollywood (Robert and Kurt Siodmak, Billy Wilder, Edgar Ullmer, Fred Zinnemann). Admittedly, none were typical (but then neither was *Caligari*). As another exile, Hans Wollenberg, the former editor of the trade journal, *Die Lichtbildbühne*, commented with Kracauer in mind: 'To generalize about all German films, using these outstanding works as proof, is certainly a mistake. The vast majority of films never survived the one season for which they were intended.'[25] Indeed, it has been estimated that only 10 per cent of the Weimar film output survives,[26] an additional reason not to see the Weimar classics as representative.

Still, when compared to French or Soviet cinema during the same period, Weimar cinema was distinctive.[27] German artistic traditions, especially German Romanticism and Expressionism, were influential, especially in the early years when some German film directors were keen for film to reflect the arts. Films reflecting the Berlin milieu were also distinctive. Categorizing the films into an early Expressionist stage followed by a middle Realist stage, followed by sound which continues the realism but now includes musicals and historical spectacles, though useful, still ignores the exceptions and those films that do not fit the chronology.

The best known Expressionist film is *Caligari* which appeared early, opening in February 1920. *Mise en scène* was especially important in Expressionist films, with camerawork less so. In German films generally, the staging – sets, lighting, acting and directing – was more important than montage, which, it has been suggested, reflected its links to the theatre. Unusually, in *Caligari* the sets were painted, though this would not be true for other Expressionist films. Expressionism, an anti-realist style in literature, theatre and painting – in painting, the emotions often permeate the landscape – began *before* the war but was mainly manifest in film in the immediate post-war years. Some of the classic Weimar films up to the mid-1920s were Expressionist, either because of the sets, the acting style or because an Expressionist text was the source, but Expressionist films only comprised a fraction of German film output.

As a more realistic or 'objective style' in the arts, the *Neue Sachlichkeit* (the New Objectivity), emerged after the period of hyper inflation, Expressionist films disappeared. The former often focused on social issues. The so-called street films revealed the dangers of the street, where bourgeois men were undone by women of the street, as in Karl Grune's eponymous *Die Strasse* (1923) which anticipates the *Neue Sachlichkeit*, or G.W. Pabst's *Die Freudlose Gasse* (*The Joyless Street*) (1925), in which Greta Garbo appeared in her second film role. The lead was the Danish actress, Asta Nielsen, a star of pre-war German films. Subgenres include the 'prostitute film', such as *Dirnentragödie* (*Tragedy of a Prostitute*) (1927) with Nielsen again as an aging prostitute, or Pabst's *Tagebuch einer Verlorenen* (*Diary of a Lost Soul*) (1929) with Louise Brooks. Other films focused on the criminal world. Some, set in working-class Berlin, showed conditions of dire poverty, such as Piel Jutzi's silent *Mutter Krausens Fahrt ins Glück* (*Mother Krausen's Journey to Happiness*) (1929), influenced by the popular Berlin artist Heinrich Zille. Sponsored by the Communist Party, it also contained sequences influenced by Soviet film, in particular the masses on the march. *Kuhle Wampe* (1932), co-scripted by Brecht with music by Hanns Eisler, was produced by the Soviet-funded Prometheus. Many of these films were set in public places: the street, the office, the cabaret or the brothel. Emblematic of the modern and of the urban landscape, the street also proved particularly problematic in Germany.[28]

Even homosexuality was treated with some sympathy, which was not the case in other countries. When the war ended, film censorship was abolished as a result of the revolution and not reintroduced until May 1920. Up to that date a spate of 'sexual enlightenment' films appeared about prostitution, venereal disease, drugs and homosexuality. Fears that this constituted little more than pornography led to the reintroduction of censorship.[29] Compared to Britain in the same period, censorship was still liberal. In later years it tightened up, but that had more to do with films with a left-wing message like *Kuhle Wampe*.

Anders als die Andern (*Different from the Others*) (1919) starred Conrad Veidt and was made with the help of Magnus Hirschfeld, who had founded the Institute for Sex Research to oppose the law criminalizing homosexuality and co-wrote the script. Danish director Carl Dreyer, known for his *Kammerspiel*, made *Michael* (1924). Wilhelm Dieterle directed *Geschlecht in Fesseln* (*Sex in Chains*) (1928), in which he also starred. He later worked in Hollywood as William Dieterle. Abortion was an issue in *Kuhle Wampe* and the Abortion Law came under attack in *Kreuzzug des Weibes* (*Women's Crusade*) (1926) an later in *Cyankali* (*Cyanide*) (1930), based on the eponymous play by the Communist doctor and writer Friedrich Wolf.[30]

The *Kammerspiel* concentrated on intensely psychological situations such as a crisis in the life of an individual. Often ending unhappily, they were strongly influenced by the great German director Max Reinhardt, known for his intimate, psychologically nuanced melodramas.[31] An early example was Murnau's *Der letzte Mann* (*The Last Laugh*) (1924), though an ironic happy ending had to be added (script by Carl Mayer, who co-scripted *Caligari*).[32] Starring Emil Jannings, it brought him as well as Murnau to Hollywood. By the late twenties this genre had disappeared. Jannings later returned to Germany for the Ufa–Paramount dual language co-production, *Der blaue Engel* (*The Blue Angel*) (1930), directed by another returning Paramount employee, Joseph von Sternberg.

The mountain film has been described as the German Western. The genre is closely associated with the geologist turned documentary filmmaker who then turned to feature film, Arnold Fanck. The antithesis of street films with their urban squalor, mountain films showed man battling but not conquering nature, in awe of the sublime. Such films proved popular, and not just with those on the political right.[33] As well as male characters, they also featured one tough and resilient woman, a Berliner and former dancer willing to learn how to ski and rock-climb, Leni Riefenstahl. She starred in films like *Der Heilige Berg* (*The Holy Mountain*) (1926) and *Die weisse Hölle vom Piz Palü* (*The White Hell of Piz Palu*) (1929), the latter in sound with the flying ace Ernst Udet. She could count both Hitler and Goebbels amongst her fans. In 1932 she made her own feature film, *Das blaue Licht* (*The Blue Light*), which loosely belonged to this genre insofar as it was set in the mountains, though the story had elements of a fairy tale.

The first German sound film was Walther Ruttmann's feature-length compilation documentary, *Melodie der Welt* (*Melody of the World*). It was a sequel to his silent documentary *Berlin: die Symphonie der Grossstadt* (*Berlin: Symphony of the Big City*) (1927) which celebrated urban life and helped to inspire Vertov's Soviet documentary *Man with a Movie Camera* (1929). *Melodie der Welt* opened in March 1929. The year was almost out before a sound feature film appeared.

Sound brought operettas and musicals to the screen, the former often set in Vienna. Ufa's popular *Kongress Tanzt* (*The Congress Dances*) (1931), which ranked first at the box office,[34] had a Viennese setting and starred Willi Fritsch and Lilian Harvey. Even unemployment served as a subject in another popular Ufa musical comedy, *Die Drei von der Tankstelle* (*Three at the Filling Station*) (1930), also with Fritsch and Harvey. It too ranked first at the box office,[35] though it did not travel well, a reflection of how sound had limited the audience range. *Der blaue Engel* did travel well and made Dietrich a star; she left for Hollywood the night of the première, but her songs, specially composed for the film by Friedrich Hollander, lived on in Germany as hits. Goebbels, a fan, later tried to lure her back, without success.

Of special significance for the early thirties are the so-called 'national epics', usually made by Ufa, which was never noted for gritty realist films or mournful melodramas. This was a genre which glorified times when Germany (or usually Prussia) had been great and, above all, victorious on the battlefield. Two historic periods were especially popular: the national uprising against Napoleon in the early nineteenth century; and, several decades before that, the life, times and character of the Prussian king Frederick II (Frederick the Great). Films about Frederick, which became a genre in their own right, the so-called '*Fridericus*' films, had already appeared during the Wilhelmine period.

Ufa's first '*Fridericus*' film was the four–part *Fridericus Rex* (1922–23), directed by the Hungarian Arpad von Czerepy. Given the context of military defeat, failed revolution and Versailles humiliation, it was taken at the time as a blatant call for the restoration of the monarchy.[36] Frederick was played by Otto Gebühr, who continued to take that role throughout the 1930s (with only one exception) until the very last '*Fridericus*' film in 1942.

More '*Fridericus*' films followed: Gerhard Lamprecht's two-part *Der alte Fritz* (*The Old Fritz*) (1927–28); *Das Flötenkonzert von Sanssouci* (*The Flute Concert of Sanssouci*) (1930); *Barbarina, die Tänzerin von Sanssouci* (*The Dancer of Sanssouci*) (1932); and *Der Choral von Leuthen* (*The Chorale of Leuthen*) (1933). Submission to authority remained the theme, but to an admirable authoritarian leader rather than to the monarch per se. During the Third Reich there were others, Frederick's mantle, by implication, having fallen to Hitler: Hans Steinhoff's *Der alte und der junge König* (*The Old and the Young King*) (1935) and Johannes Meyer's *Fridericus* (1936). With one exception – *Der alte und der junge König*, where Jannings took the role – Gebühr played Frederick.[37] His last appearance in the role was in Veit Harlan's *Der grosse König* (*The Great King*), a wartime rallying call to rely on the King's (Führer's) military judgement. It was Hitler's personal intervention which ensured that Gebühr rather than Krauss secured the role since he, unlike the director, grasped the value of continuity.[38]

Frederick also appeared in the background in films such as *Trenck*, a Phoebus production (1932), in which he opposes his sister Amalie's marriage to his aide-de-camp, Trenck, forcing her to become the abbess of a convent. Trenck goes to Russia, becomes one of Catherine the Great's favourites, but later returns to Prussia where he is imprisoned as a deserter. After his release many years later, he is banished, but returns on Frederick's death. Though a broken man, he submits to his now dead ruler, giving Amalie his memoirs, which contain the dedication: 'To the Spirit of Frederick the Unique, King of Prussia, my Life'. Submission and obedience came before personal happiness – a happy end for 1932.

Another period popular in the Third Reich was the early nineteenth century, when the Germans, after being overrun and occupied by Napoleonic forces, rose up and expelled the French. This had been a formative moment in German national consciousness since the defeat had sparked calls for the German states to unite and expel the enemy. It provided the setting for another wartime Harlan film, *Kolberg* (1945).

Yorck (1931), also a Ufa production, concerned the historic Prussian General von Yorck (Werner Krauss), so devoted to his weak king that he even obeys his order to support the French enemy. After Napoleon's defeat in Russia in 1812 he breaks his vow and launches the Prussian war against Napoleon. He has rebelled for the sake of the nation. Queen Luise of Prussia (1776–1810), the heroine of several films, was played by the popular actress, Henny Porten. *Die letzte Kompanie* (*The Last Company*) (1930), another Ufa production, was set during the Battle of Jena when Prussian soldiers fight to the last man against overwhelming Napoleonic forces. Set in the same period was *Die elf Schillsche* (*The Eleven Schillsche*) (1932), a remake of a silent film concerning a group of eleven officers. Well received, it included in its cast the young Harlan. Both the saintly Queen Luise and the officers would reappear in *Kolberg*.

Not all national epics were about leadership and obedience. Some went further than *Yorck* by advocating rebellion. The Nazis trod a thin line between obedience and rebellion: obey the leader, accept his authority but rebel against the unacceptable, including Weimar parliamentary democracy and the Versailles *Diktat*. On the eve of the Nazi takeover, heroic sacrifice coupled with rebellion was the subject of a film based on the life of the South Tyrolean hero, Andreas Hofer, who led the uprising against the French and also (inconveniently for twentieth-century Germans) against their then allies, the Bavarians. Hofer, who died a martyr to the cause, was the hero of the aptly named film *Der Rebel* (*The Rebel*) (1932), made by the South Tyrolean alpinist-turned-actor Trenker (though not for Ufa), who himself played the lead. Trenker returned to the same theme shortly before the outbreak of war, in a film which he also directed and starred in, *Der Feuerteufel* (*The Fire Devil*) (1940), an obvious attempt to cash in on his earlier success. For political reasons, however, that film had to be transposed to Austrian Carinthia, with Hofer reduced to a cameo role.[39] Hitler had abandoned the Germans of the South Tyrol when striking a deal with Italy and recognizing the Brenner Pass as the frontier with Italy, one of the rare occasions when Hitler resorted to *Realpolitik* at the expense of the self-determination of German peoples. *Der Rebel* was not the only film to feature Hofer. Less well known is *Der Judas von Tirol* (*The Judas from the Tyrol*), made by a small production company, which had its première on 21 November 1933 and included in the cast the attractive, blonde half-Jewish Camilla Spiro, in her last German screen appearance.

National epics, which as costume dramas had high production values, found a ready audience. They also found favour with the Nazis since they neither preached against war, espoused internationalism, admired foreigners or alluded to sexual deviancy or to the criminal underworld – to mention but a few failings of some of the better-known Weimar classics. Both national epics and heroic films about the First World War provided continuity. In terms of the kinds of films being made, the break came, it has been argued, not in the winter of 1932–33 but fully one year earlier, in the winter of 1931–32, not after the Nazis were in power but when they were on the brink.[40] Despite the exodus of more than 2,000 film personnel after the Nazi takeover, the films made in 1932 were not appreciably different, apart from a few exceptions, from films made in the early years of the Third Reich. They were, however, considerably different from the silents.

5

The German Film Industry 1933–1945

The *Reichsfilmkammer* (Reich Chamber of Film) or RFK was provisionally created on 14 July 1933, two months before the *Reichskulturkammer* (Reich Chamber of Culture) or RKK of which it became a part and which indeed served as its model.[1] Its earlier creation was an indication of the importance Goebbels attached to cinema; its provisional status disappeared once the RKK was set up. A committee of lawyers and economists had already met on 7 April with party leaders and representatives of the film industry with a view to devising a rescue plan for the industry. This led to the setting up of a Film Credit Bank (*Filmkreditbank*) in early June.[2] An announcement about the Film Chamber came three weeks later. It was part of the policy of *Gleichschaltung* (coordination) and would reflect the close links between the Propaganda Ministry and the film industry.

The RKK organized all areas of cultural life. Initially, it comprised seven chambers: film, literature, theatre, music, fine arts, the press and broadcasting. The last was dissolved at the outbreak of war. In any case the Reich owned the broadcasting system and could do its own vetting. Goebbels made himself president of the RKK, while each chamber was headed by a prominent individual artist, notably Richard Strauss for music. In the case of the *Filmkammer* the president was Dr Fritz Scheuermann, a lawyer who before 1933 had been a major figure involved in film finance.[3] He had only joined the party in March 1933, being later forced to resign and leave in disgrace, suspected of having made anti-Nazi comments.[4] The vice-president was Arnold Raether, an Ufa executive, who had been active in the antisemitic wing of the right-wing DNVP (German National People's Party), until he left to join the Nazi Party in 1931.[5] He was also deputy head of the Film Department within the Propaganda Ministry, deputy to the chief film censor and head of the Central Film Office within the Nazi Party's Central Propaganda Office. Within a short time Raether would be trying (unsuccessfully) to thwart Leni Riefenstahl on the grounds of her lack of party credentials.[6] Both men were only in post for two years. Later the RFK was headed by a film director, the elderly Carl Froelich.

The RFK's advisory council, selected by Goebbels, was drawn from the Propaganda Ministry, the Finance Ministry and the major banks. There was also an administrative council, which consisted of representatives from different branches of the film industry. This was similar in some respects to the Weimar umbrella organization which had covered much of the fragmented film industry, the SPIO (*Spitzenorganisation der Deutschen Filmindustrie*), set up in 1923 and headed by Ludwig Klitzsch, a director at Scherl publishing, who continued to play an important role down to 1945.[7] The RFK consisted of ten sections which covered film artists, film production, film distribution, cinemas and technical developments to name but a few. Trade unions were banned and the main film industry trade union was ultimately absorbed into the German Labour Front (*Deutsche Arbeitsfront* or DAF).

The film industry was closely observed and controlled by the Propaganda Ministry, not only in terms of suitable personnel but also in the kinds of films it could make. All the chambers regulated who could or could not work, by issuing work permits and keeping a register. Anyone seeking employment had to complete a questionnaire, proving political and racial desirability. This included evidence not only of one's parentage but also of the parentage of one's spouse. If everything was in order, admission to the chamber followed; only then could one seek work. The denazification questionnaires introduced twelve years later were not so very different, though obviously being a *Mischling* or not having belonged to the Nazi Party had by then become a desirable qualification.

On 28 June 1933, Goebbels passed a decree stating that for a film to qualify as 'German', everyone involved in its production had to be 'German', not merely hold a German passport but be of 'German descent and nationality', by which was meant not Jewish.[8] Goebbels was, in fact, making use of a quota regulation, passed three years earlier, which had tried to limit the number of imported films. Now any German-made film could be classified as foreign if anyone involved in its production was Jewish.

Just over two weeks later the 'Law on the Foundation of an Interim Film Chamber' was introduced, making it absolutely clear that Jews were to be excluded from the film industry. Finding work meant proving 'Aryan' descent as well as loyalty to the regime. Surprisingly, the director Curtis Bernhardt was brought back at this time from Paris exile to direct for Bavaria Film *Der Tunnel* (*The Tunnel*) (1933), most likely because it was also being made in a French version.[9]

Even marriage to a *Mischling* second degree (one Jewish grandparent) proved problematic, as in the case of Alf Teichs, a dramaturge at the Terra film company, who played an ambivalent role in the early stages of *Jud Süss*.[10] His records indicated that he had divorced his half-Jewish wife two months after the Nuremberg Laws were announced, but rumour had it that he was still living with her.[11] In 1933 he had offered as referees the actress Emmy Sonnemann, later Frau Goering, and the writer Rainer Schlösser, who in October 1933 was made *Reichsdramaturg*. Goebbels was impressed with him and in late 1940 made him head of production at the Terra film company, which had just produced *Jud Süss*.[12]

Those seeking work who were partly Jewish, the *Mischlinge*, had to fight their way back. Some did so successfully. Goebbels did issue exemptions.[13] Obviously, such successes were also dependent on contacts and well-placed referees. The director Erich Engel was one quarter-Jewish (*Mischling* second degree), a difficult position compounded by his having been on the political left – he had directed the first theatre production of Bertolt Brecht's *Die Dreigroschenoper* (*The Threepenny Opera*). Yet after 1933 he continued to direct films, mainly comedies. The stage actor Horst Caspar was also one-quarter Jewish. Initially forced to work in the provinces, by 1940 he had worked his way back to the centre and to film when he took the title role in *Friedrich Schiller*.[14] Later he played the Prussian General Gneisenau in the Veit Harlan blockbuster *Kolberg* (1945). Reinhold Schünzel, classified as half-Jewish, was allowed by Goebbels in 1933 to proceed with the gender-bending comedy *Viktor und Viktoria*, including a French version to be made simultaneously. Another comedy, *Amphitryon* (1935), poked fun at the Greek gods, who move on roller skates. It was as close to the Kleist play as that had been to the play by Plautus.[15] A sequence showing Jupiter descending from the heavens down a marble staircase parodied a sequence in *Triumph of the Will*. Despite sailing close to the wind, as it is not difficult to see that the target was Nazi pomp, he got away with it, but was less fortunate with another film in 1937, *Land der Liebe* (*Land of Love*), which was banned, after which he left for Hollywood. Fritz Lang, who was also half-Jewish, left for Hollywood earlier, though it is untrue that shortly after the Nazis came to power Goebbels summoned him for an interview after which he decided to leave the country. That was only a story Lang put out during the war. His last German film, *Das Testament des Dr Mabuse* (*The Testament of Dr Mabuse*), was banned in March 1933. Since his earlier Weimar films, in particular his two-part *Nibelungen* films (1924) and *Metropolis* (1926), had been considered so very German, he dallied but left for good in late July 1933 after the exclusion of Jews from the film industry.[16] As if life were not hard enough for out-of-work Jewish actors, or actors refusing to divorce their Jewish spouses, in the autumn of 1936 Goebbels set up the 'Dr Joseph Goebbels Foundation for Actors', a fund for actors in need. Excluded from benefits were 'full' and 'half-Jews', those 'married to Jews' and political undesirables.[17]

Henny Porten, a popular film star since 1910, refused to divorce her Jewish husband. This did not please her fans Hitler, Goebbels and Goering. She rarely appeared in films during the Third Reich, and on the occasion of her birthday the press was instructed to give it little prominence.[18] The handsome romantic lead Joachim Gottschalk refused to divorce his Jewish actress wife. She was unable to work, while he took leading roles. When in late 1941 she and their son faced deportation, they killed their son and jointly committed suicide. Some actors braved disapproval to attend the funeral. Their story became the subject of the second post-war German film, *Ehe im Schatten* (*Marriage in Shadows*) (1947).

A year after Gottschalk's death, Goebbels commented in his diary that he faced a 'difficult question' concerning the treatment of members of the *Reichskulturkammer* who were married to half- or quarter-Jews.

> If the usual measures in public life were applied, a large part of cultural life would be in disarray. Therefore for the time being I must try to make do with a compromise even if I am of the opinion that naturally the *Reichskulturkammer* cannot become a haven for half-Jews and those related to Jews.[19]

Full Jews had no choice but to seek work outside Germany unless in the early years they were content to give up their profession and find other means of employment. Actors choosing Austria, where they could still use the German language, were not always welcome, as jobs were scarce in a much smaller industry and antisemitism not unknown. Hitherto, the traffic had been in the opposite direction: Vienna to Berlin. Directors and technicians, whose foreign accent mattered less, had, to some extent, more options. If fortunate, they could find work in France or Italy as did Max Ophuls, who only later went to Hollywood. They could find some work in the much smaller British film industry, where their technical skills and aesthetic confidence were not always welcome.[20] Elisabeth Bergner, who was Jewish, as was her director husband, Paul Czinner, did find a British vehicle, *Catherine the Great* (1934). She starred (with Douglas Fairbanks, Jr); Czinner directed. Widely publicized in the German film press, and then screened in Germany, it was soon withdrawn after protests from Nazi diehards.[21] This incident suggests some uncertainties in the film industry, even after the exclusion of Jews. The actor-turned-director Kurt Gerron was less fortunate. As early as 1 April 1933, the first day of the Jewish boycott, when he turned up at the Berlin-Babelsburg studio to direct his next film, *Kind, ich freue mich auf dein Kommen* (*Child, I am Pleased at your Arrival*), starring Magda Schneider, he and other Jewish colleagues were summarily expelled from the studio by the production manager. He went to France where he found work, and then Holland, where he made a landmark film, *Merijntje Gijzen's Jeugd* (*Merijntje Gijzen's Youth*) (1936), and it was from there that he was later deported to Theresienstadt and then Auschwitz.[22]

This exodus left a vacuum. Actors like Veit Harlan could soon become directors. In the words of the Austrian-born half-Jewish playwright and scriptwriter, Carl Zuckmayer, it was a 'revolution of the extras'.[23] Those who remained benefited. To counter the temptation of emigration, salaries rose.[24] Attempts were often made to bring back 'Aryans' who had chosen exile. The actor Conrad Veidt's second wife was half-Jewish; he officially emigrated in April 1933. Engaged by Gaumont British to star in *Jew Süss*, based on the best-selling novel by the banned Jewish writer Lion Feuchtwanger, he returned to Germany in early 1934 for some location scenes for *Wilhelm Tell*, scripted by the Nazi writer Hanns

Johst and starring Emmy Sonnemann. His biography was being advertised in the German film press that month.[25] He also went back to visit his daughter from his first marriage. Briefly detained for 'health reasons', he was allowed, after some string-pulling at the British end, to return to Britain to star in *Jew Süss*.[26] Veidt later went to Hollywood, where he met the fate of so many anti-Nazis: being consigned to play the Nazi enemy, as in *Casablanca* (1943), in a sequence, interestingly, eliminated by the West German censors when the film was released in Germany after the war.[27]

Actors found life outside Germany hard. Some returned. Rudolf Forster, a fine actor who had played Mack the Knife in *Die Dreigroschenoper* and the captain in *Morgenrot*, divorced his Jewish wife and wrote direct to Goebbels from America several months after the war had started.[28] He soon went back to Germany and, with Goebbels's backing, found work. G.W. Pabst, who directed so many Weimar classics – *Die Freudlose Gasse* (*Joyless Street*) (1925), the antiwar *Westfront 1918* (1930), the internationalist *Kamaradschaft* (1931) and the films starring Louise Brooks, *Die Büchse der Pandora* (1929) (based on Frank Wedekind's *Lulu*) and *Tagebuch einer Verlorenen* (*Diary of a Lost Soul*) (1929), to cite only a few – worked in France and then briefly in Hollywood where he made only one film. He also decided to return to Germany or rather to his birthplace, Austria, at much the same time as Forster. He made two films, both belonging to the National Socialist genius film genre – a Nazi variant on the Hollywood biopic – in which historic figures act as Nazi role models,[29] *Komödianten* (*Travelling Players*) (1941) and *Paracelsus* (1943). A third film, *Der Fall Molander* (*The Molander Affair*) (1944–45), he did not complete.[30]

A new cinema law (the *Reichslichtspielgesetz*) came into force on 16 February 1934 to replace the Weimar cinema law. Not surprisingly, censorship increased. During the first year of the Weimar Republic all forms of censorship had been abolished, but by 1920 had been introduced for film. A censorship office (*Filmprüfstelle*) had been created with two branches, one in Berlin and one in Munich, each with a chairman, assisted by four members drawn from the legal and teaching professions and the film industry. A higher office (*Oberprüfstelle*) in Berlin dealt with any appeals, and all three offices were under the jurisdiction of the Ministry of the Interior. In addition, the police had the power to ban a film if they believed it threatened public order. The 1934 law combined the two offices into one which was now moved from the Ministry of the Interior to the Propaganda Ministry, where it became a part of the Film Department. Some senior Weimar censors had proved their worth (in Nazi eyes), and kept their positions.[31] The head of the *Oberprüfstelle*, Dr Ernst Seeger, was made head of the ministry's Film Department.[32] Involved with censorship since 1917, he held this post until his death in 1937.

Previously, the censors had had the power to ban any film likely to 'endanger public order or security, harm religious sensibilities, brutalize or deprave, or endanger German prestige or Germany's relations with foreign states'. In 1931 this was broadened to include endangering 'the essential interests of the state'.[33] Paragraph 1 protected the authority of the state, including the military, judiciary and civil service, professionals such as doctors, and legal relations, including the institution of marriage.[34] In 1934 this was extended to race and politics, and also to taste, including 'the violation of artistic feeling'.[35] Films could now be censored on a variety of grounds, some spurious: endangering vital state interests, public order or security, German prestige or its relationship with foreign states; or offending National Socialist, religious, moral or artistic sensibilities. This even extended to foreign films with German actors. A Hollywood film, *The Song of Songs* (1933), based on a novel, *Das hohe Lied* (*The Song of Songs*) by the German writer Hermann Sudermann, was partly set in Berlin, and starred Marlene Dietrich as a German peasant girl. It was banned, deemed an insult to German womanhood, since previously she had demonstrated a predilection for playing prostitutes.[36]

Censorship was now under the control of the ministry. In many cases this meant the direct control of Goebbels who always took an active interest, especially in the ninety-six state-commissioned films (*Staatsauftragsfilme*), and in wartime newsreels.[37] In 1935 the Reich Cinema Law was amended to allow the Propaganda Minister to forbid any film independently of any decision reached by the censorship board, if it was in the 'interests of the public well-being'.[38] Prior to 1935 the minister's role had not been made explicit, though it was hardly a secret.

Films were now not only censored but could, through a form of pre-censorship, be prevented from being made. An office of *Reichsfilmdramaturg* was created within the Propaganda Ministry's own film department to act as a pre-censor. All film treatments or synopses had to be submitted to the *Reichsfilmdramaturg*. If approved, the script had subsequently to be submitted. Only after that could shooting commence. Thus at several stages the project could be stopped to 'prevent in a timely fashion the treatment of material which runs counter to the spirit of the time'.[39] But, within a short time, by late 1934, the submission of scripts had become optional.[40] The film dramaturge acted less as a critic and more as a patron; he represented the state's point of view to ensure that no project was approved which jeopardized the state's interest. There was also a financial advantage, since less censorship would be required for a completed film and money would not be wasted on unsuitable projects. The first holder of the office was the twenty-six-year-old critic and fellow journalist from Goebbels's Berlin weekly, *Der Angriff*, Willi Krause, with no knowledge of film but well versed in National Socialist principles. He also wrote under the pseudonym Peter Hagen. He soon had the opportunity to gain film experience through directing and scripting the 1935 film, *Friesennot* or *Dorf im roten Sturm* (it had two titles). By 1936 he had been replaced by another twenty-six-year-old from *Der Angriff*, Jürgen Nierentz.[41] Eventually, the post disappeared.

Given the other controls now in place, the censor no longer played the most important role. Indeed, some films passed the Censorship Office only one or two days before their première.[42] Only twenty-seven films were censored after production, while eighty to one hundred films experienced cuts after opening.[43] Altogether this amounts to less than 10 per cent of the approximately 1,100 films produced.

In addition to censoring films, the Film Department gave them a rating. A new system of film classification was introduced which awarded *Prädikate* (marks of distinction) to individual films, according to their artistic or political value. The more marks of distinction a film collected, the less entertainment tax its makers had to pay, and the more profitable the film was likely to be, since classifications brought a progressive tax exemption. Films enjoyed a sliding scale of taxation, the *Prädikate* acting as a 'form of negative taxation'.[44]

Prädikate had existed during the Weimar era but had been mainly educational in nature, offered as guidance and issued by an office attached to the Central Institute of Education, separate from the office of censor. Though leading to some form of reduction in the entertainment tax, essentially they were an honour.[45] These educational classifications were retained, but new ones were added, several in 1933: 'politically especially valuable'; 'artistically especially valuable'; a combination of both; or merely 'politically valuable'; 'artistically valuable'; or 'culturally valuable'. In 1938 'valuable for youth' was introduced, in 1939 'nationally valuable' and 'Film of the Nation'. Only two classifications ('valuable for youth' and 'Film of the Nation') did not lead to a reduction in entertainment tax.

Prädikate offered financial incentives, since the more prestigious the classification, the greater the profit. And if a film received the *Prädikat* 'politically and artistically especially valuable', the entire programme was exempted from entertainment tax; other classifications brought proportionate reductions. On the other hand, if a film obtained no classification whatsoever, its screening was jeopardized, since permission for exhibition had to be applied for. After 1938 no exhibitor was allowed to refuse to show a film designated politically valuable. While censorship was an active form of intervention, *Prädikate* provided the financial inducement to make the right kind of film.

The ninety-six *Staatsauftragsfilme*, feature films commissioned by the state, were treated with greater generosity, being given more time, more money and more publicity. Such films were characterized as *Tendenzfilme*, rather than propaganda films, as that term was used to describe non-feature films produced by the Propaganda Ministry or the Nazi Party, which were in effect commercials for the party. *Tendenzfilme* were feature films (not all *Staatsauftrag*) which reflected 'strong national socialist tendencies', without necessarily directly referring to National Socialism.[46] Indeed, few films actually did the latter. Covertly rather than overtly political, they provided entertainment while also promoting Nazi values, on subjects such as great leaders and militarism. No film was allowed to express a viewpoint incompatible with National Socialism. Having said that, there was leeway, since most films were expected to entertain, and films promoting the National Socialist point of view generally had little entertainment value. Goebbels was fully aware of this, a reason why, for example, early on he made efforts on behalf of Schünzel. Moreover, even when a film was considered on-message, it still might fail to deliver, since this depended on the response of the viewer. Audiences were far from uniform and were – to cite the most obvious – divided by age, gender, geography, class, religion and politics. Some filmmakers were also not necessarily on-message: again Schünzel in the early years, and during the war years a case has been made for Helmut Käutner. Once the war began, the Security Service attended screenings to monitor audience response, an indication that, even in a controlled state, audiences were not predictable and gave concern to those in power.

In 1936 Goebbels forbade film criticism. Henceforth reviewers were confined to providing descriptive reports. In an aptly entitled article, 'The Critique of Criticism', Wilhelm Weiss, the editor of the Nazi newspaper, the *Völkischer Beobachter*, who also happened to be head of the Reich Press Association, wrote:

> The critic of today is no longer a private individual who arbitrarily determines his attitude to art according to some personal or other point of view; today's critic has a public duty assigned to him by the National Socialist state and the National Socialist ideology.[47]

A similar view was expressed in the *Völkischer Beobachter* by Alfred-Ingemar Berndt, Goebbels's press chief. He told the RKK that 'The only possible standard for judging a work of art in the National Socialist state is the National Socialist concept of culture. Only the party and the state are in a position to determine standards according to this National Socialist concept of culture.'[48] Nevertheless, within such constraints, differences could still be detected. The liberal *Frankfurter Zeitung*, for example, continued to give guarded reviews. Clearly no film having been approved for exhibition could be damned outright, unless it was frivolous, or if a few hints from on high had already been given, but what was not said was often as significant as what was said, as well as how it was said.

At the time of the Nazi takeover, the German film industry had been in dire financial straits, particularly hard hit by the Depression since Germany had been the nation hardest hit. Ticket sales were down. The number of cinemas also dwindled from 5,000 in 1929 to 2,196 in 1932.[49] Production companies, distributors and exhibitors were in conflict, the last being in the weakest position. As small businessmen, they had shown sympathy for the Nazis, especially during 1932.[50] In February 1933, however, their association failed to elect the preferred Nazi candidate, though second time round their resistance was overcome.[51]

The introduction of sound had also made it difficult to recoup costs. The first German sound film, Walther Ruttmann's documentary *Melodie der Welt*, had its première several months before the Wall Street crash. Filming began on *Der blaue Engel* one week after the crash, in one of the four newly built Ufa sound studios. Production costs had risen since sound equipment was expensive and studios required adaptation. Sound also affected the export of films at a time when imports were on the increase. Making the same film in three languages with different actors on the same set was not the way forward. Nor was nationalization, which neither the film industry nor the new government wanted.

The 1934 Cinema Law helped exhibitors at the expense of distributors. Contracts between distributors and exhibitors were standardized. Block bookings or blind bookings were abolished, as were double features. All cinemas were now required to show a short and a newsreel. A wage scale was also set and advertising came under closer control.[52] Entry prices were standardized: no price-cutting was allowed and a minimum ticket price was introduced.[53]

Production companies were also strengthened. Ufa, by far the largest of the four major production companies, fortuitously had as its head Alfred Hugenberg, who was also head of the right-wing DNVP which was allied with the Nazi Party. A media tycoon, he had earlier bought up Scherl publishers, and before that had been a director at Krupps. He served as Minister of Economics until late June 1933. Even after he lost his post, big business did not lose out since Hitler had no wish to alienate it and indeed could not afford to do so.

The idea of a *Filmkreditbank* (FKB), a special bank for the film industry, which was announced in June 1933, at the same time that the trade unions were being destroyed, had originated with the umbrella organization for the Weimar film industry, the SPIO, which had included it in their 1932 rescue plan for the film industry.[54] The revival of the idea was well received by investors in the film industry,[55] especially because things had actually worsened since the Nazi takeover: international distributors, often Jewish-influenced, were now unwilling to show German films.[56] The man most responsible for the bank's creation was Walther Funk, a financial journalist who had Hitler's confidence and who was made Secretary of State at the Propaganda Ministry, in effect Goebbels's deputy, with responsibility for the business side. In 1938 he was appointed Minister of Economic Affairs and in 1939 president of the Reichsbank. He was also a personal friend of Klitzsch who had headed the SPIO. Several banks including Deutschebank were also involved, as was Ufa.[57]

Although the film bank operated from within the RFK, the loans still came via the banks at highly competitive rates. The banks also acted as a censor at the pre-production stage since they could demand dramaturgical changes given their brief to encourage 'a truly German art'.[58] Not only did the producer have to demonstrate that he could raise 30 per cent of the production costs, but he also had to make a case that the film would make a profit. Until the film turned a profit, and the loan was repaid, it remained the property of the *Filmkreditbank*. By 1936 the bank was providing finance for over 73 per cent of all German feature films.[59] Nevertheless, film companies still remained in private hands – but not for very long, though this was not made public. Only on the eve of the war did audience numbers begin to increase.[60] And in autumn 1940, Goebbels banned American films, though this was not implemented until early 1941, giving a boost to German films.[61]

Although the *Filmkreditbank*'s function was to provide credit to the cash-starved film industry, and it was originally heralded as a means of helping small and medium-sized film companies by freeing them from their dependence on a distributor, it was the four big film companies, Ufa, Tobis, Bavaria and Terra, which benefited most. They found it easier to meet lending criteria by providing secure collateral, such as a firm distribution deal, while the smaller companies found this difficult and disappeared. But even the large companies experienced problems. There was a sharp rise in production costs – stars demanded high salaries – while film exports declined (down to 7 per cent in 1936–37), not only because of the unpopularity of the Nazis and a decline in the quality of films but also because of protectionist policies elsewhere which introduced quotas on foreign films. American films, however, were screened in greater numbers until 1940.[62] Since nationalization was not an acceptable solution, least of all to big business, which had invested so much in the film industry, another way had to be found: some form of state intervention, but one in which state financial control was not apparent. The state needed to encourage film production but not subsidize it.

The Cautio Treuhand GmbH, or Cautio Trust, was the brainchild of Dr Max Winkler, then aged sixty, who joined the party in 1937. He had acted as a trustee on behalf of German governments since 1919, responsible for creating a complex system of interlocking trusts designed to help ailing but deserving businesses surreptitiously, most recently German newspapers. Having already served eighteen chancellors, he saw no reason not to serve the nineteenth.[63]

The Cautio Trust was now called on to act as a majority shareholder and administer the assets of film companies which changed from public to private limited liability companies. Cautio bought up a majority of shares in separate deals; their representatives administered the film companies; the film companies were answerable to the trust; and the trust was answerable to the Propaganda

Ministry for whom it was holding the shares in trust, while the Finance Ministry provided the funds to buy the shares. The intention was to reduce competition between the companies, encourage cooperation and make them more profitable while maintaining even greater control over film content.

The two largest film companies, Ufa and Tobis, were the first to be taken over in this way. It was barely mentioned in the film press, though it was in the *New York Times*.[64] Goebbels did not want this aspect of the state's activity publicized. Similarly, Riefenstahl's film company was founded at this time to film the Berlin Olympics. It too operated under a subterfuge.[65] In March 1937 Ufa was taken over, along with the entire Scherl publishing empire; Hugenberg was bought out. Shortly after that, Tobis was broken up, though it later reappeared under a slightly different name. Terra was taken over next and in early 1938 Bavaria. With *Anschluss* the Austrian companies were incorporated to form Wien-Film; and after the destruction of Czechoslovakia the following year Prag Film AG was created. By 1939 all the major film companies had become *Staatsmittelbar*, state-funded, under indirect state financial control, though technically they were not state-owned. These six companies dominated film production but, to disguise the role of the state and to confuse the public, the names of the film companies were retained in slightly modified form. Film distribution and theatres were also taken over. Film finance was also reorganized through the creation of a new company, Film Finanz GmbH (Fi Fi), with representatives from the Propaganda Ministry, Cautio, the Finance Ministry, the state-funded film companies and the Reich Credit Company. This new body allocated funds to the companies.[66]

The war brought larger audiences: more Germans began attending the cinema, and more frequently.[67] Conquest then brought not only access to non-German audiences but also the acquisition of many more theatres. Against this, however, production costs had risen, labour was short, as well as materials, in particular film stock, and production itself was slowed down through an increase in censorship. Then bombing began driving audiences away. Goebbels was also concerned to protect the wartime film industry from the predations of other ministries, especially the Finance Ministry, which saw it as a source of tax revenue. The latter also wanted to exercise some control over film finance.[68] Further change was needed: again Winkler came up with a solution.

In February 1942 Goebbels announced a further reorganization of the film industry. A giant state-owned holding company, Ufa-Film GmbH, otherwise known as Ufi, to prevent confusion with the defunct Ufa, was set up to control and finance all film companies, in Germany as well as in occupied countries, though names were retained to disguise the change. Vertically organized, it had Winkler in charge, but with Goebbels above. Goebbels could rightly describe himself as *Schirmherr* or 'Patron' of the German Film. An office of *Reichfilmintendanz* (Reich Film Supervision) was created, responsible for the artistic control of film production. The first to head the new body was Fritz Hippler, who had headed the Propaganda Film Department and had directed *Der ewige Jude* (*The Eternal Jew*). He fell from grace in 1943. Later, in June 1944, Goebbels appointed Hans Hinkel, a high-ranking member of the SS and an important figure in Nazi cultural affairs. He had been vice-president of the RKK and also had had special responsibility for matters concerning Jews, excluding them as well as overseeing their separate cultural activities.[69] Financial and administrative aspects remained in Winkler's hands. This new arrangement allowed for even closer regulation: each firm could only devote 20 per cent of its resources to high-budget films. By 1943 the process of nationalization was completed. Every aspect of filmmaking was now under state control, though the extent of the state's role was not made public.

What was given publicity was the twenty-fifth anniversary celebration of the founding of Ufa, a gala occasion on 3 March 1943 at which Hugenberg, Winkler and Klitzsch, amongst others, were honoured for their services to German film. They had a long track record. (In 1944, it has been noted, seven out of the ten members on Winkler's executive had held leading positions in the German film industry dating back to before 1933.)[70] The jubilee celebration for the now defunct Ufa included the première of the colour extravaganza, *Münchhausen*. But the occasion was marred by military setbacks: the German defeat at Stalingrad had taken place a few weeks earlier and Berlin was also being bombed. Nevertheless, during the previous weeks while the German army faced disaster on the Eastern Front, Hitler had to be consulted over the precise titles to be accorded to film personnel.[71]

6

The Kampfzeit Films, 1933

The Nazi takeover on 30 January 1933 was not immediately apparent in film. Films take time to make: from idea to scenario to production to distribution. It was far easier to ban an undesirable film than to make a desirable one. In any case, films made in 1932 (compared to 1931) were less likely to offend Nazi sensibilities. Those that did were banned outright such as Fritz Lang's *Das Testament des Dr Mabuse* in March (Mabuse was a sinister manipulator). On the other hand, a filmmaker's racial origins were not yet grounds for a ban: Max Ophuls's *Liebelei* (*Dalliance*), set in nineteenth-century Vienna, opened in March 1933 when its 'non-Aryan' director had already gone into exile, its subject matter not being considered offensive. Two films were singled out for red carpet treatment: a '*Fridericus*' film, *Der Choral von Leuthen* (*The Chorale of Leuthen*), was one and *Morgenrot* (*Dawn*), a tale of heroism and sacrifice during the First World War, was the other. Both had gala openings early in 1933.

These two films could awaken the right sentiments, though to a discerning viewer (that is a Nazi) they were nationalist rather than National Socialist in alluding to German past greatness by focusing on German heroes and heroines. (Goebbels found *Der Choral von Leuthen* 'nauseating' as well as 'patriotic kitsch'.)[1] National Socialist films, on the other hand, would focus on National Socialist heroes – not heroines, for National Socialism was short of them – and would be set in the very recent German past (the Weimar period) when the Nazis were struggling to achieve power, a time which they always referred to as their *Kampfzeit* (time of struggle).

Der Choral von Leuthen is set in 1757 when Frederick the Great, against the advice of his generals, decided to fight the Austrians at Leuthen. Though out-numbered, the Prussians won the battle, at which point the surviving Prussian soldiers spontaneously sang a hymn, the 'Chorale of Leuthen', written the previous century during the Thirty Years War. Otherwise known in German as '*Nun Danket alle Gott*' – in the English-speaking world this hymn goes under the title 'Now Thank We all our God' – it became closely associated with the Prussian victory. It also belonged to the concluding part of the solemn military ceremony known as the *Grosser Zapfenstreich* (the great military tattoo), which symbolized 'the Holy Trinity of God, the Prussian king and the Fatherland'.[2]

Though in production well before the takeover, the film had passed the censor on the day of the takeover (30 January), with the première following four days later on 3 February in Stuttgart. When it opened in Berlin one month later on 7 March, just three days after the Reichstag election, it was in the presence of Hitler and most of his cabinet as well as major cultural figures. Surprisingly the audience also included Max Reinhardt, Head of the Prussian Theatre, and soon (but not yet) to be relieved of his post on racial grounds.[3] The film chimed well with Nazi efforts to play on the Prussian link. On 4 March 1933, the day before the election, Hitler, associating himself with President Paul von Hindenburg, the liberator of East Prussia and victor on the Eastern Front, gave a speech broadcast from Koenigsberg, the capital of East Prussia. At its close the bells of Koenigsberg Cathedral could be heard, an event orchestrated by Goebbels and relayed all over Germany. Those marching in torchlit processions heard it from loudspeakers on the streets.[4]

Produced and directed by Carl Froelich, *Der Choral von Leuthen* had been made in collaboration with the director of the first *'Fridericus'* film, thus providing continuity with the Weimar genre which Goebbels was keen to exploit: several more *'Fridericus'* films appeared between 1935 and 1942. Froelich (1875–1953) had a very long career in the film industry, beginning in 1903. He became a cameraman and in 1910 directed his first film. He began working for Ufa in 1920 and eventually was given his own production unit which produced mainly costume dramas and in 1929 one of the first German sound films. He supported the National Socialists, but joined the party only in June 1933.[5] The first film director to be honoured with the title of professor in 1936, he was made president of the *Reichsfilmkammer* in 1939 and was twice awarded the National Film Prize.

German heroism and sacrifice in the First World War was the subject of *Morgenrot* (*Dawn*), another film which opened shortly after the Nazis came to power. Passing the censor on 26 January, just before the takeover, with the new *Prädikat*, 'artistically valuable', it had its première on 31 January in Essen, the Krupp stronghold. Two days later it opened in Berlin, where Hitler graced it with his presence, his first cinema visit since becoming Chancellor – and a choice of film that might be thought apt at the dawn of his own regime. He attended in the company of two non-Nazi cabinet members, Vice-Chancellor Franz von Papen and the Minister for Economics and Agriculture, Alfred Hugenberg.[6] *Morgenrot* was not in fact a Nazi film[7], as is evident from the fact that, at the outbreak of war, it was subject to a few judicious excisions before re-release.[8] At this time, however, nothing in the dialogue was felt to detract from the occasion. There was enough in the film to justify Hitler's presence.

Herbert Windt, the classically trained composer for many Third Reich films, including most of Leni Riefenstahl's, provided the music. A Nazi Party member since 1931, this was his first film commission and established him as a specialist composer for 'heroic' films.[9] The script was by Gerhard Menzel, a winner of the prestigious literary Kleist prize.

The director was Viennese-born Gustav Ucicky (1899–1961), an illegitimate son of the painter Gustav Klimt.[10] A fervent nationalist, he was a founder member of the Austrian National Socialists, but never joined the German party, though he did enter the SS in March 1933.[11] He began working for Sascha Films in Vienna in 1916, becoming a camera operator, and continued to work for them in this capacity at the front while serving in the Austro-Hungarian infantry during the First World War. (The founder of Sascha Films, Count Alexander Kolowrat-Krakowsky, headed the army's film division.) After the war, Ucicky continued at Sascha until its demise and was soon working with two recent arrivals from Hungary (of Jewish origin), Alexander Korda and Michael Curtiz; he served as cameraman for the latter. Later, he turned his hand to directing. The two Hungarians left for Hollywood in 1926 – Curtiz would later make *Casablanca* (1942) – while Ucicky left for Berlin two years later to work for Ufa.[12] In 1939 at the request of the Propaganda Ministry he returned to Vienna where he remained throughout the war. His well-made films, notable for good camerawork and fluid editing, were in the heroic mould, usually with a hero, though occasionally a heroine as in some of his more obviously propagandistic films such as *Heimkehr* (*Homecoming*) (1941) and *Mutterliebe* (*Mother Love*) (1939). The former was marred by wordy speeches, while the latter verged on the sentimental. Prior to 1933 Ucicky had also directed 'national epics': a '*Fridericus*' film in 1930, *Das Flötenkonzert von Sanssouci* (*Flute Concert at Sanssouci*) with Frederick the Great in musical mode, and *Yorck* (1931), about the Prussian military hero during the Napoleonic Wars. There followed well-made literary adaptations such as Kleist's *Der zerbrochene Krug* (*The Broken Jug*) (1937), though this was at the request of Emil Jannings and not liked by Goebbels.[13]

Morgenrot is an early example of the submarine disaster genre. Dedicated to the 6,000 sailors who died in 199 seagoing coffins, its purpose was clear: to display German self-sacrifice and heroism.[14] A German submarine sinks a British cruiser, then falls into a British trap and is rammed. Ten men survive, including the captain, but there are only eight life-jackets. The captain proposes that he and his first lieutenant go without, but the men will have none of it. In the end, after the first lieutenant learns that his girl prefers the captain, he offers himself up for the supreme sacrifice and dies along with another crew member, a loner with no close relatives, wanting to give meaning to his life. The problem of an insufficient number of life-jackets is solved with two shots – a happy end with a distinctly German twist that it is good to die for one's country. Without any intended irony, the Captain declares: 'Perhaps we Germans do not know how to live, but we are wonderful at dying.' The more conventional happy end is reserved for the sailor, who returns to his wife, played by the soon to be excluded Camilla

Spira. Her performance was singled out for praise by the *Völkischer Beobachter*, then unaware that, although blonde, she was not 'Aryan' but half-Jewish.[15] Already apparent in this film is a cult of heroism more tied to death than to life. However, in the 1933 version the captain's mother, having already lost two sons, puts the pacifist case after learning that the ship has been sunk, leading a British reviewer, when the film opened in Britain in 1934, to conclude that the film contained 'subtle propagandist value upon the futility of war'.[16] The mother's lines were cut when the film was re-released in 1939, as were some lines belonging to the suicidal sailor which revealed his precarious mental state; the rest of the film proved highly suitable for German wartime audiences.[17] The need for such excisions supports Kracauer's view that this was not a Nazi film.[18]

Later in 1933, Ucicky directed for Ufa *Flüchtlinge* (*Refugees*), a *Staatsauftragsfilm* (state-commissioned film). With music again by Windt, and another script by Menzel, this time based on his own novel, it was the first film to win the *Staatspreisfilm* (state prize for film), recently set up by Goebbels for cinematic contributions to National Socialism. Set in Manchuria, it focused on the sufferings of *Volksdeutsche* (ethnic Germans), refugees from Soviet Russia, pursued by Bolsheviks, and was the first of a series of films about Germans attempting to return to the Fatherland. In June 1934 the British Board of Film Censors banned it as anti-Soviet propaganda. More accustomed to banning Soviet films, on this occasion they felt unable to pass a film that attacked a country with which Britain had diplomatic relations. However, the London County Council, which three months previously had fallen to Labour, approved the film. One year after its German première, it opened at the Curzon cinema in London's West End with Alistair Cooke singing its praises: 'just about the most exciting film there has ever been'.[19]

Few of the approximately 1,100 feature films produced during the twelve years of the Third Reich can be characterized as 'Nazi'. The numbers vary, but propaganda films comprise at most 20 per cent (229) while those that were state-commissioned (*Staatsauftrag*) films numbered only ninety-six, or less than 10 per cent. Of these, very few were Nazi in the sense of depicting Nazi heroes. The dearth of Nazi characters and suitable plots is striking. Films with political content might be costume dramas, heroic dramas or domestic dramas. They did not show Nazis – proto-Nazis perhaps, often in costume, but not real Nazis living either in the Weimar Republic or in the Third Reich. From a Nazi perspective, nationalist films were still not Nazi films.

In only three films was the main character at the outset a Nazi Party member: they were set in the *Kampfzeit*, the years prior to the takeover. In several other films set in the Weimar Republic, it was obvious that the main characters were likely to become Nazis, but such films were still nationalist rather than Nazi.

The three films with Nazi Party members as the leading character went into production and had their premières in the year that Hitler came to power. State-commissioned, they were nevertheless not the only state-commissioned films opening that year. Achieving political power was one thing; making successful films in the new image proved elusive.

SA-Mann Brandt, the first film to open, as its title indicates, was about an SA hero, or the 'unknown SA man', akin to the unknown soldier in an analogy made by Goebbels.[20] According to the *Völkischer Beobachter* it was: 'The first film about unknown soldiers in brown shirts'.[21] Passing the censor on 9 June, it was awarded the *Prädikat* '*künstlerisch besonders wertvoll*' (of special artistic value) as well as '*volksbildend*' (educational) – a category dating from 1924 – and opened on 14 June.[22] *Hitlerjunge Quex* (*Hitler Youth Quex*) passed the censor on 7 September and was awarded the new classification of *künstlerisch wertvoll* (artistically valuable); its première came twelve days later. As its title indicates, its hero was a member of the Hitler Youth. The third film, *Hans Westmar*, originally entitled *Horst Wessel*, was about a Nazi 'martyr', another SA man, but known rather than unknown, and for this reason experienced teething problems. Eventually it passed the censor on 23 November, and opened on 13 December, but it was never awarded a *Prädikat*, despite being deemed suitable for youth.

SA-Mann Brandt, subtitled *ein Lebensbild aus unser Tag* (*A Portrait from our Time*), was directed on a low budget for Bavaria Film in Munich by Franz Seitz, who had previously directed Bavarian *Heimat* comedies starring Weiss Ferdl. The subject of the SA was filmed in the style of a *Heimat* ('folksy') film and was even publicized as an 'authentic *Volksfilm*' (popular film).[23] Brandt's father was played by Otto Wernicke, who had appeared as Detective Superintendant Lohmann in Fritz Lang's *M* (1931) and again as the same character in *Das Testament des Dr Mabuse* (1933). Brandt's female friend was played by Wera Liessem, who also had a part in *Mabuse*, a film which had just been prevented from opening as scheduled in March 1933.

Set in Munich, the film opens in April 1932, just prior to the introduction of a ban on the SA. The SA then numbered 300,000 men, treble the size of the Reichswehr, which was limited to 100,000 by the Treaty of Versailles. After two months, that restriction was lifted. The film ends in 1933 with Hitler's triumph. The focus is on four neighbouring families of varying political persuasions, one Communist, one Nazi and two split. In the opening sequence Communists stone SA Headquarters while the police stand idly by. Later we see Fritz Brandt, the eponymous hero, at home with his parents, reading the paper, *Der SA-Mann*. His father is a tyrannical and unemployed Social Democrat with one redeeming feature, namely he fought in the last war. His mother, in contrast, is secretly pleased with her son's choice of political party. After a scuffle between

Communists and Nazis, Fritz has a heated political discussion with his father (and for the benefit of the audience).

Nearby lives a Nazi widow, whose husband died in the war. His last request had been that his infant son be brought up with a love for the Fatherland. That son, Erich, is now celebrating his sixteenth birthday and is shown his father's last letter. Fritz also gives him a picture of Hitler. 'Our Hitler!' sighs Erich, who is already a member of the Hitler Youth – well before the time it had become obligatory. Erich's mother takes in sewing so that her son can afford the uniform (her birthday present) as well as attend their weekend camp. The police arrive and frisk Brandt as a member of the recently outlawed SA. To his great disappointment, Eric is now warned that he cannot wear his new uniform.

Eric and mother have a sympathetic landlord, who is henpecked by his unpleasant wife. They are the third family. The wife reminds Eric's mother that the rent is due, leaves her husband with the dishes, as she announces that she is off to her women's meeting. The landlord offers Erich's mother some money, which he removes from his copy of *Mein Kampf*, whistles the '*Horst Wessel Lied*' and also gives her their pot roast. The wife on her return is outraged; he blames the cat. Only at the end do we learn her precise political affiliation – though earlier she had told her husband to go to church. She votes for List 6, that is for the BVP or *Bayerische Volkspartei*, the conservative Catholic Bavarian People's Party. She instructs her husband to do the same but he votes List 1 (the Nazis).

The fourth family is the Communist Baumanns. Their daughter, Anni, works in a tobacco kiosk; she has fallen in love with Fritz. The feeling seems not to be reciprocated, as Fritz's mind is on higher things. Anni pulls him to safety after an accident but must defend her actions to her family. Her father beats her for being a traitor to the working class while her brothers look on approvingly with her mother trying to restrain him. The Communists, wearing cloth caps, are coarse and crude. They are led by a Soviet agent, Alexander Turrow. With a penchant for vodka, luxury and women, he speaks in a thick Russian accent and wears on occasion a Russian blouse and at other times spats.

Fritz is fired from his job. His manager informs him, but is unwilling to give the reason, which leads Fritz to confront his Jewish employer, Neuberg. We know he is Jewish because of his exaggerated gestures. Neuberg takes exception to Fritz even entering his office. Fritz learns the reason: it is because he is a Nazi. In fact Turrow has the local council in his pocket, and a councillor had rung the boss to tell him to sack any Nazis on the payroll.

However, Turrow also realizes that Brandt can be useful as an informer and orders Anni to lure him. Fritz meets the Communists while keeping his SA colleagues fully informed, and later divulges to them the location of the Communist arsenal. In the ensuing skirmish Fritz is wounded and taken to hospital where father and son become reconciled, the father being won over to the son's politics, a typical Nazi solution to generational conflict. To Fritz's joy he learns that the ban on the SA has been lifted. The SA is legal again; Fritz encourages Erich to join him in a triumphant and provocative march through the working-class district. A sniper fires; Erich, wearing his new uniform, falls to the ground. Fritz carries him back to his mother, and Erich dies in her arms in a second hospital scene, a Nazi *pietà*.[24]

Aroused by Communist outrages, the people turn to the Nazis who sweep to victory at the polls (though to be precise, even after the Communists had been outlawed, the Nazis never obtained an absolute majority). Brandt arrests the Communist agitators, as well as the trade union officials involved in his dismissal. The Nazi Labour Front captures the trade union offices. The Baumann males are also arrested. The pusillanimous Jewish employer is forced to reinstate Fritz and is warned: 'We have not forgotten!' As soon as the Nazis have left his office, he reaches for the telephone and, with trembling hand, asks his secretary to find out about the next train to Switzerland. The film concludes with a torchlit parade of the SA. The crowds shout '*Sieg Heil!*', their arms raised in the Hitler salute. Anni is in the crowd. The final low-angle shot shows a happy Fritz leading the SA, his face superimposed against the swastika, which then dissolves to marching columns of SA. The '*Horst Wessel Lied*' is on the soundtrack.

The message is so obvious it hardly requires explanation. The villains are primarily the Communists, brutal, cruel, uncouth or, in the case of their non-German leader, degenerate. But there are also non-Communist villains: they include the Jewish employer and the feminist landlady. On several occasions, it has been claimed, crowds are heard to shout '*Juda Verrecke!*' ('Perish Jewry!'). (References to Jews, along with shots of Hitler and snippets of his speech at the end, were cut from the American version which was shown in the German section of New York in 1934.)[25]

Fritz's father, though tyrannical, is a mere Social Democrat. But having fought in the war, he has the potential to be won over to the cause. Generational conflict reinforces the notion that the Nazis represent the vital younger generation. There is no such thing as an old Nazi in these films. The landlord's wife, who dared to henpeck a Nazi sympathizer, is beyond redemption. Accordingly, she does not change party allegiance. Playing on the Nazi rallying cry, 'Germany awake!' ('*Deutschland erwache!*'), her husband rises up against her tyranny as he tells her that he, Anton, has also awakened ('*Anton erwache*'), possibly the director's suggestion since he had been used to directing comedies. Nazi males are kind to women – who must know their place – but are never obsessed with them, for that would be a sign of weakness and lack of resolve; their love is for the Fatherland, for which they will gladly give their lives.

Prior to its opening, *SA-Mann Brandt* had been bitterly attacked in the Nazi press, on the grounds that the rise of the SA was 'too sacred a theme' for commercial film producers, especially when such producers, although 100 per cent Aryan, 'had not minded mixing with Jews and Marxists'. Shortly before the première the name of one of the three scriptwriters was removed from the credits.[26]

Surprisingly, the film found more favour with film critics in what until March 1933 could be considered the non-Nazi press. Even the émigré critic from the US trade paper, *Variety*, Heinrich Fraenkel, who was previously the Hollywood correspondent for the German trade paper, *Lichtbildbühne*, liked it. A scriptwriter, mainly for the German versions of US and British sound films, he worked on the British *Jew Süss* (1934). Possibly it was with tongue in cheek that he claimed to have 'personally advised the London Film Society' to book the film 'for their highly select and highbrow members'.[27] The film he found well made, the photography good and the crowd scenes 'excellently handled', but he reserved criticism for the actor playing the Jewish employer: 'No Jew was found to take the part and the Christian made a bad job of the accent'.[28] The *New York Times* reviewed the film the following year in its US cut version, finding it 'from the technical standpoint' to be 'one of the best pictures made in Germany'.[29] In contrast, Goebbels's own paper, *Der Angriff*, found it 'cheaply produced' and 'badly researched', with the director and his team lacking 'talent' and 'competence'.[30] Whether Goebbels penned the review is unknown but it would not have appeared without his knowledge. He had had little to do with either the film's commission or production; it was made before he and the Propaganda Ministry had firmly established film policy.[31] In more than one speech, Goebbels made clear that 'we absolutely do not want our SA men marching across the screen or on the stage. They should be marching on the streets'.[32] The film accorded more with Hitler's views about film.

Hitler attended the film at its second showing at the large Berlin cinema, the Ufa-Palast am Zoo, in the company of Goebbels and General Werner von Blomberg, the Defence Minister. An organ recital preceded the screening. The audience was packed with SA plus 'thousands guarding all the avenues of approach'.[33] But disaster struck on the following day when the film opened in Frankfurt at the Gloria-Palast. The *Frankfurter Zeitung*, a respected liberal paper prior to 1933, under the headline 'The Screening Prevented' reported an incident which took place shortly before the screening. The SA Group Leader, Beckerle, had stood up and informed the audience that the poster advertising the film had been designed by a Polish artist, and that despite his request, the cinema owners had refused to remove it. He thereupon demanded that the SA and SS leave the cinema, which they promptly did, and the screening was halted.[34] Three days later the *Frankfurter Zeitung* printed in full a letter from Beckerle protesting at their coverage of the incident. He now claimed that the Polish artist had been a Jew. The newspaper's response was to republish their previous report, giving the source (the Wolf wire press agency), reproducing Beckerle's letter in full, and concluding with a factual statement, namely that the film had now been withdrawn from the cinema. Reading between the lines, for that no doubt was what the newspaper hoped its non-Nazi readers would do, the SA was being held up to ridicule.[35]

Hitlerjunge Quex, subtitled 'a film about youth's spirit of sacrifice', was directed by Hans Steinhoff (1881–1945), an accomplished film director and party member. Steinhoff directed many films, including the anti-British propaganda film, *Ohm Krüger* (1940). *Hitlerjunge Quex* was the first film made by the new production unit within Ufa headed by Karl Ritter, a long-standing party member who arrived at Ufa in January 1933 and later turned his hand to directing. Apparently, without prompting from the Propaganda Ministry, Ufa was now trying to prove that it could make a better film than *SA-Mann Brandt*.[36] The cameraman was the versatile Moscow-born Konstantin Irmen-Tschet, who had worked on *Metropolis* and had just completed work on Reinhard Schunzel's gender-bending comedy *Viktor und Viktoria* (*Victor and Victoria*). Later he would be chief cameraman on the first colour film and after that *Münchhausen*.

Hitlerjunge Quex, or *Hitler Youth Quex*, was based on a novel by a neurologist and writer, Karl Aloys Schenzinger, which was published in December 1932 and serialized in the *Völkischer Beobachter* from January to February 1933. It was a fictionalized account of the life of Herbert Norkus, a Hitler Youth member, killed in a Communist quarter of Berlin in early 1932 while distributing Nazi leaflets.[37] Renamed Heini Volker by Schenzinger, Volker then acquires a nickname Quex (quicksilver). Schenzinger altered many facts, then co-scripted the film which changed the story yet again.

According to the credits, members of the Hitler Youth played themselves. This even extended to those with speaking parts, including the lead, Jürgen Ohlsen. The intention was to lend an air of authenticity as neither Ritter nor Schirach wanted actors confused with the Hitler Youth.[38] The acting is of a very high order, especially by Ohlsen, which suggests hidden talents amongst the anonymous Hitler Youth. Baldur von Schirach forbade any mention of Ohlsen's name, as allegedly Ohlsen had no plans to continue with acting, having just begun a joiner's apprenticeship. Such secretiveness was abandoned when he subsequently obtained leading roles.[39]

One of the young Communists is played by Rolf Wenkhaus. In *SA-Mann Brandt*, he had played the martyred Hitler Youth, Eric, his performance being singled out for praise by the *Völkischer Beobachter* as the 'embodiment of the naïve and fresh youthful spirit'.[40] Two years previously Wenkhaus had played Emil in a charming film based on Erich Kästner's best-selling novel, *Emil and the Detectives*, directed by Gerhard Lamprecht with a script by Billy Wilder. Siegfried Kracauer characterized the juvenile sleuthing in that film as 'a democratization of [German] everyday life' and 'a triumph of light over darkness', as the young pursue the shadowy thief through the streets of Berlin.[41] Transformed and unrecognizable in *SA-Mann Brandt* with his blonde hair slicked back, Wenkhaus returns more to type in *Hitler Youth Quex*, though only in a minor role. His pert, freckled face, with a shock of blond hair hanging low on his forehead, now suggests criminality or youthful independence taken too far. He steals an apple at the film's outset, passes a bottle of schnapps to a female Communist, provocatively shoving it in her mouth, and later emerges from the shadows after spying at night on the Hitler Youth headquarters. This piece of casting sent out a confusing message, for in less than two years Wenkhaus had run the gamut from non-political youth (Emil), to Hitler Youth, to delinquent Communist.

Hitler Youth Quex is the story of the martyrdom of the fourteen-year-old printer's apprentice, Heini, whose over-eagerness leads other Hitler Youth to nickname him Quex (moves fast like quicksilver). Against his Communist family's wishes, he turns to the Nazis and joins the Hitler Youth, who are mainly blond, clean-cut and upright while the non-Nazi youth are undisciplined, slovenly and steal when necessary. The pretty, blonde, fun-loving Communist female, who makes a play for Heini, smokes, drinks and often wears trousers. (In contrast, the female Nazi wears a tie but with a skirt, a sartorial subtlety now lost.) The Nazis are drawn to the forest while the Communists frequent a fairground. As often observed, the fairground has provided a sinister setting in numerous German films including *Das Cabinet des Dr Caligari*; a site of disorder akin to carnival, impermanence, intoxication and desire.[42] It is there that Heini develops a desire for an eight-blade knife; it is the Communist villain, Wilde, however, who wins it and ultimately will use it on Heini.

Not all Communists are deemed bad in the turf war between Communists and Nazis in a Berlin working-class district. The exception is the family friend, Stoppel, played by Hermann Speelmans. Amiable, well-meaning, with sound instincts and his heart in the right place, he tries to help Heini, first by smoothing over relations with his irascible father (Heinrich George), and at the end by pointing his Communist comrades in the wrong direction, as they hunt down Heini for daring to invade their territory to distribute Nazi election material.

The corpulent George was another significant piece of casting, providing continuity with Weimar film. He also underwent a political conversion. Previously known for his proletarian roles – the foreman in *Metropolis* (1927), Franz Bieberkopf in *Berlin-Alexanderplatz* (1931) – and his work in the radical Berlin theatre, he was, in taking on this role, signalling his support for the new rulers. Several months later in November 1933 in an open letter to Goebbels he declared his allegiance to Hitler:

> I must, forgive the boldness, tell you that as if waking from a nightmare, I gave a sigh of relief, when our Führer, our great People's Chancellor, and his government gave the world

again a clear, divine and unambiguous answer to what was apparently insoluble and with that stirred the hearts of millions of unawakened *Volksgenosse* here and abroad.[43]

This, in turn, inspired an open letter to him from the exiled Bertolt Brecht, clearly intended for those who had once known and worked with George.[44] George became a stalwart of the new regime. He took on a range of important acting roles and was also appointed director of the Berlin Schiller Theatre, a plum job. His real-life wife, another well-known Weimar actor, Berta Drews, took the role of Heini's mother.

Stoppel wears the cloth cap, like his other comrades, a sign that he is a true member of the working class (in the novel Stoppel wears a sailor's cap, identifying him with the 1919 Communist sailors' and soldiers' councils). He stands in stark contrast to the real villain, the sinister and aptly named Wilde (Karl Meixner), a devil-like character, wearing his fedora cocked at an angle in Hollywood gangster style. These are political fashion statements and enable the audience to make a distinction between Communists. Further, Meixner's physiognomy, combined with his shrill voice, suggests malice. Not only is it he who, in the final scene, kills Heini but he even discusses the need to kill him in the presence of Heini's father. Wilde has no redeeming qualities.

There is no Wilde character in Schenzinger's 1932 novel. Stoppel is there but he is not the film's amiable character. For the film the Communist figure has been split in two: Stoppel, who is good, and an authentic member of the Berlin working class, and Wilde, who is bad, and leads the working class astray. In the novel a Communist, by definition, is bad. Though Schenzinger co-scripted the film, many changes went well beyond the need to adapt from one medium to another. The film reflected the fact that the Nazis were no longer aspiring to power but were in power. One might assume that they could afford to be generous to their defeated enemies, but there was more to it than that: 10 per cent of all German Communists lived in the German capital, Berlin, and in the last Weimar election nearly a third of Berliners had voted Communist.[45] The film suggests that Communists are not inherently bad but have been misled by their leaders.

Meixner's portrayal of the Communist villain ranges from the rabble-rouser whipping up the crowd in the opening sequence, exhorting them to steal, to the sinister gangster in later sequences. Whether gangster or rabble-rouser, his voice, physiognomy, body language and attire suggest a threat, in contrast to the genuine Berlin worker.

Is Wilde a Jew? He is not usually described as such, but significantly that is how Kracauer describes him. This appears in his analysis of the film for the Museum of Modern Art, written in 1941 (in very poor English, as he had only recently arrived in the US from France). The description appears not in the actual transcription of the dialogue, where Wilde merely 'looks fanatically, a little tuberculosis – the type of an instigator' (sic), but in the accompanying synopsis where Kracauer writes: 'There is no hopeless villain, except for the one who actually kills and who is made up as a jew [sic] and talks [with an] Austrian accent.'[46] The Austrian accent is slight – Meixner was in fact Viennese-born. That he may seem tubercular can only relate to his physiognomy – hollow cheeks, accentuated by high cheekbones – since he never once coughs. Could Kracauer be wrong? If Wilde, who is both gangster and agitator, is not a Jew, what then is he? Given that the film's purpose was transparent – to woo Communists and distinguish good Communists from bad, the former redeemable, the latter not – then the good Communist had the potential to belong to the *Volksgemeinschaft*. The bad Communist, by definition a foreigner or a Jew, could not. Even if it is not made explicit, Wilde is likely to have been a Jew, given that German is his native language. At one point he even shrugs his shoulders in what can be considered a Jewish gesture. This doubtless informs Kracauer's view. That he mentioned it in one description but not in the other is likely to have been an oversight.

The film borrows from several Weimar films. The mother, depressed at the family's plight since the violent, alcoholic father is out of work, is under pressure from Stoppel about Heini's weakening Communist allegiance. She tries to gas herself and Heini. The sequence, especially powerful because of the soundtrack, is reminiscent of the suicide sequence in the Communist-produced *Mutter Krausens Fahrt ins Glück* (*Mother Krausen's Journey to Happiness*) (1929), in which both grandmother and granddaughter die. As the darkened screen fills with billowing fumes Mahlerian music becomes more and more insistent on the soundtrack. It then subsides into a lament which we soon recognize as the Hitler Youth song, '*Unsere Fahne*' (Our Flag), now played in a minor key. That song was composed specially for this film by the Hitler Youth leader, Schirach, with music by film composer Hans Otto Borgmann.[47] Heini survives (there is a quick cut to a bright hospital ward where Heini is cared for by the surrogate mother/nurse). He will live to die another day, at the hands of the Communists, for this film is about sacrifice and martyrdom. His dying words are the first line of the Hitler Youth song: 'Our flag billows before us.' When he dies, a chorus takes up the rest of the song:

> Our Flag is the new epoch
> And the flag leads us into eternity
> Yes, the flag is more than death.

The image slowly dissolves to the billowing flag emblazoned with a large swastika. Columns of marching Hitler Youth merge with columns of SA. The film ends with the flag filling the screen, its large swastika becoming a cut-out through which we see marching columns of uniformed men and boys.

Heini's graphic murder in an empty fairground is reminiscent of the final sequence in Lang's *M* (1931), where the child murderer (Peter Lorre) is hunted down and killed in a fairground. Now, in a reversal, it is the child who is hunted and killed by Communists. At one point, Meixner even makes his voice sound like Lorre's. In Schenzinger's novel, Heini merely dies at night at the edge of the Berlin park, the Tiergarten, as his friends hear his scream. In the film, Heini's death is closer to that of the real-life Norkus, who died from multiple stab wounds after being chased by Communists, though this did not take place in a fairground but on the streets of working-class Berlin. (His Communist killers were caught and given three years.)[48]

One aim of the film was to persuade German Communists that they had a home in Germany after all, as made abundantly clear in one particular sequence often commented on. Heini's father is questioned by a Hitler Youth *Bannführer* (Brigade Leader), a role taken by the lanky, blond actor, Claus Clausen, in another significant piece of casting. Two years previously he had played the officer in G.W. Pabst's anti-war film, *Westfront 1918* (1930). Heini's father explains that he has not got fat from eating too much but from sitting around without work:

Father:	'So where do I belong? I belong with my class comrades. And where I belong, so does my son.'
Youth leader:	'With your own class comrades? With the *Internationale*?'
Father:	'Yes, of course, with the *Internationale*.'
Youth leader:	'Where were you born?'
Father:	'Berlin.'
Youth leader:	'But where does it lie?'
Father:	'Why, on the Spree.'
Youth Leader:	'Yes, but where? In what country?'
Father:	'In Germany, of course.'
Youth Leader:	'In Germany, yes, in our Germany. Then think that over!'

But it is not just the dialogue that provides the message. What is happening on the screen is important.[49] The camera, the acting and the casting of actors indicates who holds the answers in this sequence: it is not the portly, defeated, irascible Communist father but the tall, blond, clear-headed, kindly *Bannführer* whose figure commands the frame. Still, the father has a future since the *Bannführer* treats him with kindness and understanding. The mother is dispensable. (Norkus's mother had died in a mental hospital in 1931.)[50]

Gregory Bateson, a cultural anthropologist who later became a psychoanalyst, examined this film from an anthropological perspective for a project on propaganda at Columbia University during the Second World War. He was particularly interested in Nazi ideas relating to parenthood, adolescence, cleanliness and death.[51] Though some of his comments may now seem obvious, given greater familiarity with Freudian ideas and feminist film theory, a film idealizing Nazis provided fertile ground for an anthropologist. It is the failure of the family which enables the young to be wooed. One obvious message is that mothers are weak – they prevent boys from growing up – while tyrannical fathers can still be reformed. (In *SA-Mann Brand* the father is sympathetic to the Nazis while his wife is less so. But since she is not in actual despair with her son's politics she is allowed to live to experience the Nazi triumph.) Male Nazis are surrogate parents, a theme found in other films belonging to this genre directed at youth, of which this was the first.[52] Even the well-behaved Nazi brother and sister, Ulla and Fritz, have no parents, or rather they do not put in a screen appearance (apparently their father is a doctor). Their appearance would weaken the message that it is the party that provides good parenting. Moreover, it can tame unhealthy adolescent desires, something at which the Communist Party signally fails. After the *Bannführer*'s discussion with his father, Heini moves into a Nazi Youth home. It is from there that he goes to meet his death.

Set in Berlin and filmed there, the gala première took place in Munich while *SA-Mann Brandt*, set in Munich and filmed there, had its première in Berlin. This was clearly deliberate.[53] The première of *Hitlerjunge Quex* also took place in Hitler's presence. Other dignitaries present included Marshal Hermann Goering, now Prussian Minister-President, Rudolf Hess, the party's deputy leader, SA leader Ernst Röhm, Vice-Chancellor von Papen and Defence Minister von Blomberg. Young Reichswehr officers were known to refer disparagingly to Blomberg as 'Hitlerjunge Quex'.[54] Thousands of Hitler Youth lined the streets leading to the cinema, which was lit by searchlights. An orchestra played Bruckner's Fourth Symphony, after which the Hitler Youth Leader, Schirach, addressed the audience, he warning them of the need both for heroism and sacrifice and reminding them of an earlier meeting when he had addressed two thousand Berlin Hitler Youth members. He described it thus:

> An oppressive atmosphere hung over this assembly, we had a premonition of a terrible event … I said that tomorrow there might be one whom I would not see again … Next morning, Herbert Norkus fell at the hands of the Marxist terrorists.[55]

After the screening, Ohlsen (Heini) came on stage and saluted Hitler, who smiled and returned the salute. As the Führer left the theatre, the Hitler Youth played his favourite 'Badenweiler March'.[56] According to one reviewer:

> *Hitlerjunge Quex* is a German film, produced not with the aim of making money, but with the goal of recreating the genuine atmosphere and deeply-felt experiences of those days, a film which is a fanfare of German youth and of the German future.[57]

The best crafted of the three films and the most successful at the box office, it was also the only one to please Goebbels.[58] Viewed by over twenty million people via commercial and party outlets, it was still being shown during the Hitler Youth film hour in 1942, though by then dying for Hitler was no longer confined to the screen.

Hans Westmar, Einer von Vielen (*Hans Westmar, One of Many*) was subtitled *Ein deutsches Schicksal aus dem Jahre 1929* (*A German Destiny from the Year 1929*). Originally entitled *Horst Wessel*, it was directed by the inexperienced Franz Wenzler for the newly created *Volksdeutsche Filmgesellchaft* (German People's Film Company) with the assistance of the Berlin SA.[59] Leni Riefenstahl claimed it was first offered to her but she declined it.[60] That the title had to be changed indicates a problem with presenting the life and death of a real-life Nazi martyr.

Hanns Heinz Ewers (1871–1943) wrote the script, basing it on his hagiographic *Horst Wessel* (1932), a report commissioned by Hitler on the death of the hero.[61] Then over sixty, and a recent recruit to the Nazi cause, Ewers was treated with suspicion in some quarters, some of his works being considered akin to pornography, but Hitler wanted him.[62] He hoped that a book by a popular author would reach a wider audience.[63] So great was Ewers's enthusiasm for his new-found cause that he even took a minor role in the film, playing an elderly member of the student fraternity.[64] Nevertheless, despite the Führer's patronage, the writer's pre-Nazi writings never left the various equivalents of a Nazi index.[65]

The author of popular Gothic novels such as *Alraun* (*Mandrake*), filmed by Henrik Galeen in 1928, and *Vampyr* (*Vampire*), Ewers had also written the film scripts for both versions of *Der Student von Prag* (*The Student of Prague*), in 1913 starring Paul Wegener and in 1926 starring Conrad Veidt and Werner Krauss. On *Hans Westmar* Ewers worked again with Wegener, though not with Galeen who had been forced into exile. Wegener, the only prominent actor in the film, was closely identified with his role of the Golem (the monster who, according to Jewish legend, was conjured up by the Prague Rabbi Loew), having taken that role in the three Golem films. He also co-directed and co-scripted with Galeen *Der Golem* (1915) and *Der Golem und die Tänzerin* (*The Golem and the Dancer*) (1917). With Carl Boese he co-directed the best known of the three, *Der Golem: wie er in die Welt kam* (*The Golem and How He Came into the World*) (1920). He also appeared in *Alraune*. Typecast as a monster, his large head, broad face, high cheekbones and heavy body had made him ideal for the outsized Golem. Now in *Hans Westmar* he played the Soviet agent, wearing a beret and goatee to reinforce a resemblance to Lenin.[66]

The composer was Giuseppi Becce, but the wealthy, piano-playing Ernst ('Putzi') Hanfstaengl (1887–1975), then a friend of Hitler, also provided and arranged well-known melodies and supervised the film. Munich-born but

Harvard-educated – he had an American mother – Hanfstaengl was an early admirer of Hitler, for whom he helped open the doors of Munich society. During the hyper-inflation he lent the party money and participated in the 1923 Beer Hall putsch. Appointed Nazi foreign press chief in 1931, a post he held while composing for this film, he later lost favour. Fleeing to England in 1937, he was interned at the outbreak of war, then transferred to Canada. His 'old Harvard Club friend', Franklin Roosevelt, interceded and he was released to US custody where until 1944 he claimed to have advised the American government on psychological warfare.[67]

The film was scheduled to appear under its original title, *Horst Wessel*, at Berlin's largest cinema, the Ufa-Palast, on 9 October 1933, on what would have been Wessel's twenty-sixth birthday. The completed film minus the final scene had in fact been shown earlier, on 12 September, to SA leaders to great applause: 'the old warriors found that some sequences were so faithfully reproduced that they felt themselves transposed to old times.'[68] The complete version had a closed screening on 3 October for prominent representatives from the arts, politics, journalism and the diplomatic corps, and included Goering, the conductors Wilhelm Furtwängler and Erich Kleiber, and the Nazi playwright Hanns Johst.[69] Thus its failure to pass the film censor a few days later on the morning of the première met with surprise. The 'inadequate depiction of the heroic life' of Horst Wessel had 'endangered the interests of the state and Germany's reputation'.[70]

Goebbels was behind the ban, attempting to put his stamp on film production. Eventually he was forced to back down and allow the film, subject to a change in title and some cuts. Shortly after the ban was announced he felt the need to explain his opposition to the film, thus implicitly revealing his links to the censor's decision. He reiterated his preference for the SA on the streets rather than on the screen, emphasizing that were they to appear on the latter it must only be in a film of the highest artistic quality. He had known Wessel, and the figure in the film neither resembled him nor conveyed his character. Its real failure, however, was artistic, though he was careful to say that the music was outstanding as were the scenes with the SA.[71] The film finally passed the censor on 23 November under a new title, *Hans Westmar*, and the première followed three weeks later on 13 December, but was denied any *Prädikat*.

Horst Wessel's main contribution to the Nazi movement was to write the words of the Nazi party anthem or signature tune, which subsequently became known as the '*Horst Wessel Lied*' (Horst Wessel song). During the Third Reich it was Germany's second national anthem after '*Deutschland über Alles*', which the Social Democratic President, Friedrich Ebert, had made the national anthem in 1922, after Germany became a republic. Wessel's verses were a hymn to the SA.

> Hold the flag high! Close the serried ranks!
> The SA marches with firm, bold step,
> Comrades shot by the Red Front and the Reaction
> March in spirit in our ranks.
>
> The street free for the brown battalions,
> The street free for the storm troopers!
> Millions full of hope look up to the swastika
> The day of freedom and bread dawns.

The dead comrades marching in spirit was an allusion to 'the Blood Myth', so important to Nazi belief and ritual, whereby defeat is turned into a spiritual victory. Though the noble warrior may die, he is resurrected to return 'in spirit to the fighting columns of Brown Shirts'.[72] Wessel immortalized this in words later set to an old army tune or sailor's song, though Goebbels tried to present Wessel also as the composer. Subsequently the party adopted it as their own anthem.[73] It would be their first song to be released as a recording.[74] But soon Wessel himself became a dead noble warrior and this gave the song greater resonance. Nevertheless, a film based on his life ran into difficulties.

Nazi martyrs are the subject of all three *Kampfzeit* films. Two were based on actual cases (Norkus and Wessel) and conclude with a cinematic spiritual return. Having died, the hero's spirit lives on: his ghost marches with his comrades across the screen through a superimposition of shots – a cinematic trick, incidentally, not pioneered by the Nazis. The Tyrolean alpinist, Luis Trenker, ends *Der Rebell* (1932) this way. The rebel, played by Trenker – he was fond of starring in his own films – was shot by the Napoleonic invaders, but returns at the end to march in spirit. Trenker claimed Hitler saw his film four times.[75] Much earlier, in Abel Gance's celebrated anti-war film, *J'accuse* (1918–19), the dead rise from their graves with a similar superimposition, though here the director's intention was different in that the ghosts belong to a dream sequence in which the dead judge the living.[76] Ghosts in films were one of the earliest cinematic tricks.

Much has been written about the real Horst Wessel, who died at Communist hands, some of it based on Communist disinformation portraying him as a pimp. Born in 1907, Wessel came from a solid bourgeois background: his father was a Lutheran clergyman who during the First World War was chaplain to Field Marshal von Hindenburg's headquarters. In the same year that Wessel began his studies at the University of Berlin (1926), he joined the SA, having found the conservative student fraternity insufficiently radical. He soon abandoned his studies to become a construction worker and chauffeur. His sympathy for the unemployed enabled him to challenge the Communists on their home ground in the working-class areas of Berlin. His success at converting Communists – many in his SA unit were former Communists – combined with his obvious qualities of leadership, led to his rapid promotion within the SA. It also made him a Communist target. His verses, now set to music, became popular in Berlin and were enthusiastically received at the 1929 Nuremberg party rally. That same year he became enamoured of a prostitute, Erna Jaenichen, whom he had first encountered in a bar when being beaten by pimps. He began living with her and took offence at any disrespect shown his future bride. To Goebbels's alarm (Goebbels was then Gauleiter of Berlin), he began to spend less energy on party matters. While supporting the ex-prostitute, he ignored his mother's pleas to return to his studies. After his younger brother, also a member of the SA, was killed skiing, Wessel's mental and physical condition deteriorated.[77]

Hunted by the Communists, Wessel was killed early in 1930 when still only aged twenty-two.[78] His widowed landlady, in dispute with him about the rent for his live-in girlfriend, helped arrange the killing. Her husband had been an active Communist and she sought party help. When they realized that her dispute was with an SA leader, they took immediate action, hoping to discover useful documents relating to SA activities. Wessel was shot as he opened the door, and died six weeks later in hospital of septicaemia; his SA comrades had delayed medical treatment by refusing to summon a Jewish doctor living three doors away.[79] Street battles erupted on the way both to and from his burial. Given the tense atmosphere, Hitler decided not to attend, something Goebbels held against him.[80] Hitler had once admitted that he preferred addressing a crowd and was no good at a funeral.[81]

The Communists attempted a cover-up, presenting the murder as the result of a dispute amongst pimps; hence the legend of Horst Wessel the pimp, rather than Horst Wessel the unstable idealist. The murderer and the network of Communist accomplices were caught and tried. To the Nazis' dismay, the murderer and his main accomplice received light sentences (six years and one month), though ten other Communists who were implicated (including the landlady) were also sent to prison for shorter terms.

By 1933 Wessel had become a source of myth and legend, in which Goebbels had a hand.[82] On the third anniversary of his death, three weeks after the Nazis took power, and during the election campaign, a memorial service was held at his grave, with Hitler, Himmler and Goebbels in attendance. But Goebbels experienced difficulties with Wessel's mother. Shortly before the film went into production, he commented: 'She wants to privatize Horst's song: I refused this point blank. The song belongs to the nation. The mother is insufferable. She does not deserve this heroic young man.'[83]

The Wessel case was reopened in 1933, along with other Weimar 'miscarriages of justice'. The murderer was brought to Berlin from prison and, under the pretext of returning him to prison, then turned over to the SA and shot by members of Wessel's brigade. His body was found in a forest clearing east of Berlin on 20 September,[84] just over three weeks before the film (under its original title) was scheduled to open. His 'summary execution' had Goering's and Röhm's approval, though allegedly it was Hitler who gave the order.[85]

Accompanying the film titles is a musical motif befitting the death of a hero, also used in the 'Ceremony of the Fallen' sequence in *Triumph of the Will*. On each side of a swastika a candle burns, above which appear the letters HW and the caption 'a German fate from the year 1929'. The film opens in a Viennese beer garden. Westmar, played by tall, clean-cut Emil Lohkamp, a provincial stage actor in his first film role,[86] tells friends that he must return to Berlin where unemployment is rife. The film cuts to a dole queue, as someone hums the '*Horst Wessel Lied*', and then to a dosshouse where a character states: 'in Moscow you have your own villa.' In the next sequence the camera pans upward to the Communist leader, Kuprikoff (Wegener), in beret and bow tie and with a cane and goatee, who stands on a hill overlooking a shanty town. A low-angle shot emphasizes his high cheekbones and narrow eyes. Twirling a flower, he tells his assistant in a thick Russian accent: 'misery is our best friend'. The film cuts to Karl Liebknecht House, the Communist Party headquarters, awash with red flags emblazoned with the hammer and sickle. Kuprikoff is chairing a Communist Party committee meeting and proclaims: 'the Soviet is in Russia, the Soviet is in Germany, the world belongs to us, Hitler and the Nazis are children and fools.'

The characterization of the Communists is clear: while the boss is Russian, his dignified, businesslike and not unsympathetic young assistant is German. By the end of the film, the assistant will have seen the light. To confuse matters, he is given the name Camillo Ross. That was the name of a seventeen-year-old Communist shot a few hours before Wessel's murder. In court Wessel's murderer cited revenge for this murder as his motive for killing Wessel.[87] Ewers is likely to have created the part of Kuprikoff for Wegener, since he had worked with him previously and the character does not appear in his novel.

Two other Communist characters are Jews and depicted as grotesques. The Reichstag deputy, Kupferstein, also wears a bow tie, but askew, for he is a comical Jew: short, with frizzy grey hair, a large nose (probably false), spectacles, jerky body movements, a rasping voice and a silly grin. The real Josef Kupferstein was a Communist party functionary, a young brigade leader for Berlin-Mitte, implicated in Wessel's death. He was reported to have given a fiery speech in a piercing voice at the trial and was sent to prison for four months.[88] In the novel he is the main Communist villain, the evil presence, even when in Warsaw pulling strings. Ridiculed in the film, he appears less powerful.

The other Jew is Kuprikoff's female assistant. Smartly turned out, small in stature, her short dark hair in a bob, with a prominent nose, she hangs on his every word.[89] Later we see her harangue a Communist meeting. She is a

conflation of several figures, linking Jewish women with the radical left such
as the short, dark-haired Spartacist leader, Rosa Luxemburg, killed in January
1919 in the Spartacist uprising in Berlin, and the half-Jewish Ruth Fischer (born
Elfriede Eisler), an attractive smartly turned-out Communist firebrand of
bourgeois background, sister of the Communist composer Hanns Eisler. Later,
in American exile, she turned against the Communists, denouncing both her
brothers (the other was the journalist, Gerhart Eisler) to the House Un-American
Activities Committee.[90] During the Ruhr crisis in 1923 she appealed to right-
wing students by attacking 'Jewish capital' along with 'French imperialism' but
was finally stopped by the party for distributing posters displaying the Soviet star
with the swastika.[91] The most obvious source, however, is Else Cohn, whose name
indicates a Jewish origin. She was implicated in Wessel's death: it was she who
reported back to the Communists that Wessel had returned to his flat, for which
she was later sentenced to one year in prison.[92] In the film, as also mentioned at
the trial, she hovers around Wessel's flat.[93] In the novel, which is closer to the trial
as reported in the press, she is also the person who knocks on his door.[94] She is
not mentioned by name in the novel, though she is described as 'small and ugly'.
Those familiar with the press coverage of the case would assume it was Cohn.[95]

Hans returns to Berlin; under the eyes of his kindly bourgeois mother we
see him unpack. He attends a lecture where internationalism and peace are
praised: Germany may have lost territory but she is 'frontierless', 'European', a
'*Kulturnation*', and Germans are 'world citizens'. Wessel was studying law and this
is likely to have been a lecture on international law. The middle-aged, grey-haired,
slightly dishevelled lecturer, with his spectacles atop his head, stands in front of a
map of Europe while paraphrasing Ebert's comments when opening the Weimar
Assembly in February 1919.[96] Some have concluded (wrongly in my view) that he
must be a Jew.[97] Not every enemy of the Nazis was a Jew, especially those accused
of 'stabbing Germany in the back' or of accepting Versailles. What, however, has
been missed in this sequence is a swarthy student with a prominent nose who
is taking copious notes. He sits in the first row in the foreground of the frame;
behind him in the next row an angry Hans is pointedly not writing. The point
has been made: only Jews accept a weakened Germany. Next to the note-taker sits
a brunette wearing spectacles, one of only three females. This highlights another
Weimar failing: that emancipated women aspire, and are allowed, to study the
same subjects as men.

The sequence concludes with the lecturer declaring: 'Down with war! Down
with weapons!' The film then cuts to a shot of crossed swords as a voice shouts:
'Weapons up!' Two young men, members of a student corps (fraternity), are about
to start a duel, now illegal, when the police arrive, after which the students sing
a rousing nineteenth-century student song about brotherhood. Young men have
been deprived of their birthright to train to defend the nation. This is Weimar

law, enforced by the police who in Berlin are under Social Democratic control. In the next sequence, Hans gazes down from a window at Communist marchers shouting 'Death to the Fascists!' 'The real battle is outside … on the streets', he tells his friends. 'The whole of Germany is at stake. We must fight hand in hand with the workers.' A friend reminds him that he is not a worker, but Wessel counters that there must be no more class distinctions: 'We are workers too. We work with our brains. Our path is now beside our brothers, the workers.'

Hans meets a German-American who had left Berlin for the USA twenty years previously. He is travelling with his attractive blonde daughter. They traverse Berlin in a taxi, affording the viewer the opportunity to see Berlin through the emigrant's eyes. Neon lights flash. Signs proclaim that French, English, Spanish and Russian are spoken; restaurants offer Hungarian, Chinese and Italian food. 'I do not recognize it,' says the father. 'It looked different twenty years ago.' The daughter is impressed and declares Berlin truly international, to which her father adds: 'But not German'. They enter Chez Ninette. A black man takes their coats. Posters on the wall advertise plays such as *A Jew Goes into the World* at the (left-wing and avant-garde) Piscator theatre and *Moscow Cries and Laughs* at the Volksbühne. A black singer appears on another poster. The dance band plays a Yiddish tune. They order a beer, but an Indian waiter tells them that only English beer is available along with Russian caviar, but nothing German. This nightclub is a Nazi nightmare. It is also an indictment of the degenerate tastes of the German bourgeoisie. An obese businessman requests the nationalist 'Wacht am Rhein' (Watch on the Rhine), which is then played in jazz style. The banjo player begins to dance; the waiter and the dark-skinned jazz singer dance together. Rising up in a rage, Hans puts a stop to the sacrilege. He tells the Americans 'that is not Germany – it is somewhere else'.

A dissolve to the trenches and then to a cemetery, after which we see Hans seated on a bench with a friend to whom he declares: 'Three million have died, and all we can do is dance, booze and bawl.' The film cuts to a Communist meeting addressed by Kupferstein. In a comical Jewish accent he shouts: 'Long live the Fatherland of the worker! Long live the Soviet Union!' and calls Hitler a madman standing in their way. The camera picks out Hans in the audience, accompanied by several other Nazis, including a friend who a few hours later will be murdered. The dignified Ross announces that, as promised, a representative of the Nazis will be allowed to speak: 'Which one of the brown shirts would like to?' Hans stands up, adopts a Hitler pose, addresses the audience as 'Fellow Germans'. He tells them that everyone is guilty – the middle classes, the workers, but most of all the Communists – and shouts 'Germany awake!' and 'Long live the Fatherland!' This sets off a brawl which spreads to the streets. The police arrive; shots are fired, after which the cowardly Kupferstein creeps out from under a table bedecked with the red flag – confirming an antisemitic jibe that Jews are cowards.

Hans and his friend take leave of each other with the Hitler salute. The friend is then set upon by the Communists, knocked unconscious and his body thrown into the canal. It has been assumed that his death is based on that of an SA man by the name of Kütemeyer who drowned in a canal and who, despite lack of evidence of Communist involvement, was posthumously honoured at the 1929 Nuremberg Party Rally.[98] The character is not, however, mentioned by name in the film.[99] He does not appear in Ewers's novel, which mentions a fight between the SA and the Communists on the Jannowitz bridge in which Communists shout: 'Beat the fascist dogs to death, throw the Nazis in the Spree!'[100] He is played by Adolf Fischer, who the previous year had appeared as the upright Communist in the film *Kuhle Wampe: oder wem gehört die Welt* (*Kuhle Wampe: or To whom does the World Belong*) which opened in New York after 1933 as *Whither Germany?* Funded from Communist sources, co-scripted by Brecht with music by Eisler, it was directed by Slatan Dudow. Doubtless, in the changed circumstances, Fischer considered it a wise career move to accept this small part, though his name is absent from the credits. Casting him in the role of a Nazi martyr was less about giving him a job and a chance to redeem himself and more about targeting cinema-goers who had seen *Kuhle Wampe*. Fischer had changed sides; shouldn't they?

Switching sides is the theme developed in the next sequence. At a Communist committee meeting, a visibly upset Ross tells his boss that Communist behaviour will make fanatics of the other side. 'Your opinion does not interest me. Let Moscow deal with this!' he is told. The transformation of the good Communist has begun.

The SA plan to march in protest. The Communists round up their supporters. Hans leads the marchers. In a low-angle shot against a backdrop of clouds – soon to become familiar in Riefenstahl's documentaries – we see him marching. He looks to the left. The camera leads us to the object of his gaze: in the front row of the crowd of spectators, directly behind a policeman stand three bearded men in black hats, *Ostjude* – the implication is that they enjoy police protection. It is only a three-second shot, but telling. The Berlin Police President, Karl Zörgiebel, and his Vice-President, Bernhard Weiss, were Social Democrats, hated by the paramilitary SA for maintaining order on the streets. Weiss was also a Jew, and since 1927 Goebbels had had him in his sights, giving him the nickname 'Isidor', a typically Jewish name, or 'Vipoprä', an abbreviation for Vice-Police President, and had had some success in publicizing Weiss's shortcomings amongst the wider public.[101] The sequence concludes with the singing of '*Deutschland erwache*' as another street battle erupts.

Hans rescues a girl, Agnes, from a pub where her drunken Communist step-father is beating her, a deviation from both the novel and the Wessel murder trial where the culprit is a pimp. Her name has also been changed, along with her occupation. Interestingly, the name change only occurred after filming had begun.[102] In the novel she appears as Erna, and initially as a prostitute. She also shares the flat with Wessel.[103] Given his previous literary endeavours, Ewers was unlikely to shy away from such information as detailed in the court records and in the press coverage. Communist fathers of females (as in *SA-Mann Brandt*), or stepfathers as in *Hans Westmar*, made easy targets. Hans gives Agnes some money and advises her to go away for a time. He is observed by Ross, who introduces himself to Hans. He asks what can he know about the workers and accuses him of impinging on Communist territory: 'The East is ours while you have the West.'

To his mother's consternation, Hans has given up his studies to become a worker: a construction worker by day and a taxi driver by night ('I am going to be a worker with my brains and hands. He who wishes to lead must serve'). He gives a ride to the German-Americans whom earlier he had befriended. They recognize him and invite him to America. He rejects their offer as he has a great mission: 'We are a small race but have a great message for all. We must be like the masses.' When the daughter asks how long this will take, he replies: 'a few years'.

Worried at Hans's success at recruiting, the Communists call in Agnes. They tell her to see Hans often. Instead, she warns him. Their relationship deviates from the biography since they do not actually live together, though she is around a great deal. She can be relied on and tells Hans: 'I don't want to go back to them [meaning the Communists], but I also don't want to join you either [meaning the Nazis].' (Apparently Wessel's 'fiancée' allowed herself to be financially supported by the Communists until 1933.)[104] Given her previous occupation, however, it would not have done to have Erna/Agnes be seen as a Nazi supporter. In any case, Nazi heroes do not have sexual liaisons and, in contrast to the real Wessel, cannot be seen to show weakness in succumbing to a female. Wessel's behaviour caused Goebbels great concern. Still, the film allows Agnes to try and save Hans. At his funeral the camera picks her out briefly as a spectator rather than a participant, peering through iron railings as the cortège passes.

In the 1931 Reichstag election, the Berlin Nazis do well at the expense of the Communists. Hans, however, remains disappointed since his eye is on total victory. By now he is also ill, presumably due to overwork. Feverish in bed, he is nursed by Agnes. A furious Kuprikoff pronounces a death sentence on Hans. His female sidekick harangues a crowd and liaises with Hans's landlady. Hans leaves to stay with his mother and, as his car drives off, the Communists (including the character based on Cohn) fail to kill him. Later he returns to his room to collect his things. Agnes and a female Nazi arrive to help. He gazes out of the window, pleased that the streets now belong to the SA. But the landlady has observed his return and has sent word. A knock at the door, he opens it and is shot. He dies later in hospital, attended by a doctor and his mother. In the novel Goebbels puts in an appearance at the hospital, but not in the film, though his voice is heard on the soundtrack at the end.[105]

The film concludes with a grand funeral, filmed in semi-documentary style, full of the Nazi pageantry soon to become familiar in Riefenstahl documentaries. This sequence is in stark contrast to the eight-second clip from newsreel footage of the 1930 funeral of Wessel.[106] That revealed a comparatively modest affair with two open carriages, a hearse and some cars containing prominent Nazis though not Hitler. Crowds lined the streets; some individuals gave the Hitler salute; riots broke out and the police charged. A fragment also showed the coffin being lowered into the grave, with Goebbels's tiny figure clearly visible. The actual funeral took place in winter, while in *Hans Westmar* the extras are lightly clothed for a summer day, the actual time of filming.[107] In *Hans Westmar* a large funeral cortège processes through the streets of Berlin. The flag-draped coffin is covered in flowers, obscuring the Nazi flag underneath. The Social Democratic-controlled police had ordered that the flag not be displayed. As the cortège passes Karl Liebknecht House, Kuprikoff looks out from a window. Street fights break out. Communist attempts to disrupt the funeral procession fail; the SA restores order. Hans is finally buried.

For the apotheosis, the Horst Wessel song is finally sung. At the film's outset its melody was briefly hummed, but this is the first time the words are heard.[108] Possibly this was due to copyright problems with the words rather than with the music.[109] From the left of the screen the SA marches. High in the sky, striding towards the left, Hans appears carrying the flag. He comes towards the camera, his form juxtaposed against clouds, after which there is a quick cut down to earth and to the actual footage of the historic torchlit parade on the evening of 30 January 1933 which Goebbels organized. It shows the SA and SS marching through the Brandenburg Gate.[110] The crowd salutes. Communist clenched fists slowly unfurl to the Hitler salute. The camera picks out Ross in the centre as his clenched fist also slowly opens to the Hitler salute. The film cuts back to the Berlin crowds on 30 January 1933 with rousing music on the soundtrack: 'Deutschland Marschiert' (Germany Marches). The mission has been accomplished: good Communists have become Nazis. Their moral and racial qualities allow them to belong to the *Volksgemeinschaft* from which, by definition, bad Communists are excluded.

Compared to *Hitlerjunge Quex*, this film is heavy-handed, the acting earnest, though the camerawork on occasion is good. The battle for the streets sometimes attains a documentary quality; from a propagandist's point of view, the final sequences are effective. But ultimately the story is told both literally and figuratively in black and white.

Jewish characters appear in these three films which glorify the *Kampfzeit*. This is not surprising, given the context: at the end of March the Nazis called for a boycott of Jewish businesses, and in April the new Civil Service Law with its 'Aryan' paragraph was introduced. By July, Jews were excluded from the film industry. The amount of screen time accorded to Jewish characters varies from film to film, as does their depiction. In two of the films the characterization is crude. One would not expect it to be otherwise in films whose purpose was overt propaganda. However, in the most successful of the three, *Hitlerjunge Quex*, the characterization is so subtle as to have been missed by most critics.

The *Kampfzeit* films did not point the way forward. This was not because of the quality of the two SA films. Nor was it because of the temporary ban on *Hans Westmar*, or because Goebbels believed that the SA belonged on the streets rather than the screen. It was the elimination of Ernst Röhm, the SA leader, just over six months after the opening of *Hans Westmar*, which effectively put paid to the genre, for it would have been difficult to make a film about the *Kampfzeit* without reference to the SA. Films set in that period were not excluded altogether, but nationalist films fitted the bill better than *Kampfzeit* films. On the other hand, the better-made Ufa film about the Hitler youth martyr had a future. There the uniformed adult Nazi did not belong to the SA but was a Hitler Youth leader. *Hitlerjunge Quex* ran for at least another nine years, that is until 1942, when reality began to catch up with what was on the screen, and escapism became the order of the day.

7

Leni Riefenstahl's Triumph of the Will

Triumph des Willens (*Triumph of the Will*), Leni Riefenstahl's 1934 film on the Nuremberg party rally, is undoubtedly the best-known example of Nazi documentary. It has provided the stock images of the Third Reich or, to be precise, the Third Reich prior to the outbreak of war. Beginning with Allied wartime film propaganda, clips from this film have been used as shorthand for Nazi Germany.[1] Such clips have become very familiar: a godlike Hitler descending from the clouds; adoring crowds of women, some in folk costume; children shyly gazing up at the Führer; Hitler's motorcade moving slowly through the Nuremberg streets lined with admirers; wave upon wave of uniformed men goose-stepping to martial music; torchlit parades; low-angle shots of Hitler addressing his followers from the podium against the backdrop of a large swastika flag or the Prussian eagle.

A film spectacle on a grand scale, this film shows the Nazis as they wished to be seen, and as they continue to be seen, long after the demise of the Third Reich. Both Führer and director display a mastery of the crowd; he is adored not only by the crowd but also by the director in his dual role as Führer and film star. This was the only film in which Hitler took the leading role. After this, it has been rightly claimed, there was no need to make another about Hitler.[2] A 'prototype Nazi film',[3] it was by no means typical and had no followers, except for those documentaries subsequently produced by Riefenstahl. Hitler admired her work and chose her to be his film director. But before the takeover she had already sought him out, and after the takeover lost no opportunity to advance her career. Through her preferred medium she expressed her admiration for Germany's new leader. It was a case of mutual admiration.

Not only is *Triumph of the Will* not a typical Nazi film product, its director was not a typical Nazi director. Exerting considerable stylistic control over her product, Riefenstahl can, for this reason, be considered the film's *auteur*, though objections can be raised to the term in that a director is part of a team. Nevertheless, it is as an *auteur* that Riefenstahl acquired her large post-war following of *cinéaste* admirers, adept at separating style from content. However, she was never a free agent and, especially as a documentary filmmaker, worked within constraints. Her claims to independence can partly be discounted on the grounds that there were no independent filmmakers in the Third Reich; even if a case can be made for one or two who avoided political content in films, this hardly applies to someone filming a party rally.[4] Riefenstahl was certainly free to make technical and stylistic decisions. In so doing she helped contribute to the Hitler myth or Führer cult, imbuing him with godlike qualities which served to protect him when things began to go less well.[5] Nevertheless, it is still worth pointing out that by the time *Triumph of the Will* was ready for viewing in March 1935, Hitler's position was secure.[6]

No other film produced during the Third Reich became a 'classic' in quite the same way. Unlike any documentary made at that time, it was purportedly a document of the Sixth Party Congress, itself a staged event, greatly facilitated by both the set-designing skills of the architect Albert Speer and a lavish budget.[7] Propaganda masquerading as documentary is a more apt description, though in an interview in *Cahiers du cinéma* in 1965 Riefenstahl denied this:

> But my film is nothing more than a document. I showed then what everyone had witnessed or heard of. And everyone was impressed. I am the person who fixed that impression, who recorded it on film ... But if you see the film today you will agree, that it does not contain a single reconstructed scene. Everything in it is genuine. And there is no tendentious commentary for the good reason that there is no commentary at all. It is history. A purely historical film ... It is *cinéma verité*. It reflects the reality of what in 1934 was history. It is therefore a document. Not a propaganda film.[8]

There was of course no need for commentary, given the camera, her direction, the editing and the soundtrack. Furthermore, propaganda can exist in a variety of genres and forms. Documentary and propaganda are by no means mutually exclusive.

Nazi Party rallies were a gathering of the party faithful to behold their leader and hear his word; or to quote Goebbels, they were the party's 'high mass'.[9] Held in September, the traditional time for party congresses, Nuremberg had been the setting for the fourth rally in 1929, and for subsequent rallies, all of which took place after Hitler was in power. Nuremberg was in Franconia or northern Bavaria, a territory incorporated into Catholic Bavaria during Napoleonic times. Franconia was mainly Protestant and rural, a hotbed of Nazi support, in contrast to the Catholic areas to the south where there was still some loyalty to the Catholic Centre Party. The city, however, had a strong social democratic tradition. A *Reichstadt* or independent imperial city in late medieval and early modern times, it was the birthplace of Albrecht Dürer and the setting for Wagner's *Die Meistersinger*. Symbolic for the Nazis, as it had been for the nationalist Wagner, its selection was also a triumph for the Gauleiter (District Leader) of Franconia, Julius Streicher, the editor of the virulently antisemitic weekly, *Der Stürmer*.

A picturesque and historic city, Nuremberg proved ideal for Riefenstahl's film, affording a variety of suitable images: late medieval spires and bridges, evidence in stone of German greatness and prosperity. Visually and ideologically acceptable, it also had a geographic advantage, for if not the actual geographic centre of Germany, it was still sufficiently central and convenient – the junction of seven main railway lines – for those travelling from east and west and north and south. It was estimated that half a million people participated in the 1934 rally.

In September 1934 Hitler, who had been in office only twenty months, was in the process of consolidating his power. The purpose of this particular rally (and of the film) was propaganda on behalf of Hitler, confirming him in his role as supreme leader of the party and of Germany. Two momentous events had immediately preceded the 1934 party congress. Two months earlier, in the so-called 'Night of the Long Knives', Hitler had purged his opponents within the party and from among his non-Nazi allies. The most important casualty was Ernst Röhm, leader of the SA, the Brown Shirts or storm troopers, a paramilitary force which, in controlling the streets, had helped ensure his rise to power. The other important event was the death, one month before the congress, of Field Marshal Paul von Hindenburg, who had been President since 1925. It was he who had appointed Hitler Chancellor and ensured the constitutional legality of his accession, though Hitler had run against him unsuccessfully in the 1932 presidential election. Having decided to abolish the presidency and combine the separate offices of President and Chancellor, Hitler was now presenting himself to the party faithful in his new role. The purpose of both rally and film was to demonstrate Hitler's enhanced position within the party and within the state. In contrast to the previous year's rally, this year's was 'consciously devised as a vehicle of the Führer cult', with Hitler 'now towering above his Movement which had assembled to pay him homage'. Riefenstahl's film 'made its own significant contribution to the glorification of Hitler. It was Hitler himself who devised the title *Triumph of the Will*. But his 'triumph' owed 'only a little to will [and] … far more to those who, in the power-struggles of the summer, had much to gain – or thought they had – by placing the German state at … [his] disposal'.[10]

Given Hitler's opposition to the emancipation of women, it is surprising that he chose a woman to film the Nuremberg rallies, overwhelmingly male gatherings of party members. Women would rarely obtain such work in other countries. Directors were in the front line, and also in a position of power, something normally deemed inappropriate for a woman. Women did work in many film industries but rarely as directors. They could act as editors – behind-the-scenes work, involving the managing of material rather than people – but subordinate to the director. A good editor helped ensure a director's artistic reputation, though this was rarely acknowledged. Riefenstahl herself spent many months editing her films, demonstrating her skill. Indeed, she was fortunate to be able to combine both roles of directing *and* editing.

The paradox is that Riefenstahl, the best-known female director in the inter-war period, and indeed Germany's first, was able to advance her career in a very hostile climate, when government policy was committed to returning women to *Kinder, Kirche, Küche* (children, church and kitchen).[11] Many professional women were in the process of being relieved of their civil service jobs or right to practise as lawyers. Promoting Riefenstahl is a supreme example of the Nazis not practising what they preached. Furthermore, Riefenstahl was not a Nazi Party member, and never became one, a fact she and her defenders in the post-war period never tired of pointing out, though significantly her father did join shortly after the takeover.[12] Many directors, however, never took out party membership and never found it an obstacle to career advancement.

Aside from being a woman in a male-run industry, Riefenstahl was also an outsider to the film industry, in that she was not associated with any film company. Before 1933 she had directed only one independently made film, in the sense that it was not produced by one of the major German companies. Originally a film star, she was able to put her earnings towards making her own film. She was exceptional in this respect and obtained her position of director of the party congress films by a back door or possibly even the front door, since as a film star she was welcomed in Nazi circles. Knowing how to manage her own career, she was unstoppable in seizing each and every opportunity.[13] It is clear that it was she who first sought out the Nazis in 1932, possibly because some of the negative reviews for her first feature film, *Das blaue Licht* (*The Blue Light*), came from German critics of Jewish origin.[14]

It was Hitler, not Goebbels, who then chose her for what was a highly important task. Her film style suited his purposes. Every Riefenstahl documentary film was made with Hitler's backing and indeed could not have been made without his support. That she was a woman does not seem to have mattered to him. Though Hitler selected her, her own self-promotion played a role. If we are to believe her version of events, which she was keen to promote after the event, i.e. post-1945, she landed the commissions in the teeth of opposition from the Minister of Propaganda.[15] However, one should not confuse any difficulties she may or may not have experienced with political difficulties. She was making a different kind of film, unlike the usual fare promoted by Goebbels: it was not a feature film but a documentary about a carefully orchestrated event for public and international consumption. But most importantly, Riefenstahl was beyond Goebbels's control, responsible directly to Hitler, ensuring that this was one area of film activity over which the Propaganda Minister did not have control. His opposition to her, if indeed there was any – and his diary entries indicate otherwise – proved useful to Riefenstahl in her post-war strategy to obtain rehabilitation.[16] In 1929 Goebbels described her as '*die wunderschöne Leni Riefenstahl*'; in May 1933 he picnicked with her after making her the offer to film the party rally; he found her 'beautiful' and 'a woman who knows what she wants'.[17] That Riefenstahl has felt free to criticize Goebbels but not Hitler also demonstrates the power of the Hitler myth, which in her case seems to have outlasted the Third Reich.[18] Never denying her original support for the Führer, tellingly she never thought this placed her in a bad light.[19]

Born in Berlin in 1902, Riefenstahl first trained as a dancer, starting at the ripe age (for a dancer) of sixteen, if we are to believe her memoirs, and also attended art college. Her first attempt at memoir-writing appeared as early as 1933, suggesting self-promotion in an important year when new opportunities beckoned. It was published by the Jewish-owned Ullstein, which is why, it has been suggested, she initially kept quiet about her Nazi sympathies.[20] Riefenstahl was a solo dancer (in the style of Mary Wigman who herself was influenced by Isadora Duncan), but switched to films after a knee injury temporarily ended her dancing career, a wise move, on the evidence of her dancing in her second and last feature film, *Tiefland* (*Lowlands*) (1954). Energetic and highly ambitious, between 1926 and 1933 she starred in a number of mountain films (*Bergfilme*), directed by Arnold Fanck. These action melodramas, set in rugged and remote landscapes (usually mountains), were not incompatible with Nazi beliefs – escape from urban life and the mundane, and a longing for purity – but their appeal to non-Nazis should not be overlooked.[21] Thanks to new camera techniques, mountain films included some sensational pieces of filming for the late 1920s. With an uncanny knack for being in the right place at the right time, Riefenstahl was able to advance her career with great single-mindedness: she learned to rock-climb, on occasion even barefoot. She also learned to ski, eventually reaching Olympic standard, coming seventh in a downhill race which qualified her for the 1932 winter Olympics.[22] Whether trapped in alpine blizzards, or on a Greenland ice floe, she displayed her athletic prowess and daring, her physical strength and stamina far exceeding her acting talent.

In 1931 she turned her own hand to directing *Das blaue Licht*, for which she also co-wrote the script with the Hungarian poet, Bela Bártok librettist (*Duke Bluebeard's Castle*), film theorist and scriptwriter, Béla Balázs. As he was of Jewish origin, his name was removed from the credits after 1933, and, to avoid paying him his fee, Riefenstahl enlisted the services of Streicher to deal with 'the Jew Balázs' who was now in Moscow.[23] The film opened in early 1932. The story, she claimed, was based on a legend, but its similarity to a 1930 novel, *Bergkristall* (*Rock Crystal*), by the Swiss author Gustav Renker is very close.[24] It has been suggested that she may not have been in a financial position to purchase the rights.[25]

Set in the Dolomites, the outcast, wild woman Junta, played by Riefenstahl, guards a treasure that emanates a blue light and lures young men to their death. A Viennese artist falls in love with her but inadvertently causes her death when he provides the villagers with details about the location of the treasure. The loner, Junta, scales the heights (literally), and it was in this role that Riefenstahl attracted Hitler, another loner intent on scaling the heights.[26] It was said to be one of his favourite films. No matter that Junta was a woman whose place, according to prevailing Nazi (and conservative) precepts, was in the home. Before plunging to her death, Junta/Riefenstahl demonstrates amazing rock-climbing skills – scaling Dolomite peaks, dressed in rags and unsecured – and this was not trick photography.[27] Even if the film might be understood as replete with German Romantic clichés, one must not underestimate the contribution of Balázs, who, though a Communist, was a maverick and an author of numerous tales or fables. His imprint is unmistakable in the film.[28] In contrast to 'realist' mountain films, this film was based on a legend, the telling of which appealed to Balázs. For Riefenstahl the appeal was that, in contrast to mountain films, the female character was at the centre.

Even before Hitler had become Chancellor, Riefenstahl, by now his ardent admirer, had sought him out, made easier by his admiration for *Das blaue Licht*.[29] It was she, we learn from her gushing autobiography, who made the first move. After hearing him speak in Berlin during the 1932 presidential election, she wrote him a letter and met with him before he became Chancellor.[30] A film magazine of August 1933 includes a picture of Riefenstahl seated behind the wheel of a smart convertible, the epitome of the modern woman, elegant, sporty, independent. Such women are not wholly absent from Third Reich films, though they hardly conform to the image of the *Hausfrau*.[31] The picture appeared one week before her latest film, *SOS Iceberg*, opened, directed by Fanck and filmed in Greenland.[32] To attend its Berlin première she was forced to interrupt work on the Nuremberg party rally, the first to take place since the Nazi accession.[33]

After the 1933 rally came several other important commissions: the 1934 and 1935 rallies and the Berlin Olympics in 1936. Riefenstahl would also be involved in lesser-known productions made by the film company she formed (with Hitler's blessing for services rendered) after the Berlin Olympics. Riefenstahl-Film GmbH, it is assumed, was funded from Hitler's *Kulturfond* (Cultural Fund), which itself was the recipient of payments to Hitler including royalties from *Mein Kampf*.[34] Shortly before the outbreak of war she was in consultation with Speer about plans to build her a gigantic complex to include a studio and a processing laboratory on land donated by the state near to her home in Berlin-Dahlem. Discussions continued until 1942,[35] but the war prevented the project from being realized. She neglected to mention this in her memoirs.

Once war began, and with no major commissions pending, she turned again to feature film. Her plan for a film about Penthesilea, the Amazon queen, she claimed, proved too costly for wartime. But her main reason for abandoning the project may have been that she had lost her taste for the battlefields after returning from the Polish front at the end of September. Though she claimed to have been in Poland to film for the Wehrmacht, she was probably there to make a new documentary for Hitler about his triumph there. Some footage is likely to have been used in Fritz Hippler's *Feldzug in Poland* (*Campaign in Poland*) (1940).[36] After witnessing her first atrocities, the execution of nineteen Jewish male civilians in the town of Konskie on 12 September 1939,[37] she abandoned plans to film at the front and returned to Berlin and to an earlier project, another feature film, *Tiefland*, on her preferred theme of mountain versus valley life. She claims to have first begun work on this in Spain in 1934, which she had to abandon after falling ill and was then called away to work on the 1934 party rally.

Based on an opera of the same name, *Tiefland* was fourteen years in the making and became the Third Reich's third most expensive film, the first two being in colour. This film confirms Riefenstahl's privileged status as a director. Though costly, the film could hardly be construed as central to the war effort.[38] However, Riefenstahl could call on Hitler's help indirectly via his deputy Martin Bormann.[39] Unlike other film directors, she was not working for a company but always had her own (three in all) and more financially independent of the state. Had the war not intervened, she would also have had her own studio, funded by the state. Thus she had no need to work to deadlines, and money seems to have been unlimited, or so Hitler's underlings thought.[40] Goebbels complained about the money being 'frittered away' but expressed relief that he had no responsibility for the film.[41]

Tiefland was finally released in 1954. Five years previously, Riefenstahl had sued the publisher of a Munich weekly illustrated over claims of abusing Gypsy extras. Altogether fifty-one of these from a nearby Austrian holding camp, Maxglan, were used in 1940 and 1941; many later died in Auschwitz. For indoor filming at Babelsberg in 1942 sixty-six extras were taken from the Berlin Gypsy holding camp, Marzahn, many of whom also died in Auschwitz.[42] Though Riefenstahl won her first libel case in 1949 she mainly lost a second in 1987 when the court rejected her claim that they had not been compelled to work and had been paid. She was, however, cleared of knowing at the time that they were destined for Auschwitz. Nevertheless, the accusation that she had abused these extras rankled.[43] In 2002 after claiming in an interview that all her extras had survived, she was forced to retract her words or face being taken to court. For the first time ever she made a retraction.[44] She died the following year, age 101.

Of the three Nuremberg party rally films, *Der Sieg des Glaubens* (*Victory of Faith*) (1933), *Triumph des Willens* (*Triumph of the Will*) (1934) and *Tag der Freiheit* (*Day of Freedom*) (1935), it is *Triumph of the Will* which is the best known and rightly so since it is the longest and the most lavishly produced. Riefenstahl's first documentary on a party rally, *Der Sieg des Glaubens*, was a more modest effort (approximately fifty-one minutes), and not as well made – also her view.[45] This may account for her reluctance to acknowledge the film until its discovery in the 1980s. Admitting to having made three party rally films – during denazification she admitted to only one – was a distinct disadvantage after the war. The film, however, had been withdrawn for a political reason, namely that Röhm, the leader of the SA, had co-starred with Hitler. It was pulled on 1 July 1934, the day after Röhm's death, when Hitler ordered the print destroyed. Compared to *Triumph of the Will*, *Der Sieg des Glaubens* also received less publicity, although it was still widely viewed for the seven months after its release.[46]

The film celebrates Röhm. It is he who stands alone with Hitler in an open automobile while Himmler is left standing below on the street shaking his leader's hand. Only Röhm accompanies Hitler through the massed groupings of the SA when they pay their respects at the Ceremony for the Fallen (the next year it would be Heinrich Himmler with Hitler, accompanied by the new SA leader, the nonentity, Viktor Lutze). The film was also keen to promote the approbation of outsiders and includes shots of foreign dignitaries, especially from countries friendly with Germany (Italy and Japan), as well as Spanish fascists three years before the outbreak of the Spanish Civil War. A longish speech in Italian by Professor Marpicati would have been incomprehensible to most members of the audience, except for his final words in German: '*Heil Hitler*! *Heil* Mussolini!' In the 1934 film non-Germans will have a minimal presence.

It is not a polished film: shots are out of focus; figures dart in and out of the frame; the numerous party members accompanying Hitler as he arrives at the field seem unsure about the pace and keep step miserably. Many shots should have been edited out, though not at the expense of those party luminaries who needed to make a screen appearance. Röhm adjusts his belt, nervously feels his pocket, then scratches himself. Hitler arrives to address the Hitler Youth, carrying his brimmed military hat which he places on the rostrum ledge. Introduced by the plump and gauche Hitler Youth leader Baldur von Schirach, Hitler begins to speak. Schirach, backing away in the confined space, knocks his leader's precariously placed hat off the ledge. The camera remains on Hitler who is still speaking, but the hat is now missing from the foreground of the frame. Schirach remains unaware. The cameraman makes no adjustment. Presumably, Riefenstahl includes this sequence because it is her leader speaking.[47] Amongst the young men, we see some with very dark hair, some even wearing glasses, including one bespectacled trumpeter. It is not only the Hitler Youth in 1933 who wear glasses, but also older party members, some of whom also have swarthy complexions. It is also evident, judging from their faces, that some of these men in uniform are not young. Such obvious physical failings (deviations from the 'Aryan' norm) will be excluded in 1934 as will be the female presence; in 1933 there is a two-second shot of two attractive Hitler Youth girls.

At times *Der Sieg des Glaubens* is close to newsreel coverage of public events, especially in the close-ups of Röhm and the shots of the foreign ambassadors; these are static images. Riefenstahl was dismissive of newsreel but was forced to rely on many newsreel cameramen. This, her first documentary, is quite removed from the aestheticizing tendencies apparent in her subsequent documentaries. However, it also contains a number of sequences and shots that will be repeated in the 1934 film: the blessing of the flags and the visit to the Monument of the Dead to cite but two. In none of the three rally films does the director deviate from the prevailing party line. Thus in 1933 Röhm is glorified, in 1934 Hitler and in 1935 the armed forces. Despite her claims to be apolitical, a young woman who knew nothing about politics,[48] Riefenstahl does not put a foot wrong. She was certainly attuned to advancing her career with an uncanny sense of getting it right politically.

For *Triumph of the Will*, Riefenstahl had lavish resources at her disposal, hitherto unknown in the making of a documentary film. Preparations began in May, though she claims to have tried to escape the commission and to have lost precious time. She and some of her team arrived in Nuremberg two weeks before the rally. Her staff of 120 included (depending on one's sources) sixteen to nineteen cameramen, sixteen to eighteen assistant cameramen, some dressed in SA uniforms to enable invisibility amongst the crowds, nine aerial cameramen, sixteen (or seventeen) newsreel cameramen from Ufa, Fox, Paramount and Tobis-Melo (the latter especially for sound), as well as twenty-two chauffeur-driven cars, SA and SS bodyguards, and field police officers.[49] One of the iron masts in the Luitpoldhain stadium behind the rostrum was fitted with a lift to hoist a cameraman to a height of 125 feet (visible in one of the shots). At Nuremberg's Adolf-Hitler-Platz a sixty-foot ramp was built at first-floor level to allow a trolley for cameramen to take bird's-eye views of the marching soldiers. Other cameramen were even equipped with roller skates or were perched precariously on rooftops or on fire truck ladders.[50] Some inadvertently appear in the film, at least twelve instances having been identified.[51] Working closely with Speer, 130 anti-aircraft searchlights (requisitioned from the Luftwaffe) had been placed around the Zeppelin Field at forty-foot intervals to create a 'cathedral of light' and 'dramatise the spectacle'. A reluctant Goering was won over by Hitler with the words: 'If we use them in such large numbers for a thing like this, other countries will think we're swimming in searchlights.'[52]

Over a period of five months, sixty-one hours or nearly 100,000 metres of film were edited down by Riefenstahl to just under two hours. The rally, which began on 5 September and lasted six days, was reduced to highlights. Even then, and despite her best efforts, it still has its longueurs. But that was in the nature of the project, which included the need to please the patron. Ingenious editing,

camerawork, and soundtrack attempt to overcome the repetition of men marching and marching. Movement becomes dynamic, the tempo quickens, the camera
looks up, the camera looks down and picks out the patterns of marching troops.
Indeed the whole spectacle looks as though choreographed, possibly a legacy
from her dancing years. There is a rhythm to the editing, a constant change in
camera angles, shots and images which is complemented by the music which
flows seamlessly from motif to motif. It also had a purpose, namely to alleviate for
the viewer the monotony of columns of marching men, which had to be included
as evidence that Germany was again on the march. Less could be achieved with
the sequences in which prominent Nazis delivered speeches, despite the skilful
editing and the provision of the equivalent of what then constituted a soundbite.
There was a limit to what could be cut without giving political offence. What did
end on the cutting room floor included Walter Ruttmann's section on the history
of the party (but this was, apparently, with Hitler's approval) and a sequence on
the Women's Association.[53]

Riefenstahl's abilities have been questioned. The success of *Triumph of the Will*
has been attributed to the lavish resources put at her disposal, or to help from
the documentary filmmaker Ruttmann. Ruttmann had pioneered a film genre,
the city documentary, with *Berlin, die Symphonie einer Grossstadt* (1927), and
excelled at film montage.[54] The genre influenced the Soviet filmmaker, Vertov,
and his celebrated avant-garde city film, *Man with a Movie Camera* (1929),
though Ruttmann, in turn, had been influenced by Eisenstein's montage. He
died in 1941, making it impossible to establish the extent of his assistance to
Riefenstahl, though it has been suggested that initially he contributed more than
one-third of the film. An official in the Ministry of Propaganda, Leopold von
Gutterer, originally proposed that the film not only focus on the events of the
rally, but also provide a history of the movement. Ruttmann was assigned to the
latter. But after a visit from Hitler to the cutting room in December 1934, possibly
at Riefenstahl's invitation, Ruttmann's contribution disappeared.[55] Hitler clearly
preferred Riefenstahl's version, which in concentrating on the events of the rally,
had emphasized his dual role as film star and Führer. In any case, a history of the
party had become a delicate matter after the demise of Röhm.

The film is divided into a number of set-pieces, punctuated by fade-outs and
dissolves. Unequal in length, they do not necessarily appear in chronological
sequence, which negates Riefenstahl's post-war claim that the film was 'pure
history' and a 'record' of the rally. Thirty years earlier she had rejected placing
sequences in correct chronological order, as her brief was to make an 'artistically
significant' film.[56] An examination of the rally's schedule, as detailed in the
press, confirms that the film is quite unchronological.[57] Filming took place in
Nuremberg itself: its streets and buildings, its congress hall or Luitpoldhalle,
the Luitpold stadium and the Zeppelin Field and tent city on the outskirts

(though a few indoor speeches were subsequently shot in a Berlin studio).

The music for *Triumph of the Will*, about which there are a number of misconceptions, especially that it was based on borrowings from Wagner and Bruckner, was exceedingly important. Herbert Windt's contribution should not be undervalued. A party member since 1931 and a classically trained composer, he did the music for the previous year's *Der Sieg des Glaubens*, some of which he would recycle for *Triumph of the Will*. He did not do the music for *Tag der Freiheit* the following year, but between 1933 and 1945 provided music for just under fifty films. For *Triumph of the Will* he composed seven consecutive sections of music: an overture, a brief musical interlude which comments on a few captions; a longer two-part section which he called the 'Horst-Wessel – Variations'; 'Arrival of the Führer'; 'Drive through Nuremberg'; 'Nuremberg Awakening' which includes a brass arrangement of Wagner's 'Wach auf' chorus (*Die Meistersinger*, Act III). Windt also composed two further brief musical interludes: a repeat of the Hitler arrival music as Hitler leaves his hotel, and a very theatrical and operatic musical build-up to his arrival at the central market square for the main military parade. In all, Windt provided twelve and a half minutes of original film music for a film which ran to one hour forty-six minutes.[58] In the other ninety minutes much of the music is diegetic, that is music which is presumed to have arisen from within the film story itself. Comprised mainly of military marches or folk songs, it reinforces the image; at times it even clarifies or dominates the image. German audiences, familiar with the words of a particular song or aware that a particular march was Hitler's favourite, would be in no doubt about the message.

One established view is that *Triumph of the Will* begs for Wagnerian music. This has led to an assumption that the music must therefore come directly from Wagner, or possibly Bruckner. There are good reasons, however, why this was not the case. Firstly, the conservative *Reichsmusikkammer* or RMK (Reich Chamber of Music) considered classical German music sacrosanct, the 'most German of the arts' which could not be used for lowly film purposes or tampered with in any way. An aggressive debate about the citation of 'original' music raged in the daily and specialist press between film composers, affiliated to the more lenient film chamber (RFK), and the RMK. Secondly, 'serious' film composers like Windt publicly rejected the idea of quotation. They could do better. (Windt even claimed to have objected to using the '*Horst Wessel Lied*' as too primitive for film.) The RMK criticism was directed primarily at newsreels which raided the classical music cupboard for their soundtracks.[59] Just as Riefenstahl hoped to 'transcend' the newsreel cinematically, Windt hoped to do the same musically.

Furthermore, one must not overestimate Wagner's appeal: Nazi Party members displayed less enthusiasm than Hitler or Goebbels, as Speer has recounted. *Die Meistersinger*, conducted by Wilhelm Furtwängler, was the first event of the Nuremberg rally. In 1933, much to Hitler's annoyance, it had been poorly attended by party functionaries. Few seats had been taken before his arrival at the opera house, and party members had to be rounded up from nearby beer halls. In 1934 Hitler ordered his officials to attend, though they displayed little enthusiasm, some being observed to fall asleep. By 1935 tickets went on sale to a more appreciative public.[60] Wagner did not enjoy mass appeal and the film was intended for a mass audience. Windt's own initial sketches for the film music indicate that he had planned a composition of his own rather than take anything direct from *Die Meistersinger*, for which Riefenstahl would subsequently (in the 1960s) take credit. However, it is more likely that Goebbels (or another party official) overruled the composer. The 'Wach auf Chor' (the wake-up chorus) had been a party favourite since the early days of the Nazi movement, when it was appropriated as a political wake-up call.[61] It is thought that Windt was forced to drop his own composition in favour of this sole Wagner quotation. Nevertheless, by substituting a brass arrangement for the original, he made the quotation less obvious, which he could probably justify in that brass provides a sound more like the early morning bugle call. Aside from this, there is no other direct quotation from Wagner. Appearances, or in this case sound, can be deceiving. *Siegfried* or *Rienzi* are often mentioned as other examples, but they were not used. The confusion arises in that some passages are merely reminiscent of passages from these operas. This is partly by virtue of their function: a fanfare for the hero/Führer's arrival is not dissimilar to the fanfare from *Rienzi* for the leader Rienzi's arrival, and the Führer, as a Siegfried-like hero, has a *Siegfried*-like motif. Furthermore, the musical style is composed in the Nazis' preferred heroic (and German) nineteenth-century style.[62] The viewer/listener is prompted to make a connection encouraged by both context and musical style. This in turn helps legitimate the Nazis by anchoring 'their' music in a familiar German musical tradition, thus making the film doubly effective as propaganda – both visually and aurally.

The absence of commentary prompted Riefenstahl to proclaim disingenuously that the film was not propaganda. But the music functions as a kind of commentary. And there are words, mainly, though not always, in the form of truncated speeches. Moreover, the film begins with a written commentary: the opening titles (prepared by Ruttmann) declare that *Triumph of the Will* is a 'record' (*Dokument*) of the 1934 Party Congress, that it is produced by 'order of the Führer' and directed by Leni Riefenstahl.[63] Before any image appears on screen, we hear only music, then a drum roll followed by ominous music; after this a short text puts the rally in context:

> Twenty years after the outbreak of the World War, sixteen years after the suffering began [the 1918 defeat], and nineteen months after the beginning of Germany's rebirth [accompanied by a Wagnerian motif], Adolf Hitler again flew to Nuremberg to rally his followers.

The Wagnerian-sounding motif mutates into the '*Horst Wessel Lied*', Windt's 'Horst Wessel Variations'. Through a pilot's window we see clouds which soon cover the entire screen through which Nuremberg (in an aerial shot) begins to emerge below. The plane flies lower, its shadow passes across the city. Down below troops march in formation along roads and across bridges. Nazi flags hang down the front of buildings. The plane taxies to a halt; Hitler appears at the door, followed by other members of his entourage, including Goebbels. He is greeted with shouts of '*Heil!*' from a waiting crowd, which is by no means large, and consists mainly of women, children, and boys in Hitler Youth uniform. He smiles at them benignly. This is the effective opening sequence in which the leader or god descends from the clouds (Valhalla) but, in a concession to modernity, by airplane.

As Hitler's motorcade travels through the flag-bedecked streets, the music changes to a well-known military march followed again by a Windt contribution. One of Riefenstahl's critics has noted that sometimes Hitler's windscreen is up and sometimes it is down, evidence of being filmed on different occasions and prompting again the question of authenticity.[64] With the camera held just behind Hitler's head – permission for the cameraman to be so placed had been given the previous year – we see ecstatic crowds of women, young and old, some in folk costume, and children. From a window, women and children look on; a cat suns itself. The car stops for Hitler to collect flowers from a child held by her mother. Nice touches. Some male faces can be picked out in the crowd, though rarely are they young: for young men should be more than spectators. Carefully composed shots of young male heads encased in swastika-emblazoned helmets – Hitler's guards – resemble 'statues on film'. To form a human chain, SS men interlock hands by gripping each other's belts: the camera picks out the insignia on the belt buckles.[65] On the soundtrack a *Burschenschaft* (nationalist student fraternity) song reaches a crescendo. Hitler arrives in triumph at the Hotel Deutscher Hof to greet his admirers. He appears at a window, below which the words 'Heil Hitler' are set in lights. These will be turned on in the next short sequence which takes place in the evening at Hitler's hotel: trumpets and drums play hunting music in flickering light.

The next sequence is Nuremberg at daybreak: rooftops, a window opens; Nazi flags flutter in the breeze; the camera lingers on the distinctive architecture, which is also reflected in the river. Wagner is now on the soundtrack: a brass arrangement of the 'Wach auf Chor' from *Die Meistersinger*. Church bells, heard faintly, strike seven. Next an aerial shot of a tent city on the outskirts: the drums roll and we soon see young drummers and trumpeters playing reveille. Young men shave, wash, hose each other down, and scrub each other's backs to shrieks of laughter, while on the soundtrack we hear a jolly *Burschenschaft* song about friendship. Smiling SA men drag firewood, which has been loaded on carts, for heating the great vats of porridge and sausages. Laughing boys (not girls) participate in horseplay – a boy is thrown high in a blanket – expressions of male bonding and male aggression channelled and sublimated. What has been cut is footage from the Women's Association. Another procession: to the accompaniment of an accordion playing regional dance music, peasants in folk costume arrive in Nuremberg. Some women wear elaborate head-dresses; many men carry agricultural implements – rakes and scythes. Amongst the onlookers, a child contentedly munches an apple, a boy stands on a column to obtain a better view, a girl wets her lips in expectation. We see Hitler inspecting the massed ranks of his young uniformed male supporters; he shakes hands, steps forward to ask one a question, then returns to his car. He and other leading figures depart in separate vehicles; this sequence has obviously been edited from material filmed at different times.[66]

After this, Rudolf Hess opens the Sixth Party Congress in the Nuremberg Luitpoldhalle or Congress Hall. He refers to the revered memory of Germany's President, 'the first soldier of the Great War who has crossed over to eternity', and adds 'at the same time we think of our fallen comrades.' He then welcomes the 'esteemed representatives of foreign countries', not missing the opportunity to point out the propaganda value of their presence, 'who by participating in this rally, honour the party'; but they get less coverage than in the preceding year's film. Hess refers to the army and to recent changes: 'In a spirit of real comradeship the movement gives a special welcome on behalf of the movement to the army representatives, now directly under the Führer's command.' On the rostrum sit Wehrmacht chief General Werner von Blomberg, Grand Admiral Erich Raeder, as well as delegates from friendly countries such as Italy and Japan. The Nazi leadership, individually featured in close-up, are now allowed characteristic one-liners, a compilation of excerpts not necessarily taken from the opening session. On each occasion, across the screen a name flashes in lights, followed by audience applause. In the case of Streicher: 'A people that does not maintain the purity of its race will perish' – the only allusion to the Jewish Question. This was filmed later in a Berlin studio due to equipment failure.[67]

The next sequence opens with a distance shot of the Zeppelin Field, with its massive construction of the German (Prussian) eagle, designed by Speer in the Nazi-approved 'modern' style, its clawed feet resting on a swastika. On the rostrum is Hitler, with him Konstantin Hierl, head of the Labour Corps, created by Hitler as a solution to unemployment. The 52,000 uniformed and militarized men are making their first public appearance. For this sequence Riefenstahl coined the phrase 'Hitlerwetter' (Hitler weather) when she wrote: 'Unfortunately the sun disappeared behind a cloud. But when the Führer appeared rays broke through the clouds. Hitler weather!'[68] Nature obliged, but the sequence is obviously dramatized and rehearsed, and not unrelated to a theatrical genre pioneered by Nazi playwrights, the *Thingspiel*, a heroic play with a religious quality, a cast of thousands with much recitation in unison. To a drumbeat the Labour Corps shoulder their spades, and a *Sprechchor* or speaking chorus pledge themselves to be 'labour soldiers', ready to carry Germany into a new age. One of the men asks: 'Comrade where do you come from?' A telescopic lens picks out the faces of individuals who then identify themselves according to their place of origin. In most cases they come from the periphery: Friesia, Pomerania, Königsberg, Silesia, the Black Forest, the Danube, the Rhine and, finally, the Saar, which was to be returned to Germany in a plebiscite five months later by an overwhelming vote, in which just over 90% chose dictatorship. In unison they chorus: 'One people' (shot of one of the men), 'one leader' (shot of Hitler), 'one Reich' (shot of eagle), 'Germany' (shot of flag). They build dykes across the North Sea, fell forests, plough and sow seeds, and sing to words set to a folk tune: 'We are the men from the Farmers' Guild, true to our homeland and to the earth.' The drums roll; we see Hitler on the rostrum; the chorus continues: 'Though we did not stand in the trenches, nevertheless we are the soldiers with hammers, axes, spades, scythes as once at Langemark, Tannenberg' (German battles of the First World War). A soldier dips a flag in memory of the fallen, which is intercut with another brief shot of Hitler and entourage on the rostrum.

On the soundtrack is 'The Good Comrade' also known as '*Ich hatt' einen Kamaraden*' (I Had a Comrade), a haunting song about the death of a comrade in battle. Invoked as a lament for the First World War dead, Riefenstahl uses it more than once in this film to great effect. It begins: 'I had a comrade, a better one you will not find.' The second verse continues:

> A bullet came flying
> Is it for me or for him?
> It tore him away
> He lies at my feet
> As if he were a part of me.

Often described as a folk song, the words in fact were composed by the Swabian ballad poet, Ludwig Uhland, first published in 1815 and later set to a folk tune. Uhland, who had immersed himself in French and German medieval poetry, later gave up poetry for politics, and was a Liberal member of the abortive Frankfurt Parliament of 1849. Nazis and others on the right, however, either preferred to ignore, or were oblivious of, this inconvenient fact. For many it was the authentic voice of the *Volk*.

At the mention of those killed by the Red Front (an infinitely smaller number than those killed in the war) the guns go off, the flags are raised high with a great flourish, the fabric swirling like a dancer's skirt. The camera pans the rows of men whom Hitler addresses: 'No one should be despised for doing menial work,' he tells them and predicts that a time will soon come when everyone will pass through their ranks. A slow dissolve across Hitler's upraised arm in salute is superimposed against a shot of the 52,000 with spades on shoulders.

From day to night or semi-darkness at the SA camp: lit by bonfires and magnesium torches, shadowy figures appear in silhouette to roars of '*Sieg Heil!*' Through the billowing smoke, bayonets are held high; on the soundtrack 'Volk ans Gewehr' (People to the Defence), a rousing fighting song from the early nineteenth-century nationalist movement. Fire was an important symbol, and also politically significant in the early German nationalist movement: bonfires on the Wartburg in 1817 protested against Metternich's crushing of the nationalist movement. It is also apparent that the SA were enjoying themselves, while the director was probably drawn to the aesthetic possibilities of filming a night-time scene with fire. This sequence has also been singled out as the only sequence which was not *for* Hitler, in which people were not waiting in anticipation for Hitler, and which was also not mentioned in the official programme.[69] Now in the process of being sidelined, the SA are addressed by their new, unassuming leader, Lutze. The sequence concludes with a grand firework display, including a splendid Catherine's Wheel.

Next comes the turn of the Hitler Youth in a more typical sequence constructed around the arrival of Hitler, his speech, and his exit from the stadium. It begins with a drum roll and shots of young drummers and fifers. Boys cling to a flagpole, others crane to get a better look. They wait in anticipation. Hitler, Schirach and others (Hess, Goebbels, Himmler, von Blomberg) arrive. Schirach addresses the rally, after which Hitler begins his speech with the words: 'My German Youth'. His long speech is broken up with cross-cutting to the faces of the boys, picked out by a telephoto lens. None is dark-haired. Hitler admonishes them to be obedient, peace-loving, courageous, but adds that 'a people should not be forgiving.' He departs to thunderous applause. The sequence concludes with the Hitler Youth song composed by Schirach on the soundtrack, '*Unsere Fahne*' (Our flag waves before us). The camera dollies away from the massed ranks, arms in salute, the flags fluttering.

In the next, very brief, sequence the Wehrmacht (armed forces) appears on the parade ground. If Riefenstahl is to be believed, their leaders were disgruntled at its brevity. She blamed this partly on inclement weather and later on spoiled footage, which forced her to rely on footage first shot by a Ufa newsreel crew.[70] But, such a sequence was constrained by the Versailles Treaty and the restrictions placed on military equipment. This would all change by the following year, once Germany was rearming. In silhouette we see Hitler, Hess, Goering, von Blomberg and Raeder; on the soundtrack we hear military marches and hunting music as well as original sound. The cavalry gallop past, followed by motorized vehicles, followed by more horses. It was a poor showing for the military, possibly even sending out a message that Germany was still fighting the last war.

The next sequence is the gigantic rally of party functionaries on the Zeppelin Field. It takes place in early evening with a torchlit parade. It is also lit by searchlights and often filmed at a great distance. The gigantic Speer eagle construction just above the rostrum is lit by Klieg lights. Given the lack of light, close-ups with telephoto lens were technically impossible.[71] Speer claims to have suggested night-time filming because it would hide the paunches of the middle-aged men, so evident in the previous year's film.[72] Estimates vary as to the numbers present: 180,000 to 200,000 marchers carrying 21,000 standards, a veritable forest of flags, with 250,000 spectators. Accompanied by marching music, the political leaders approach the rostrum but it is only Hitler, bathed in searchlights, who can be identified. He takes the salute and proclaims: 'It is not the state which commands us but we command the state. It is not the state which has created us but we are creating our own state.' The sequence concludes with rows of marching men carrying flags and torches.

The impressive Ceremony of the Fallen in the Luitpold arena begins with a silent soundtrack and a panoramic view filmed by cameramen from the purpose-built lifts on the flagpoles. Massed to the left are vast numbers of SS and to the right similar numbers of SA, separated by a wide aisle down which three figures slowly walk, so small in the distant shot as to be unidentifiable. A brass band begins to play a funereal motif associated with the death of a hero.[73] The camera slowly moves in, allowing us to identify the figures: Hitler in the centre with Himmler on his left and Lutze on his right, walking towards the eternal flame at the war memorial. They pause, and as they turn to walk back 'I Had a Comrade' replaces the funereal music.

This ceremony is followed by an SA and SS rally in the arena, with an estimated 97,000 SA led by Lutze and 11,000 SS led by Himmler. Hitler stands on a stone rostrum into which a swastika has been carved. Cameramen are visible at the corner of the rostrum, and on one of the lifts constructed on a flagpole a camera can be glimpsed. Lutze speaks, though Himmler does not. Hitler refers to 'the dark shadow' which has passed over the movement, a reference to Röhm, and warns that if anyone sins against the spirit of 'my SA' this will not break the SA but will break them, to which there are cheers and a cannon salute. The Horst Wessel song is now on the soundtrack, while a Nazi ritual takes place, the consecration of flags. With one hand Hitler shakes the hands of flag-carrying SA men, giving each man a hard look. In his other hand he clutches the *Blutfahne*, the alleged blood-stained flag from the 1923 Munich putsch which he presses against each flag as it is presented to him. Thus he blesses each flag and its bearer.

The final sequence reaches a crescendo. This is Hitler's review of troops, more or less a filmed record of the interminable marching of Third Reich organizations, the monotony only broken by constant changes in angle of vision – aerial shots, shots from rooftops and windows, and at eye level – as well as very skilful editing and a rhythmic montage. To match the tempo of the music to the cadence of the marching troops, Riefenstahl makes an unlikely claim to have conducted a studio orchestra herself.[74] After an initial sequence in the stadium, the film quickly cuts to Hitler driving through the streets of Nuremberg; from a window two women and a boy look out, the latter wearing a Hitler Youth armband. Every detail is telling. Crowds line the streets. On the soundtrack are snatches of trumpet, a medley of musical motifs: military music, folk songs, Nazi songs. Contingents of naval recruits goose-step to the 'Badenweiler March', allegedly one of Hitler's favourites marches. Wave after wave of goose-stepping men in uniform make their way through the Nuremberg streets, through tunnels, across picturesque bridges, weaving patterns, beautifully choreographed and edited. SS men goose-step down wide steps, reminiscent of the famous Eisenstein 'Odessa steps' sequence in *Battleship Potemkin* (1925), a film Riefenstahl much admired.

The last sequence contains the closing ceremonies in the Luitpold Hall, with the 'Badenweiler March' again on the soundtrack. Hitler, Hess, Himmler, Streicher, Goebbels and others proceed down the aisle, hailed by their followers, whose arms are upraised in the Hitler salute. They ascend the stage to observe the SA and SS carrying their standards and banners. SS and SA men, no longer segregated, now sit together. Hess introduces Hitler. These are the first spoken words.[75] He swallows and after a few seconds' silence, as the cheers continue and then subside, begins to speak: 'Soon the party will be for all time the leading elite of the German people ... Our aim must be that all good Germans become National Socialists ... that this state shall endure for thousands of years'. We have a distant shot of the audience, after which the camera dollies into the speaker, followed by an out-of-focus shot of a uniformed Goering adjusting his belt – another poor piece of camerawork cited against Riefenstahl by her critics.[76] Hess declares that the party is Hitler, Hitler, however, is Germany, just as Germany is Hitler. With this the Sixth Party Rally comes to an end. Arms in salute, the audience sings the Horst Wessel song; even Goering in medium close-up is observed singing. The camera pans to the swastika above the stage which dissolves into close-up and then dissolves again, this time to the Reich Labour Corps marching on the parade field.

There can be no doubt as to why this film was made. It assured the party that all was well despite recent events. It showed the German people the benefits of having at the helm a strong leader and of belonging to a *Volksgemeinschaft*, a community of the *Volk*, to which only physically and mentally fit 'Aryan' Germans could belong. It captured on celluloid the importance of vast rallies as first adumbrated in *Mein Kampf*: the 'mass meeting', Hitler wrote, was 'necessary' because in it the individual at first 'feels lonely and easily succumbs to the fear of being alone', but then gets the picture of a larger community, which in most people has a 'strengthening, encouraging effect'.[77] The viewer of course saw an idealized image of the party. In advance of the rally, party newspapers warned participants that Nazis do not get drunk and must comport themselves accordingly. Nothing untoward was filmed or reported in the censored press.[78]

There was much that the film did not show. Aside from the Nazi leadership, the physiognomy of the film's participants conforms to Aryan stereotypes and to acceptable images of young, old, male, female. This was conformity, for in a *Volksgemeinschaft* there can be neither difference nor individuality. Faces are blank, bland, uninteresting. Expression of emotion is limited: adoration from females; determination and obedience from males, especially from those in uniform; excitement from the young. If Eisenstein invented and used typage, selecting particular faces to suggest character, Riefenstahl selected faces to deny character and individuality. A 'dehumanized mass' constitutes the *Volksgemeinschaft*: crowds and troops choreographed by the director. Enemies, 'the dark shadow', are rarely alluded to in this film and visually are wholly absent.

It is not the faces but the shots that are memorable. That they are sometimes out of focus or reframed in mid-shot has been noted by critics.[79] Even one of Riefenstahl's greatest post-war champions found the film crew's work unimpressive.[80] What Riefenstahl excelled at was shot composition, especially when taken from a low angle, possibly the most prevalent in the film. But then a low-angle shot was appropriate to a film extolling the Führer principle. The camera constantly looks upward not only at the Führer, but also at other faces in the cast of thousands, though the faces in the crowd lose their individuality even when viewed in close-up. Her choreography of large crowds is also impressive. It is on an even grander scale than earlier epics. It is documentary, not feature film: she is not employing film extras, though she could be accused of forgetting this at times.

This choreography of the masses, gigantism and the overuse of the low-angle shot are ingredients in what has come to be known as fascist aesthetics, a contentious concept which implies that specific qualities can be found in works produced by or on behalf of fascists. Against this, others argue that such qualities belong to a Western aesthetic tradition.[81] The low-angle shot, though overused in this film, and favoured by fascist artists, especially sculptors, derives from an aesthetic practice originating in Italian Renaissance statuary, in particular the leader on horseback, the *condotierri*. A pre-fascist artistic convention has been employed by fascists to emphasize political inequality, the powerlessness of the individual and the power of the leader.

The film had its première on 28 March 1935 in Berlin at the Ufa-Palast am Zoo, Germany's grandest and largest cinema. Speer had transformed the theatre's façade for the occasion. Nineteen outsized twelve-metre-long swastika flags covered the entire front; the flagpoles, made out of raw steel, were anchored in the roof. Above the marquee a splendid imperial eagle was anchored in the masonry.[82] Hitler was in attendance, along with top party dignitaries, high-ranking military and foreign diplomats.

Riefenstahl was also awarded the National Film Prize by Goebbels, who declared:

> The film has successfully avoided the danger of being merely a politically slanted film. It has translated the strong rhythm of these great times into convincing artistic terms; it is an epic, beating the tempo of marching formations, steel-like in its conviction, fired by passionate artistry.[83]

That the film won an award in Germany should occasion no surprise, nor that it won one at the Venice Film Festival, but it also enjoyed success in Paris at the 1937 International Exhibition, notwithstanding protests from French workers. Surprisingly, the French press did not single it out as a propaganda film.[84] The London *Observer*'s correspondent did not miss the political message, indeed he was taken in by it, when he noted that this 'film "document" offered convincing proof that the passionate, dynamic, explosive energy displayed by Chancellor Hitler this week in the diplomatic talks is the concentrated personal expression of a national energy, equally passionate and dynamic'.[85]

German cinema owners were encouraged to screen *Triumph of the Will* as a main feature. This proved unpopular with the public, and after a week many cinemas replaced the film. It continued, however, to be shown to both party and Hitler Youth, in churches and halls.[86]

The most successful propaganda film ever made, as so often described, was an advertisement for and on behalf of the Nazi Party and its leader. For an apolitical animal, Riefenstahl was remarkably attuned to the needs of the Nazi Party, able to display in all their glory Nazi iconography, symbols and rituals. On cue, she wrote at the time – though later insisting it was her ghost writer, Ernst Jäger, editor of *Film Kurier* – that from the Führer's will his people have triumphed.[87] But the film was also her triumph, enabling her to become the Third Reich's leading documentary filmmaker.

Her next triumph was *Olympia* for which plans were being laid in 1935. Before that, however, she made one more rally film. For many years the 1935 rally film existed in an incomplete print. Only German reunification made possible a complete print, the West Germans (and the US and Britain) having held reels one and three while the East Germans held reels one and two.[88] Crucially, what was missing for those in the West was the Hitler speech on reel two. Though this film is much shorter than *Triumph of the Will*, only twenty-eight minutes, it does not abandon the style of its predecessor. Its focus, however, is different, not surprisingly given the brief to make a film about the military and especially about military technology. Entitled *Tag der Freiheit – Unsere Wehrmacht – Nürnberg 1935*, it can be and often is translated as *Day of Freedom, our Wehrmacht, Nuremberg 1935*, but a more accurate translation is *Rally of Freedom*, for 'Tag' has two meanings: rally and day. The rally itself had been billed as the 'Reich Party Rally of Freedom', hence the film's title. Riefenstahl's own account might lead one to think that the military had been put out by their low profile in the 1934 film.[89] This is not quite the whole story. The real purpose of the 1935 rally film was to inform the world that Germany was once again a military power, in the process of rearming and in defiance of Versailles.

What was not communicated in the 1935 film was another major decision. The leader of the Reich Doctors had raised the issue of banning marriages between Jews and non-Jews, which led Hitler to announce in Nuremberg, during the rally though not at the rally itself, that laws would soon be introduced to regulate relations between Jews and non-Jews. He had summoned the Reichstag to Nuremberg for a 'symbolic meeting' to take place during the rally – it had not met there since 1543. Its purpose was to approve a new Flag Law whereby the swastika replaced the imperial flag, beloved by the conservative military. Hitler called on the Reichstag to approve three laws: the Flag Law, the Citizenship Law and the Blood Law, the last two subsequently becoming known as the Nuremberg Laws.[90] In her memoirs Riefenstahl claimed not to have been in Nuremberg that day, but she was in fact at the congress for the entire period.[91]

In March 1935, six months before the 1935 rally and twelve days before the première of *Triumph of the Will* in which the military made its brief appearance, Hitler denounced the disarmament clauses in the Versailles Treaty. The Wehrmacht replaced the Reichswehr, the military force dating from the Weimar Republic, the army, navy and air force were expanded, and conscription was introduced. *Tag der Freiheit* had its première in December 1935 along with a lavish star-studded Ufa feature film, a patriotic costume drama set in 1809 in occupied Prussia and thus a *Preussenfilm* (Prussian film). *Der höhere Befehl* (*The Higher Command*) was directed by Gerhard Lamprecht, who in the closing years of the Weimar Republic had directed the delightful *Emil and the Detectives*. *Tag der Freiheit* was thus in good company, appearing in first-run cinemas alongside a feature film which became one of the box office successes of the 1930s. It continued to be shown in the following two years (up to 1938) and also in schools, and was thus widely viewed.[92] Its message was unmistakable: Germany's 'higher command' was to ignore her international treaty obligations. Three months after the première, Germany entered the Rhineland. However, some foreign contemporary observers who attended the rally overlooked another message, namely that the German people had to be sold the idea of rearmament and that the high command had to be won over to work with the Nazi hierarchy.[93] *Tag der Freiheit* was also a vehicle for wooing the military, and that was why it was given star billing.

Once again an 'artificial day' was constructed by taking a number of events and putting them together not necessarily in temporal order.[94] Thus the film was not a re-creation of the rally: shots of the armed forces in historic Nuremberg were dispensed with in favour of those taken on the Zeppelin Field (*Zeppelinwiese*), where in 1909 Count Ferdinand Zeppelin had landed his third airship (*Zeppelin* in German). The destruction of the *Hindenburg* airship, which caught fire over New Jersey, was still two years in the future. After that disaster, Germans had less cause to feel triumphant about airships.

The 1935 film was a 'symbolic depiction of the value of rearmament'.[95] Some sequences are not dissimilar to those in *Triumph of the Will*: instead of a civilian tent city at daybreak, it was a Wehrmacht tent city. With reveille we see soldiers waking, washing, fooling about and then eating. The cavalry mount their horses and ride off into the distance, watched by a crowd. Hitler addresses the armed forces. An elaborate military review follows, with equal time for each branch of the service, a display of military equipment, staged manoeuvres, tank formations, cavalry – also in motorized units – and aircraft. This film has been described as 'the first Nazi official film to aestheticise the battlefield'.[96]

The film was also pioneering in terms of the soundtrack. Though music played a smaller role than in *Triumph of the Will*, the sounds were freshly recorded. The composer was Peter Kreuder rather than Windt.[97] Classically trained and a successful composer of film music, he had his own jazz band during the 1930s, which at times verged on the impermissible, given the hostility to jazz and swing.[98] Riefenstahl collected sounds of shells and other equipment after the event, which she cut to the images. After that, Kreuder composed the music, which included songs and marches used by the Wehrmacht in 1935. An innovation was that each piece of military equipment was introduced by its own sound which came prior to its image appearing on the screen.[99]

The focus is on the military, rather than on the party, and the Nazi hierarchy is less prominent.[100] Armed with field glasses, Hitler, Goering and Hess stand on a rostrum alongside General Blomberg, the monocled Prussian head of the Wehrmacht who three years later will lose his post for marrying a prostitute less than half his age. (Hitler attended the wedding.) They observe the manoeuvres as spectators rather than as participants. Hitler addresses the assembled crowd, informing them that every German is needed, at which point the camera travels along lines of soldiers in profile. Men in a variety of uniforms cling to flagpoles in an attempt to gain a better view. Children also climb flagpoles; their evident excitement signals to the viewer the importance of the sequence. After Hitler's speech, soldiers march past on the field. Hitler salutes them from the podium. Then the Navy marches past, followed by the Luftwaffe, the cavalry, the motorized cavalry, trucks, tanks and so on. The film concludes with planes flying overhead in mass formation. Their image is then superimposed against fluttering swastika flags. On the soundtrack is '*Deutschland über alles*'. Some planes regroup and fly off into the distance in a swastika formation. The image of the old Reichswehr flag, emblazoned with a cross, is then replaced with an image of the new Wehrmacht flag with the swastika in the centre and the cross, reduced in size, relegated to a corner. The party has triumphed. The party flag (red flag with the black swastika in a white circle in the centre) had also just been made the national flag. This was one of the laws promulgated at Nuremberg. Riefenstahl well understood the significance of that year's rally.

In less than a year Riefenstahl was filming the two-part *Olympia* or *Olympiade* – *Fest der Volker* (*Festival of People*) and *Fest der Schönheit* (*Festival of Beauty*) – a three-and-a-half-hour documentary on the Olympic Games held in Berlin in the summer of 1936. The Olympic Committee had decided on Berlin before Hitler had come to power; indeed the games would have taken place there in 1916 but for the outbreak of war. That the committee did not go back on its 1931 decision to hold the games in Berlin was a propaganda coup for the Nazis, even though some Nazi sporting associations were not happy with the internationalism and pacifism associated with the Olympic ideal.[101] The committee insisted that the Nazis tone down some of their antisemitic propaganda by, for example, removing antisemitic posters lining the roads as well as providing assurances that Jews would not be excluded from the German team.[102] Nevertheless, a seal of approval had been given to a regime which, amongst other things, had withdrawn citizenship from 'non-Aryan' Germans and would not allow them to attend the games.

Riefenstahl was to film the event, in which Hitler for tactical reasons kept a low profile but was by no means absent. She made the film via the Olympia Film Company in which she and her brother were partners. Founded and funded by the state for the purpose of making this film, it was eventually liquidated by the state. The Propaganda Ministry's intention was to distance itself from the film: 'The government does not wish to appear publicly as the producer of this film.' *Olympia* was therefore, despite Riefenstahl's claims and rights to royalties, no less an official production than her previous documentaries.[103]

In some respects *Olympia* is not dissimilar to *Triumph of the Will*: the 'Aryan' *Volksgemeinschaft* replaced by athletes and athleticism, a community of sportsmen, though not all 'Aryan'. Admiration for young bodies, beautiful bodies, especially male bodies, permeates Riefenstahl's work from *Triumph of the Will* onwards, and is not absent in her post-war African photography.[104] In this she had much in common with Nazi sculptors such as Arno Breker, known for his outsized, idealized, asexual male nudes.

Her attempts to sell *Olympia* in Britain and the US met with failure. She arrived in the US to promote her film, which she brought in three different versions (one had deleted all shots of Hitler),[105] just before *Kristallnacht*, news of which she claims to have greeted with disbelief. Shunned thereafter by film people – one exception was Walt Disney – she returned to Germany empty-handed. After *Kristallnacht*, no one wanted to do business with a 'saleswoman for Nazi Germany'.[106]

Riefenstahl then founded her film company, Riefenstahl GmbH which made *Kulturfilme* and *Tiefland*. For the purpose of making *Triumph of the Will* she claimed to have been forced to rename her earlier film company, Leni Riefenstahl Studio-Film GmbH, as the Reich Party Rally Film GmbH.[107] In all she had during the third Reich three different film companies, none financially independent of the state. Unlike other directors she always had her own company, and had war not intervened her own studio.

Riefenstahl's real difficulties came with German defeat and the end of her filmmaking career.

8

A Judenfrei *Cinema: 1934–1938*

Despite the Nazi commitment to antisemitic policies and the cleansing of the film industry of non-Aryan personnel, German films were surprisingly slow to reflect government policy on the Jewish Question. Few films were produced which featured Jewish characters. If anything, Jewish characters were significant by their absence, for which there were good reasons. The process of excluding Jews from society and from the economy was one contributing factor. Jews could no longer work in the industry, either on or off screen. The industry had become *entjudet* (dejudaized). What remained was a cinema without Jews, in contrast to the classic Weimar cinema which, in Nazi eyes, was not only a cinema with Jews but one which had been completely *verjudet* (judaized). Now not only had the industry become *judenfrei* but so also, it seems, had the screen.

The exclusion from the screen need not have extended to negative Jewish characters. One might have expected to find some examples, yet this was not the case. Aside from the three *Kampfzeit* films of 1933, and one or two others, there was little inclination to make propaganda films, antisemitic or otherwise. In this respect, Germany's industry was no different from that in other countries, excluding the Soviet Union. Many in the entertainment industry were keen to provide (as the name suggests) entertainment, and this is what they felt comfortable with. Until the outbreak of war, that is until the summer of 1939, no German film was made in which Jewish characters had more than a marginal role. They were not totally absent from the German screen in the period 1933–39: they had had their uses in the 1933 *Kampfzeit* films and – on very rare occasions – continued to make an appearance, though usually fleeting.

Um das Menschenrecht (*For Human Rights*) had its première in December 1934, co-directed and co-scripted by the celebrated prize-winning Nazi author Hans Zöberlein (1895–1964), an exceptionally brave soldier and shock troop leader during the First World War who won the Iron Cross First Class.[1] He recounted his wartime experiences in *Der Glaube an Deutschland* (*The Belief in Germany*), published in 1931 with a foreword by Hitler. It was intended as a rebuttal of Erich Maria Remarque's *All Quiet on the Western Front*, and emphasized the importance of comradeship and love of the Fatherland.[2] It served as the basis for Zöberlein's first film, *Stosstrupp 1917* (*Raiding Party, 1917*), which opened in February 1934, which he co-directed with Ludwig Schmid-Wildy. *Um das Menschenrecht* was Zöberlein's second film, based on a manuscript in which he described his immediate post-war experiences in the *Freikorps* (Free Corps). That subject served as the basis for another book, published after the film, in 1936, *Der Befehl des Gewissens* (*The Command of Conscience*), though the period covered extended to 1923. Doubtless and for good reason, Zöberlein felt more comfortable with books than with films.

The heroes in *Um das Menschenrecht* were members of the *Freikorps*, marauding bands of anti-Communist volunteers who took up arms in the immediate aftermath of the First World War. Formed from disbanded army units as well as volunteers responding to military defeat, they fought Communist uprisings in Germany; in the Baltic region they played a decisive role against the Bolsheviks (1919) and in Upper Silesia against the Poles (1921). Once things settled down, the *Freikorps* was dissolved. The Nazis considered *Freikorps* members their honorary forerunners. Many, like Zöberlein himself, then entered the Nazi Party; he joined very early, in 1921, as indicated by his membership number 869.[3] He also joined the SA and was active politically in Munich. After the Second World War he was sentenced to death, later commuted to life, and in 1958 was released on health grounds. His crime was that he had headed an execution squad of the Werewolves Commandos, formed in the last year of the war, whose mission was to shoot anyone preparing to surrender. On 28 April 1945, shortly before the arrival of the Americans, he shot defenceless civilians in Penzberg, Bavaria, including a pregnant woman and the Social Democratic mayor.[4]

Um das Menschenrecht is about the making of a Nazi during the immediate post-war revolutionary years, a formative period for the party. Opening one year after *Hans Westmar* and six months after the assassination of Röhm, it loosely belonged to the *Kampfzeit* genre, in that it was set in a period when the Nazi Party was in the process of formation, though the party is not mentioned, and (conveniently) prior to the formation of the SA. That made it possible to argue the Nazi case without entering dangerous waters.

Produced by Arya-Film (like Zöberlein's previous film), under the patronage of the Care for Nazi War Victims, *Um das Menschenrecht* was dedicated to the unknown volunteer soldiers of the *Freikorps*, and set, according to the opening titles, 'in a time of German disintegration and powerlessness'. It deals with the fate of four comrades who return home at the end of the First World War to discover Germany in revolutionary turmoil. Max, the painter, finds his studio occupied by an attractive Soviet agent, a *femme fatale*, who persuades him to serve the revolutionary cause and promote world revolution. Fritz finds his family starving and believes that only the International will fight for human rights. A discontented Girgl, worried by the new spirit, retreats to his mountain farm and his wife and children. The main character, not surprisingly, is named Hans, and we can assume that he is based on Zöberlein himself and his experiences. He is a former student who, appalled by the poverty and political conflict, is unable to accept either bourgeois patriotism or the call of the International. Fearing that Bolshevism will destroy Germany, he joins the *Freikorps*, who are depicted as disciplined and orderly, in stark contrast to the Communists. The latter sing the 'Internationale' when drunk, smash shop fronts (this film was made after the SA had become closely associated with such activity) and enjoy the support of emancipated women who advocate free love, further evidence of social disorder.

In the ensuing street fighting, innocent people are killed until the *Freikorps* restore order. Suddenly Hans comes face to face with his one-time comrades, Fritz and Max. After some hesitation he lets them go free, and then spends a sleepless night (he has also just fallen in love). Fritz and Max run for their lives. On reaching home, Fritz learns that his wife and child have been killed in the street fighting and his world collapses. He and Max escape to the mountains and to their comrade, Girgl. Subsequently, Girgl is tried for high treason for harbouring his friends and given six months. In the end, Girgl, Fritz and Max decide to emigrate to Brazil, having lost faith in the new (Weimar) Germany. Hans remains; an image of his fallen comrades has appeared to him, and he has also married. The audience knows there will be a happy end and that one day the friends will reunite on German soil.

Jewish characters appear in a variety of guises. When a doctor tries to rescue a woman from the revolutionaries, and asks them why they are fomenting revolution, they reply that they no longer want to be treated as second-class citizens and in any case 'what would a bourgeois know about human rights?' To this the doctor replies that he has spoken to front soldiers, not to Jews. (The implication here is that Jews had not served at the front, an antisemitic slur that developed during the war and prompted an official investigation. This found that Jews had in fact volunteered in large numbers, in relation to their proportion of the population, but its findings were not published.) The leader of the revolutionaries is obviously a Jew since he wears glasses, an indication that he is an intellectual, and is smartly turned out, an indication that he is of bourgeois background. Overhearing the doctor's remark, he declares him 'a dangerous chap' and gives the signal to two of his men to shoot him. They hesitate for a moment, then take the doctor out of the building after which a shot is heard.

The boss of a housing society is obviously a Jew. He smokes a large cigar – always a bad sign in Nazi (and Communist) films – has a moustache and a high-pitched voice. He advises Hans that if he seeks work he must join a party, by which he means the Majority Socialists, who were closely associated with the creation of the republic in 1919. Hans then learns at a building site that he has no hope of work if he does not belong to a trade union, closely associated with the left. Hans has been dispossessed. The left controls Germany. In a nightmare a hook-nosed Jewish businessman with a funny voice appears.

As the film ends, when Hans and his wife see his friends Fritz and Max embark for the West, *Ostjude* (Eastern Jews) disembark from the East. In traditional black coats and hats, they carry wicker suitcases and sacks like the peddlers they are likely to be, in a shot both fleeting and telling. Max comments: 'Front soldiers are emigrating, Germans!' To which his wife replies: 'They are immigrating, Jews, they are coming here, aliens.'

Um das Menschenrecht provides a gamut of Jewish types: revolutionaries – though of the bourgeois variety – Social Democrats, trade unionists, Jewish businessmen and *Ostjude*. Made by the most committed of film directors, a virulent antisemitic writer who briefly turned his hand to film, without much success, this film though made in 1934 counts as the last of the films set during the *Kampfzeit*.

Jewish characters were absent from the German screen during the years 1935–37, with two minor exceptions. In *13 Stühle* (*13 Chairs*) (1938) comedians Heinz Rühmann and Hans Moser pursue a shop owner whose beard, spectacles and hat identify him as an orthodox Jew.[5] Towards the end of the following year another Jewish character appeared peripherally and fleetingly: that was in the *Staatsauftragsfilm*, *Pour le Mérite*.

An Ufa film, *Pour le Mérite* was directed by Karl Ritter who had recently turned his hand to directing and whose third film this was. It opened on 22 December 1938 in Hitler's presence. Hitler publicly congratulated Ritter for making 'the best film of contemporary history'.[6] With a large cast, it received the *Prädikat* 'of political importance and artistically of special value' and was judged suitable for youth.

The film concerns the fate of several air force officers who during the First World War had won the high military honour, *Pour le mérite*, a Prussian order of merit for gallantry dating from the eighteenth century. Ritter himself, a former pilot, had won it as had Hermann Goering, to whom the film was intended as a tribute, and on whose post-war exploits apparently the story was based.[7] (During the First World War the largest number of recipients of the award came from the Luftwaffe.)

Germany's enemies, namely those who stabbed her in the back – the Jews, the Communists, the pacifists, the supporters of the 'shameful' Weimar Republic – are castigated while the military, which, in defiance of Versailles, supported illegal rearmament, comes in for praise. Those awarded the *Pour le mérite* turn out to be closet Nazis who, towards the end of the film, reveal their swastika badges hidden under their lapels. They will come into their own when the Nazis take power and German honour is restored. The film concludes with a

Luftwaffe song rising above the sound of engines. Goebbels's voice is heard on the soundtrack reading Hitler's proclamation of 16 March 1935 announcing the introduction of conscription and the creation of the Wehrmacht to replace the Reichswehr. Defying Versailles, Germany has remilitarized.

The film begins in November 1918 when German pilots are ordered to deliver their planes to the Allied victors. One squadron leader refuses and instead orders his pilots to deliver their planes to Darmstadt. Two pilots lose their way and are forced to land at Mannheim airport, now in the hands of the workers' and soldiers' councils, depicted as noisy, undisciplined and disorderly. The council's leader, who makes a very brief appearance, is obviously a Jewish Bolshevik stereotype. Interestingly, though completely unrecognizable, he is played by Karl Meixner, previously Wilde, the Communist villain from *Hitlerjunge Quex*. Short, bespectacled, though not dark-haired, he has a faint resemblance to the Russian communist active in Germany, Karl Radek. We see him twice, though on each occasion only for several seconds, addressing an unruly meeting held behind closed doors at the airport. Later the two pilots are rescued by their squadron leader who, having just landed, orders the revolutionaries to release them and return their belongings. The revolutionaries comply, but one of the pilots notices that his *Pour le mérite* is missing. He soon discovers the culprit: a tall, dark-haired, slovenly, comical revolutionary. The pilot slaps his face and retrieves his medal. As the pilots take off in their planes, the 'Jewish-Bolshevik' leader runs onto the field, shouting angrily but too late. He then barks at the revolutionaries and gets his own face slapped by the comical revolutionary. At this all the men laugh. The appearance of the 'Jewish-Bolshevik' leader is so fleeting that the film's antisemitic tendency, in contrast to its anti-revolutionary tendency, may have been lost on the audience, though one film programme actually described the leader of the revolutionaries as a 'Jewish-looking reserve officer'.[8]

Ritter was one of the few German directors known to be antisemitic. His contact with antisemitic circles dated from before the First World War. Born in 1888, to an opera-singer mother, he had married the daughter of Wagner's great-nephew. A fanatical antisemite, he subsequently became an ardent National Socialist. He and his wife joined the Nazi Party in 1925. With access to Bayreuth circles, Ritter met Hitler and became a personal friend.[9] He had worked in the film industry since 1925 as a commercial artist, even at one time for a Jewish-owned production company about which he subsequently made disparaging remarks.[10] Initially involved on the technical side, he was called to Ufa as producer in January 1933. *Hitlerjunge Quex* was made under his supervision, but it was not until 1936 that he directed his first films, *Weiberegiment* (*Women's Regiment*) and *Verräter* (*Traitors*). The latter, an anti-British thriller about a spy ring operating in Germany, won him a medal at the Venice Film Festival for outstanding achievement and had its première at the 1936 Nuremberg Party

Congress. The idea for the film came not from Ufa but from the Propaganda Ministry, with the involvement of the War Ministry and the Head of Military Espionage, Admiral Wilhelm Canaris, later executed for his role in the 20 July plot against Hitler.[11]

A significant figure in the Nazi film industry, Ritter was honoured in 1938 with the title of professor. His films, fourteen in all, were technically assured. Considered 'the finest exponent of the militarist feature film set in a contemporary context',[12] he was responsible for creating the genre of the *Zeitfilm*, a theatrical and episodic film with documentary qualities which delivers the propaganda message not through character but through fast-moving action scenes. Ritter described the genre as follows:

> The pure entertainment film is only one aspect of our *Weltanschauung*. The *Zeitfilm* is about tanks, aircraft, and the troops at the front. It must bear the characteristics of contemporary Germany, it must be heroic, as our fate at this time demands. At the same time it must show humour and a positive attitude to life in accordance with our new found beliefs.[13]

Goebbels was not keen on the genre, and later not on Ritter, but this had more to do with Ritter's personal limitations than with actual political differences.[14] For propaganda purposes, Goebbels preferred the past as a setting rather than the present, feeling on safer ground when exploiting historical myths.[15] Moreover, he would not have approved of Ritter's demand for a reduced role for the 'pure entertainment film'. Despite such differences, Goebbels still defended Ritter to Hitler. According to the Nazi ideologist Alfred Rosenberg, who had no brief for Goebbels, Hitler had complained in late 1939 that there were no films reflecting National Socialism. In reply, Goebbels mentioned the 'good (Ritter) national films' which Hitler then dismissed as 'generally patriotic but not National Socialist'.[16]

Given the strength of Ritter's antisemitism, one might expect to find some evidence of it in his films. Yet only three feature Jewish characters, of which *Pour le mérite* was the only one to appear before the war. In that film, as we have seen, the Jewish character appears only fleetingly. The suggestion that in the earlier film, *Verräter* (*Traitors*), one of the characters is Jewish is incorrect.[17] The German informer, Geyer, played by Paul Dahlke, is not a Jew. There is no indication in the dialogue that he is. Moreover, this is confirmed by the manner of his death since drowning in a swamp or bog was an old German form of punishment meted out to tribal members who had transgressed. He was not the only German to meet such a fate in a film.[18]

In a film made during the Third Reich it is not surprising that a villain with dark hair might be mistaken for a Jew. This happened on occasion. Victor Klemperer, a keen cinema-goer, recorded in a diary entry for 11 September 1935:

After many months to the cinema, Prinzess Theatre; *The Cossack and the Nightingale*; such awful trashy rubbish that it is not worth making any note of it. But in it the role of a gun-running Levantine monster. Immediately a girl beside me whispers: 'The Jew!'[19]

Interestingly, this spy film was not German-made, but Austrian. Initially banned in Germany, and then subjected to cuts and changes, it was directed by Phil Jutzi, now in exile, who had directed two proletarian films, *Mutter Krausens Fahrt ins Glück* (*Mother Krausen's Journey to Happiness*) and *Berlin Alexanderplatz*.[20] Here the 'Levantine monster' (Klemperer's words) has been confused with a Jew.

A similar confusion has arisen with another film, *Mit versiegelter Order* (*With Sealed Orders*), a spy and adventure film set in the Middle East. Directed by Karl Anton for Majestic-Film, it opened in January 1938, and received the *Prädikat* 'of artistic value'. The story concerns a conflict between German and international interests. The villain is the unpleasant bar-owner, Ibrahim Speere, short, fat, with black hair. Despite the Arabic spelling of his first name, he has erroneously been taken to be a Jew.[21] In German, *Levantiner* suggests a '*Mischling*' – European father and Middle Eastern mother, as indicated by the villain's name. Levantine was also a synonym for wily and devious –not unlike the negative characteristics associated with Jews. And Jews of course originally emanated from the eastern Mediterranean. But in Germany Jews were more often associated with the east of Europe than the east of the Mediterranean. That Levantine and Jew might be confused is not surprising. Nevertheless, in Third Reich feature films Jews are readily identifiable by specific markers such as their name; their physiognomy – dark hair, prominent nose, short and/or fat, wearing glasses; their body language; or their speech – a particular intonation or the sprinkling of Yiddish words. Though this villain is short and his hair is dark, nothing else indicates that he is a Jew, though he is played by Hans Stiebner, whose girth, stature and hair colour destined him for other villainous roles, including Jewish villains, such as Nathan Rothschild's agent, Bronstein, in *Die Rothschilds* (1940) and the obviously Jewish journalist – he utters a Yiddish word – in the anti-British *Ohm Krüger* (1941).

Not every villain in a film made during the Third Reich was necessarily a Jew. On occasion the villain could be an 'Aryan' traitor to the nation or to the *Volk*, or not a pure German. However, propaganda emanating from other quarters had primed audiences to perceive villains as Jews and Jews as villainous. Even when antisemitism was absent on the screen, it was never absent elsewhere. Audiences may have begun to assume that every villain was a Jew, even when the script indicated otherwise.

Films made for propaganda purposes, that is for a particular political purpose with a particular message, were a minority of the films produced in the Third Reich. This is not to say that the many films not specifically belonging to this category did not have a political meaning or were free of ideology. But Jewish characters appear more frequently in films which can be classified as overt propaganda films, even when antisemitism per se was not central to the overall message. They could be foreign – emanating from the 'East' as Bolsheviks or as 'primitive' ghetto Jews – or infected by ideas from the 'East', namely Bolshevism. Or they could be associated with shady business practices, which were of course 'non-German'. Often peripheral, but occasionally instrumental to the plot, such characters served to remind audiences of the decadent Weimar period as well as the threat of external danger because Jews, even if German-born, as 'non-Aryans' posed an external threat to the German *Volk*.

Since we can exclude these two films, *Verräter* and *Mit versiegelter Order*, we can conclude that no Jewish characters appeared in any German film for four years, that is from the première of *Um das Menschenrecht* in December 1934 to the première of *Pour le mérite* in December 1938. Prior to the outbreak of war, the years 1933, 1935 and 1938 are turning points in the history of the persecution of German Jews. Yet only the *Kampfzeit* films and *Um das Menschenrecht* had obviously negative Jewish characters. These films, however, as well as *Pour le mérite*, had committed directors who were early party members. Such films were still the exceptions. The German film industry was intent on doing what it liked to do best, producing films which, to some extent, could have been produced prior to 1933.

In the year that the Nazis came to power, a number of measures were taken against the Jews. Negative Jewish characters appear in the three *Kampfzeit* films made that year and again in the Zöberlein film the following year. In 1935–36 as the Nuremberg Laws were being introduced, we find German films *judenfrei*. Again in 1938, when persecution was stepped up prior to *Kristallnacht*, we have the fleeting appearance of one Jewish character in one film. In the two crucial years, 1935 and 1938, the Germans had to resort to a foreign film which they believed presented the case against the Jews. In 1935 the Swedish comedy, *Petterson und Bendel* (*Petterson and Bendel*) (1933), was shown with German subtitles. Shortly after *Kristallnacht* it was re-released, now dubbed into German.

In early 1935, party radicals became restless. By the end of March, anti-Jewish incidents erupted which quickly spread to major cities, Munich being the first in April and May. By mid-July, further incidents took place in Berlin, mainly on the fashionable Kurfürstendamm. On 15 July, Jewish shops were vandalized and Jews beaten up.[22] This was purportedly in response to an incident two days previously in a Berlin cinema, which resulted in the dismissal of the Berlin police chief, Magnus von Levetzow, something long desired by Goebbels.[23]

On 14 July 1935, a Sunday, the Nazi newspaper, *Völkischer Beobachter*, stated that a Swedish comedy, *Petterson und Bendel* (the Swedish title is *Pettersson &*

Bendel), produced two years previously, was the first foreign film to appear in its original version and to have received the highest *Prädikat*: 'of political value to the state'.[24] The reason for this became apparent in the accompanying review: the film offered 'new practical proof' of 'unscrupulous Jewish "competence" … repugnant to any normal, sensitive Aryan'. Aryan and non-Aryan characters were depicted in striking contrast: the Aryan lead was 'fresh and natural' while the two Jewish characters were 'portrayed in an unfavourable light'. These Jewish roles were taken not by 'made-up Aryans' but by 'two original representatives of the Chosen People who performed with an authenticity that leaves out nothing'.[25]

Brief mention was made of catcalls mixed in with the applause at the Ufa cinema on Berlin's Kurfürstendamm. This was attributed to 'Jews getting impudent and friends of Jews as long as the cinema remained darkened'.[26] Fuller coverage appeared on the next day's front page under the headline 'Jewish Impudence: The Incident at the Première of a Swedish Film in Berlin':

> On the occasion of the première there were incidents instigated by a large, apparently organized, number of Jewish patrons which make certain things plain. Even if this Jewish impertinence wisely took place in the dark, it proves – especially with regard to the official categorization of the film – that Jewry shamelessly takes advantage of the new Reich's position on the Jewish Question which ought not to remain without consequences.[27]

A second review on the second page again referred to the incident: 'The Kurfürstendamm, on the whole Jewish, was very angry on yesterday's Shabbes [sabbath]'.[28] Now it was no longer described as a spontaneous response of Jews and 'friends of Jews' but one 'organized' solely by Jews.[29]

The leading Swiss newspaper, *Neue Zürcher Zeitung*, reported the catcalls at the première (the 9 pm showing apparently) and also that some members of the audience had left, which had not disrupted the screening. It would be difficult, the Swiss paper suggested, to establish after the event who had been responsible, but the National Socialist press was convinced that they were dealing with 'a Jewish demonstration', and consequently had 'devoted columns to the incident'. The provocation was all the more serious, the report suggested, since the film gave 'an unflattering picture of the dealings of an Eastern Jew' and had received the official classification, 'of political value to the state'.[30] A German daily also reported some whistling and the whispering of mocking comments.[31]

The *New York Times* reported extensively on the violence that broke out on the Kurfürstendamm on the evening of 15 July: it 'seems to have been the direct result of a report which had appeared in the Nazi official party organ, the *Völkischer Beobachter*, that Jews had booed a Swedish antisemitic film running in a photoplay house in the Kurfürstendamm'. The Nazi paper had warned that 'such insolence was not to be endured' and a 'fiery editorial on the subject' followed in the afternoon edition of Goebbels's *Der Angriff*. According to the American paper, the rioting began 'in front of the cinema mentioned in the Nazi press', the first victims being those leaving the theatre who were 'seized, beaten and chased'.[32] The 'beating and bullying' quickly became 'indiscriminate'; some Americans and other foreigners fell victim. A statement issued that evening by the official German news bureau was also quoted:

> Attempts by Jews to disturb presentation of the film *Petterson and Bendel* in a Berlin photoplay house on Kurfuerstendamm resulted Monday evening in demonstrations before the theatre. A large crowd expressed displeasure with the provocative behaviour of the Jewish patrons of the photoplay house.[33]

In his diary entry for 15 July, Goebbels recorded that that evening he had received a telegram from Berlin about 'Jewish demonstrations against an antisemitic film'. Doubtless, in his eyes, or in those of the author of the telegram, catcalls were tantamount to a Jewish demonstration.[34] He made no further comment, which might suggest that Goebbels was not directly involved, but it has been argued and with good evidence that he was behind the demonstration. Several years earlier he had taken a prominent role in the demonstrations against *All Quiet on the Western Front*.[35] Now he was flexing his muscles, if that is not a misplaced metaphor – getting his own back on the Interior Minister Wilhelm Frick who opposed demonstrations against films that had been passed by the censor. He was also getting his own back against those in the Economics Ministry who believed that such actions were bad for Germany's relations abroad and could lead to economic boycotts.[36] (Even Goebbels could sometimes be wrong-footed as when in February 1935 the Ministry had to declare that Pola Negri was an 'Aryan' to avert possible disruptions from Nazi hotheads who thought otherwise.)[37] As mentioned, Goebbels was also determined to be rid of the Berlin police chief, von Levetzow, whom he replaced with his friend the young SA Group Leader, Wolf-Heinrich Graf von Helldorf.[38] (His trust proved misplaced since later Helldorf was active in the 20 July plot.) The events of July 1935 can be seen as a dress rehearsal, albeit on a much smaller scale, for *Kristallnacht*. The Berlin SA had long held Goebbels in high esteem, and it is likely that the demonstrators on the Kurfürstendamm were SA members in civilian dress.[39]

The Kurfürstendamm demonstrations were a continuation by party radicals of the anti-Jewish incidents which had begun earlier in the year. A minor incident, a few catcalls, albeit by Jews, became inflated. Nazi members of the audience were alert to any hostile acts: sniggering, whispering and catcalls. A darkened cinema lent itself to a unique form of protest. During the war this would be repeated in some occupied countries.[40] Whether those leaving the cinema did so because the film offended them or because the catcalls made them fear violence is not known. Though some Berlin Jews unwittingly played into the hands of their enemies, the incident was blown up and became part of the campaign of escalation.

One month later, the press reported that the Propaganda Ministry had examined copies of the film, and found that in four Berlin cinemas, two of which had previously had Jewish owners, the film had been tampered with, which suggested that the previous 'non-Aryan' owners were still exerting influence.[41] Thus the furore over the film served as a pretext for further Aryanization.[42]

Two months later, Hitler mentioned the incident in his address on the 'Jewish Question' to the reconvened Reichstag at Nuremberg:

> This international unrest in the world unfortunately appears to have given rise to the opinion among Jews in Germany that now perhaps the time has come to set Jewish interests up in clear opposition to the German national interests in the Reich. Loud complaints of provocative actions of individual members of this race (*Volk*) are coming in from all sides, and the striking frequency of these reports and the similarity of their content appear to indicate a certain method behind the deeds themselves. These actions have escalated to demonstrations in a Berlin cinema directed against a basically harmless foreign film which Jewish circles fancied was offensive to them.

Hitler threatened that 'should these incidents lead to quite determined defensive action on the part of the outraged population, the extent of which cannot be foreseen, the only alternative would be a legislative solution to the problem.'[43] That the film had not been considered 'basically harmless' was reflected in its *Prädikat* and the attendant publicity in the *Völkischer Beobachter*. That Jews, and not Nazi hotheads, were being taxed with provocative behaviour was merely a pretext for the next stage of persecution. That to instigate this the Nazis had to make do with a Swedish film, however, is telling.

After the introduction of the Nuremberg Laws, Hitler became somewhat reticent on the subject of the Jews, even after the murder in Davos of the Swiss Nazi leader, Wilhelm Gustloff, by a Yugoslav Jewish medical student on 12 February 1936. This has been attributed to his concern about the pending Olympic Games. Once they were over, he reverted to type: when Herschel Grynspan murdered the German attaché in Paris in November 1938 the result was *Kristallnacht*. Just over three weeks later, on 2 December 1938, *Petterson und Bendel* enjoyed its second German run, again in Berlin. The original subtitled version – a form unpopular with German audiences – had been withdrawn and dubbed into German. This version satisfied Goebbels: the dialogue was now more pointed than in the Swedish original,[44] though apparently the German subtitles had not been that faithful.[45] Dubbing also allowed greater freedom: the voice could be changed as was done with the main Jewish character, Bendel, played by the Swedish Jewish comic actor, Semmy Friedmann. Peculiar and unpleasant, it set him apart from the others, which hardly seemed necessary, given the opportunities afforded by the script and (in retrospect) even Friedmann's performance, though to some viewers, apparently, it communicated charm.[46] Nothing, however, was left to chance, in case German audiences, like Swedish audiences, found the character amusing, rather than repugnant.[47]

The script, as well as Friedmann's appearance and performance, conform in many ways to a negative Jewish stereotype. Swedish cinema during this period was nativist: Jews were the 'Other', perceived as foreign, even though they had lived in Sweden since the seventeenth century; they were 'identified by specific ethnic markers such as dark curly hair, hooked noses, extravagant gestures, or foreign accents'.[48] Friedmann was criticized by the Swedish *Judisk Krönika* (*Jewish Chronicle*) both for taking on the role as well as for his performance – his exaggerated make-up and gestures, and his use of 'unappealing jargon'. Subsequently, he conceded privately that it had been a mistake.[49] The *Völkischer Beobachter* was able to cite Swedish reviews in support of racial difference including even one from the Stockholm *Social Democrat*: 'Bendel is no figure in a novel but the very embodiment of this race.'[50]

Based on Waldemar Hammenhög's popular novel of 1931 and directed by Per-Axel Branner, the story concerns the partnership of two rogues, the Swede, Petterson, played by a well-known, dark-haired Swedish actor, Adolf Jahr, who lightened his hair for the part, and Bendel, played by the Swedish Jewish comedian Friedmann. Dark, small and nimble, Bendel arrives in Stockholm harbour on a ship from Eastern Europe, obviously a stowaway. The ship glides into the harbour – a dark hulk from which a furtive Bendel emerges attempting to evade two officials. But this is Sweden, not the USA. For American audiences a ship reaching US shores reached a haven, the Promised Land, where one day the immigrant would feel at home. The poor and puzzled immigrant, portrayed by Charlie Chaplin, is the obverse of the poor and knowing Bendel arriving in a Sweden where he does not and never can belong. To ridicule Jewish speech, Bendel's voice dubbed into German is squeaky and grating; in Swedish apparently he spoke with a German-Jewish accent, though in the novel he is said to speak 'virtually perfect Swedish' with the exception of one vowel.[51] He meets the down-and-out, happy-go-lucky Petterson while sheltering under a tarpaulin in the dock area. The latter enquires if he is a Jew, which Bendel vehemently denies, though eventually he admits to having a half-Jewish mother. However, Petterson seems to have nothing against Jews, though intuitively he finds Bendel different. The film clarifies what the novel never does: it makes Bendel Jewish by putting klezmer-style music on the soundtrack. This becomes his leitmotif.[52] The impoverished pair soon team up in money-making ventures. In contrast to the novel, the film emphasizes the differences between Petterson and Bendel, making the latter a more negative character. Together they plan a number of scams. Petterson has the charm and looks to impress the women he plans to dupe. Bendel has the brains and appears greedy, devious and cowardly, in stark contrast to the guileless Petterson.[53] An implicit antisemitism plays on the notion that Jews are unattractive but smart, good at business but unscrupulous.

It all ends happily. Bendel departs by boat for a destination unknown while Petterson gets the girl, marrying his pregnant girlfriend after a few misunderstandings, in contrast to the novel where she commits suicide.[54] Also eliminated from the film is the romantic competition between the two men for the girl.[55] Though Bendel may appear as the outsider, he is never singled out for abuse. Nevertheless, he does sail away to other climes, a happy end for 1930s Sweden where outsiders cannot belong. It was also a happy end for Nazi Germany since up to 1941 emigration was the preferred means of solving the Jewish problem.

One cannot escape the conclusion that the film industry was dragging its feet, not out of any resistance to National Socialism per se but simply because their brief was to entertain and they selected scripts accordingly. Goebbels was unwilling or unable to force the purged industry to make films that directly reflected the government position on the Jewish Question. Though dissatisfied with two of the three 1933 *Kampfzeit* films, he would not have been averse to more skilfully made films with a message but also with entertainment values, something he would eventually get in 1940 with *Jud Süss*. Still, providing pure entertainment was not without its political uses: it could encourage people to turn a blind eye, while censorship also ensured that nothing untoward appeared on the screen which might encourage dangerous thoughts. It would, however, be a mistake to regard the film industry during the 1930s as an instrument of government anti-Jewish policy. What occurred was much subtler. The overwhelming majority of films could be classified as entertainment films, though that by no means implies that they were without political value. In a negative sense, their value consisted in what they excluded because of censorship or self-censorship; in a positive sense, in what they promoted, which was usually not at odds with the beliefs of the new rulers.

Films are not necessarily a good source for the historian. During this same period it would be difficult to find a film in Britain or in the US which reflected the problem of unemployment. In America it was thought unemployment was bad box office, while in Britain the censors would not allow a film on the topic.[56] In Germany the problem was different. Though one would be hard put to find films reflecting the persecution of the Jews, this was not because of the government but because the industry was slow to respond, despite *Gleichschaltung* and Aryanization. From the introduction of the Nuremberg Laws in late 1935 to the second half of 1939, Jewish characters are significant by their absence from the German screen. One will look in vain in German feature film to find evidence for the persecution of the Jews: the only film in which a Jewish character had more than a marginal role during this period was a Swedish import. But by 1938 the industry began to respond: plans were underway to produce German comedies in which Jewish characters would no longer be peripheral.

9

Two German Comedies (1939)

At the beginning of January 1938, all German Jews were forced to add a middle name to their identity cards: Sara for women and Israel for men. In March the annexation of Austria (*Anschluss*) brought many more Jews under German rule. The well-publicized persecution of Austrian Jews – public humiliation, expropriation and forced emigration – exceeded anything which had taken place in the *Altreich* (Old Reich).[1] Aryanization of Jewish property continued apace in Germany, and in April and May of that year anti-Jewish violence also erupted.[2] In the autumn the Munich agreement brought a further increase in the number of Jews under German control when the Czech border areas (the Sudetenland) with their German minority were annexed. Finally, in November in a greatly expanded German Reich a pogrom was unleashed: *Kristallnacht*, the night of broken glass. The pretext was the assassination of the German attaché in Paris by a Polish-born Jew whose parents, under the new anti-Jewish measures, had recently been expelled from the Reich. The Jews were held responsible for the damage and required to pay RM1 billion. Some 30,000 Jews were rounded up and put in concentration camps. Before the year was out, Jews were forced to cease any business activity and to sell businesses, land and valuables. They were excluded from the welfare system and forbidden access to cultural institutions. In Berlin, and shortly thereafter elsewhere, they could no longer attend cinemas and theatres. They also could not drive cars. Jewish children still attending school were expelled. The aim was to make life so intolerable that Jews would seek to emigrate. Large numbers began seeking refuge elsewhere.

Two comedies were in the pipeline in 1938 but had their premières in 1939. In them Jewish characters occupied more space than in previous German films, though not centre stage in the sense of playing the lead – that would come the following year in two films which were not comedies. By definition, Jews were unsuited for the romantic lead, but well suited to play villains. In one of the two comedies the Jew meets his come-uppance when seeking the hand of the 'Aryan' heroine. This would also be the case in *Jud Süss* the following year. In both comedies, as in *Petterson und Bendel* earlier, an 'Aryan' romance occupies centre stage. It was only on the eve of the war that the first comedy opened; shortly after its outbreak the second comedy had its première. Thus it was not until the second half of 1939 that German audiences were given the opportunity to see two German-made films with Jewish characters in more central roles. The degree of antisemitism in both films however is open to interpretation.

The première of *Robert und Bertram* took place in July 1939. The film had been planned since April 1938, that is well before *Kristallnacht* and a subsequent Goebbels directive to film companies to produce antisemitic films. It thus was not made in response to any specific directive.[3] Nevertheless, even without a directive, directors were not ignorant of what was required as the persecution of the Jews intensified. *Robert und Bertram* was mild in comparison to the second German comedy, *Leinen aus Irland* (*Linen from Ireland*), which appeared two months later. That partly relates to the circumstances of its production but also to the source on which it was based.

Films take time for completion: from idea to scenario, to production approval, to pre-production, to production, to the censor's approval, to première and finally distribution. During this long period a film can be overtaken by events. This was the case with *Robert und Bertram*. By the time it opened, eight months after *Kristallnacht*, Jewish emigration had accelerated; there was talk of war, which was to break out six weeks later. At the beginning of 1939 Hitler had made clear that, were this to happen, it would be the fault of the Jews.

Based on a well-known farce, also entitled *Robert und Bertram*,[4] this comedy remained closer to its source than *Leinen aus Irland*, the second antisemitic German comedy. This may explain its shifting post-war reception. Forbidden by the Allies but subsequently passed by the West German censor in 1979 with minimal cuts, it was released on video in the early 1990s in the series '*Die grossen Ufaklassiker*' (The Great Ufa Classics), but after an outcry was withdrawn.[5] Very little was cut, at most two and a half minutes.[6] There is disagreement about its virulence.[7]

When discussing films made during the Third Reich, it is important to be aware that there have been different versions. This is important less for artistic reasons or for evaluating a director's competence, than for being aware that cuts have been.[8] The Allies forbade outright some films such as *Jud Süss*. Such films we can now view uncut. We might call them Type A films. Other films were cleared for viewing but subject to cuts, either at the time or subsequently; the last mentioned applies to *Robert und Bertram*. These we might call Type B films. What has been cut has often been lost forever. Type C films are those films deemed so harmless as to be offered uncut. Aside from the viewing context having changed, films that now may seem harmless are often available only in a cut version. This should be borne in mind with regard to this film.

Taken out of context, what purports to be a light-hearted comedy might seem harmless. Put in context, it is obvious that it had a purpose: to present Jewish characters in a negative light. In this it partly failed because it remained close to its source. Comedy can be difficult to control. According to the *Reichsfilmarchiv*, which catalogued all films made in the Third Reich, it was a 'harmless rogues' farce'.[9] Such a description is not that dissimilar to Hitler's disingenuous description of *Petterson und Bendel* as 'basically harmless'. Why not simply describe the film as a 'rogues' farce'? Why add 'harmless'? It would not be wrong to conclude that its purpose was anything but.

Based on a popular nineteenth-century musical comedy (comedy with singing and dancing) by Gustav Raeder (1810–68), *Robert und Bertram oder die lustigen Vagabunden* (*Robert and Bertram, or the Merry Vagabonds*) remained on the German stage for decades. The third generation of an acting family, and a member of the Dresden court theatre, Raeder was a singer, comedian and playwright, who usually took the leading comic role in his own plays. It is not clear when this comedy was first performed.[10] In Raeder's day it was not unknown for Jewish actors to take some of the roles: Ludwig Barnay, a distinguished actor, proudly recalled that at the beginning of his career he had taken the role of the young Jewish lead to prove that one could play a Jew not wearing a false nose and using gestures to suggest the character's ethnicity.[11] Nevertheless, the presence of Jewish actors does not in itself attest to the absence of antisemitism, as is clear from the case of Semmy Friedmann playing Bendel.[12] Actors take roles for a variety of reasons, doubtless the most important being financial. Furthermore, they cannot know in advance the likely audience response. Since the Second World War, and especially since the 1960s, we have become more sensitive to issues of race and ethnicity. But that was not the case earlier: then some Jewish characters conformed to what would now be considered negative Jewish stereotypes.

There was comic potential in making fun of the Berlin *nouveaux riches* and in satirizing 'salon Jews' for their cultural affectations; this followed a long theatrical tradition which began in the early nineteenth century and *was*, however, antisemitic. The Jew as parvenu was one antisemitic stereotype and not confined to Germany. (Parvenus who were not Jewish were also considered comic material.) Salon Jews, along with other Jewish characters, are ridiculed in *Robert und Bertram*, but, it can be argued, this alone is an insufficient indicator of antisemitism. The depiction of Jewish characters is not hostile nor does it differ from the depiction of non-Jewish characters, who are also ridiculed. The rogues, though loveable and amusing, remain rogues, while the non-Jewish characters, especially those they dupe, remain stupid throughout. Laughter is had at the expense of both Jewish and non-Jewish characters. A light-hearted farce, *Robert und Bertram* was meant to entertain.

Raeder's characters are not actually described as Jews, though this is hardly necessary since the dialogue makes it clear that they are. The servant is specifically described as speaking a 'Jewish dialect', which partly means pronouncing German vowels in a Jewish manner and speaking in singsong. Early on, the slovenly

servant, Jack, wearing livery, addresses his master, Ipelmeyer, in 'Jewish dialect'.
Offended, Ipelmeyer (who speaks high German) warns him: 'I have taken you
into my service after many requests from your mother, on the condition that you
give up the Jewish dialect.' Jack replies, 'As you command', but mispronounces
'immediately' (*sogleich* as *sogleuch*, a recognizably Jewish distortion, giving an
oy vowel or Yiddish pronunciation). 'An intolerable dialect', declares Ipelmeyer,
'could ruin my enjoyable evening.'[13]

Making fun of the Jew's inability to speak German properly was an element
in antisemitism, a term commonly thought to have been coined in the 1870s.
It suggested that Jews spoke a Semitic language, Hebrew, rather than an 'Aryan'
(Indo-European) language, German, or the Yiddish dialect which was also
Germanic, and that this, rather than religion, accounted for their difference.
Language was then linked to 'race'.[14] For Wagner, Jews could never speak German
properly.[15] This belief in the Jew's linguistic failure was not confined to Germany;
it indicated their outsider status and foreignness at a time of growing linguistic
nationalism.[16] Nevertheless, there is a world of difference between what Wagner
was writing in the 1850s and the fun that Raeder, at a similar time, was having
with his Jewish characters. There is, however, a tenuous link: Wagner's first foray
into antisemitic cultural politics was 'Judaism in Music',[17] an essay published
anonymously and directed at the Berlin-born Jew, Giacomo (Jakob) Meyerbeer,
who dominated the opera scene and composed in the French style.[18] Raeder often
parodied Meyerbeer and grand opera: even the names Robert and Bertram, it
has been suggested, may have been taken from his opera *Robert le Diable* (1831),
where Robert (tenor) is warned to be on guard against his friend Bertram
(bass).[19] But Raeder's purpose was to make his audiences laugh. His target was
the absurdity of grand opera; there is no evidence that he was interested in
relating Meyerbeer's work to his Jewish origins.

Raeder's play belongs to a theatrical genre: the local farce which originated
during the wars of liberation and died out sometime after the revolutions of 1848.
Initially, its regional character had a political dimension, since speaking a dialect
was an indication of belonging to a specific region and that brought with it a
licence to bear arms, especially important during the wars of liberation, though
not during the Restoration period which followed. Nevertheless, the relationship
between the local and the centre was ever present in the period prior to German
unification.[20] By using dialect, the genre created categories of who belonged and
who did not. It also appealed to a local audience who attended theatres in the
suburbs. In contrast, the tragedies of Goethe and Schiller and their successors
were performed in urban rather than suburban theatres and in High German,
hence the term 'stage German' (*Bühnendeutsch*). Speaking the local dialect was
a sign of authenticity while High German often suggested pretension, ambition
and moral laxness.

Yiddish also was a dialect, but Western Yiddish, which was what many Jews in the German areas then spoke and which disappeared later in the century, was not confined to a particular locality; for this reason, it has been argued, it never won for itself 'the status of a genuine dialect'.[21] Thus the deployment of Yiddish in a 'local farce' had a different purpose to that of other regional dialects.[22] The 'local farce' which included Jewish characters *was* antisemitic; it played on notions of Jewish cowardice, military unfitness and sharp practices.[23] Moreover, when a salon Jew spoke High German, it indicated a lack of authenticity.[24] Nevertheless, shortly after 1848, a change has been noted: Jewish characters in farces were no longer treated as alien. This reflected an attempt to assimilate the more inclusive ideals of the Enlightenment, but this only took place as the genre itself was dying out.[25]

Where does Raeder's play fit in? Its dating is important. It is not known when it was first performed, but it was *after* 1848. A number of stock Jewish stage characters are included. All are found in Berlin, which Robert and Bertram visit, though that constitutes only one of several episodes. One feature, in particular, links the play to the later development since the Jewish servant, who mangles the language, is revealed to be on the side of the law: it is he who works with the police to find the rogues, recover the jewellery, and bring them to justice. This is the most convincing piece of evidence in favour of Raeder's lack of antisemitic intent.

The film, however, is another matter. There is little doubt that the intention was to treat the Jewish characters with hostility, even if this doesn't always work. It is mild, however, when compared to the other antisemitic comedy of 1939. The 1939 *Robert und Bertram* was not the first film version. A twenty-five-minute German silent film had been made in 1915–16 by the underrated director of early German comedies Max Mack, with the young and gifted comedian Ernst Lubitsch, also of Jewish origin, playing Ipelmeyer's assistant.[26] During the First World War Lubitsch appeared in a number of comedies before turning his hand to directing comedies and costume dramas such as *Madame Dubarry* (1919) and *Anna Boleyn* (1920), which then brought him to Hollywood in 1923. A silent version of the same title made in 1928 had little to do with this farce.[27] Prior to 1939 *Robert und Bertram* had not been considered a vehicle for antisemitism.[28] That it was selected by Hans Heinz Zerlett, the film's director and scriptwriter, who also wrote the libretto under the name of Hans Hannes,[29] suggests that he recognized its potential but also the need to make changes. It is the extent of these changes and whether they were sufficient or insufficient which account for the disagreement about the film's antisemitism.[30]

A comparison of the film script with the play is instructive. Raeder's play consists of four parts (not acts), loosely related through the antics of the two eponymous characters, the two jolly rogues or vagabonds, Robert and Bertram. In the first part they escape from jail. Humorously entitled 'The Liberation', it contains a spoof on Beethoven's *Fidelio*. Two old friends are reunited in jail after Bertram bores a hole through his cell floor which, unbeknownst to him, happens to be the ceiling of Robert's cell below. Together they make their escape, easily outwitting their bumbling jailers. This scene is not dissimilar to the film's opening sequence since in both the jailers are depicted as incompetent. A swipe at those in authority, it will not have gone down well in some quarters. Part two of the play is entitled 'The Wedding'; it takes place in a village inn where the escaping Robert and Bertram have come in quest of a meal. In the film it is very different, not because of the need to adapt to a different medium, but because of the need to rework the German characters to make them seem less like country bumpkins.

The third part takes place in Berlin at a soirée and masked ball given by the social-climbing Berlin Jewish banker, Ipelmeyer, played by Herbert Hübner from whom Robert and Bertram steal jewellery. Though this, to some extent, has been changed in the film, the changes are fewer than for the previous sequence. A linking sequence between the second and third parts has also been added: in the play Robert and Bertram merely appear at the Ipelmeyers – how that happened is never explained. Robert takes on the disguise of the singing Count of Monte Cristo. Fun is had at the expense of Italians, and especially how they speak German, a gift to the playwright or actor. The pretensions of Berlin society and the admiration for all things Italian are also satirized. Though the Berlin sequences form only one part of a four-part play, in terms of actual playing time they comprise just over a third. In the film this has been reduced to less than a quarter of the playing time (eighteen out of eighty-seven minutes).

The last part finds Robert and Bertram returning to the village for the *Volksfest* (festival). When recognized by the police, they escape in a balloon. Again this too is very different from the play where Jack, the servant, in pursuit of the two thieves, links up with the police.[31] In 1939 a Jew could not be seen to be on the side of the law, nor could the theft from a Jew be deemed a crime.

It is worth looking more closely at some of Zerlett's changes. A sour note, absent from the play, is struck in the linking sequence which is added to the film to explain why Robert and Bertram go to Berlin. Now elegantly clad from the proceeds of selling the horses they have stolen from the police, Robert and Bertram identify Ipelmeyer in the fashionable Café Kranzler; he bears, as has been pointed out, a faint resemblance to the German-born composer Jacques Offenbach, of Jewish origin, who worked much of the time in France, and whose music has been considered quintessentially French.[32] They take a nearby table and converse loudly, with the deliberate intention of being noticed. Pretending that Robert is a famous singer, the Count of Monte Cristo, and that Bertram is his singing teacher, Professor Müller, they impress Ipelmeyer, who invites them to join him at his table. He then extends an invitation to an evening of entertainment at his grand house which is to conclude with a midnight masked ball. Robert takes his leave; Ipelmeyer now confides in Bertram: 'I'll let you in on a secret: I am an Israelite.' Bertram points to his own large belly and replies dryly: 'I have a belly.' The implication here is that there is no need to spell out who is a Jew since by definition it is obvious. In any case, Ipelmeyer was already identified as a Jew with the remark: 'That's him, to judge by the profile.'

The film emphasizes that Ipelmeyer's money has been ill-gotten: a Jewish guest comments that Ipelmeyer's palatial town house must have cost him a fortune, to which another guest replies: 'It has cost even more, though not Herr Ipelmeyer, but the people he conned.' This disparaging comment has been cut from the video. What is heard instead is only: 'it cost several people a fortune.' That Jewish wealth is based on overcharging is made clear in an earlier remark also partly cut from the video. Having stolen a purse, which contains a note signed by Ipelmeyer foreclosing on a debt, Robert and Bertram come to Berlin to seek him out. Upon reading the note, one says to the other: 'He'll go to another Jew, who will charge a higher rate to pay Ipelmeyer.' The word Jew has been cut from the video; instead one hears a blip.

Also eliminated from the film is Ipelmeyer's cousin, Frau Forchheimer, who loves all things Italian. Another female character replaces her: Ipelmeyer's wife. She is having an affair with a character named Forchheimer. Wearing a mask, Forchheimer is surprised that Frau Ipelmeyer recognizes him. She informs him that his feet gave him away (she says 'an die Fiss' – distorting the vowel from Füss to Fiss, giving it a Yiddish sound). She is also alluding to the antisemitic charge that Jews were flat-footed, thus making them poor soldiers, and unfit to defend the nation.[33] The significance of this line may have been lost on the West German censors who allowed it to pass. Both Ipelmeyer and wife (along with several other Jewish characters) speak German throughout but with a Jewish intonation; in the play it was mainly Jacques, thus suggesting that the Ipelmeyers were more assimilated.

Overweight and overdressed, Frau Ipelmeyer is, aside from the racial overtones, not too dissimilar to matrons in other plays and films – she is a stock comic character. At the masked ball she appears as Madame de Pompadour, with Ipelmeyer as 'Louis Quatorze the Fifteenth' (Louis Quatorze der fünfzehnte) – in the Raeder play it was Louis Quatorze the fourteenth (der vierzehnte).[34] Their daughter appears as Cleopatra, whom Jack calls 'the Queen Kleptomania', a double-edged joke added by Zerlett, alluding to Jewish money as theft. In the play she came as 'La Pucelle d'Orléans' (Joan of Arc).

The Count of Monte Cristo is now French, rather than Italian, to whom a proud Ipelmeyer shows off his daughter's knowledge of the language. This change had a purpose. Bourgeois Jews were Francophile, as France, Germany's historic enemy, was the first country to emancipate the Jews. Thus Jewish disloyalty could be emphasized, while Germany's new ally, Italy, would not be subject to ridicule.

Another Zerlett addition shows Ipelmeyer planning to seduce a ballerina, but his rival, the sinister doctor, renamed in the film Dr Cordvan (Dr Corduan in the play), deliberately administers him a sleeping potion.[35] A similar scene in *Jud Süss*, interestingly played by the same ballerina, suggests lasciviousness on the part of her patron – lasciviousness and wealth going together. The patron, however, is the Duke while in *Robert und Bertram* he is a Jew though in *Jud Süss* it is the Jew who procures for the Duke.

The film has also dispensed with the heroic potential of Samuel Bandheim, Ipelmeyer's bookkeeper. In love with Ipelmeyer's daughter, he is too poor to meet her father's approval: the father complains about his poor prospects though it is he who bears the responsibility for his poor pay. In the play Bandheim is astute (like the rogues) but also moral (unlike them). He has the potential to be a romantic hero, though Raeder does not develop this, disinclined as he is to stay with any one character for too long. Raeder does, however, make him the most sensible as well as the most honourable character: not only does Bandheim see through Robert and Bertram, but he warns an outraged Ipelmeyer to come to his senses before it is too late. In the film he appears sad and ineffectual, put upon both by Ipelmeyer and his spoiled, petulant and not unattractive daughter, who is quickly taken with the Count of Monte Cristo (Robert), thus revealing the absence of another feminine virtue, fidelity. Bandheim's costume for the ball is a suit of armour, in which he can barely move. With his room for manoeuvre constrained, his attempt to warn Ipelmeyer not to trust Robert and Bertram appears feeble; when challenged, he also quickly backs down. He is not the stuff of which heroes are made. Conforming to an antisemitic stereotype, a Jew must be shown to be cowardly. Raeder's Bandheim proved unacceptable to Zerlett, who modified the character accordingly.

Jewish characters are ridiculed in the film: the daughter comes over as distinctly unpleasant, shrieking hysterically when she discovers that her jewellery is missing. In between songs Robert has managed to rob her while Bertram, flirting with Frau Ipelmeyer and stroking her hand, has removed her jewellery. Together Robert and Bertram make their escape through a window. The sequence ends with a distraught mother and daughter (Ipelmeyer has fallen asleep). The slovenly and put-upon servant shrugs his shoulders and turns to camera (as though on stage) to address the audience with the words: '*Schluss galop mit der jüdischen Hast, Nu.*' ('That's it, the Jewish fast dance is over, so.' '*Jüdische Hast*' means Jewish pushiness and the '*nu*' is Yiddish for so). These lines are not in Raeder and are delivered by Robert Dorsay, a former cabaret artist later executed for making anti-Hitler jokes.

Other changes to the script are subtler, introduced to ensure that no Jewish character has positive qualities, while the non-Jewish characters are made less negative. Whereas in the original Michel is thoroughly stupid from beginning to end, here he is a loveable country bumpkin. We first see him carving on a tree the name of his beloved inside a heart while on the soundtrack we hear a Schubert *Lied* of undying love.[36] Stuttering and stammering when visiting his uncle, the jailer, he is comically ineffectual as Robert and Bertram make their escape. Though at the beginning he appears stupid, he does not end stupid. He enters the army with great reluctance but they make a man of him: he is briefly glimpsed in uniform marching down Unter den Linden, in the linking sequence when Robert and Bertram meet Ipelmeyer. By the end, his military experience has transformed him and he returns, polished, confident and passionate, to get the girl. Aptly named Michel after *der deutsche Michel* (the German Michel), an early nineteenth-century caricature personifying Germany – akin to John Bull for England – he is simple and slow on the uptake, embodying a Germany easily taken advantage of by other nations. Such a character appeared in other farces.[37] Zerlett retains Michel for some laughs, but his triumphant return at the end confirms that the image of a weak Germany is long out of date.

Another addition is the love interest between two 'Aryan' characters and a villain named Herr Biedermeier, presumably because the film is set in the Biedermeier period (1839), a time of German political weakness, and exactly one century prior to the making of the film. The innkeeper, Lips, has a daughter, Lenchen (in the play she was merely a waitress at the inn but not the daughter). She is in love with Michel. Biedermeier seeks Lenchen's hand. He has taken a loan from Ipelmeyer in order to buy the lease on the inn which enables him to put pressure on Lips by refusing to extend the lease. Lenchen's father is therefore in no financial position to allow her to marry Michel. Lenchen and her father are the only characters not treated satirically.

It is Biedermeier who has provided the link to Berlin. Robert and Bertram who, after entertaining the village wedding guests with a spoof sentimental Viennese song, steal his purse. Finding no money in it, but a note from Ipelmeyer foreclosing on Biedermeier's debt. They go to Berlin to aid 'Aryan' true love, and send later anonymously their illicit takings to Lenchen's father to enable him to pay off the mortgage. They also provide instructions on how to deal with Biedermeier. With her father's debt now cleared, Lenchen is free to marry Michel. Thus Robert and Bertram's only crime has been theft to aid 'Aryan' true love; but stealing from a Jew is hardly a crime since, by definition, Jewish wealth is ill-gotten.

At the annual village fair the police recognize Robert and Bertram and give chase. As they are about to be caught, they jump into a basket attached to a balloon which immediately lifts off. A Zerlett addition is that Michel stays the hand of the police who are about to shoot and puncture the balloon as it floats upwards. Soaring to heaven, Robert and Bertram finally escape the law. Lovely chorus girls appear as angels. The staircase to heaven is lined with a bevy of beauties, Busby Berkeley-style, though minus the dancing. The pearly gates open and the film ends. The previous year, Zerlett had also made *Es leuchten die Sterne* (*The Stars are Shining*), a revue with an attempt at Busby Berkeley choreography. He had also studied *Broadway Melody* of 1931.[38] This final sequence is absent from the film script; it will have been added during filming.[39] Possibly it also had a German antecedent: Reinhold Schünzel's *Amphitryon* (1935) where in one sequence the gods journey through the clouds.[40]

God was on their side: Robert and Bertram have not paid for their crimes. But were they crimes in 1939? With Aryanization in process, stealing from Jews was not, though escaping from prison and from the arm of the law was. The film began with the declaration that 'This is the story of two vagabonds who, in spite of their misdeeds, went to heaven because they possessed the most beautiful of all human virtues: gratitude.' This is a bit forced, since helping Lenchen and her father in return for a free meal after escaping from prison hardly merits such a reward. But a happy end was necessary. Compared to subsequent antisemitic films, especially *Jud Süss*, the Ipelmeyers got off lightly.

An entertaining freewheeling, anarchic musical comedy, with a light touch, the opening shots emphasize the links to nineteenth-century theatre: a proscenium arch with Robert and Bertram suspended as puppets. Some critics took this amiss, criticizing the film for failing to disguise its theatrical origins.[41] Yet cinematic voyeurism is also emphasized. As the characters dress for the masked ball, the camera playfully peers through one window after another as each character then draws the curtain, shutting out the camera. The music may also have caused offence. The characters sing well-known arias from Mozart, Beethoven, Weber and Schubert, but often with different words, spoofing the sacred German classical music tradition. This will have offended members of the *Musikkammer*. Folk song – so differently deployed in *Triumph of the Will* – is also parodied, which for some again was no laughing matter. The actors playing Robert and Bertram also dance. Both had experience in musicals, operetta and vaudeville (the last, in contrast to America, hardly ever transferring to the German screen). Rudy Godden (Robert) was especially talented, a superb singer, dancer and comedian. Nevertheless, he did not enjoy the same kind of success that his Hollywood counterpart would.

The comic touches are quite even-handed. Most characters, including the Jews, the military, the administrative officials and the villain Biedermeier, get their come-uppance. The exceptions are the two vagabonds, Lenchen, her father and Michel, though the rogues do have to exit this world to gain their just reward. Arguably, the Jews are no more ridiculous than the administrative officials, while Herr Biedermeier remains distinctly unpleasant, the true villain of the piece.

Ipelmeyer remains good-natured; the fun at his expense never turns nasty, and is not dissimilar to ridicule in a Molière play, which never gets out of control. Despite the changes to the script – negative with regard to Jews and positive with regard to non-Jews – the film retains enough of the spirit of the original and of the light-hearted character of a popular farce. At times it is malicious, but never vicious. Taking a popular farce with Jewish characters could misfire. Comedy is difficult to control: it can be subversive. An undercurrent of the original material wells up from time to time and subverts the film's purpose. *Robert und Bertram* often misses its target; it was not effective antisemitic propaganda.

The film opened on 7 July 1939 in Hamburg and one week later in Berlin. Having a première outside the capital was not unusual, but suggested it was not a prestige film. Reviews in the controlled press play on the fact that the film's purpose was to enlighten Germans about the Jewish danger, but reviewers required no prompting on how they should respond when they heard the word Jew. Advance publicity hardly mentioned the Jewish Question, though one member of the cast, the actress playing Ipelmeyer's daughter, alluded to the problem of acting a Jew. Her comments, used to publicize the film, reveal some confusion about the film's target:

> I almost cried, when filming came to an end, as I had enjoyed it so much. At first the role caused me some sleepless nights before I saw the script … It is a strange feeling to enter the public's consciousness as a Jewish girl, and during filming I got some horrified looks from visitors. We really looked like real *Mischpoke* [Yiddish for tribe].[42]

1939 was different from 1859; it was also different from 1940. In the summer of 1939 the jokes would have paled somewhat: German Jews (aside from the *Ostjude* immigrants) did not speak Yiddish, and were desperate to leave Germany, subject to obtaining visas. For them speaking a language other than German became a distinct advantage. Had they been in the audience – and Berlin Jews had been banned since 28 November 1938, a ban which soon extended to the rest of Germany – they would not have been amused, nor would non-Jews unsympathetic to the regime. To diehard Nazis, the Jews would appear grotesque, confirming them in their prejudices, though they might not have been amused by the antics of the non-Jews. That the Ipelmeyers and their friends got off so lightly might even have baffled them. For the apolitical viewer, the message might have missed the target; many may have enjoyed themselves. The nineteenth-century origins of the film are not wholly disguised: a rich comic vein has been tapped.

Goebbels was displeased with the film, recording in his diary: 'Examined film *Robert und Bertram*: a weak piece of work by Zerlett … The Jewish problem is touched upon very superficially, without any real sense of empathy.'[43] Zerlett (1892–1949) was trying to please his master but, given his career hitherto, it is not surprising he failed. Originally a stage actor, he also wrote plays, revues and reworked operettas. It was always light material. He had begun working in film in the early 1930s, directing his first film in 1934 and thereafter always writing scripts for the films he directed as well as libretti too, if necessary. Membership of both the Reichsfilmkammer and the Reichsschriftumskammer (the chamber for writers) created some confusion about his classification since membership of both chambers was not allowed. In 1937 Goebbels made him production chief for Tobis, in the hope that he could improve the artistic side of things, but Zerlett failed to make headway against his adversaries on the business side.[44] It was also at this time that he joined the party.[45]

Robert und Bertram was one of Zerlett's comeback films, one of four he made after giving up the post of production chief. In an interview in January 1939 he claimed that the 'Ipelmeyer scene already had a strong antisemitic tendency in Raeder and is central to my film'. Feeling a need to justify his choice of material, he added: 'it goes without saying that these Jewish roles must be taken by non-Jews.'[46] In other interviews he also emphasized the film's antisemitic aspects.[47] He made one other antisemitic film: Venus vor Gericht (1941).

Zerlett was a good friend since youth of Hans Hinkel, a high-ranking member of the SS, and an important figure in Nazi cultural affairs in the Reich Chamber of Culture (RKK), a bureaucrat in the Propaganda Ministry for Jewish affairs, and from 1943 Reichsfilmintendant after the fall of Hippler. Zerlett was in intimate correspondence with Hinkel. Shortly after Robert und Bertram opened, he asked Hinkel to find out if Goebbels was against him. The latter replied that Goebbels had nothing against him personally, though he had not liked Robert und Bertram and one other of his films, but was satisfied with the rest of his work and was not opposed to his continuing as a scriptwriter and as a director. Later Zerlett suggested to Hinkel that Goebbels should visit him in the resort of Bad Saarow, where he had a house. It was now judenfrei, so Goebbels could enjoy the improved atmosphere. Still trying to curry favour with Goebbels in July 1944, he asked Hinkel to relay to Goebbels his suggestion for raising morale: the word Deutsch in future should always be written in capital letters – since the English always write the first person singular with a capital letter.[48]

Zerlett's light touch combined with his light head, made him unsuited for making effective propaganda films; nevertheless he did his best. Aware that antisemitic films would help advance his career, he was not so much an antisemite as a careerist – the second of his three wives (before 1933) had been a Hungarian Jew. In 1946 he was arrested by the NKVD; Bad Saarow was in the Soviet sector. Already suffering from tuberculosis, he died three years later in Buchenwald.

According to Goebbels's enemy, the Nazi ideologue Alfred Rosenberg, Hitler was also displeased with Robert und Bertram. 'The new Robert und Bertram does down the German', he is reported to have declared.[49] Humour is difficult to control. The film received no Prädikat and barely recovered its production costs.[50] Eventually, it was withdrawn from circulation, as unsuited to wartime, but later apparently reissued in 1942 with cuts and a different ending: instead of ascending to heaven in a balloon, audiences are informed that Robert and Bertram have joined the Wehrmacht.[51] Despite this change, a still publicizing the film appeared inadvertently alongside the announcement showing the two rogues making their heavenly ascent.[52] The image had retained its appeal.[53]

Leinen aus Irland (*Linen from Ireland*) was less light-hearted, though also based on a comedy. In some respects it is closer to the antisemitic films of 1940. Indeed, the actor Siegfried Breuer, who played the unpleasant manipulative Jew, was considered for the role of Jud Süss.[54] Had he been given the role, the assessment of that film might have been even harsher. As an actor Breuer knew how to be sinister, a villain through and through: he brings to his role in this film, as in others, a steely coldness.

Leinen aus Irland was based on a play of the same name by Stefan von Kamare but subtitled *A Comedy from Old Austria*, which opened in Munich at the Residenztheater in 1929.[55] It was then not perceived as antisemitic, nor should it have been. Indeed, the play was criticized from a Nazi perspective for taking 'the path of a Jew in a corrupt egotistical world relatively lightly'.[56] But significant changes were made to the film script to ensure that it was antisemitic. It is quite different from *Robert und Bertram*, with which it is sometimes coupled.[57]

After *Anschluss* the Austrian film industry was quickly made *judenfrei*. Persecution moved at a much faster pace: Aryanization proceeded with extraordinary speed as Jewish emigration was encouraged, with a central office being set up for that purpose that summer.[58] In the autumn the production company Tobis-Swascha, along with other Austrian film companies, was amalgamated into Wien-Film, at first majority-owned by Tobis.

Leinen aus Irland was intended to show that the Austrian industry had been truly *gleichgeschaltet*.[59] Goebbels visited the set during filming in Vienna in June 1939 and expressed himself satisfied.[60] And after viewing the finished product in September 1939, he recorded in his diary: 'it has turned out very well.'[61] The film opened on 16 October 1939, receiving the classifications: 'of political value to the state' and 'of artistic value'. The director was Herbert Helbig and the script was by Harald Bratt, who later co-scripted the anti-British *Ohm Krüger* (1940). Bratt's script did rather more than merely adapt from one medium (the stage) to another (the screen): it was an extensive rewrite.

Irish linen refers to an attempt before the First World War to reduce tariffs and import cheap linen from Ireland to the Habsburg Empire. This would benefit the local textile manufacturers, and in particular one company, Libussa, by reducing the cost of materials. It would result in some unemployment, which in the play would have affected the Czechs. Though only alluded to, unemployment is a matter sufficiently serious for one character, Dr Goll, to consider it a cause for resignation from the civil service.

In the play, the director of Libussa, Brennstein (Kettner in the film, the name of another character in the play), meets Schlesinger from Scutari, an absurd and comical figure who has a number of money-making projects up his sleeve, as well as insider knowledge about shares in another company. He displays some negative Jewish 'characteristics' – smart with money and duplicitous – but is not shunned by the non-Jewish characters and is ultimately rewarded for his efforts. He announces himself as the proud owner, founder and editor of Albania's only newspaper, though he concedes that given the high illiteracy rate the paper has few readers. Nevertheless, this does not prevent him from soliciting advertising revenue.

Brennstein's independent-minded daughter Lilly is in love with Goll, an incorruptible civil servant opposed to the Irish linen project because it will result in unemployment. Goll is the obstacle to the profitable deal Lilly's father hopes to conclude with Schlesinger. Thus the father asks Lilly to persuade the high-minded Goll to see things his way, namely turn a blind eye to the unemployment problem. If Goll agrees, Brennstein will consent to his daughter's marriage. Initially, the headstrong and indulged Lilly shows willingness, as she is beginning to find her fiancé too staid for her tastes. It even looks as though the engagement will be called off, but Lilly then undergoes a change of heart and comes to respect her fiancé's principles. She is forced to run after him (literally) as he is about to board a train to leave the country. Her father in turn comes to appreciate Goll's integrity: a good quality in a son-in-law, he concedes, though not necessarily in business.

With Goll temporarily out of the picture, there is no obstacle to the ministry's approval of the Libussa project. An overjoyed Brennstein proposes to Schlesinger that they now work together in the Balkans selling ladies lingerie.

Earlier Schlesinger himself had been planning to propose marriage to Lilly, but before he could formulate the words she lets him know of her sudden change of heart towards Goll. In any case, the audience knows that Schlesinger would have been refused, not because he is a Jew but because Lilly prefers Goll. Lilly's father has had no qualms about working with Jews: his secretary, Dr Körner, is one. Lilly calls him her dearest friend. Körner confides in her: 'You know, Fräulein Lilly, how difficult it is to free myself from the bonds of the little ghetto there in Galicia,' adding that it is not so easy to be a gentleman 'if you still feel the ghetto inside you'.[62] Lilly offers her sympathy and even calls him her soulmate:

Dear Doctor, you really were not born for good fortune. Accept that. You will always fight with yourself and will only advance if someone with integrity leads the way. I also have something similar in me and this is why I like you and speak to you as though to myself … Don't misunderstand me, Dr Körner, you are a gentleman, one of the finest I know.[63]

A play with dialogue like this, even if not breaking the taboo of intermarriage, would have had to be heavily adapted. And so it was. Dr Körner becomes the villain, Dr Kuhn, the scheming capitalist. Schlesinger's name is retained for a minor and very different character.

The film opens in the Sudetenland. Sudeten-German weavers in peasant dress are on the march – a conflation of the Sudeten crisis of the previous year (when the Czechoslovak border region with its large German minority was incorporated into the Third Reich) and the Silesian weavers' uprising of the previous century, familiar to audiences from Gerhart Hauptmann's play, *Die Weber* (*The Weavers*). An arrow on the road points in the direction of Varnsdorf, a border town in the Sudetenland, previously a crossing point on the Czech–German frontier. There the owner of an old Sudeten-German family textile firm – we see from the sign above the entrance that it was founded in 1751 – is tricked into signing over control on unfair terms to Libussa, a textile firm now specifically located in Prague. The prime mover behind this takeover is not the director of the company, Lilly's father, but the company general secretary, Kuhn, the sinister Jew played by Breuer. It is he who is behind the move to persuade officials in the Ministry of Trade to remove the tariffs imposed on linen imported from Ireland. According to the film publicity:

> in 1909 and 1910 in the economic life of the Danube state ruthless, Jewish, shady characters could accomplish much – their goal was to seize control of the Central and East European textile market … The film shows how Jewish freeloaders destroyed the existence of Sudeten German weavers' families, supported by a half-rotten morality, which was even present in the ministries. With the introduction of tariff-free linen from Ireland the last means of a livelihood will be taken from the honest weavers in the Sudetenland.[64]

Opposing Kuhn's move is the upright civil servant, Goll, who also provides the love interest. The only character to remain substantially unchanged from the play, he stands in stark contrast to the other civil servants, who appear as idle, cynical Habsburg time-servers, though not without humour in the acting. The sub-text is that their time will soon be up with the arrival of the new men following *Anschluss*. Only here does the comic element surface; in the play the comedy lay elsewhere, with Schlesinger and with Lilly's friends. The only politician in evidence in the film is the minister, naturally a corrupt socialist. The Sudeten German owner of the textile firm, in financial difficulties, dismisses the Habsburg machinery of government as 'the royal, imperial pigsty'. In contrast to the play, Lilly and Goll initially do not know each other. It is the devious Kuhn, trying to overcome Goll's opposition, who engineers the introduction. It is his hope that Lilly will soften up Goll. As in the play, Lilly's father asks her to try and persuade Goll to give up his opposition. In the film she is unhappy with this request, but complies, in the hope that Goll will refuse. Less independent-minded, less frivolous and less headstrong than in the play, she has the makings of a good Nazi *Hausfrau*, though, in a concession to modernity – as in the play – she smokes.

Kuhn is distinctly unpleasant, but dapper and suave. He has an uncle, Sigi Pollack, who makes a surprise visit. Fat and ugly, the uncouth *Ostjude* who speaks with a German Jewish intonation, he is impressed by Kuhn's new-found wealth. Both are on the make and together they plot and plan. There are some similarities in the script to *Jud Süss*: for instance, the contrast between the urbane assimilated Jew (Kuhn or Süss) and the unassimilated and primitive *Ostjude* (Sigi or Levy). The implication is that behind every assimilated Jew lurks the unassimilated horde. Kuhn himself, fully aware of this, wants to keep hidden his links with his cousin. Much to his annoyance, he returns to find Sigi sitting in a bubble bath in his elegant bathroom. This plays on an image of the *Ostjude* as uncouth and in need of a wash. Kuhn asks for Lilly's hand. Not only is he rebuffed by her outraged father, who would never under any circumstances want him for a son-in-law, he is also summarily dismissed and thrown out. Her father has finally caught on to his unsavoury business schemes.

This film does much more than subvert the play: the script is a major rewrite. Its antisemitism is qualitatively greater than that in *Robert und Bertram*, perhaps a product of the Austrian context where antisemitism flourished. The comic elements are provided by the decadent but ineffectual Habsburg civil servants. To the extent that there is comedy in the portrayal of Sigi, it is vicious. Missing is the light touch, but Goebbels was pleased: the repellent Sigi and the villainous Kuhn were closer to his ideal Jew than Ipelmeyer. Both character types would reappear the following year in eighteenth-century dress in *Jud Süss*, a project which, at the time that *Leinen aus Irland* opened, Goebbels was trying to get off the ground.

Thus to the outbreak of war German cinema-goers had only been exposed to three films in which Jewish characters made more than a marginal appearance. The first was a Swedish import, the second was German-produced but failed to satisfy either Hitler or Goebbels, and the third, which was made in Austria, now part of the Greater German Reich, showed the way forward. Solving the Jewish Question was now moving to the top of the agenda, and this urgency would be reflected the following year in a small number of films.

The Rothschilds and Jud Süss

Just before *Kristallnacht*, or possibly just after – we do not know the exact date as no document has ever been found – the Propaganda Ministry issued a directive that each film company should produce an antisemitic film.[1] The persecution of the Jews had intensified, and the film industry was expected to play its part in preparing Germans for their removal; but it should be emphasized that, at this stage, it was expulsion from Germany rather than extermination. The comedies, then in production, which merely ridiculed Jews, would no longer suffice. Two and a half months later, on 30 January 1939 (the sixth anniversary of the Nazi seizure of power), Hitler delivered his oft-quoted Reichstag speech, in which he prophesied 'the destruction of international Jewry from the face of the earth'.[2] He was, it has been argued, making a conditional threat, conditional on war breaking out, for which he would hold the Jews responsible.[3] Elsewhere in the two-hour-long speech he threatened to make antisemitic films in retaliation for an announcement made by American film companies that they planned to produce anti-German films. It is not clear exactly what particular announcement he had in mind, though *Confessions of a Nazi Spy* was nearing completion and *The Great Dictator* was in preparation.[4]

In response to the Propaganda Ministry directive, one company, Ufa, obliged with *Die Rothschilds* (*The Rothschilds*). Another company, Wienfilm, based in Vienna, proposed *Wien 1910* (*Vienna 1910*), though filming did not begin until 1941 and, after further delays, it was not released until 1943.[5] Another company, Terra, made *Jud Süss*, which was by far the most successful of the state-commissioned propaganda films. It had little competition from the other antisemitic films.

Die Rothschilds opened on 17 July 1940, directed by Erich Waschneck, a Weimar director best known for *Acht Mädels im Boot* (*Eight Girls in a Boat*) (1932), which touched on the highly controversial topic of abortion. It was shown only in Berlin and a few other cities and was withdrawn from circulation after only two months either because of its poor box office performance or because it might have competed with *Jud Süss*, which opened in late September.[6] It was re-released one year later in July 1941 with the subtitle, *Die Rothschilds Aktien von Waterloo* (*The Rothschilds' Shares at Waterloo*). Goebbels remained dissatisfied with the film. It never received any *Prädikate*, and the press was forbidden to discuss it.[7]

There were good reasons for Goebbels's dissatisfaction. It was a flat, undramatic and wordy film, with a complicated plot about playing the stock market during the Napoleonic wars, having as its target not only Jews but also the British. The film's production history suggests that it oscillated between these two enemies. Several discourses are closely linked: anti-capitalism, Anglophobia and antisemitism.[8] At one stage (in December 1939) Mirko Jelusich, an Austrian writer, who first proposed the subject though he did not write the script (that was done by C.M. Köhn and Gerhard T. Buchölz), described the project as anti-British. Seven months later, on the day before it opened, Hitler issued the directive for Operation Sea Lion (the invasion of Britain), though two days after the première he announced to a specially summoned Reichstag his conciliatory offer to Britain. Thus the film appeared at a time when anti-British propaganda was reaching a new crescendo.[9] The relationship with Britain has been aptly described as one of 'love–hate'. While previously Hitler had expressed sentiments of 'Nordic similarity', by June 1940 Goebbels, despite an earlier admiration, was portraying the British as 'the Jews amongst Aryans'.[10] Between December 1939 and July 1940, however, the film was closely linked with *Jud Süss*, then also in production. The press was instructed to characterize neither of the 'Jewish films' as antisemitic, but rather as 'objective representations of the Jews, as Jews are in reality'.[11] Both films focused on well-known historic characters, wealthy German Jews in positions of economic, and thus political, power. In so doing they illustrated the belief of many antisemites in the existence of a world Jewish conspiracy in which Jews pulled the strings of their puppets, who occupied the actual seats of power. Intended to expose how the British plutocracy, in their eagerness to do business with the Jews at the time of Waterloo, had become fully judaized, the film expended its energy on two enemies rather than one. This was not a recipe for effective propaganda.[12] Furthermore, its antisemitism was relatively feeble (relative that is to *Jud Süss* or *Der ewige Jude*). Both Jews and British are presented as posing an economic threat, but significantly in this film the Jews do not pose a racial threat, except in so far as their propensity to corrupt was predetermined, inherent in their very nature.

Nathan Rothschild, an *arriviste* (played by the portly Carl Kuhlmann), is sent to London from the Frankfurt ghetto by his wily father, Meyer Amschel Rothschild (played by Erich Ponto). His other brothers are sent to other European capitals, as part of a Jewish capitalist international. Shunned by high society, his low point comes when no one attends his lavish banquet. We see him humiliated, dining alone in a hotel, with faint sounds of tinkling laughter coming from a distant banquet in another room where his guests prefer to enjoy themselves. His grotesque agent, played by Hans Stiebner, warns him that he will always be a 'boy from the *Judengasse*' (Jews' Alley). That would seem to be the extent of his sufferings. But soon he will triumph, as he hedges his bets and plays both sides, buying and selling shares while the battle of Waterloo rages, which incidentally is won by the Prussians rather than by Wellington (portrayed in this film as a womanizer). Most importantly, Nathan Rothschild has spread the rumour that Wellington has been defeated, thus creating panic on the stock exchange, which enables him to buy up shares cheaply. When news spreads of victory, his shares soar in value. Now almost everyone wants to do business with Rothschild. The exception is one important female character, the elegant Mrs Turner, who is Irish and whose banker-husband Rothschild has ruined. He is played by Herbert Hübner (Ipelmeyer) in an exception from typecasting. She abandons England for Ireland, with the damning words: 'You say Rothschild and I say England which is the same thing and I am leaving this country.' This pro-Irish theme appears in other films made at this time such as *Der Fuchs von Glenarvon* (*The Fox of Glenarvon*) (1940) and *Mein Leben für Ireland* (*My Life for Ireland*) (1941).

Displaying more social than political venom, the film failed as a vehicle for virulent antisemitism. But, in case the audience missed the point, a statement was appended to the end of the re-released version. Superimposed on a large map of England, a Jewish star sparkles above the following words: 'As work on this film ended, the last of the Rothschild descendants is abandoning Europe as refugees. The fight goes on against their helpers in England, the British plutocracy.' This is further evidence, were that needed, that the purpose of this film (re-released in summer 1941) was still to demand the emigration of Jews rather than their extermination, though the geographic area from which emigration was possible had now widened to include Occupied Europe. Emigration would be halted in October.

This was by no means the first time that the Rothschilds had featured in fiction. The Nazi poet, playwright, novelist and second scriptwriter on *Jud Süss*, Eberhard Wolfgang Möller, had written a play first broadcast and then performed in the theatre in 1934 and finally published in 1939, *Rothschild siegt bei Waterloo* (*Rothschild Triumphs at Waterloo*). It was inspired by a play from 1808 (antedating Waterloo) that associated Jews with betrayal. *Die Sauvegard* (*Safe Conduct*) by Julius von Voss, was about a Jew (not Rothschild) who spread rumours to boost the price of shares.[13]

From the very beginning, legends proliferated about the origins of the Rothschild fortune, creating 'a myth of immense wealth; of meteoric social ascent; of limitless political and diplomatic power; and of some enigmatic *ultima ratio*, connected with the family's religion'.[14] Often but not always this narrative was told in pejorative terms, and the same applies to its cinematic representations: the German version was pejorative, while an American version became a tale of 'economic over-achievement, social success, legitimate power and moral ends'.[15] This of course was not remote from the American dream, which is why it became the subject of a Hollywood film in 1934, *The House of*

Rothschild. Starring the British actor, George Arliss, as both Meyer Amschel and Nathan, it was very much an Arliss vehicle. Following his triumph as Disraeli in *Disraeli* (1929), a sound remake of a 1921 silent, he held the film option. Benign when compared to its German counterpart, it was nevertheless not wholly free of traces of antisemitism: it assumed that Jews were clever with money and were also bent on domination. In the American context, their wiliness could be perceived as a virtue, however, especially when it enabled them to avoid paying taxes, as in an opening sequence which would later be incorporated into *Der ewige Jude*. Its influence on the German Rothschild film, however, is hardly discernible, aside from both films beginning in the Frankfurt ghetto, from which the dying Meyer Amschel sends his five sons to seek the family fortune in the major European capitals. It also includes an unfortunate image: over a map of Europe the capital cities mark out the points of a Jewish star, an image reused in the German version. But its dual themes of love triumphant and assimilation triumphant involve intermarriage between Nathan's daughter and a British officer, after they overcome Nathan's initial objections that she should marry someone of 'our own race'. The Germans do not fare well: the villain is a Prussian minister, Baron Ledrantz, played by Boris Karloff, and the film concludes with the 'Hep-Hep' riots of 1819 directed against Frankfurt's Jews. Throughout, the evils of prejudice are emphasized. Love triumphant is also a theme in the German version but for obvious reasons involves 'Aryans'. The daughter, Phyllis Bearing (sic), also defies her banker father in her pursuit of true love; but as proof of her love, in an act wholly unacceptable for a Hollywood heroine, she produces a child born before marriage.

Synonymous with Jewish wealth and power, the Rothschilds' ascendancy also paralleled the demands for Jewish emancipation, which was eventually achieved in 1867 in the North German Confederation, and in 1870 in the Second Reich, but removed by the Nuremberg Laws. A suitable subject, one might think, for a Third Reich film on Jewish domination, but nevertheless one with pitfalls: the story could not be told without some mention of those non-Jews who had aided and abetted their rise, including German princes. In the German film's opening sequence we observe an Elector, the Landgraf (Count) of Hesse, in flight from Napoleon. He leaves his ill-gotten wealth with the Rothschilds (ill-gotten because it was payments received from the British for his sale of Hessian mercenaries, when it goes without saying that Germans should be fighting alongside Germans). This then forms the basis of the Rothschild fortune. In exposing the Rothschilds' network of business relationships, too many non-Jews were caught in the net.

Of those feature films produced in response to the Propaganda Ministry directive at the time of *Kristallnacht*, only *Jud Süss*, the best known, became both a political and box office success. Indeed, the film's subsequent notoriety stems from the latter. No expense was spared on this well-made film, a lavish star-studded costume drama. Though closely linked to the persecution of the Jews, it illustrates well Goebbels's dictum that the most effective propaganda should come in the guise of entertainment. However, the idea for the film did not originate with the Propaganda Ministry. Indeed, very few Nazi Party members were involved in its making, and few were known antisemites. The director's first wife had been Jewish; the lead actor's stepdaughter was a *Mischling* First Degree (her Jewish father, the Czech-born actor, Julius Gellner, taking up employment with the BBC German Service in January 1941, while her stepfather starred in this most antisemitic of propaganda films).[16]

Jud Süss is not only a costume drama (fictional characters set against an historical background) but, in so far as it takes as its subject an historical figure, it is also an historical drama (based on an actual historic figure).[17] Joseph Süss Oppenheimer (1698–1738), otherwise known pejoratively as *Jud Süss* or *the* Jew Süss, was court Jew to the Duke of Württemberg during his brief reign (1734–37). Süss's meteoric rise and fall, and spectacular execution in an iron cage, soon became the subject of legend, then literature, and finally in the twentieth century, film. Indeed, his execution was what for the eighteenth century constituted a media event, with the production of numerous pamphlets, poems and illustrations. Court Jews (with privileged status) were neither numerous nor typical. From the late seventeenth to the late eighteenth century they acted as agents to the numerous German petty princes who ruled the principalities that then constituted Germany, offering them financial advice, outfitting their armies, and procuring for them and their families jewels and other luxury items.[18] Süss Oppenheimer engaged in all these activities, but nevertheless was most untypical, in that, according to contemporary accounts, he was an elegant courtier, libertine and freethinker, yet significantly chose not to convert to Christianity. A powerful private adviser, he often behaved as though he were a government minister, though he was not one. In the German film he is addressed at one point as 'Herr Finance Minister', but he was never actually in government, and indeed as a Jew could not have been a civil servant. As a private adviser, however, he was responsible for introducing a number of harsh financial policies, the aim of which was to sort out the Duke's precarious finances. This made him very unpopular and contributed to his brutal end. After the Duke's sudden death he was tried, convicted and executed for high treason, despite many legal irregularities.[19]

A German novella on the subject, entitled *Jud Süss*, by the young Württemberg writer, Wilhelm Hauff (1802–27), appeared in 1827; there is a plagiarized English version by Anne Elizabeth Ellerman, *The Prince Minister of Württemberg* (1897).[20] Better known, however, is Lion Feuchtwanger's best-selling novel, also entitled *Jud Süss*, published in 1925. Translated into many languages, the novel appeared in Britain as *Jew Süss*, its title translated literally, though in the US it was changed to *Power*, Jew being too strong a word in the American context. The Feuchtwanger novel served as the basis for a British film, *Jew Süss*, on which the Jewish Feuchtwanger, now in exile, advised. Produced by Michael Balcon at Gaumont British in 1934, with the exiled German actor Conrad Veidt in the title role, the film opened shortly after *The House of Rothschild* which it trailed at the box office. It was soon banned in Vienna, where it was deemed philosemitic propaganda, by the antisemitic but anti-Nazi Christian-Social government of Austria, while the Rothschild film, causing no offence, continued to be screened.[21] The ban was gleefully reported in the German press.[22] In America, outside major cities such as New York (with a large Jewish population), it was not a box office success, with critics also finding the film far too long. Failing to match the recent success of Alexander Korda's costume drama, *The Private Life of Henry VIII*, it disappointed its British producers, the Ostrau brothers. But it did well in Britain, ranking sixth at the box office for 1934, the second most popular British film after Korda's *Catherine the Great*.[23] Political propaganda was banned from the British screen, but the film passed the strict British censors despite dialogue alluding to the contemporary plight of the Jews: 'They did it in 1430, they can do it in 1730, they can do it in 1830, they can do it in 1930. Who is going to stop them?' says one character to Süss (and of course the audience). This was the closest that any British film came to touching on the subject of Nazi Germany prior to the outbreak of the war.[24]

Several years passed before the Germans decided to make their own version. Why this took so long can partly be explained by certain aspects of the story, which proved awkward for anti-Jewish propaganda, especially after the passage of the Nuremberg Laws. Sexual attraction between the races posed problems, though the delay may also reflect a lack of eagerness within the industry to produce propaganda films, especially antisemitic ones. The Germans were also slow in deciding to make a film about the Rothschilds.

In January 1939 a scriptwriter at the Terra film company, Ludwig Metzger, responded to the Propaganda Ministry directive with the subject of *Jud Süss*. Hitherto he had not been involved in writing scripts for propaganda films, and he was then at work on a musical, *Zentrale Rio*, directed by a former colleague of Bertolt Brecht's, Erich Engel, the director of the first stage production of *Die Dreigroschenoper*.[25] When Metzger met with a lukewarm response at Terra, he rushed to the Propaganda Ministry, where, according to one witness, 'it went off like a bomb.'[26] It was taken up by Goebbels himself, and became a *Staatsauftrag* (state-commissioned) film, which was subsequently also described as *Staatswichtig* (important to the state). Metzger received his contract for a treatment in February 1939 and shortly thereafter, accompanied by the film company's dramaturge, made a brief visit to the Stuttgart Archives to conduct some historical research.[27] Not surprisingly, there is little evidence of this in the film, despite the statement, following the titles, that 'The events described in this film are based on historical fact.' Such a statement reflected Goebbels's directives and was not unusual in Third Reich films based on historical subjects. Aside from the execution, the story is pure invention; this is also true of the Feuchtwanger and Hauff versions, but this version, in addition to offering a good story, had the additional burden of complying with the needs of the state.

Metzger planned to base his script on the Hauff novella, as film publicity in the summer of 1939 made clear.[28] After war broke out, another scriptwriter was brought in: the diehard Nazi Möller, who had inspired the Rothschild film. A high-ranking member of the SS, and consultant to the Propaganda Ministry, he was held for a time after the war in the same Württemberg fortress, Hohen Asperg, that had once housed Süss Oppenheimer.[29] With no previous experience of writing film scripts, he was brought in by the State Secretary for Film in the Propaganda Ministry, Leopold Gutterer, doubtless to ensure that the film met Nazi requirements. Metzger was not delivering what was wanted, possibly because he relied too heavily on the Hauff novella, though a synopsis indicates he was in fact free with the story.[30] It goes without saying that he had to leave out a character that Hauff, under the influence of Walter Scott's *Ivanhoe*, had invented, namely Süss's lovely sister, Leah, the beautiful Jewess. Metzger and Möller were closeted together at the latter's home in Thuringia for ten weeks, which was doubtless uncongenial for both, with Metzger subsequently complaining about not getting his expenses for this and the archive visit.[31] Though Hauff's racial credentials (unlike Feuchtwanger's) were impeccable, his ideological suitability was doubtful, according to Möller in an interview in late October 1939.[32] Apparent in all of this is the uncertainty as to what constituted a truly antisemitic film, as well as the ad hoc nature of mounting this major film, the idea for which was not hatched in the Propaganda Ministry. One might go so far as to say that it was almost in desperation, and then with some relief, that the idea of basing a film on Hauff was initially agreed. Only after the publicity had gone out was it decided that he was not suitable. By then, the original idea had been overtaken by events, as the war had begun, and Möller stepped in. Dismissing Hauff's attitude to Jews as sentimental, Möller excused him on the grounds that he had had the misfortune to be living in a time which was favourably disposed to the emancipation of Jews *and* Poles. Coupling Poles with Jews reflected the opening stage of the Second World War.

The script was not the only problem. The director assigned to the film at Terra-Film company, Peter Paul Brauer, had no reputation as a director and thus had little success in finding actors willing to take on the roles, especially that of the lead.[33] At this stage, a fine stage and film actor, the Austrian-born Ferdinand Marian, who had played Iago on stage and had caught Goebbels's attention, rejected the role.[34] Indeed, Marian turned down the role on several occasions, only accepting it after a personal audience with Goebbels. Gustav Gründgens (the target of Klaus Mann's satirical novel, *Mephisto*) was also considered, but as Intendant (Director) at the Prussian State Theatre could call on his protector, the Minister of Prussia, Hermann Goering, to support his refusal.[35] Eventually, several actors including Marian auditioned: if we accept Marian's account, each out did the other in execrable acting to avoid the role.[36]

Goebbels's diary entries make clear that the conquest of Poland with its large Jewish population made urgent a film on the 'Jewish Question'. After flying to Łódź (31 October 1939) for a one-day visit, presumably to advise on film sequences for *Der ewige Jude*, he returned horrified. For what he had seen was 'indescribable'; these were 'no longer human beings', but 'animals', and 'the task' would not be 'humanitarian' but 'surgical'. 'One must make the cut here, and a very radical one at that. Otherwise, Europe will perish with the Jewish disease.' The Polish streets were described as already 'Asia' and he worried that they would have much to do to 'Germanize'.[37]

Shortly after Goebbels's return, Brauer was sacked, and was forced to inform Veit Harlan (1899–1965), who worked for another film company, Tobis, that it was Goebbels's wish that he be his replacement.[38] After the war, Harlan would claim that he had tried in vain to escape the appointment, even threatening to enlist to go to the front.[39] That he was not keen to produce propaganda films may well have been true, for up to that time he had mainly directed melodramas; but as a result of this film and the subsequent state-commissioned films, he was to become the Third Reich's leading director. An actor since the early 1920s, he had turned to directing in 1935, able to avail himself of the new opportunities in the *judenfrei* industry. One of his final acting roles was to utter the line often misattributed to Goering: 'When I hear the word culture I reach for my gun.' This was in Hanns Johst's play *Schlageter*, about the eponymous Nazi martyr condemned to death by the French in 1923 for an attack on a railway line in the occupied Ruhr. Opening at the Prussian State Theatre on Hitler's birthday in 1933 and in his presence, it also included in the cast Emmy Sonnemann, later Frau Goering.[40] Harlan appeared in another politically significant play the following year, which also opened in Hitler's and Goering's presence: *Hundert Tage* (*The Hundred Days*), a play by Mussolini (with some help from Giovacchino Forzano) about Napoleon's return from Elba. Harlan's first wife, to whom he had been briefly married in 1923, was Jewish; his second wife, whom he divorced in 1939, had become a good friend of the Czech actress Lida Baarova, with whom Goebbels conducted an affair in 1937–38, and Harlan was involved in the subterfuge.[41] Harlan was no stranger to Goebbels, as the latter's diary entries make clear,[42] and so far had not found it a disadvantage.

Insisting on reworking the script, Harlan still retained a great deal from Möller and Metzger, acknowledging them as scriptwriters – the credits read 'script by

Harlan, Möller and Metzger' in that order – but dispensing with their services. After the war, Harlan insisted that his script was less antisemitic than the one he inherited, and in some respects this is true. However, he did add one important sequence which intensifies the hatred for Süss: the execution of the smith, Bogner, a new character, Harlan's invention. Goebbels was pleased with Harlan's 'new ideas' and thought he had done a 'splendid reworking' of the script.[43]

Completing his script very quickly, Harlan made a visit to Poland with two other members of his team in January 1940. They went to Lublin, where he claimed to have consulted a rabbi on Jewish rituals and practices, but where he also hoped to find Jewish extras to add an element of authenticity.[44] The outbreak of typhus, or possibly an unwillingness on Goebbels's part to allow these Polish Jews entry into the Reich at a time when Jews were being expelled, even to participate in a film which called for their expulsion, meant that Harlan had to look elsewhere. It was probably typhus, however, which put paid to the plan: the press was instructed to say nothing about the arrival of these Jews, which suggests that they were in fact on their way.[45] The sequences with Jewish extras were then filmed in Prague in the Barrandov studios in March 1940. Of the several sequences involving Jewish characters, only one was played by non-Jews. That was the Frankfurt ghetto sequence, which appears early in the film and was filmed in Berlin.[46] The other two sequences – the entry of the Jews into Stuttgart and the synagogue scene – were filmed with Jewish extras recruited in Prague who were bussed daily to the studios. The synagogue service is not performed correctly. Nevertheless, the performers were Jews, desperate in many cases for work, and it even seems that they were paid. Most were Czech, but in the synagogue sequence the solo singer apparently was a German refugee.[47] The voice on the soundtrack accompanying the film titles most probably comes from a recording, since the voice has a slight Hungarian accent.[48] Harlan wanted these Jews to appear strange, and believed that he had staged a Chasidic service, a service unfamiliar to the Czech Jewish extras, for they belonged to western rather than eastern Jewry. Only one of the extras survived to testify against Harlan at his 1949 trial, and recounts how Harlan was keen for them to behave in a wild and abandoned manner. Subsequently Harlan described this as a 'demonic effect', comparable to an 'exorcism', words which the editor of his posthumously published memoirs prudently excised.[49]

Goebbels also intervened in casting, insisting that Harlan's new wife, the blonde, Swedish-born, Kristina Söderbaum, play the female lead. The portly film and stage actor, Heinrich George, was cast as the Duke. A former Communist, turned ardent Nazi, castigated in an open letter from Bertolt Brecht in 1933, he had played the foreman in Fritz Lang's *Metropolis* (1926), the father in *Hitlerjunge Quex* (1933) and now headed two Berlin theatres (the Schiller and the Renaissance).[50] Goebbels had insisted that Marian and Werner Krauss accept the roles, with considerable pressure put on the former. Eventually, Goebbels was forced to issue a disclaimer to the effect that those actors playing the parts of Jews were in fact of pure 'Aryan' blood.[51] This of course did not extend to the non-speaking Jewish parts. Taking on Jewish roles was fraught with danger, touching on questions at the heart of antisemitic propaganda. Could a Jew be easily recognized? How could a non-Jew impersonate a Jew? Moreover, it could cast doubt on the actor's 'Aryan' pedigree. In a context where the Jew was constantly reviled, it was felt that playing one could blight one's career. This seems to have been one of Marian's concerns.[52]

Krauss, Dr Caligari in *The Cabinet of Dr Caligari*, was a very distinguished character actor. He took on two important roles, Levy, the secretary to Süss, as well as the rabbi. He also appears in two smaller speaking parts in the early sequence set in the Frankfurt ghetto, as an elderly Jew at a window who tells his attractive, slatternly granddaughter to cover herself up, as well as the butcher on the street below with whom he converses. He revelled in playing these Jewish roles. After the war both he and Harlan maintained that he had agreed to take the larger roles on condition that he also be given the smaller roles, assuming that Goebbels would object to an actor showing off his tricks and thus release him from the film.[53] But Krauss was foiled, though Goebbels agreed to his request that he would not wear a false nose but rely on his acting skills to create character. After the war George Bernard Shaw came to Krauss's rescue. Shortly after being made vice-chairman of the newly formed Actors' Chamber, Krauss came to Britain in 1933 to play opposite Peggy Ashcroft in Gerhart Hauptmann's play, *Vor Sonnenuntergang (Before Sunset)*, filmed four years later by Harlan as *Der Herrscher (The Ruler)*. On one occasion, some members of the London audience, protesting against his appearance, demonstrated on stage, but the show went on after a speech by the young Ashcroft. After the war Krauss contacted Ashcroft, hoping for her support.[54] She did not respond, in contrast to the ninety-one-year-old Shaw, to whom he also wrote about being 'put under pressure' to act in *Jud Süss*. Collaboration, Shaw wrote to Krauss, was not a crime:

All civilizations are kept in existence by the masses who collaborate with whatever governments are for the moment established in their country, native or foreign. To treat such collaboration as a crime after every change of government is a vindictive stupidity which can [sic] cannot be justified on any ground.[55]

Harlan's script was dense, economic and fast-paced. Detailing the meteoric rise and fall of Süss, the story is quite different from Feuchtwanger's and Hauff's. It would be wrong to think that it had been directly influenced by the Feuchtwanger novel. Nevertheless, after the war Feuchtwanger, who had never actually viewed the film, believed that it had, and indeed his widow even attempted to claim copyright on the Harlan film, though this may have been a legal ploy to prevent the circulation of the Harlan version.[56] It is true that both Harlan and his predecessor had been invited to watch the British film in Goebbels's viewing studio. Harlan and others also had the opportunity to watch newly captured Yiddish film from Poland, such as *The Dybuk* (1937). Copies of *Yidl mitn Fidl* (*Yiddle with his Fiddle*) (1936) were already available.[57] But there are no visual similarities, aside from the final execution scene, where in falling snow Süss enters the cage at ground level to be hoisted up. It would have been historically accurate (in both films) for him to ascend the gallows first and then enter the cage.

The story, according to Harlan, was as follows.[58] The cash-strapped Duke, thwarted by the Württemberg Diet (not parliament) in his plans for a ballet, and shamed into being unable to offer his wife more jewels, sends an emissary to the Frankfurt ghetto to seek out the financial wizard Süss. To the accompaniment of ominous music on the soundtrack, the coat of arms of Württemberg dissolves to the nameplate of Süss, partly in Hebrew lettering, which hangs outside his door in the ghetto. This was the first of several significant dissolves, which make those connections the innocent viewer might otherwise fail to make.[59] Dressed in black traditional dress and wearing side-locks, Süss tempts the awed emissary with precious jewels and only agrees to help on condition that he be allowed entry into *judenfrei* Württemberg, where a *Judenbann* (ban on Jews) has been in force for over a century. A dissolve soon removes the side-locks. Instead we now have the face of an eighteenth-century gentleman, seated in a carriage hurtling across the countryside: the Jew in disguise, released from the ghetto, and bent on reaching Stuttgart, the capital. Unfortunately, his carriage overturns but, fortunately, the occupant of a passing carriage offers him a ride. She is Dorothea, the daughter of the leader of the Diet. Played by Söderbaum, she soon reveals her weak racial instinct when she does not recognize him for a Jew. Furthermore, she is impressed by the fact that he has travelled widely, another bad sign, for a German girl's heart should be in the *Heimat*, though to her credit she does persist in questioning him as to where his *Heimat* or home or native land actually is. Beaming as he moves closer to her, he says that he is most at home sitting beside her. Jews are cosmopolitan, rootless and thus dangerous is the message. Together in her carriage they enter the gates of Stuttgart. A captivated Süss visits her at home to thank her but is immediately denounced by her fiancé, Faber, who is also her father's secretary. The film's proto-Nazi, he has heightened racial instincts. Stealthily moving forward, his eyes narrowing as he utters in astonishment, 'But that is a Jew!' Taken aback, she feebly responds: 'Nonsense! They let him through the city gate without ado.' 'I am not mistaken, that is a Jew!' he replies and, confronting Süss, informs him that there are no inns for Jews in Stuttgart. Süss flinches, lowers his eyes and thanks him for his knowledge of human nature, one instance of several where Marian tries through gesture to humanize the character.

Despite this initial setback, Süss soon ingratiates himself with the Duke and becomes his financial adviser, for Jews of course were believed to have a talent for this. Through his control of finances he is now the power behind the throne and in effect runs the country. He soon brings ruin to Württemberg (for Württemberg read Germany). Throwing coins on the table, which dissolve into the tulle skirts of ballerinas (another important dissolve), he now also pimps for the Duke. Thus the Duke has got his wish, a ballet as well as a ballerina. Rising ever higher, Süss becomes ever more powerful. The Duchess likes him. He has a mistress. His financial policies, designed to fill the Duke's coffers, lead to outrage and protest from the people of Württemberg. He also displays his cruel as well as calculating side: he taxes the smith, Bogner, for having his house abut the road and then destroys half his house. When Bogner is later executed for smashing Süss's carriage, the crowd is enraged; Süss becomes fearful. The tide is beginning to turn.

An image of a drum cuts to a ragged band of Jews entering Stuttgart; the drum roll cuts to strange oriental music. It is in fact a recently composed song in Hebrew, '*Shir Hagamel*', better known as '*Gamal Gamali*' (about a camel), and is being sung in an untypically mournful style. The composer, Yedidiya (Gideon) Admon-Gorochov, was a Russian-born Zionist émigré to Palestine, who in his commitment to expunge European influences from Jewish music had borrowed a Bedouin melody. Thus in a film whose purpose was to show that Jews were not European, the music chosen was by a Jewish composer attempting to do just this very thing. Who selected this song composed some twelve years previously, though published in Berlin in 1935, is not known.[60]

The music has been carefully and ingeniously used to underline the difference between Jew and German. Not only were Jewish extras recruited to perform Jewish rites, but Jewish advice may have been solicited in selecting the music. The distinguished film composer Wolfgang Zeller was assigned to the film before Harlan's appointment. He probably was not responsible for the specifically Jewish music, but he provided ominous music for Süss and eerie music for the rabbi when impersonating an astrologer. The latter is aptly named Rabbi Loew, after the Prague rabbi who conjured up the Golem. For Dorothea he chose a motif, a fourteenth-century German folk song rearranged by Brahms, '*All mein Gedanke*' ('All my Thoughts') which in various mutations appears as her theme, for all her thoughts are with Faber, while the Jew has arrived to disrupt the peace and security of a German home. Dorothea's motif is often followed or preceded by an alien-sounding Jewish motif. Just as a Zionist composer was intent on expunging European influence to justify a Jewish return to Palestine, so a Nazi composer was required to provide alien or ominous music to reinforce the point that Jews did not belong in Europe. Zeller was well qualified for the task, having provided music for Carl Dreyer's *Vampyr* (*Vampire*) (1932) and the Nazi documentary *Ewiger Wald* (*Eternal Forest*) (1936).

There is now no stopping Süss: he even attempts to marry Dorothea, but she rejects him as does her outraged father. On her father's advice she and her fiancé hastily marry, though they do not consummate the marriage. Faber is now arrested for sedition and tortured. Dorothea visits Süss to intercede for him, is raped and drowns herself in shame. Her husband and the crowd seek revenge. They march on Süss's town house, while inside his secretary cowers, for Jews are also cowardly according to antisemitic lore. Meanwhile, Süss encourages the Duke to quash the rebellion by staging a coup against the Diet, which will enable him to seize absolute power. The Jews will finance the coup as Süss has negotiated a deal with them during a synagogue service, having warned them that if they refuse they may pay with their lives. Unfortunately for Süss, the Duke suddenly dies at a palace celebration. As he is pronounced dead, we have a close-up of the frightened face of Süss, who is immediately placed under arrest. In the film's final dissolve the face of the bewigged eighteenth-century courtier reverts to the face of a bearded poor Jew on trial for his life. Süss is condemned and executed, which for Fritz Hippler, head of the Propaganda Ministry Film Department, was a Nazi 'happy ending'.[61] The film concludes with one of the judges, Dorothea's father, played by the dignified Eugen Klöpfer, announcing that all Jews must leave Württemberg immediately and uttering the warning: 'And may our descendants honour and adhere to this decree which will spare them great harm to their property, their lives and their blood.'

The film's message is unmistakable. If Jews are allowed entry to Württemberg (for which read Germany) they bring in their wake pain, suffering and disorder. Peace, prosperity and order will only be restored upon their expulsion. The Jewish characters are all villains: not only Süss, but also his secretary and the rabbi. Devious, cunning, ingratiating, Jews are depicted as smart, though not that smart. They can be outwitted, as the leader of the Diet at one point informs a despairing Faber. Krauss is fierce and sharp as the secretary who delights in outwitting simple but virtuous Germans, though at the end he is shown to be a coward. Jews are the 'other' – their religion strange but also not spiritual, with financial transactions taking place in the synagogue, as when Süss meets the rabbi. Süss panders to the Duke and is himself also lascivious, though Marian makes his character complex. Indeed, according to Harlan, Marian received fan mail which, if true, might suggest that the film was not achieving its purpose, though such fans were unlikely to be resisters.[62] Presenting Süss as a sexual predator, and the proto-Nazi Faber as almost asexual, it would not be surprising if females in the audience were drawn to Süss, particularly as played by Marian.

However, it is hardly credible that in late 1940 women would send fan letters to an actor playing the evil Jew. It was also in Harlan's interest to make such a claim, implying as it does that the film was not so antisemitic, not so lethal. By the time of Harlan's trial, Marian was dead, following a car crash in 1946 after he had been drinking. Marian's widow rallied to Harlan's support, but during his trial drowned in mysterious circumstances.

Harlan's film includes a number of negative characteristics associated with Jews, but its antisemitism is not of a specifically German variety. Indeed, the film adds nothing new in this respect. We see Jews depicted as cut-throat capitalists: Süss is initially an ingratiating salesman and later a grand bourgeois. At the opposite extreme, we also see Jews as shabby immigrants – but they are linked by blood to the Court Jew. The one negative Jewish stereotype that is absent, for obvious historical reasons, is that of the Jew as Bolshevik. But in encouraging and planning a coup, Süss is in fact sowing disorder: the fear of Bolshevism was also a fear of breakdown, as well as a fear of the abolition of private property. On the German stage, Jews had often been depicted as intriguers.[63] Courtiers have also been closely associated with intrigue even when they have not been Jewish, and feature as stock characters in many an eighteenth-century German bourgeois tragedy, especially in Schiller's plays, which can be read as a critique of despotism. Schiller, who was born in Württemberg, even alludes to Süss in *Die Räuber* (*The Robbers*) as the unnamed minister, a man of great personal wealth, the seducer of women and the agent of despotism.[64] In this respect the Harlan version, rather than the Feuchtwanger version, is closer to the historic Süss in addition to displaying a number of features associated with the genre of bourgeois tragedy.[65] Finally, the contempt for the effete courtier is not wholly unrelated to antisemitism, for the courtier is a parasite and Jews too were accused of parasitic behaviour, of not doing useful work.

Clever with money, Jews are unscrupulous. Rootless, they insinuate themselves where they are not wanted. Acquiring enormous power secretly, they are able to dominate. They also prey on women. If they fail by seduction first time round, they will turn to other methods; lurking behind the clever financier, and seducer, is the rapist. As poor immigrants, they bring disease, only briefly hinted at in this film, especially when Krauss playing the rabbi, coughs excessively, suggesting that he is the carrier of disease from the ghetto, a point made much more strongly in *Der ewige Jude*. A still from the rape sequence in *Jud Süss* was also used in a Nazi anti-smoking campaign of 1941. It shows the louche Süss, dishevelled in his silk brocade dressing-gown, his bejewelled hand resting on the innocent Dorothea's shoulder, above which the caption reads: 'The Jew has his victim by the neck.' In another poster the cigarette is actually referred to as 'a Jud Süss'. 'May I offer you a Jud Süss?' asks a grinning devil depicted with a chain-smoker.[66] To emphasize his unwholesomeness, the film was publicized by a notorious poster, which depicted Süss as a traditional Jew in close-up in sickly green. Designed by a Social Democrat, Erich Knauff, he was executed in 1944 for anti-Nazi remarks overheard in an air-raid shelter.[67]

These negative Jewish stereotypes are almost always associated with the male Jew. Rarely do we see female Jews: only in an early sequence, when we get a brief glimpse of a half-dressed, sexually provocative, attractive woman who appears at the window in the Frankfurt ghetto. This may just be a Harlan touch; he liked to titillate, as in the brief shot at the beginning of the film when a woman in the crowd, for no obvious reason, has her bodice ripped. One can over-interpret film. Given their inferior status, Jewish females seem not to have constituted the same sort of threat as Jewish males. *Rassenschande* (race defilement) usually involved Jewish males with 'Aryan' females and not vice versa.

'Aryan' women do not fare well in this film: they appear in a negative light in varying degrees. For it is primarily women, the aptly named weaker sex, who let the side, or race, down, proving susceptible to the predator, the Jew who preys on 'Aryan' womenfolk. They are not to be trusted is one message, the anti-feminism supporting – and indeed often serving as the vehicle for – the antisemitism. The Jew still remains the target throughout the film, but it is mainly women who unwittingly aid and abet him in his rise to power.[68]

Of the female characters, the most important is Dorothea. Though far from frivolous in demeanour and attire, she is nevertheless naive and dangerously so, lacking a sound racial instinct. Her mother is non-existent, she is looked after by an almost mute nurse-housekeeper, a role which downgrades that of the older, experienced woman. The absence of the mother in this and other propaganda films is not accidental: an authoritative female presence is dispensed with, allowing the vulnerable younger female to be protected and controlled by males. With her baby face and childlike voice, Söderbaum suggests an infantilized woman, which suits the film's ideological purpose. Her face, voice and manner reinforce the notion that she has not come of age and indeed never will. Gender differences are exaggerated by making the female immature in contrast to the male. She appears even more infantilized in the earlier script. Like almost all the other female characters in this film, she is easily deceived by the Jewish villain. Indeed she seems congenitally incapable of recognizing danger, and thus will herself constitute a danger to society, and to the race. That women require male control nevertheless is not an idea originating with the Nazis.

The other female characters (with one exception) also suggest female unreliability. The flirtatious Duchess, halfway through the film, crucially persuades her husband to trust his Jewish financial adviser and to do as he advises. Charmed by the Jew and his ability to procure items of luxury, she acts as temptress to her husband, while at the same time she is herself easily tempted. It is her desire for luxury which at the outset of the film shames the Duke and spurs him on to seek the services of the Jew. Once one Jew is allowed entry to *judenrein* Württemberg, others will follow.

Other female characters also display moral weakness: Süss's mistress is thrilled at the sight of the smith's house being demolished on his orders: 'Half a house, like a toy, like a puppet theatre, how sweet' (a play on his name since sweet in German is *süss*). Later, as the smith is executed, shouts from a crowd call her a Jew's whore and warn Süss that his turn will soon come. A mother tries to persuade her husband to allow their adolescent daughters to attend a masked ball which Süss has arranged on behalf of the Duke. At the ball Süss will pimp for the Duke, with one of the daughters falling victim. The mother suspects nothing, while the father instinctively remains suspicious; again the wife overcomes the husband's misgivings, thus bringing ruin on her daughters. In contrast to Dorothea, these female characters are frivolous and pleasure-seeking. The only positive female character in the film, aside from the mute nurse-housekeeper, is the wife of the smith: with her child clasped in her arms, she pleads with Süss (and with the audience's sympathy) not to destroy their home and her husband's livelihood. Her duty rightly is to child and husband: she serves others rather than seeks her own pleasure.

Conveniently, Dorothea's father appears only as a father but not as a husband. By dispensing with a mother altogether, even in the home, the power of the father is enhanced, making gender differences starker. This father is a patriarch, the leader of the Diet and father of his country. Though not the hereditary father of his country, he is nevertheless his country's true leader, in so far as it is he who safeguards the race, something the hereditary leader, the Duke (the bad father), has failed to do. Dorothea's father embodies the law, the law of the race. With his assistant, Faber, he has a dual relationship: he is both his master and his surrogate father, in that soon he will become his father-in-law. When that happens, his authority will extend further, even to advising the newly wed couple as to when or whether they should consummate the marriage. This proto-Nazi father, both wise and kind, never puts a foot wrong. But he remains dependent on his hot-headed future son-in-law, who has youthful energy and is keen to do battle. Together they will work to rescue the country.

In contrast to the female characters, almost all the male characters uphold the law and safeguard the nation (for nation read race). The exception is the debauched Duke, who in his pursuit of luxury is destroying the country. He signifies the old order and must be overthrown. Though this might seem like revolution, it is a nationalist revolution, the Nazis believing themselves heirs to the early nineteenth-century German nationalists who, against the wishes of the princes, participated in the popular uprising against the French occupation. Thus the only bad 'Aryan' male characters are the Duke and his courtiers.

That Dorothea should be confined to the domestic rather than the public sphere is reinforced early on in the film when she emerges from the kitchen, the only instance in the film when we actually see a kitchen. The Nazis adhered to the first and the last of the three Ks, *Kinder, Kirche, Küche* (children, church and kitchen). Carrying the roast goose, Dorothea displays her ignorance when her father asks to whom they should offer a toast. 'To the Duke!' he gently chides her, since it is his coronation day. Her ignorance does not place her in a bad light but merely confirms that her place is in the home. The dumb-blonde stereotype is acceptable in Nazi films, as long as she does not neglect her duty to the race. But here Dorothea will fail. Raped, she must drown herself in shame.

The rape is an important element, as it is in mythology: it drives the plot forward and delivers the message. Innocence defiled – the woman as victim in contrast to a child as victim – is powerful, given the sexual overtones, and appropriate in a film devoted to *Rassenschande*. Unusually, Dorothea happens to be both married *and* a virgin. But, once she has lost her purity, she has lost her value, and thus cannot die a martyr to the cause, unlike Nazi male heroes. Her death, however, does trigger a call to arms: the battle between males is now conjoined, especially over who owns her body, for the Jew, as is his wont, had taken it from the 'Aryan'. 'Aryan' males are awakened to the coming battle. Honour is at stake. Tapping into a variety of sources, the film drives home the point that the fight against the Jew is deadly serious, and also biological. It can be read as a parable of what will happen if the Nuremberg Laws are transgressed, and if Jews are allowed to live in Germany, where they do not belong.

Harlan and others mention Goebbels's interventions in the film, and that rushes were sent to him on a daily basis. Aside from casting and Harlan's own appointment, there is little evidence of significant interference. Certainly, Goebbels was responsible for getting the project off the ground, sacking the director and securing Marian and Krauss in the major roles. And of course after the war it was in Harlan's interest to lay the blame on Goebbels. He also refers to a curse by way of exoneration, which Süss utters as he is being strung up, and which was cut from the final version; but such a curse does not actually appear in the script.[69]

The film had its première at the Venice Film Festival on 5 September 1940, where it did not win a prize, but many Italian film critics, including Michelangelo Antonioni (a critic before he became a director), singled it out for praise.[70] It opened in Berlin three weeks later at the Ufa-Palast am Zoo, Berlin's largest cinema, with a clamour for tickets. Some of the SS who had helped recruit the Jewish extras were put out at the shortage of tickets for the opening night, which Goebbels and other Third Reich dignitaries attended (though not Hitler, who had forsworn films for the rest of the war).[71] It was a gala occasion, but, shortly before midnight, British bombs, which had been falling on Berlin since 1 August, killed eleven civilians.[72] The Battle of Britain had commenced the previous month and the London Blitz the previous week.

Advance publicity catered to two distinct audiences: antisemites and fans of melodrama.[73] This ensured large audiences, as did the rave reviews in the censored press, and the best possible *Prädikate: staatspolitisch* (of political importance to the state), and *künstlerisch besonders wertvoll*, (of special artistic value). Surprisingly, given its subject matter, it was also deemed suitable for youth, presumably to warn them of the Jewish danger, though some parents and teachers objected.[74] It continued to be shown in occupied countries, as well as in pro-German countries such as Spain,[75] and in 1944 was re-released in Germany and in occupied countries as part of a new antisemitic and anti-Bolshevik propaganda action.[76] Of the thirty most popular films between 1940 and 1942 *Jud Süss* ranked sixth, as one of the most popular of the state-commissioned films. It grossed RM6,200,000 and was viewed by 20,300,000 people between 1940 and 1943.[77] Of course Germany, through conquest, had a captive audience, with German films dominating the cinemas.[78]

There was no mistaking the purpose of the film, which was clear to the Nazi leadership: Himmler made it compulsory viewing for the SS and the police. It was also clear to some journalists. The *Berlin Illustrierte* juxtaposed a still from the execution scene against American wire press photographs of Polish Jews being deported with the words:

> The Jews are leaving Cracow. After the end of the Polish military campaign the solution of the Jewish Question in the General Government was one of the most pressing problems … A century's defensive battle against Jewry's penetration comes to a conclusion.[79]

Reports from Budapest in March 1941 that the film had sold out, that tickets were being ordered four or five days in advance, and excited audiences were shouting during the execution scene that this is what should be done to Budapest's Jews went down well with Goebbels. He wanted this particular report to go direct to Hitler.[80]

The film's impact on audiences is harder to gauge. The Security Police, who attended showings, recorded favourable comments, but people would have been guarded about saying anything too negative. That so many people saw the film still raises questions. What were they seeing? To what extent did the film's popularity also relate to its being a well-made film with a racy story, which for an unpolitical viewer was a mixture of 'sex and crime'?[81] For an antisemite it illustrated the Jewish danger and the desirability of removing the Jews from Germany. But what about members of the audience who were not so inclined? Would the film have persuaded them?[82] This we cannot know with certainty. The writer Ralph Giordano, then in his teens, attended the film in Hamburg though Jews were banned from cinemas. He went with a non-Jewish friend and was struck by the silence of the audience when the film ended. He and his friend walked home together in silence. Finally his friend spoke, suggesting to a shocked Giordano that there must be something in it. Giordano survived the war and later covered Harlan's trial for crimes against humanity, while his friend provided testimony against Harlan that the film had been effective propaganda.[83]

We do know that this film boosted Harlan's career: he became the Third Reich's leading director with a commensurate large salary. For this he paid after the war, when he was the only Third Reich film director to face trial. This only took place once it seemed likely that a denazification panel would clear him, thus enabling him to resume his directing career. At his subsequent trial for crimes against humanity he was acquitted, on the grounds that the 'Final Solution' would have taken place with or without this film, and that the decision to launch the 'Final Solution' had been made after the film's release.[84] What was not in dispute at that time was the film's antisemitism or that the Nazi leadership believed it was effective propaganda. In dispute was only its direct link to the 'Final Solution'.

The film cannot be divorced from its context. Its effectiveness was influenced by other forms of propaganda, stringent censorship, which did not allow for alternative views, and a wartime situation which singled out the Jews both as the internal and the external enemy. On numerous occasions, Hitler and other leading Nazis had made the Jews responsible for the outbreak of war. Nevertheless, it is still difficult to assess the film's effectiveness as propaganda, precisely because it came in such a highly palatable form. That it was a box office hit and pleased the Nazi leadership is incontestable.

Right: 1. A Hitler Youth (Jürgen Ohlsen) plays a Hitler Youth, *Hitlerjunge Quex* (1933). (*British Film Institute*)

Below: 2. University student Hans Westmar (Emil Lohkamp), second row with arms folded, refuses (for political reasons) to take notes in a lecture on internationalism, in contrast to other students, as in front row. (*Hans Westmar* (1933). (*Imperial War Museum, London*)

Above: 3. The leader of the German Communists (played by Paul Wegener) with his female assistant who hangs on his every word. *Hans Westmar* (1933). (*Imperial War Museum, London*)

Left: 4. Leni Riefenstahl (in white coat) instructing cameramen filming *Triumph of the Will*, Nuremberg, 1934. (*British Film Institute*)

Above opposite: 5. A low angle shot of Hitler with arm raised in 'Hitler salute'. *Triumph of the Will* (1935). (*British Film Institute*)

Right opposite: 6. A delighted child among the Nuremberg crowds enjoys the parade. *Triumph of the Will* (1935). (*British Film Institute*)

7. The leader of the revolutionaries wearing glasses (the Jew as Bolshevik played by Karl Meixner) barks at fellow revolutionaries. *Pour le Mérite* (1938). (*Imperial War Museum, London*)

8. At the Ipelmeyer Ball. From left to right: Fräulein Ipelmeyer, Frau Ipelmeyer, Herr Ipelmeyer (in the centre wearing glasses) Robert, Bertram. *Robert und Bertram* (1939). (*Deutsche Kinemathek, Berlin*)

9. An assimilated Jew played by Siegfried Breuer with his unassimilated uncle played by Fritz Imhof. *Leinen aus Irland* (1939). (*British Film Institute*)

10. Nathan Rothschild (Carl Kuhlmann) forced to dine alone. *Die Rothschilds* (1939). (*British Film Institute*)

11. Jew Süss (Ferdinand Marian), his mistress (Else Elster) and secretary, Levi (Werner Krauss) (left) watch an execution but become alarmed as the crowd turns hostile. *Jud Süss* (1940). (*British Film Institute*)

12 and 13. Young Jewish male before and after his hair and beard are cut. *Der ewige Jude* (1940). (*Imperial War Museum, London*)

14. A Jewish shopkeeper berates a bemused ethnic German (Berta Drews) for not buying from him. *Heimkehr* (1941) (*Imperial War Museum, London*)

15. Journalists gather in a Swiss hotel foyer seeking news of Krüger; the *Berliner Tageblatt* journalist, played by Hans Stiebner, is in the centre. *Ohm Krüger* (1941). (*Imperial War Museum, London*)

16. Theresienstadt: children resting while enjoying bread and fruit. *Theresienstadt, A Documentary Film from the Jewish Settlement Area* (1944). (*Yad Vashem*)

17. An unidentified member of a Theresienstadt concert audience. *Theresienstadt, A Documentary Film from the Jewish Settlement Area* (1944). (*United States Holocaust Memorial Museum*)

11

Der ewige Jude *(1940)*

A third film on the Jewish Question opened in Berlin two months after *Jud Süss*, and four months after *Die Rothschilds*. This time audiences were not roused. The *Sicherheitsdienst* (Security Service) attributed the lack of enthusiasm to timing, given that it came so soon after the successful *Jud Süss*. In support they cited audience comments such as: 'We have seen *Jud Süss* and have now had enough of Jewish filth!'[1] However, this negative response probably had less to do with audience saturation with the Jewish Question than with the nature of the film. For, unlike *Jud Süss*, *Der ewige Jude* was not a feature film but a documentary, which the author of the report conceded would have more appeal to 'the politically active part of the population' than to the 'typical film[-going] public'.[2] Certainly the documentary contained none of the entertainment on which Goebbels set such store. Yet it was made under his auspices and with his encouragement.

Sometimes translated into English as *The Eternal Jew*, and less frequently as *The Wandering Jew*, the latter is a more accurate rendition. *Ewige* in German does mean eternal, but *ewige Jude* refers to the legend of the Wandering Jew, the French *Le Juif errant* being close to the English. The medieval Christian legend from which it derives contains both elements of wandering *and* of eternalness: a Jew, who drives Christ from his doorstep when carrying the cross to Calvary is condemned to *wander* the face of the earth for *eternity* or until the Second Coming.[3]

At some point the legend lost its Christian character. In much nineteenth-century romantic writing even its anti-Jewish character is diluted, as in Eugène Sue's five-hour play, *The Wandering Jew*, where the Jew became universalized, a symbol of suffering humanity. But in Germany such a version held no interest for antisemites. There the anti-Jewish legend had been revived and reinvigorated during the Reformation. It continued down the years to retain its anti-Jewish character, and was used to explain the presence of the Jewish nation long after it should have been redeemed or destroyed. Opponents of Jewish emancipation used it to support their view that the Jews lay under a curse. After emancipation was granted, the legend continued to surface in debates about the Jewish Question. The Nazis transformed the legend, the Jews now being guilty of not being 'Aryan' rather than not being Christian. Lacking roots (unlike the Germans), unable to settle, they were a parasitic people, who roamed the earth, feeding off their host

societies and ultimately destroying those societies if not eliminated. In some
respects they were not unlike the Gypsies, another parasitic people in the eyes of
the Nazis, though the latter were considered a social menace rather than a threat
to German culture. Parasitism was closely related to vampirism: bloodsucker
was a frequent term of abuse which Hitler and others applied to Jews. Süss had
been described as such in film publicity,[4] and the earlier *Jud Süss* script contains
a ballad composed by Möller in which Süss is the 'great vampire' and Jews 'drain
[German] blood'.[5]

On 8 November 1937 Goebbels and Streicher opened an exhibition at Munich's
Germanic Museum entitled '*Der ewige Jude*'.[6] This became a touring exhibition
which visited major cities such as Berlin, Vienna, Bremen and Dresden. A Dresden
resident, Victor Klemperer, commented in his diary on 'the repulsive poster' in
a hundred shop windows and the daily newspaper references urging readers to
visit the exhibition to find out about 'the most odious race'.[7] The Jew was held
responsible for usury, Bolshevism and degenerate art. The exhibition catalogue
includes 265 pictures of Jews, ranging from two of the historic Jud Süss to one
of a chubby ten-year-old Yehudi Menuhin with conductor Bruno Walter. On
18 July 1938 the censors approved a compilation film made for the Propaganda
Ministry under the title *Juden ohne Maske* (*Jews without Masks*), the purpose of
which was to unmask the Jew in disguise, namely the assimilated Jew. Intended
for internal party consumption,[8] it included extracts from the Munich exhibition,
some of which also ended up in *Der ewige Jude*.[9] Again there were links with *Jud
Süss*, the publicity for which belonged to this propaganda campaign directed at
assimilated Jews. Süss was a Jew to be unmasked, that is 'unmasked before the
camera',[10] or 'in film without a mask',[11] or 'a typical example of the Jew who poses
a real danger to his host country not through the external characteristics of his
race but because he conceals his Jewishness through assimilation'.[12] This may in
part explain why ultimately *Der ewige Jude* became the preferred title rather than
Jews without Masks.

With the outbreak of war, the newly appointed head of the Ministry of
Propaganda's Film Department, Fritz Hippler, began work on a film entitled *Der
ewige Jude*, a response to the number of Jews now brought under German rule,
which had increased from 300,000 to two million. This film, which brought him
justified notoriety, was sandwiched between two other documentaries for which
he was also responsible: *Feldzug in Polen* (*Campaign in Poland*), the official film
of the Polish campaign, followed by *Sieg im Westen* (1941) (*Victory in the West*)
about the campaign in the West. *Feldzug in Polen*, it is now thought, was probably
begun by Leni Riefenstahl as a record of Hitler's triumph in Poland, which she
abandoned after experiencing the reality of a battlefront.[13]

Born in 1909, Hippler had joined the Nazi Party in 1925 at the age of seventeen
and received his doctorate from Heidelberg in 1934 for a dissertation on John

Stuart Mill and Karl Marx. In the previous year he had participated in the Berlin book-burning. He began working with newsreel and film in 1935, and in 1939 became the director of the central Nazi organization which controlled newsreels, the same year he also became head of the Promi Film Department, subsequently holding the title of *Reichsfilmintendant* (Reich film director).[14] In 1943 he fell from grace due to intrigues, having amongst other things enabled Erich Kästner, a banned writer, whose books had been burned in 1933, to work on a film, *Münchhausen*, under an assumed name. Subsequently, it was also discovered that he had a Jewish great-grandmother, though as Obersturmbannführer in the SS a thorough check would have been conducted prior to his joining.[15] At the end of the war he got off lightly: his two-year prison sentence and 5,000 Mark fine were for belonging to the SS.

Who should take credit for this film? Hippler was taking his orders from Goebbels, but since the titles list it as his 'creation' (*Gestaltung*), it is his name which has come to be associated with the film. Hippler considered it Goebbels's 'very own work', though it was in his interest (post-war) to say this.[16] He has been aptly described as merely Goebbels's 'production manager'.[17] The idea for a film on the subject, however, may have come from Dr Eberhard Taubert, as the film credits indicate. Taubert, a consultant (*Referent*) in the Propaganda Ministry on the Jewish Question, collected the data on Jews used in the film. It is thought that he also wrote the script.[18] In 1934 he had set up the Institute for the Study of the Jewish Question, and had had frequent discussions with Goebbels about how to raise public awareness on the issue. So opposed was he to so many things – earlier he had been involved with anti-Bolshevism – that he was also known as 'Dr Anti'.[19] Now that the war against Bolshevism had been suspended, he could concentrate on the Jewish enemy. The film had been in the pipeline since shortly after *Kristallnacht*, as had *Jud Süss*. The outbreak of war led Goebbels to take a far more active interest in getting both projects off the ground. Pre-war plans to film Jewish life in Poland had foundered on the refusal of the Polish authorities to allow in German cameramen.[20] Now no such objections could stand in the way.

The film was to be a compilation documentary. This has been described as a 'parasitic genre' because it takes footage from other films, often for didactic purpose, to edit and create a different meaning not inherent in the original shots.[21] It was pioneered by the Soviet editor Esfir Shub in her first film, *Fall of the Romanov Dynasty* (1927), in which she intercut pre-existing footage, including the tsar's home movies, to justify the Bolshevik Revolution. Originally an editor and still in effect acting as an editor, she used montage, a form of editing, to create relationships between shots through a juxtaposition of images. She is even credited with influencing Eisenstein's use of montage when he initially observed her editing, though she also learned from him when observing him film *October* (1927).[22]

In cinematic terms, *Der ewige Jude*, however, was a very crude compilation film, especially if compared to the work of the pioneer of the genre. Its theme was the parasitism of the Jews, and to illustrate this it (aptly) used a parasitic genre. Material from a variety of sources was utilized: stills, newsreel (both German and non-German), documentary, feature film (Weimar and Hollywood), and new footage sent back from German cameramen in occupied Poland, mainly from the newly created ghetto in Łódź. Three years earlier, the *Reichsfilmarchiv* had been set up to collect film material (feature, newsreel and documentary) for possible use in *Tendenzfilme*, including antisemitic ones, and a special catalogue was created which included a register of stock shots.[23] This collection would be drawn on. It would be quite different from a Riefenstahl documentary; indeed it went against almost every one of her artistic principles even though extracts from *Triumph of the Will* were eventually incorporated into the film. One notable difference is that Riefenstahl did not use a narrator, having confidence in the image, the editing and the sound to relay the message. Hippler and his team were incapable of making that kind of film. Unlike Riefenstahl, and for good reason, Hippler has had no post-war admirers: he was able to lead a peaceful life in some obscurity, remaining unrepentant.[24] Whereas Riefenstahl made a feelgood picture about a harmonious *Volksgemeinschaft* in which the enemy never puts in an appearance, Hippler made its mirror-opposite, both in style and in content. Intended as a documentary on 'World Jewry', it focused on the enemy, both within and without, in Germany, Poland and the US, for this Jew was everywhere. The ideal German type only put in the occasional appearance and then solely for the purpose of contrast with the Jew.

On 2 October 1939, the Wehrmacht propaganda company cameramen Heinz Kluth was ordered to film stories of Jewish life in Warsaw.[25] On 8 October Goebbels informed Hippler that he was to leave for Łódź the next day with a team of cameramen: 'Convince yourself of how these Jews live, how they are at home. Shoot life in the Polish ghetto.' He was instructed to film

> everything which comes before you, life, trade and bartering on the street, the synagogue and the rituals and don't forget the slaughter. We must capture everything in its original state, for soon we will have no more Jews. The Führer will have all of them settled in Madagascar or some other area. Therefore we need film documents for our archive.[26]

Hippler left on 10 October with six cameramen and began filming the following day, returning to Berlin on 13 October. The footage was shown at once to Goebbels, who reacted with disgust, recording in his diary that some scenes were 'so horrific and brutal in their explicitness that one's blood runs cold'; such 'barbarism' made him 'shudder'.[27] Hitler was also kept fully informed about progress and even made suggestions.[28] Some footage was used immediately (16

October), in a newsreel, but the Łódź shots were intended for a documentary propaganda film.[29] In late October, Goebbels flew to Poland to see with his own eyes the conditions in Łódź.[30] It was then that he reached the conclusion that the task would have to be 'surgical' rather than 'humanitarian', for the people he saw were 'no longer human beings'.[31]

The film was edited and reworked over and over and subjected to test screenings before the final version was ready for public viewing. In February 1940 it was discussed in *Der deutsche Film*, accompanied by twenty-six illustrations. As several sequences were missing – part of Hitler's January 1939 prophetic speech and the contrast between German and Jew (with the *Triumph of the Will* borrowings) – it is clear that this was not the final version.[32] This did not stop publicity. Like *Jud Süss*, the film had been advertised well before the final version was ready. What this publicity achieved (in both cases) was to keep the project before the eyes of the public and thus raise public consciousness about the Jewish Question.

A test viewing was organized by Hippler and Hans Hinkel, State Secretary in the Propaganda Ministry for Anti-Jewish Questions, previously concerned with excluding Jews from cultural life. On 1 March 1940 the film was shown to an invited audience of academics, civil servants and members of the Nazi leadership. In response to heated discussions, more changes were made. From this discussion also came the suggestion that the Jew should be contrasted with the German. More changes were made and the film was finally shown to Hitler on 4 April. He must have withheld his approval, since these were additional changes.[33] Only on 3 September 1940 did Goebbels express himself satisfied: 'absolutely splendid, sublime creation'.[34] Six days later it was shown to an invited audience of representatives from the party, military, foreign press, SA, SS, Hitler Youth, women's groups, film personnel, along with a sprinkling of academics. They made the suggestion, which Goebbels then acted on, that the film was only suitable for people with 'strong nerves' and should therefore come in two versions. The milder one for women and children was soon ready on 10 October 1940. Both versions passed the censor on 4 November and received a number of *Prädikate*: *Staatspolitisch wertvoll* (politically valuable), *Künstlerische wertvoll* (artistically valuable), *volksbildend* (national education), *Lehrfilm* (instructional), and the youth version was classified as *jugendwert* (valuable for youth). A slightly shorter version (fifty-six minutes) was also made for foreign audiences, which left out the Weimar Republic sequences and a part of Hitler's prophetic speech of January 1939. Additionally, special versions were made for specific foreign audiences: a separate French one was ready in 1942 under a different title, *Le péril juif* (*The Jewish Danger*), taken from the title of the French publication of *The Protocols of Zion*. A Dutch version, *De eeuwige Jood*, was ready in the summer of 1941; a Czech version was also made.[35]

The première took place in the Ufa-Palast am Zoo in Berlin on 28 November 1940: the youth version at sixty-three minutes long was shown at four in the afternoon, followed by the longer adult version at seventy minutes at half past six. High-ranking members of the party, the civil service, as well as the cameramen were present at the evening performance. Surprisingly and inexplicably – no reason has been advanced – Goebbels was absent in Norway. Hitler did not attend films during the war, though this particular one could hardly be described as entertainment. It was part of a long programme. The first film screened was *Ostraum – deutscher Raum* (*Eastern Realm, German Realm*), a *Kulturfilm* (cultural film) whose title speaks for itself. Though Germany was not yet at war with the Soviet Union, it had already made inroads in the East with the Stalin–Hitler Pact. This film was giving advance notice that the East belonged to Germany. After this came a newsreel, followed by Beethoven's 'Egmont Overture', then finally the main attraction.[36]

Goebbels had instructed the press to discuss the film not only in cinematic but also in political terms; and of course, like its two predecessors on the Jewish Question, it was not to be described as antisemitic. Both Hippler and Taubert were interviewed in the press and on radio. Hippler emphasized that the box office success of *Jud Süss* proved that, in spite of doubts previously expressed, there was great interest in the Jewish problem. He also discussed the distinct advantages of documentary and feature film. *Der ewige Jude*, as a documentary, could expand on the feature film, and show things which a feature film could not, just as a feature film could show things which a documentary could not. A feature film could offer 'completeness' by showing the rise of Jewry, its terrible impact, and the unscrupulous business dealings of Jews. He was vaguer about documentary, which could give a 'direct picture of reality' and offer 'authenticity'.[37]

Film publicity emanating from the Propaganda Ministry linked the outbreak of war to the Jewish Question, suggesting that the Jews were responsible. However, very few critics picked up on this, while two important papers (Goebbels's *Das Reich* and the *Frankfurter Zeitung*) did not review the film at all.[38] The only paper to make the link was the *Deutsche Filmzeitung* which characterized the war as 'ultimately a conflict between the national socialist idea of building … Aryan humanity and the destructive forces and teachings of world Jewry'.[39]

What did audiences see in this film, which film historians have described as 'one of the most virulent propaganda films ever made';[40] as 'the hate picture of all time';[41] as 'probably the most evil film ever made';[42] as 'the ultimate in filmic anti-semitism';[43] which could 'turn honest citizens into mass murderers',[44] and even Jews into antisemites?[45] The film falls into several sections: it begins by observing the *Ostjuden* in their natural habitat, i.e. Poland. It then provides a history of the Jews, beginning with their origins in Asia and their migration into Europe. After this we learn about their wealth, especially in banking, their power, above all in the US, and their domination of German culture in the Weimar period. Finally, we are informed about Jewish religious beliefs and rituals; the film concludes with ritual animal slaughter.

The title, *Der ewige Jude*, dissolves to a Star of David. Accompanied by ominous music, a second title follows: 'a film contribution to the problem of world Jewry'. Then a third title: 'A documentary film from the German Film Society, based on an idea of Dr Eberhard Taubert'. Credits are duly given: director, Fritz Hippler; music, Franz Friedl; and the names of seven cameramen and two film editors. Then a final title:

> The civilized Jews we know in Germany provide only an incomplete picture of their true character. This film includes actual footage from the Polish ghettos. It shows us the Jews as they really are, because they hide themselves behind the mask of the civilized European.

After this we hear the narrator's voice, one of the two official voices from the *Wochenschau* (newsreel). This voice will be present throughout the film and will never lose its grating, hectoring tone, which bludgeons the listener. That voice (obviously) will be absent from the foreign versions.[46]

The narrator informs us that the Polish campaign has provided the opportunity to get to know Jewry well, for nearly four million Jews dwell in Poland, though never in rural areas (the first of many black marks). The second black mark is that they, unlike the Poles, have not suffered the chaos of war. In contrast to the Jews, the Poles now get off lightly, unlike their treatment in Hippler's previous documentary, *Feldzug in Polen*. As proof we learn that within an hour of the German occupation the Jews were back in business. This is illustrated by street scenes of men haggling, many of whom have in fact been driven into the cities and were bartering in desperation. The narrator now mentions that twenty-five years earlier Germans had had the opportunity to glimpse the Polish 'ghetto', and that since then their eyes have been opened by the experiences of the intervening period. What now confronts the Germans are not merely the 'grotesque elements' but a plague, and one which is a threat to the German people. Wagner is quoted: 'The Jew is the evil force behind mankind's corruption.' We see the interiors of Jewish homes and as we are told that they are dirty, we see shots of flies on the wall. But these inhabitants of dirty homes are not really poor for they have preferred to hoard their money rather than create clean and comfortable homes. Inexplicably, some blonde children are briefly glimpsed in the foreground of the frame. There is no mention that Jews have been herded together as a consequence of the policy of ghettoization, or that the viewer is unlikely to be observing normal conditions. Ghetto footage (from Łódź, Warsaw, Lublin and Cracow) is used to authenticate the daily lives of Jews when at that point life was anything but ordinary for Polish Jews, and its extraordinariness was a consequence of German policy.

Other shots include men at prayer bobbing up and down, which provides a link with Harlan's own quest for authenticity. (It was approximately three months later that Harlan, probably on Hippler's advice, went to Poland to recruit Eastern Jews for the synagogue sequence in *Jud Süss*.) We are informed that this is how Jews recite their prayers. It serves to reinforce their oddity, for this film purports to be an ethnographic tour of the original Jew, the *Urjude*, the primitive Jew observed in his natural habitat with the aim of disabusing anyone of the notion that a leopard can change its spots and assimilate. For difference is hereditary, and any attempt to go against this is to go against a law of nature, a law of blood. The film cuts again to street life, for which there must have been a surfeit of material, though some faces appear more than once. This is where, the narrator informs us, 'so-called community life' takes place. Jews rarely engage in useful work but prefer to barter and haggle. We see a few elegantly clad bourgeois women; we also see men digging who by their dress appear middle class. They look up towards the camera with some hostility. It is obvious that they are unused to manual work, indeed that they are being compelled, which only serves to illustrate the point. (Compulsory male labour for those aged fourteen to sixty had been introduced on 26 October 1939.) This sequence was taken from a newsreel (Ufa Tonwoche), which had said that only when Jews are 'really allowed to work properly do they suddenly hold back'.[47] Further shots of Jews bartering are accompanied by the accusation of 'unrestrained egoism', which is then related to religion: 'His religion makes cheating and usury a duty.' The Bible is enlisted in support, with the citing of a truncated passage from Deuteronomy. This particular passage has a long history in antisemitic literature: 'Unto a foreigner thou mayest lend upon usury, but unto thy brother thou shalt not lend upon usury.'[48] We are told that the Jew begins with a vendor's tray, then gets a stand, then a shop, then a larger shop. The most unscrupulous will own warehouses and large banks, and live in splendid houses, having escaped the ghettos of the East. But actual production is left to the workers and peasants of the host nation. To the accompaniment of heroic music we learn that the Aryan, in contrast, wants to create something of value to society, whether food, clothing, art, machinery. When there is no commentary, the music intensifies. One by one the black marks pile up. Jews are dirty, are urban, are unproductive; they are neither farmers nor workers but eternal parasites, the eternal Jew.

Having focused on Poland, the site of Eastern Jewry, the film (with pseudo-oriental music on the soundtrack) moves briefly to Palestine, where few Jews live, we are told, though it still remains the spiritual centre for international Jewry. What follows is taken from a Zionist propaganda film made in 1935, *Land of Promise*, in which the urban, orthodox Jew was negatively contrasted with the new agrarian, Kibbutz-inhabiting Jew.[49] A quick cut from a Zionist flag fluttering in the breeze to Jews at the Wailing Wall; wailing, we are told, their loss, the fall of Jerusalem. In the same breath, and to destroy any vestiges of sympathy with their plight, we are informed that nevertheless their homelessness is of their own choosing. This may seem contradictory, but the shot of orthodox Jews praying at the wall was probably too good to leave out. Furthermore, it also helps explain why the Jews left Palestine. This leads into a brief and crude history of the Jews, as well as a geography lesson. Even 4,000 years ago they were already wandering. A map indicates their travels from the Tigris and the Euphrates to Egypt, from which they were eventually expelled to Palestine for their activities in the grain trade. Always plundering on the way, they became a mongrel race. A light-skinned African face appears with the comment: 'they develop into an oriental Near Eastern race with a negroid admixture, a definitive mongrel race (*Mischrasse*)'. The cosmopolitan empires of Alexander the Great and then Rome bring out the Jews' trading and migratory instincts. They settled in large towns, spread through North Africa to Spain and France, to southern Germany and after that to England. After the peoples of Spain and France 'rose up against them', they arrived in Germany (the film ignores the fact that there were Jewish settlements prior to that). They then follow the German colonization of the East, to Poland and to Russia. Benefiting from the new and 'vague' nineteenth-century ideas about human equality and liberty, they spread across Europe, moving in the past hundred years like an irresistible tide from Eastern Europe (illustrated by another map). They are now likened to an 'equally restless animal', who wanders and also emanates from the East – the rat, bringing ruin and spreading disease: plague, leprosy, typhoid, cholera and dysentery. 'Cunning, cowardly, cruel, rats are found mainly in large packs.' From shots of rats, which were filmed in Berlin by the chief cameraman, Erich Stoll, a committed Nazi,[50] the camera returns to the faces in the Łódź ghetto. The rat sequence was left out of the French version, the Vichy government having found it too strong.[51]

Statistics relating to Jewish criminality are now provided, courtesy of Dr Tauber. In 1932, Jews constituted 1% of the world population but 34% of those involved in the drug trade, 47% in robberies, a similar percentage in card-sharping and gambling, 82% in international criminal gangs, and 98% in prostitution. We are told that the source of the language of 'international shady characters and criminals' is Hebrew and Yiddish.

Jewish physiognomy 'conclusively refutes liberal theories of the equality of men', we are told. 'Jews change their external appearance when they leave their Polish haunts … Hair, beard, skullcap and caftan make the Eastern Jew readily recognizable.' Without this only the 'keen-eyed' are able to recognize the Jew's racial origins, for 'it is an intrinsic trait of the Jew when among non-Jews to hide his origin.' Medium shots of herded Polish Jews in traditional orthodox dress are followed by close-ups of male faces, which then dissolve to close-ups of clean-shaven faces, with side-locks removed, and their owner in Western dress. One by one each Eastern Jew is transformed and Westernized. They are now ready to 'steal into Western civilization'. Dissonant music is on the soundtrack. As the camera pulls back, we see these same men now in Western dress, some wearing bow ties. They smile awkwardly to camera, and show unease which the narrator attributes to their not yet feeling comfortable in Western suits. One can imagine the conditions of screen testing – and the bafflement of the subjects. A great deal of footage must have ended on the cutting-room floor, for only the dimmest expressions were wanted on faces selected for their irregular features, protruding ears and large noses to emphasize the physical contrast between Aryan and Jew. The sequence, which began with close-ups thus imitating mug shots, ends with what looks like a police line-up; this visually links Jews to criminality which will be developed further.[52]

The narrator tells us that it is the assimilated Jews who constitute the 'dreadful danger', and of them the Berlin Jews were 'the most adept at hiding their origins, it no longer being "apparent" that their fathers and forefathers [had] lived in ghettos'. Images appear of men and women in evening dress, with nothing to indicate that they are Jews, but, according to the logic, that makes them all the more dangerous. The extent of Jewish assimilation is further illustrated by photographs and footage with subtitles: we are told that Baron Maurice de Rothschild is a Rothschild black sheep, and that Major James de Rothschild is a British Zionist and a symbol of international Jewish finance. To illustrate the Rothschild ascendancy, feature film is resorted to; for as Hippler earlier had admitted, documentary film was unable to illustrate the rise of Jewry. Thus in his compilation documentary he turned to Hollywood for authenticity and to *The House of Rothschild* (1934), a film, the narrator tells us, made by Jews – though in fact Darryl Zanuck was Hollywood's only prominent non-Jewish producer. The original, accurately translated and dubbed into German, proved insufficient to the task and had to be intercut with comments from the narrator to ensure that the audience got the right message.[53] As proof of Jewish cunning, the long sequence early in the film where Meir Amschel Rothschild dupes the tax inspector is included. In the American context this had an altogether different meaning: there it illustrated the makings of a good capitalist, who outwitted the emissaries of the state. That this film appeared during the early stages of the New Deal is not politically significant. Rather it evoked the older American belief that men are the masters of their fortune. A mild political message was apparent in the suggestion that antisemitism implicitly belonged to the Old World, that it should be combated and that Rothschild would make a good American. For the producers of *Der ewige Jude*, that was precisely what was wrong with America. Germans who longed to go to America must be disabused of their fantasy. Not only must public awareness be heightened regarding the Jewish issue, but America must be exposed as dominated by the Jewish enemy. This was well before America entered the war; but, since this film emanated from the Propaganda Ministry, it had in its sights American anti-German propaganda. America was still attractive to large numbers of Germans, many of whom had relatives there. In any case, this film was not made for an American audience but for a German one.

Traditionally, the Nazis had attacked the US as the 'playground of the Jews', but after the war began the order went out that the US was to be treated with caution to avoid provoking its entrance into the European War.[54] This however, did not exempt Roosevelt who, in Nazi eyes, was a syphilitic who had surrounded himself with Jews. He was a tool of the universal enemy, international Jewry; his membership in a New York chapter of the Freemasons was offered as evidence. He was thus unable and unwilling to seek an accord with the New Order.

A map like a spider's web illustrates the upward routes of the five Rothschild sons and the Jewish banking network. Other Jewish banking families are mentioned: Warburgs, Bleichröders, Sassoons. Jews dominate the New York Stock Exchange, for New York is today the 'centre of Jewish power', ruled by Jewish banking houses such as Kuhn, Warburg, Wertheim, Guggenheim (all, as it happens of German origin). This is followed by footage of the Exchange. Other influential Jews are also mentioned: the Presidential financial adviser and friend, Bernard Baruch; another banker, Otto Kahn, 'who behaves like an English lord'; Mortimer Schiff; 'Jewish lawyer and enemy of Germany', Samuel Untermyer, who had organized a boycott against Germany in 1933; Herbert Lehmann, 'Jewish governor of New York'; 'Professor Felix Frankfurter', a Supreme Court justice since 1939 but still described as 'Presidential legal adviser'; US Secretary of the Treasury Henry Morgenthau, Jr, and the Mayor of New York, the 'half-Jew' Fiorella La Guardia, who in 1937 had declared that Hitler belonged in a 'World's Fair of the Chamber of Horrors', which brought a protest from the German ambassador and an apology from the US State Department. Jews in positions of power in other countries are also mentioned: the British Secretary of State for War, Leslie Hore-Belisha 'whom British soldiers salute as their commander' had in fact resigned in January 1940, amidst allegations from the British Jewish community that this was because he was a Jew;[55] and the one-time French Premier, the Socialist Léon Blum, 'who tried to be a genuine Frenchman'. 'But the Jew remains a rootless parasite even when in power.'

The scene shifts to Germany after newsreel clips of the end of the First World War from which we learn that Jews profited. We see Berlin, then the National Assembly in Weimar, and are informed that the Jews now seized their chance. They included socialists like Otto Landsberg; 'the Jew Hirsch, Minister President of Prussia'; 'the Jew, Theodor Wolff, editor of the *Berliner Tageblatt*'; the left liberal author of the Weimar constitution, Hugo Preuss; Walter Rathenau, the assassinated left liberal Jewish Foreign Minister; Rudolf Hilferding, a socialist Finance Minister; and the Vice-President of the Berlin Police, Bernhard Isidor

Weiss. The non-Jew Phillipp Scheidemann, the first Chancellor of the Weimar Republic, who actually resigned over the Versailles Diktat but whom the Nazis called the 'herald of the *Judenrepublik*' (Jews' republic), is also mentioned. Such people incited the masses, fomented class war and terror, after which we see the pediment on the Reichstag, and its dedication, 'Dem deutschen Volk' (to the German people), though the anti-parliamentary Nazis were more concerned with preserving the *Volk* than preserving parliament. The attack on the socialists continues: Marx was the son of a rabbi (wrong) and had 'curly brown Negro hair'; his socialist rival Ferdinand Lassalle is referred to as Lassalle-Wolfsohn, Wolfsohn being his father's name.[56] Continuing the inaccuracies, the socialist Rosa Luxemburg, of Jewish origin, is conflated with anarchist Emma Goldman, also of Jewish origin: 'Rosa Luxemburg, real name Emma Goldman'. The errors mount up. Also mentioned are the 'Russian Jew' Eugen Leviné, 'the most notorious Communist', executed for his involvement in the 1919 Munich Soviet, and Herschel Grynszpan who assassinated the German minister in Paris, leading to *Kristallnacht*.

More spurious statistics follow. Three-quarters of German Jews live in cities but do not work in factories. Out of one hundred prosecutors, fifteen are Jews; out of one hundred judges, twenty-three are Jews; out of one hundred lawyers, forty-nine are Jews. Fifty-two out of every one hundred doctors are Jews, sixty out of one hundred merchants are Jews. While the average income of the German is RM810, that of the Jew is RM10,000. Millions of Germans were unemployed while immigrant Jews acquired fantastic riches in only a few years. Names of Jewish swindlers and fraudsters are mentioned.

Having dealt extensively with Jewish criminality the narrative turns to culture, for Jews are most dangerous when they 'meddle in a people's culture, religion and art, and pass judgement, when the Nordic concept of beauty is completely incomprehensible to the Jew ... The rootless Jew lacks a feeling for the purity ... of the German idea of art.' The Bach Toccata and Fugue in D Minor on the soundtrack, signifying German purity and greatness, accompanies images of ancient Greek sculpture, followed by medieval German sculpture, especially from the Bamberg and Naumberg cathedrals, symbols of German art. But for good measure the Parthenon is also included along with Botticelli's *Spring* and finally the Sistine Chapel. Riefenstahl's *Olympia*, especially in the Prologue, had also made the conscious link between Ancient Greece[57] and Nazi Germany, while Botticelli was considered a 'northern' artist – Houston Stewart Chamberlain and other nineteenth-century racial theorists claimed the Greeks and Romans as German. The sound of Bach fades and is replaced with African music which soon merges into jazz (degenerate music), drums and a female vocalist on the soundtrack accompanying the rapid cuts and dissolves of images of Cubism and Expressionism. 'What he [the Jew] calls art must titillate his degenerate nerves. A smell of fungus and disease must pervade it; art must be unnatural, grotesque, perverted or pathological.' Jewish art critics and dealers 'extolled the fantasies of sick minds'. We see paintings by George Grosz, Otto Dix, Oskar Kokoschka, Naum Gabo, Marc Chagall and Pablo Picasso, even Emil Nolde's *Brother and Sister* (1919). Despite Nolde's early membership of the Nazi Party, this did not prevent his work from being included in the Exhibition of Degenerate Art which travelled through the Reich from 1937 to 1939 and from which many of the above examples are taken. Shots of primitivist sculpture dissolve to film clips of black banjoists, followed by a pretty black blues singer. From the sublime to the primitive, Jewish critics, the narrator proclaims, have led the descent. Degenerate art was both Jewish and 'Negro'. Jewish critics defined what was German art and culture and included theatre critic Walter Kerr; satirist Kurt Tucholsky, 'a sick pornographer'; and Magnus Hirschfeld, 'who promoted homosexuality and perversion'. We see book jackets of Hirschfeld's works coupled with titles such as *Woman's Whip*. Under the guise of cultural and scientific debate, healthy drives were steered into degenerate paths. Next comes the turn to science, where 'the relativity' Jew Einstein hid his hatred of Germany behind his 'obscure pseudo-science'. And so on.

'The Jewish Eldorado was the stage.' Most theatre directors were Jews: Max Reinhardt is 'the Jewish dictator of the stage'. Jewish comedians are mentioned, including Max Ehrlich and Kurt Gerron, both of whom would be performing three years later at the Westerbork transit camp and the latter also at Theresienstadt both dying in Auschwitz. The distinguished actor Fritz Kortner, born Nathan Kohn in Vienna, is referred to as Kortner-Kohn. Now in California exile, he is charged with 'glorifying a depraved officer who does not shrink from murder': singled out from his many stage and film appearances is his role in the German film *Der Mörder Dimitri Karamazov* (*The Murder of Dmitri Karamazov*) (1931), based on Dostoevsky's *The Brothers Karamozov* from which we see a clip. Next come sequences from Fritz Lang's film, *M* (1932) where Peter Lorre, a Hungarian-born Jew, confesses to child murder, again implying that such crimes are committed by Jews. We then learn: 'For the Jew is instinctively interested in everything which is sickly and depraved.' Ignoring the line between art and life, these film clips count as evidence of the Jewish impulse to murder.

Weimar newsreels are discredited because they implicitly suggest that Jewish artists who left Germany before 1933 were a loss to German culture. We hear the tenor Richard Tauber's departure for New York 'mourned as a loss to German art'. We see Ernst Lubitsch light a cigar and express his joy to be back in Germany, 'especially my native city, Berlin'. We also see the 'Jew Chaplin' welcomed in Berlin. Germans, the narrator informs us, 'applauded unsuspectingly this foreign Jew', the deadly enemy of their race … A false dogma of human equality had misled the people's natural instinct.' (*The Great Dictator*, long in the pipeline, had had its première a month later in October 1940, but publicity prior to release meant that the film's contents were not secret. It suited Taubert, who regularly inflated the world's Jewish population, to accept the unfounded rumours long in circulation that Chaplin was a Jew.)

Religious education also comes in for criticism, Europeans having been taught to consider Jews as related to 'Christianity's founder'. With Bach's Toccata and Fugue in D Minor for organ on the soundtrack, icons of 'Aryan' sculpture appear including those on the Parthenon, as well as Nordic art – the Bamberger Reiter and a female figure from Naumberg Cathedral. High-minded poets and artists are reproached for their flattering depiction of what was 'Hebrew tribal history', and for considering Abraham and Isaac as 'examples of the highest morality and humanity'. Moreover, Hebrews could never have looked like this: Renaissance paintings of figures from the Old Testament are replaced with a film sequence in which Jews are celebrating the festival of Purim, which the narrator tells us was 'photographed by Warsaw Jews themselves for use in a cultural film'. What may look like a harmless family celebration, we are told, is the commemoration of the slaughter of 75,000 antisemitic Persians by the biblical ancestors of 'our present-day Jews', implying that it is the Jews who annually celebrate genocide, a 'feast of vengeance'. Both scripts for *Jud Süss* had also described the synagogue service as Purim; but, as this is mainly a children's festival and is not celebrated in the synogogue, it was replaced (doubtless based on Jewish advice) with another service.[58]

To illustrate Purim, a clip was taken not from a 'cultural film' as stated but from a Yiddish feature film, a comedy made in Poland, *Der Purimshpiler* (*The Purim Player*, also known as *The Jester*) (1937). A Nazi film critic (Erwin Goetz, pseudonym for Frank Maraun) justified using feature film in a documentary: it did not 'call into question the documentary character of the film' since the sources were stated and the viewer was not misled, but most importantly because when scenes with Jewish actors were included 'fiction becomes reality … the reality of the cultural activity of the Jews in the cultural life of their host people … Fiction reflects reality in the excerpts from films which were shot in pre-war Poland by Jews for Jews.'[59] Thus, if the purpose was didactic then the means justified the end. If Jews had found the dinner sequence in *Der Purimshpiler* humorous – Jews are shown seated at a long dinner table laughing and enjoying themselves while eating – Germans were expected to be repelled. This illustrated well the workings of a compilation documentary.

'Educated Germans', the narrator tells us, 'objective and tolerant, regarded such tales of vengeance as folklore' or 'strange custom'. Underneath the 'bowdlerized West European clothing' is concealed the Eastern origins of this celebration of a feast of vengeance. But to understand what lies underneath the customs a closer look at the 'laws and teachings of the Jewish race' is required. 'From childhood the Jew learns his ancient law in the Talmud school … Rabbis are political agitators, not peaceful theologians', for 'the politics of a race of parasites must be conducted in secret'. Talmudic law teaches cunning, to respond politely to calm the stranger's anger, and to ally oneself with those 'on whom fate smiles'. Since Jews assume no one understands their language or strange symbols, they are willing to appear before the camera even when at worship, the narrator tells us. Admitting German cameramen into the synagogue is held against them when they were hardly in a position to refuse. In fact this is rare footage, since normally Jews would never have allowed filming. It was the Germans who had closed the Great Synagogue of Łódź. After a request from some leading Jewish figures it was reopened on 10 October 1939, with the sole purpose of using it for filming.[60] We see the Orthodox in plain hats, the Hasidic in distinctive hats. We see men in the synagogue making deals, though this was staged, probably by Stoll, the chief cameraman,[61] since this was evidence that Judaism, unlike Christianity, is a materialistic religion. As the Torah scroll is opened and passages are read aloud, the narrator interjects that the Jews are proclaiming vengeance against their enemies, and God's promise that the Jews will become 'the world's sole ruler'. This is not a religion, he declares, nor a religious service but a 'conspiracy by a sick, cunning, contaminated race, against all non-Jews, against the Aryan peoples, their morals and laws'. The Jewish religion is not mysterious but dangerous. But, in its attack on religion, it was thought that the film might have gone too far for some potential viewers: concern was expressed that especially the choral singing in this sequence was too close to a Roman Catholic service and might awaken sympathy amongst Catholics.[62]

It is at this point that the shortened version, intended for 'tender souls', ended. Others could see the long slaughter sequence according to the kosher method, filmed in Łódź, among the 'most horrifying every photographed'. The ban on this method was lifted for one day to enable filming.[63] Hippler brought the footage back to Berlin on 16 October and Goebbels viewed it that night. Having ordered the footage, he was nevertheless shocked and recorded: 'This Jewry must be annihilated.'[64] This ancient method of slaughter, observed by orthodox Jews and Muslims, involves slitting the animals' throat to enable bleeding because it is forbidden to consume blood. It takes up to two minutes for the animal to die which in film time seems interminable. Modern methods stun the animal first. Twelve days later, Goebbels showed the sequences to the vegetarian Hitler and others who were 'deeply shocked'.[65]

Not only do we see the animal bleed to death but we also hear it and then see it disembowelled while still alive. Switzerland forbade this practice in 1892, we are told. Germany forbids it. Before 1933 National Socialists in Baden, Bavaria and Thuringia had proposed that it be outlawed as unworthy of a civilized nation. Supporting ritual slaughter (and doubtless recognizing the political capital the

Nazis could make out of this issue) we see headlines from communist, socialist and liberal papers, described as 'the Jewish press'. Journalists could write these things, we are told, because they had never witnessed ritual slaughter. At this point once again we see sheep being slaughtered, after which the film cuts back again to the dying cow. It is pointed out that on 21 April 1933 the Führer had ensured this practice was outlawed. This is followed by the chilling statement: 'Just as it dealt with this cruel slaughter, so will the Germany of National Socialism deal with the whole race of Jewry.' The Nuremberg Laws removed citizenship, so that 'Jewish blood and the Jewish way of thinking will never again contaminate the German people.' Newsreel footage of Hitler addressing the Reichstag on 30 January 1939 follows, and in particular the passage in the two-hour speech which refers to the fate of the Jews in the event of war. Europe, Hitler declares, cannot find peace until the Jewish question is solved.

> There is sufficient living space in the world for everyone, but the idea that the Jews were chosen by God to live by the blood and sweat of other races must be swept away. Jews will just have to get used to the idea of performing some respectable, constructive activity, as other people do, or sooner or later they will face a crisis of unimaginable proportions. For if international Jewish financiers in Europe and beyond succeed in plunging the nations into war again, the result will not be the bolshevization of the earth and the victory of Jewry, but the annihilation of the Jewish race in Europe.

This last sentence was cut from the international version. However, German cinema audiences know that war has come, and that the promise must be made good: annihilation (*Vernichtung*) from Europe. With hindsight, it is difficult to accept that at this stage it might only mean physical removal rather than outright extermination. How much significance should one attach to the incorporation of this newsreel clip in a film made after the outbreak of war, though well before the invasion of the Soviet Union after which the mass killing of the Jews began? The Propaganda Ministry's brief was to promote government policy, but what that policy was at this stage is debated.

The Manichean struggle between darkness and light is now coming to an end. In conclusion, we see the light: the Aryan – predominantly though not exclusively male – faces in mainly low-angle close-ups, some already familiar from *Triumph of the Will*. Against images of men on the march and Nazi flags waving, the narrator concludes:

> The eternal law of nature – maintaining the purity of one's race – is the legacy, which the National Socialist movement bequeaths to the German people forever … united with this resolve [they] march on into the future.

Missing from this long tirade against Jews are two negative stereotypes. One is the Jew as Bolshevik (as distinct from Jew as Socialist), doubtless out of deference to the Stalin–Hitler Pact, in force at this time. It had not been absent from the 1937 Munich Exhibition, when it was declared: 'Arrest ten Communists and you will find nine Jews among them.'[66] Also absent is the sexualized Jew, leading mainly Aryan females, rather than males, to commit *Rassenschande*. Perhaps this was because it was a theme in *Jud Süss*. But even a hint of this would have weakened the argument so strong in this film that the Jew as 'Other' is so repellent that Aryans could never be attracted. Moreoover, it would negate the purpose of the film which presents Jews as a plague.

The antisemite found no shortage of material on which to draw. Overload and overkill was the style of the film, but what was left out and what was included is significant. The target was the primitive, criminal unEuropean *Ostjude*, who camouflages himself as he leaves his native habitat for the wider world, whose culture and economy he will try to take over. The habitat of the Jew was the East of Europe: footage showed him *in situ*; but his original habitat had been the East, Asia, proving that he was not European.

In making Polish Jewry its target, *Der ewige Jude* reflects its origins in the first months of the war. But in also attacking Jewish dominance in France, Britain and the US, it went further. Germany was at war with Britain and with France, though not with the US. Throughout 1940, that is in the eleven months prior to its première, the prevailing propaganda strategy had been to maintain a 'façade of moderation towards the US', because Germany had no desire to provoke the US into entering the war on the side of Britain.[67] Two months after the film's première on 30 January 1941 Hitler warned the US that any attempt to aid the British by sea would be met with force. Six weeks later, Congress passed the Lend-Lease Act for aid to Britain. That unleashed a barrage of anti-American and antisemitic sentiments, the two merging easily. In April 1941 Goebbels wrote:

> There on the other side of the big pond an unscrupulous clique of Jews, capitalists, merchants of death, bankers, and newsmen stealthily pursue their criminal goal of maneuvering the United States into the war despite the fact that the American people does not support them.'[68]

And yet *Der ewige Jude* which is restrained in its view of the Jew as Bolshevik is not in its view of the Jew as American plutocrat. In this it reflects German propaganda policy for 1939 to 1940 towards the Soviet Union but not towards the US.

The purpose of this film is not difficult to gauge. There is no room for subtle interpretation here, no covert message. Script, image and sound leave no doubt as to the purpose. The controlled press understood the message, though some better than others. Its reception is harder to gauge.[69] One can try to relate it to the number of people who viewed the film. But how they actually received it is far more difficult to assess, especially for historians who prefer to ground this in documentary evidence. It also belongs to the larger debate about whether Nazi propaganda films were actually effective. This film is a particular case in point, because it was so crude, repellent and outrageous in its statements. Can it have worked? In contrast, *Jud Süss* had entertainment value, but one can still ask the question: did it work, or did the message wash over members of the audience attracted to the drama, the acting, the costumes, etc.? Was it 'popular not because of its antisemitism, but in spite of it?'[70] Conversely, was *Der ewige Jude* unpopular not because of its antisemitism but because of the kind of film it was? The impact of both films has often been assumed rather than demonstrated, given what we know of Goebbels's role in both productions and the subsequent fate of European Jewry. We are, however, on safer ground if we relate the film to its particular context, to what was happening then, to what was known then, to the evidence gleaned, admittedly, from tainted security police reports, and finally to viewing figures.

The reform of the ratings (*Prädikate*), which acted as a form of negative taxation, meant that after 1938 no cinema owner dared to refuse to book a film with good ratings when offered by a distributor. A film with the highest distinction meant that the entire programme would be exempted from entertainment tax, an important consideration.[71] Especially after 1938, no cinema owner could refuse to exhibit a film with a mark of political distinction. For this reason it has been assumed that no cinema owner would refuse a film with suitable ratings, which this film had in abundance. Yet this is precisely what seems to have happened, which disproves the assertion.[72]

In the week following the première the film was supposed to have been shown in sixty-six German cinemas. An examination of the listings page of the Berlin edition of the Nazi Party paper, the *Völkischer Beobachter*, reveals that in the first week it was on in thirty-six Berlin cinemas, the following week in half that number, and two weeks after opening in only one.[73] The film had to compete with feature films and was quickly replaced. Cinema owners wanted to make a profit.

It is only possible to offer a rough guess as to how many people actually viewed the film during the Second World War. Estimates vary between 2,000,000 and 4,750,000. Compared to the number who saw *Jud Süss*, *Der ewige Jude* attracted between less than one-tenth and one-quarter the number of viewers. Probably no more than one million actually paid to see the film; the rest were members of the Hitler Youth, the military and other captive audiences.[74] Not only were cinema owners 'resisting' but so also were cinema-goers. The one fed the other. As members of the audience could not leave the cinema once the film began, they chose not to go. Word got around. With takings low, other cinema owners were not inclined to take a risk. The film had a limited appeal.

This all begs the question of the extent to which Germans were or were not antisemitic on the eve of the 'Final Solution', or whether they suffered from an inherent capacity for 'eliminationist antisemitism'.[75] The film cannot serve as evidence one way or the other. What its reception reveals is that many Germans preferred entertainment, and indeed may, to some extent, have even been impervious to the message, certainly if presented in this guise. Indifference may not have been what Goebbels desired, but it was not a complete disadvantage when the first deportations of Jews began two months later from Stettin on the Baltic. Audience comments, which the Secret Police chose to include in their reports, support both sides: some of the comments recorded suggest that the film reinforced antisemitic beliefs and whipped up viewers, while others indicate that members of the audience were turned off by the film. Viewing figures tend to support the latter. Of course the question still remains which audiences and which viewers chose to make comments. About this we know much less. There remains some doubt as to whether Goebbels's, Hippler's and Tauber's creation actually worked as propaganda.

In contrast, we know a great deal about why the Propaganda Ministry made this film, though its precise relation to the 'Final Solution' is contested. Does the incorporation of Hitler's speech into the film, or the film itself, serve as evidence that a decision to implement the 'Final Solution' had been taken in the period between January 1939 and November 1940?[76] This depends upon the dating of that decision, about which historians continue to disagree. Was the actual decision to implement the 'Final Solution' made subsequent to this film? We now know that the Wannsee Conference of January 1942 merely coordinated the measures already being taken. Historians, mainly of the 'functionalist' persuasion, have argued that at some point in 1941, either just before or after the invasion of the Soviet Union in June, such a decision was made, as a consequence or function of the war.[77] Some even contend that no clear order from Hitler was ever given, as this was not necessary.[78] Alternatively, was annihilation always intended (by Hitler), as the 'Intentionalists', those who set such store on the word rather than the deed, have long argued?[79] If one explains the policy of extermination, which began in 1941, as 'the realisation of the annihilation … aimed at since 1939' then this film has a very close connection, for its making can be understood to be a part of that 'realisation'.[80] Thus the nature of the film's direct link to the Holocaust can be understood as part of a wider historical debate on the genesis of the 'Final Solution'. The Nazi contribution to the legend of the '*ewige Jude*' was to make a film with that title, the purpose of which was to ensure that the Jew would no longer be able to wander or be 'eternal'.[81]

12

The Second World War

Once the war was well underway, film output was reduced. This was partly due to a shortage of material and manpower. A few days before the outbreak of war, Goebbels had announced that he wanted to 'change the film programmes when things get serious'. What he had in mind, however, was 'apparently suitable material that is not unduly expensive'. 'Only as a last resort' did he want a reduction in the 'actual number of films'.[1] Yet in a short time this is exactly what occurred.

Estimates vary as to the number of feature films produced during the twelve years of the Third Reich, due to the use of different criteria. The higher estimate (1,356 films) includes non-feature film (feature length documentaries), as well as co-productions, mainly made outside Germany, which a lower estimate (1,094 films) excludes. On the other hand, the lower estimate only includes those films which passed the censor and had their premières in Germany. It excludes the sixty-seven international co-productions, the twenty-seven films banned prior to screening, and some films which, though banned, were permitted premières abroad. To confuse matters, the lower estimate also includes three films made prior to the Nazi takeover and several banned shortly after their first public screenings.[2] Taking the lower estimate, and deducting the Weimar films but adding in the twenty-seven films which failed to pass the censor, we then have a total of 1,118 films. If we average this out to an annual rate and a monthly rate, we have approximately ninety films per year or an average of seven and a half films per month.

Of course statistics can only be taken so far. Nevertheless, what is apparent from either list is that a greater number of films were produced in the years prior to the outbreak of war than during the war itself. The more selective list shows that in 1934 129 films appeared, in 1938 ninety-three and in 1939 107. By 1940 a dip was noticeable: eighty-five films appeared during that year. An even greater decrease occurred over the next two years: sixty-seven films in 1941 and fifty-eight in 1942. Output rose again in 1943 with seventy-six films and in 1944 seventy-five. In the first months of 1945, only six films appeared, though the more inclusive list mentions seventy-six in production for 1945 of which twenty-five had not been completed by early May when the war ended, and thirty-five, though completed, did not have premières. By 1945 of course few cinemas existed in which films could have premières. And certainly there were no gala openings in Berlin, though great efforts were made for *Kolberg*.

Once the war was over, the Allies, keen on re-educating Germans, banned a number of films on the grounds that they were racist, extolled militarism or strong leadership, glorified fascism or National Socialism or displayed anti-democratic tendencies.[3] The ban even extended to films made prior to the Nazi takeover, such as *Morgenrot* and *Der Choral von Leuthen*, both nationalist films which the Nazis had welcomed in early 1933, and a '*Fridericus*' film, *Trenck* (1932). The Allied censors were by no means consistent. A film might be suspect because of the director: many of Veit Harlan's films (though not all) fell into this category.

Nevertheless, once such inconsistencies are taken into account, as well as the variable rate of annual film production, it is apparent that the Allies found most films made during the last eighteen months of the war less objectionable. And with good reason since the film industry was no longer expected to produce rousing propaganda films but ones which raised morale and reminded audiences of better and more 'normal' times. German feature films have been divided into four categories: political (films with an obvious political message); comedy (musicals and comedies); serious (melodramas which included many but not all of the literary adaptations); and action, which speaks for itself.[4] Although categorization is not always straightforward – some films straddle more than one category – nevertheless the conclusion is inescapable that fewer political films were produced in the last years of the war. Proportionately more political films (twenty-three) appeared in 1941. This declined to fourteen for 1942, to six for 1943 and only four for 1944. Escapist fare became the order of the day as German victories became few and far between. Distraction rather than incitement was required and such films also happened to meet with the approval of the Allied censor.

In the final year of the war, several films failed to pass the German censor, a number incidentally not dissimilar to the number that failed to pass the Allied censor as unsuitable for German viewers. For obvious reasons, however, the two groups of banned films were very different. What displeased the German censor did not displease the Allied censor and vice versa.

The majority of feature films that the Allies found unsuitable for post-war German audiences originated in the period 1939 to 1943. The Allies banned only thirteen films made in 1933 and a similar number for each of the following years until 1937, when the number rose to twenty-one, although in that year slightly fewer films were produced. Such films the Allied censor categorized as nationalist or militarist. From 1938, only four films were banned; from 1939 seventeen of which *Robert und Bertram* and *Leinen aus Irland* were two. From 1940 fifteen were banned, including *Jud Süss*, *Die Rothschilds*, *Bismarck*, Trenker's *Der Feuerteufel*

(*The Fire Devil*), *Friedrich Schiller*, as well as a film based on a Schiller play, *Das Fräulein von Barnhelm*, which had a 'Nazi militarist tendency inserted into the original story'.[5] From 1941, with film production greatly reduced, eleven films were subsequently banned, including the pro-voluntary euthanasia film, *Ich Klage An* (*I Accuse*), and the anti-British *Ohm Krüger* (*Uncle Krüger*). From 1942 sixteen films were banned, two by Veit Harlan – *Der grosse König* and *Die goldene Stadt* (*The Golden City*) – as well as another Bismarck film, *Die Entlassung* (*The Dismissal*). From 1943 fourteen were banned, none of which were particularly lethal, including the anti-British *Titanic* which had the dubious honour of being banned by both German and Allied censors, though passed by the Russians.[6]

Only twenty-seven films failed to pass the German censor, for a variety of reasons, during the twelve years of the Third Reich. That was approximately two a year.[7] Given the controls, that number is not insignificant. The anti-British *Titanic* is the best-known example. Another, *Panik* (*Panic*), about the escape of animals from a zoo, was deemed unsuitable for wartime.[8] In early 1939 *Das Leben könnte so schön sein* (*Life Could Be so Beautiful*) fell foul of its title. Even when divested of its subjunctive and revised to *Life Can Be so Beautiful*, and with the première already scheduled, Goebbels still banned the film 'because it tended to sabotage the government's population policy': the social and economic difficulties experienced by the young married couple were taken to be a criticism of National Socialist policy.[9] The husband was played by Rudi Godden (Robert in *Robert und Bertram*), in his first serious role. During filming, *Titanic*'s director, Herbert Selpin, was arrested on Goebbels's orders, accused of having made on the set derogatory remarks about the military, a serious crime for 1943.[10] His death in prison sent tremors through the film industry. Selpin was the only film director to meet this fate, though not the only member of the industry: the actor Robert Dorsay (Jacques, the servant, in *Robert und Bertram*) was executed in 1943 for making Führer jokes. The press officers for Ufa (Richard Düwell) and Terra (Erich Knauff, who had designed the ubiquitous poster advertising *Jud Süss* with Marian appearing devil-like in sickly green) were executed in 1944 for making 'defeatist remarks'.[11] On the other hand, attendance at the funeral of the popular romantic actor, Joachim Gottschalk, went unpunished. He had committed suicide with his Jewish wife and young son in late 1941. After the war Harlan presented attending his funeral and defying Goebbels as forms of resistance.[12]

The most notorious propaganda films appeared in the early years of the war, in 1940 and 1941. Especially in the last year of the war, when things became desperate, some German feature films fell foul of the German censor for displaying the wrong tendencies – tendencies, however, unlikely to alarm an Allied censor. Käutner's *Grosse Freiheit, Nr. 7* (*Great Freedom Street, Number 7*) was deemed suitable for non-German audiences: it could be shown in the Czech Protectorate of Bohemia and Moravia but not in the Greater German Reich.[13]

Via Mala, directed by Josef von Baky, was banned in the last weeks of the war for its 'dreary atmosphere'.[14]

The Allies banned only seven films from 1944: the Harlan Agfacolour melodrama *Opfergang* (*Self-Sacrifice*) and the morale-boosting saga of a family united in war, *Die Degenhardts* (*The Degenhardts*), one of two films made by Heinrich George in which, not surprisingly, he also took the lead. Of the very few films which opened in the first months of 1945, only Harlan's Agfacolour blockbuster *Kolberg* met with an Allied ban.

Considering films in terms of calendar year output can take us only so far. Another approach is to relate film production and film content to the course of the war itself, though at times this can be difficult. Films could be intended as propaganda, that is to persuade to a particular point of view: that the Jews, the British, the Russians were the enemy; that euthanasia of the unfit was good; that a great leader was necessary or genius will out, etc. But raising morale was also important, especially once the war began to go badly. Escapist films offered a respite from the war or from the call of duty and enabled the viewer to emerge refreshed from the cinema, thoughts about the war having been temporarily banished. They could also suggest the possibility of happy private lives, especially important late in the war when members of the audience were likely to be female and worried about reunion with their loved ones serving at the front.

Sometimes a film could simultaneously be propaganda, raise morale *and* entertain. Films also had another function in prescribing acceptable wartime behaviour: men were to follow orders, put personal desires aside and lay down their lives, while women were to remain faithful, be good wives, fiancées, mothers, and refrain from putting pressure on fighting men.

Distinguishing which films were and which were not propaganda is not easy. In some the propaganda was overt, in others only covert; it has even been argued that in the Third Reich there was no such thing as a non-political film.[15] Against this is the argument that films were complex 'audiovisual artifacts' which contain ambiguities and contradictions.[16] Though Goebbels was clearly in charge, he could not micromanage every film. Nor could he control audience response, which was by no means uniform, as it depended on age, gender, geography, class, religion and political persuasion. Estimates vary as to the number of films which contained overt political propaganda, anything from 139 to 229, at most 20%.[17] Moreover, only ninety-six or less than 10% were actually commissioned by the state, the so-called *Staatsauftrag* films. If the state decided to commission a feature film then it (or rather Goebbels) was addressing a particular need. In return for largesse, a desirable political message was expected in a film with lavish production values.

One can get a distorted view of Third Reich film output. Notorious films such as *Jud Süss*, promoted by the Propaganda Ministry, have subsequently become closely identified with Third Reich cinema. On the other hand, well-made but relatively harmless films, often star-studded, were able to be screened after the war.[18] What has often gone unacknowledged is that such popular films were usually offered in a cut version. *Robert und Bertram* is the most controversial example, in that it had to be withdrawn even in its sanitized version.[19] Some of these films were first banned by the Allies (*Jud Süss* met with an outright ban still in place), but with some tinkering, usually cuts, were often later passed by the West German censors, either in the early 1950s or much later.[20]

Entertainment in the Third Reich was rarely innocent.[21] Lethal but well-made films – and the two categories are not necessarily mutually exclusive – constitute only a fraction of film output. The majority of films produced during the Third Reich have been forgotten. Many are neither worth viewing – not dissimilar in this respect to the film output of many other countries from that period – nor worthy of closer examination, given the political significance of that period and state. This does not downplay the importance of film propaganda; it merely puts it into perspective.

Films can usefully be related to the different stages of the war, though given that feature films take time to complete, an exact match with a particular propaganda onslaught is often impossible. A distinction also has to be drawn between production and distribution. The war moved at a faster pace than film production. While being made, a film might be overtaken by events, thus preventing it from doing the job for which it had been intended. By the time of completion, it was likely to relate to a previous stage in the war; film scenarios could not keep up with changing military fortunes. Occasionally, even the enemy might have changed. Sometimes there was a delay in release to allow a tinkering with details or fine-tuning. It could be hard, however, to disguise a film's origins. Despite these caveats, it is still possible to relate some state-commissioned films to different stages of the war, bearing in mind the impossibility of a precise match.

Initially, some films made prior to the outbreak of war, or even to the Nazi takeover, were reissued in a new version. *Robert und Bertram* (1939) appeared with a different ending: the two rogues, instead of escaping in a balloon, join the Wehrmacht. *Morgenrot*, made in 1932, which opened shortly after Hitler came to power and was the first film première to be graced by his presence after becoming Chancellor, was reissued with the mother's pacifist speech excised along with references to battle losses.[22] Militarist films made prior to the war, according to one directive of February 1940, could only be screened if they did not refer to the First World War, because that was a war which Germany had lost.[23] This affected several Ritter productions, including *Pour le mérite* as well as *Urlaub auf Ehrenwort* (*Leave on Word of Honour*), and Ucicky's *Morgenrot* which had been successfully revived in November 1939. Other nationalist films made prior to the outbreak of war and set in the pre-war period were brought back into circulation to replace some 'shallow films', in Goebbels's words. He thought comedies and newsreels did not go together and insisted that some premières be postponed.[24] Other reissued films included Harlan's *Der Herrscher* (*The Ruler*) (1937), based on Gerhart Hauptmann's *Vor Sonnenuntergang* (*Before Sunset*), about an industrialist (a great leader) who takes a young woman as his second wife against opposition from his family, and Gerhard Lamprecht's *Der höhere Befehl* (*The Higher Command*), a '*Fridericus*' film that had been shown in conjunction with Leni Riefenstahl's *Tag der Freiheit* in all cinemas during 1936 after Germany had announced rearmament.

Many propaganda feature films began life in the first few months of 1940, though some did not reach the screen until late 1941 and one not until 1943.[25] They included anti-Polish, anti-British, nationalist, militarist and authoritarian films. With one exception, however, Jewish characters were demoted from centre stage to their earlier supporting roles. This is apparent in several films that opened in 1941 and 1942, and also in one from 1943, though that was in fact a delayed release.

One anti-Polish film which had its origins in the opening stage of the war was *Feinde* (*Enemies*). Made by the Russian-born director Viktor Tourjansky who spoke Russian on the set, which did not please the actors, it had its première in November 1940.[26] Unruly, uncouth Poles are the enemies. They harass the German heroine who lives with and works for her unpleasant Polish stepmother who runs an inn, her deceased German father having made the mistake of marrying racially beneath him. The heroine seeks to escape and is eventually rescued along with other ethnic Germans by the German hero, played with dignity by the urbane Willy Birgel. Once he is on hand, the audience can expect a happy end: the Germans escape through a forest to reach German soil. An opening statement makes clear the film's purpose:

> Humanity will never forget the untold suffering of the German people in Poland, for whom the whole of the post-war period was a time of unceasing victimization. Deprived of their political rights, economically exploited, terrorized and dispossessed – this was their fate over the years. Then in 1939 the British guarantee to Poland precipitated the Polish massacres. Tens of thousands of innocent Germans were deported under threat of horrible torture. 60,000 were slaughtered like cattle.[27]

Another anti-Polish film, based on an idea suggested by Goebbels and first mentioned in early February 1940, opened two years after the Polish conquest and several months after the invasion of the Soviet Union.[28] *Heimkehr* (*Homecoming*) had a script by Kleist prize-winner Gerhard Menzel and was directed by Gustav Ucicky for Wien-Film. Later banned by the Allies, it was first shown at the Venice Film Festival on 31 August 1941, then in Vienna on 10 October and finally in Berlin on 23 October 1941. Starring the Viennese actress Paula Wessely, Attila Hörbiger (Wessely's real-life husband) and Carl Raddatz (as her fiancé), it received several *Prädikate* including *Film der Nation*, a special and rare designation. One of the more costly films, it never recouped its outlay at the box office. By the time of its release, the tribulations of ethnic Germans had less appeal to Germans suffering food shortages and bombing raids.[29]

Two days after *Heimkehr*'s opening in Berlin, Goebbels spoke about the educational value of film and suggested that, at a time when the entire nation was weighed down with heavy burdens and worries, entertainment also had particular political (*staatspolitisch*) value to the state.[30] Several months previously he had made clear the role for entertainment films: 'Entertainment can also sometimes have the task of helping to equip a people for their life struggle, of providing them with the necessary edification, entertainment and relaxation.' Film was not a 'mere vehicle for entertainment but a vehicle for education, and a force for state morality'.[31] Yet another year passed before Goebbels decided that priority must be given to 'lighter and more entertaining films'.[32]

Heimkehr depicts Poland as a place of disorder where ethnic Germans, clearly a cut above the rest, are brutally mistreated. Halfway through the film the German hero (Raddatz) is killed by Poles. The prim and proper heroine (Wessely) carries on to the end. Locked in prison with her fellow ethnic Germans – they are awaiting their dawn execution – and inspired by a Hitler radio broadcast, prior to her arrest she had listened to German radio surreptitiously, she delivers a splendid exhortatory speech, a sequence Goebbels found 'the best ever filmed'.[33] Suddenly planes thunder overhead and the prison walls are blown down. Poland has been invaded; the justification for that invasion being the purpose of the film.

> Friends, we're going to get home, that's for certain … At home in Germany people are no longer weak, and are no longer unconcerned with what happens to us. And why shouldn't we be able to go home if that's what we want? Think how it will be, friends … when everything around us is German, and when you go into a shop it won't be Yiddish or Polish you hear, but German. And it won't only be the whole village that will be German, everything all round us will be German. And we'll be right in the middle of it, in the heart of Germany … on the good old warm soil of Germany. In our own country and at home … And all around the birds are singing and everything is German.[34]

The opening titles claim that the events were based on stories told by ethnic Germans who had fled Volhynia, an area settled by Germans in the eighteenth century and which since 1919 had been divided between Poland and the Soviet Ukraine. The heroine exhorts her fellow ethnic Germans, telling them that soon they will be *Heim ins Reich* (home in the Reich). After the signing of the Stalin–Hitler pact Volhynia came under Soviet control; its German inhabitants were resettled in western Poland from which the Polish inhabitants were expelled to a rump Poland, the so-called General Government. By the time the film had its première the Germans had attacked the Soviet Union and taken Volhynia, its Jewish inhabitants falling victim to mobile killing squads in the first three weeks.

Once fighting recommenced in the spring of 1940, Goebbels demanded more political films and less light entertainment.[35] After the conquest of Denmark, Norway, the Benelux countries and France, the Battle of Britain began in July. In retaliation for the bombing of London, Coventry and industrial sites, the British bombed German civilian targets, which contradicted Goering's assurances of Luftwaffe dominance. Anti-British films did not suddenly appear – the attitude to Britain had hitherto been ambivalent – but the majority of such films originate in this period and had premières up through 1942.[36] Anti-British films included the pro-Irish *Der Fuchs von Glenarvon* (*The Fox of Glenarvon*) (April 1940) and *Mein Leben für Irland* (*My Life for Ireland*) (February 1941). They also included films which attacked Britain's role in Africa: *Carl Peters* (March 1941), directed by the ill-fated Selpin; *Ohm Krüger* (April 1941) co-directed by Hans Steinhoff (director of *Hitlerjunge Quex*); and *Germanin* (*Teuton*) (May 1942), directed by Goebbels's brother-in-law, Max Kimmich.

Goebbels lavished both money and awards on *Ohm Krüger* at a time when film costs were to be kept down. Set during the Boer War, its purpose was to play on anti-British feeling stirred up by the shock of British bombing raids.[37] The British are depicted as duplicitous and degenerate, undeserving of their empire, their record in Africa abysmal, while the Germans, historically late on the scene, deserve but are denied their place in the sun. Britain remained the enemy in Selpin's *Titanic*: the decadent owner of the White Star Line is shown as criminally responsible for the disaster. The film closes with the words: 'The death of 1,500 persons went unatoned, a lasting indictment of Britain's lust for profit.'[38] *Titanic* passed the censor in April 1943 but was never screened in Germany, although it was in neutral and occupied countries.[39]

Aside from the antisemitic films of 1940 whose origins antedate the outbreak of war, the propaganda offensive in the cinema did not really begin until late 1940. *Wunschkonzert* (*Request Concert*), a *Staatsauftrag* film, opened in December 1940 but had first been mentioned by Goebbels in March of that year.[40] A love story directed by Eduard von Borsody, it moves from one German triumph to another, beginning when the couple first meet at the Berlin Olympics (Hitler is in evidence – his sole appearance in feature film). The hero then disappears for three years after being called up to fight in the German Condor Legion in Spain; after that there is a jump to the Polish invasion. Newsreel footage of the Olympics, the Condor Legion and the Polish campaign are incorporated. Also included are a few shots of the Western campaign at the end of the film when the couple are reunited.[41]

The hero has been able to reconnect with his fiancée via the *Wunschkonzert*
or 'Request Concert', which was first introduced in October 1939. An immensely
popular Sunday evening radio programme, this was broadcast live and transmitted
to the home front and battlefront, linking the two fronts. Requests for songs and
poems were sent in, then broadcast by well-known singers and actors. Soldiers
were able to make contact with their loved ones who, in turn, were able to make
contact with them via the personal messages attached to the requests for which
one made a donation to charity. *Wunschkonzert* the radio programme was an
immense morale booster; *Wunschkonzert* the film, with its happy end, also had a
happy end for the Propaganda Ministry because it was the second most popular
film at the box office for 1940–42.[42]

The story appealed to both men and women, with its upbeat ending at a time
of German triumph – France and Poland had been defeated and the Battle of
Britain was raging. Cut from the post-war version is the final sequence when
the audience spontaneously breaks into the rousing First World War song: '*Wir
fahren gegen Engelland*' (We are going to [against] England). The moral was not
lost on viewers: military men must take orders, do their duty, behave correctly
at all times and not allow personal feelings to dominate. Women must not ask
questions, should remain patient and loyal, and all will come right in the end,
as it seemed to do for most, but not all, the characters. A music student, now
a soldier, plays the organ in a bombed-out church while German soldiers are
returning after storming the French trenches. Lost in the fog, and desperate to
avoid minefields, the music guides them. They reach safety, but the organist
dies. Someone had to in a war film, but since he is unattached, he is expendable.
Anyhow his mother feels it was a noble cause, as she makes clear when making
her request on *Wunschkonzert*. With victory on the Western front, the wrong of
the First World War has been righted; German music has not only inspired both
fronts but even saved lives.

Other films starred the military, with little reference to the home front and with
hardly a female role. Luftwaffe films such as Hans Bertram's *Kampfgeschwader
Lützow* (*Battle Squadron Lützow*) and Karl Ritter's *Stukas* (*Dive Bombers*)
appeared in the first half of 1941. Both extolled fighting and fighting men,
sending out a message loud and clear that Germans could rely on their men. Such
action films were not only directed at the home front but were also prescriptive
films. War was about winning, which Germans of course did easily, but also about
dying, which Germans could do well by meeting death with courage. Moreover,
the men could rely on their commanding officers who were shown as highly
competent, born leaders, but never remote from their men, behaving responsibly
as older brothers rather than as fathers. War provided comradeship; the bonds
amongst fighting men were the most important that men could experience. War
also enabled weak men to become brave. Such fast-paced action films, which

contained newsreel footage of, for example, Stukas attacking ships in Dunkirk harbour, offered an added attraction. For male viewers these films could even be considered recruitment and training films.

There were also war comedies. The diminutive comedian Heinz Rühmann, who began his career in Weimar, starred in *Quax, der Bruchpilot* (*Quax the Crash Pilot*) (1941, after Munich a sequel was made). Though courting disaster while getting his laughs, he triumphs (for Germany) in the end when he learns to submit to authority, becomes a good pilot and even an instructor. Even the 'little man' could become a hero, in this case a 'petit bourgeois hero'.[43]

After the invasion of the Soviet Union in June 1941, feature films began to match military events more closely.[44] The Bolshevik threat, having disappeared for twenty-two months, now surfaced in films such as Karl Ritter's Soviet espionage film, *GPU*. His earlier *Legion Condor*, about the German contingent in the Spanish Civil War, had been caught out by the Nazi–Soviet pact. In late August 1939 while on the set he was informed that the film now faced problems with the censor; after the invasion of Poland, work on the film stopped altogether.[45] Another anti-Russian film that he had just completed, *Kadetten* (*Cadets*), had been selected for a gala showing at the Nuremberg party rally on 5 September 1939. It had to be withdrawn for the same reason, but was eventually released after the invasion of the Soviet Union and had its première in Danzig in 1941.[46]

Up to December 1941, when the Germans failed to take Moscow and the US entered the war, Germany appeared invincible. Once the war continued longer than expected and a final military victory remained out of reach, films were also needed to suggest persistence and the importance of leadership. Harlan's *Der grosse König* (*The Great King*) did both. Reviving the '*Fridericus*' genre, it brought back to the screen the now elderly Otto Gebühr, who had been impersonating Frederick in most of the '*Fridericus*' films since the silent era. The leader was great, not by virtue of being a Hohenzollern, but by virtue of his actions. Unlike other Hohenzollerns Frederick the Great, happened to be a man of action too. Goebbels mentioned the film in April 1940, but the première did not take place until almost two years later, in early March 1942.[47] By then the war with the Soviet Union had begun. Set during the Seven Years War when the Prussians were fighting the Austrians, the film was also anti-Austrian, which suggests that it might not have helped morale in the *Ostmark* (Austria). But Prussia only won the battle of Schweidnitz (1762) with the help of a Russian general acting against the orders of his new queen, Catherine the Great. Since Germany was now at war with the Soviet Union, history had to be rewritten. When Harlan told Paul Wegener, the actor playing the Russian general, that this would involve more days' filming, Wegener was unconcerned, having done the number of days stipulated in his contract, he would receive additional remuneration. Harlan quotes his reply in the Berlin dialect: 'I couldn't care less what the limping Mickey Mouse (*hinkende Mickymaus*) wants'.[48]

Keeping up morale on the home front was important, as it was for other countries in the war. Once bombing began to take its toll the home front began to share some of the dangers which those at the front had become accustomed to. Conversely, those at the front now had an additional worry, namely the safety of their loved ones on the home front.

Die grosse Liebe, a *Staatsauftrag* film, opened in June 1942 at Berlin's largest cinema, the Ufa-Palast am Zoo, and proved to be the most successful of all the *Staatsauftrag* films, ranking first at the box office in the period 1940–42 and grossing RM27.2 million. It starred a leading member of the German film industry, the popular Swedish singer and actress Zarah Leander, who had made her debut in German films in 1937. A star of 1930s melodramas, several of them directed by Detlef Sierck (who left for Hollywood in 1937 to become Douglas Sirk), she made twelve films in all during the Third Reich.

Leander always played a woman with a past, and usually a singer. Her deep, heavy voice proved unattractive to some diehard Nazis for whom it was insufficiently feminine.[49] In *Die grosse Liebe* she plays a popular singer, Hanna, who falls in love with Paul, a Luftwaffe officer, played by the bland and handsome Viktor Staal. The film is not really about him but about her, with the home front at the centre, though thanks to the heroine's occupation the military are not wholly absent. They are shown being entertained by Hanna, enabling audiences to see them in a pleasant setting rather than in the act of fighting, by this date a safer proposition. Leander's songs raised Wehrmacht morale and that of cinema audiences who, while watching her, escaped the realities of the war: two weeks before the première the RAF had reduced central Cologne to rubble within ninety minutes. Via the vehicle of a love story, audiences are instructed about correct behaviour during wartime and the need to make personal sacrifices, not dissimilar to *Wunschkonzert* eighteen months previously. Newsreel footage is used on three occasions, the last of which shows a Stuka dogfight, but soon it becomes apparent that it is a cinema audience which is watching a newsreel of the dogfight. Also now included is a sequence set in a bomb shelter during an air raid with everyone behaving impeccably. A true *Volksgemeinschaft*: no grumbling; everyone pulls together.

After a few happy days together, Paul is called for duty. Hanna decides to continue with her profession, hoping to find him when, as part of the Propaganda Ministry's special entertainment unit, she next sings in Paris for the German troops. Cut from the post-war version are shots of the Waffen-SS linking arms and singing along with her.[50] Eventually she finds Paul in Rome; they decide to marry; then unofficially he learns from a comrade that they must make themselves available for duty. Hanna puts her foot down, but he, being a man and a German officer, takes no notice. He returns to the front, though officially he has not yet been ordered to do so, thus acting *beyond* the call of duty. After she sees newsreel shots of the invasion of the Soviet Union, she understands the reason for his sudden departure and relents. She has begun to think beyond her mere personal happiness. The couple are only reunited once she hears from him that he has been lightly wounded and is recovering in a military hospital.

Hanna's accompanist is also in love with her. He composes songs which punctuate the turning points in the story. The songs were actually composed by Bruno Balz while in a Gestapo prison, his release apparently facilitated by another film composer, Michael Jary.[51] The lyrics are significant. In Paris she sings the newly composed, '*Davon geht die Welt nicht unter*' ('The world will not go under'); for world read Germany. As her love grows, it becomes *die grosse Liebe*, that is a love both great and large, and sufficiently strong to withstand changes in military and personal fortunes. That a miracle may be needed becomes clear in another newly composed song: '*Ich weiss, es wird einmal ein Wunder geschehen*', ('I know one day a miracle will happen'). Once reunited in the military hospital the couple hope that their marriage can take place but look skywards for reassurance as planes fly overhead: personal happiness remains subordinate to the needs of war, a message Hanna has now taken to heart, as should female members of the audience. For male members, especially those in the military, the message was slightly different. Now they are not only fighting for the higher cause, Germany, but also for their women at home and thus for personal happiness, an admission that the Fatherland on its own no longer provided sufficient motivation. In contrast to *Wunschkonzert*, which happily combined home front with war front, *Die grosse Liebe* does not show fighting, an admission that militarily things were no longer going well.

Die grosse Liebe was Leander's penultimate film; her last was *Damals* (*Back Then*). The highest-paid actress and the highest-paid individual in the film industry, she commanded the astronomical fee of RM400,000 per year, lavish even by today's (German) standards (the Reichsfilmintendant was only paid RM18,000).[52] She also insisted that her director must be Rolf Hansen, who had run foul of the Propaganda Ministry in early 1939 when his film *Das Leben könnte so schön sein* was banned by Goebbels.[53] Goebbels had wanted Leander made a *Staatsschauspielerin* (State actress) but Hitler was opposed to this since she had refused to take out German citizenship.[54] While making *Damals* she learned that 53% of her salary had not been paid into her Swedish bank account as stipulated in her generous contract. This led to a confrontation with Goebbels. After a bombing raid in early 1943, which damaged her Berlin home, she decided to return to her native (and neutral) Sweden to sit out the war. *Damals* was pulled from the cinema five weeks after its première.[55] For the last two years of the war there were no Leander films to raise morale.

From 1943 onwards the proportion of propaganda films fell from 14% to approximately 8%.[56] *Die Degenhardts* (*The Degenhardts*) is one of the few from 1944 and focuses on the impact of the war on a family living in Lübeck. Directed by Werner Klinger for Tobis, it had its première shortly after D-Day, on 6 July 1944 in Lübeck which had been heavily bombed. It stars Heinrich George as a paterfamilias who had fought in the First World War. He is unreconciled to his son's socially inferior wife and proud of his town hall job, which, however, he soon loses because of his age. Devastated by his loss of status, he pretends to go to work, but soon, thanks to the war and civil destruction, gets his old job back and becomes reconciled to his son, though he loses another (not seen on screen, since he is far away on the high seas) – a happy end of sorts, given the year. Civil destruction is shown, its purpose being to rally audiences against Allied bombing raids. German cultural achievements are emphasized: Hanseatic architecture as well as the dance of death frieze in St Mary's church dating from 1452 and painted in the aftermath of the Black Death. The family also gathers in that church, where one son plays the organ for a performance of Haydn's 'Creation'. But in this montage sequence, bombs also rain down on Germany's cultural heritage while a radio broadcast denounces the enemy's barbarity. (The church had been destroyed by British bombs in 1942.) Was this what audiences wanted to see? The film did not fare well at the box office. By the autumn of 1944 the Propaganda Ministry called for the revival of nationalist films.[57]

Helmut Käutner's films are technically accomplished, especially in their use of the mobile camera and of light and shadow. They emphasize the private over the political, his characters usually seeking personal happiness. For this reason, on the surface at least, they seem untainted by Nazi ideology, which may account for the director's post-war reputation.[58] Uniquely, Käutner also either wrote or co-authored all the scripts of the nine films he made during the Third Reich.[59] The political is absent from most of his films, though not from an earlier one, *Auf wiedersehn Franziska* (1941), where the private and the political eventually come together.[60] The spirited Franziska may not have been the ideal Nazi *Hausfrau* for having a child outside of marriage, but she does encourage her future husband after he is drafted into a military unit involved in making newsreels.[61]

Käutner's other films, on the surface, focus on the personal. *Romanze in Moll* (*Romance in a Minor Key*) (1943), based on a Guy de Maupassant story about marital infidelity, is set in the late nineteenth century, remote from the present day. The subject, however, was not necessarily appropriate for 1943, even if the heroine behaves correctly, paying for her infidelity by committing suicide; in the story she dies of natural causes. Goebbels initially banned the film's domestic release, but allowed it to be shown in occupied territories and, surprisingly, also at the front, but not within Germany itself. He then relented. The film won best foreign film prize at Stockholm in 1944, the only Third Reich film to do so.[62] Despite Goebbels's reservations, the story is told within certain constraints. A loveless marriage may be at the centre, but the heroine's bid for happiness through an extramarital affair is doomed. The lover is a composer, played sympathetically by Ferdinand Marian, doubtless in a bid to avoid typecasting. His presence, however, ensures that there can be no happy end. Not only script, direction, acting and music delivered meaning, but also casting. Käutner dared not go too far; consequently he has been accused of creating 'illusions of escapism'.[63] On the other hand, extramarital affairs which ended happily were hardly to be found on the screen in other countries at this time.

Käutner was also responsible for two films made towards the end of the war that suggested better times and also emphasized a private world. *Grosse Freiheit, Nr. 7* (1944) was made in colour and set in Hamburg in the rough sailors' quarter of St Pauli; the harbour scenes were filmed in a heavily bombed area of Hamburg, which demand skilled camera work.[64] It starred the highly paid middle-aged Hans Albers in a sensitive portrayal of a former sailor who sings for his living. Banished from the film is any trace of the Third Reich; none of the characters would have made good Nazis; and Nazis would have spurned the clubs of St Pauli. Nevertheless, at the end the hero decides to join his sailor friends when they set sail. On the soundtrack is the folksong '*Muss I denn*', which had also been used in Käutner's only 'political' film, *Auf Wiedersehn, Franziska*.[65] It was also used in other films such as *Morgenrot* to remind audiences that men must do their duty and leave women behind, though the actual folksong alluded to men having to leave the village to find work. The words play with the idea that men will remain faithful and one day will return, reinforcing a political message that parting is necessary and, by implication, fighting is too. This film was deemed unfit for German audiences and opened in Prague on 15 December 1944.[66]

The lyrical *Unter den Brücken* (Under the Bridges) (in black and white), Käutner's last film made during the Third Reich, is set in contemporary Berlin. The influence of the French film *L'Atalante* (1932) is apparent.[67] A barge negotiates the canals of the Babelsburg studios in a make-believe Berlin, while outside in the real Berlin the bridges had been destroyed by Allied bombing; actors had to contend with bombing on a daily basis, making their journey to the studio hazardous. Absent is any talk of duty. Though set in the present, there is no indication that a war is going on. When the characters peruse a newspaper, we see nothing to suggest that this is the Third Reich. By banishing the war, the promise of better days is implicit while offering 'a false sense of normalcy' and a 'temporary illusion'.[68] Doubtless such escapism would have helped raise morale had the film been ready in time. It passed the censor but too late to be shown, and finally opened in Germany only in 1950.

Colour films were a rarity. Germany could not compete with Hollywood's Technicolor and had to make do with a German product, Agfacolor, which produced more natural colours but had not reached the stage of development of the faster Technicolor. Technicolor sequences in feature film were first used in the American-made *The House of Rothschild* (1934), which concluded with a ballroom scene in colour. But the breakthrough came the following year with the first Hollywood feature film completely in colour, *Becky Sharp* (1935), made in three-strip Technicolor, a process which involved three films running through the huge camera, each recording one of the primary colours.[69] Two years later, six colour feature films had been made and in 1938 twelve, in addition to animated films and black-and-white feature films with colour sequences. Britain also began producing films in Technicolor: a British documentary on the coronation had appeared in colour in 1937, though processed in Hollywood. Technicolor established a laboratory in West Drayton just outside London, which became operational in 1938. Several British feature films soon followed via United Artists and Alexander Korda. The real Technicolor breakthrough however came with *Gone with the Wind* which was made with a new, improved Technicolor process. It had its première in December 1939.

Goebbels was keen that Germany should make colour feature films and had obtained a copy of *Gone with the Wind*, his only regret being that it was without subtitles. He had nothing but praise for the film:

> the colour was splendid, the effect stirring ... The crowd scenes are fantastically done. A great achievement for the Americans. One needs to see it several times. We should use it as an example and work.[70]

In the early 1930s Ufa had developed its own two-colour process (Ufa-color) and made the first German colour film, the short *Bunte Tierwelt* (*The Wonderful Animal World*), which had its première during the Weimar period, on New Year's Eve 1931. I.G. Farben developed the three-colour Agfacolor process, which then made colour feature films possible. In 1938 Ufa and Agfa signed a contract to cooperate, and the Neubabelsberg film studio got its state-of-the-art colour film laboratory. It was still some time, however, before the laboratory had improved the colour quality sufficiently to enable its use in a feature film.

The first German colour feature film was a musical (operetta), *Frauen sind doch Bessere Diplomaten* (*Women Do Make Better Diplomats*), which opened on 31 October 1941. A frothy Ufa vehicle for the Hungarian-born dancer and singer Marika Rökk, who was not a patch on any of her Hollywood counterparts, it was directed by her husband, Georg Jacoby, who also directed another Agfacolour musical revue for Ufa which opened in the summer of 1944: *Die Frau meiner Träume* (*The Woman of My Dreams*). The first colour film took more than two years to make. Work began in July 1939, before the invasion of Poland, while the première took place when the war against the Soviet Union was well underway (October 1941). The studio's slogan was: 'When the film is done, the war will be over, too.'[71] Rökk recounted the difficulties of filming in colour: intense heat, actors even getting burnt and having to wear sunglasses till the clapper fell.[72] The technicians kept tinkering with improvements to shooting with colour film, which partly accounted for the delay. Another reason was the need to re-shoot some sequences because one actor in a supporting role, Karl Stephanek, defected to London to broadcast from there.[73] Taking longer than any other film in the history of Ufa – Riefenstahl's *Tiefland* which was black and white was not made by Ufa – it had by November 1944 (three years after opening) recouped its production costs three times over.[74]

The twenty-fifth anniversary of the large film conglomerate Ufa, which was reorganized into Ufi as a holding company in 1943, was celebrated with an escapist Agfacolor extravaganza, *Münchhausen*, based on the adventures of Baron Münchhausen. Opening shortly after the battle of Stalingrad and directed by Josef von Baky, with Albers playing Münchhausen, it had Ferdinand Marian in a cameo role as Cagliostro. Erich Kästner wrote the script under a pseudonym, Berthold Bürger, since he was a banned writer. Fritz Hippler arranged this and gave it as one reason for his downfall in 1943, though on other occasions he found other reasons.[75] Bringing in a banned writer for this star-studded vehicle might be seen as a sign of desperation; it was also an indication of the importance attached to the anniversary special.

Colour feature film was a war that Hollywood won, though once the war was over they were keen to obtain Agfacolour, for by then interest had grown in other film processes. In all, only nine colour films had their premières during the Third Reich, though at the war's end seven were still in production.[76] Jacoby made two films; a less well-known director, Volker von Collande, made the long forgotten *Das Bad auf der Tennone* (*The Bathing Place on the Tennone*) (1943). Käutner was also privileged to make one colour film, *Grosse Freiheit, Nummer 7* though, as mentioned earlier, it opened in Prague, and was not allowed to open in Germany.

As an indication of his privileged position as director, Harlan made four of the nine colour films: *Die goldene Stadt*, the second colour film (1942); the literary adaptation *Immensee* (December 1943); the melodrama, *Opfergang*, about a *ménage à trois* set in contemporary Hamburg, which appeared in December 1944; and *Kolberg* which opened in January 1945.

Die goldene Stadt opened in late November 1942. An anti-Czech melodrama about a country girl who goes to the big or 'golden' city (Prague), it loosely belonged to the *Heimat* genre, in that the city constitutes the 'other'.[77] Good Germans reside in the *Heimat* (by definition a city is never a *Heimat*) and, in this case, work the farm, while in the city, live inferior and degenerate Czechs. The country girl (with a German father and Czech mother), in defiance of her father, goes to the city to her aunt. Her male cousin, a dissolute Czech, gets her pregnant.

Returning home, she commits suicide, as her unhappy mother had earlier, and in the same manner, by drowning in a swamp. Drowning in a swamp was a fate meted out to wayward Germans or half-Germans, as in the 1935 film *Friesennot* (*Friesians in Peril*), re-released a year before this film under the new title *Dorf im roten Sturm* (*Village in the Red Storm*) after the invasion of the Soviet Union.[78]

Die goldene Stadt was based on a play, *Der Gigant* (*The Giant*), by Richard Billinger in which there had been no ethnic difference, all members of the family being German. There had also been no unhappy ending since the girl returned to live on the farm with her illegitimate offspring. (Billinger, who came from the same part of Austria as Hitler, had been sympathetic to the Nazi cause, though his homosexuality complicated matters).[79]

In this film the city–country conflict was racialized, the heroine is provided with a Czech mother. As befits Nazi misogyny, it is always the mother's origins, not the father's, which are tainted. Not everyone from the city, however, is bad: the engineer who comes to drain the swamps is a sympathetic character who understands rural problems. The engineer occupied a special place in Nazi thinking. Though emphasizing tradition and rejecting Weimar 'Jewish' modernity, Nazis could not oppose modern technology *tout court*, since it was needed to strengthen Germany's economic and military position. This accounts for some of the ambiguities inherent in the Nazi embrace of modernity.[80] Nevertheless, this film coincided with a series of films concerned with the exodus from farming communities.[81] Agriculture had become even more important in wartime, and women were not expected to desert, especially when men were at the front.

The father, played by Eugen Klöpfer, Söderbaum's father in *Jud Süss*, is a harsh character; his treatment of his daughter verging on the sadistic, not untypical of how young females are treated in Harlan films. The script underwent many changes: Goebbels interfered to ensure that the girl died at the end.[82] At one point the father justifies his mistreatment of his daughter on the grounds that she bore a close resemblance to her unfortunate (and wayward) mother. The poor girl is a victim: the housekeeper who encouraged her to go to the city becomes engaged to her father and joins in persecuting her. After his daughter dies, her father decides to bequeath his property to the neighbouring farmer to whom she had been engaged. 'Blood and Soil', or *Blut und Boden*, belonged to the *völkisch* ideology espoused by the Nazis; films promoting it were often referred to as '*Blubo*' films. In such films the patriarch usually wins. In this case, however, the father's final decision suggests that *Boden* (soil) has triumphed over *Blut* (blood), additional evidence, were that necessary, of the dispensability of females, since the farm will go to someone not blood-related. There are echoes here of the Nazi opposition to the hereditarian principle, which in this case has not targeted the aristocracy or the monarch, but a blood relative (female) who has committed *Rassenschande*.

The farmer bequeathed his farm to the most suited person, just as the Nazis were most suited to running the state.

Söderbaum drowned in so many Harlan films that she earned herself the soubriquet the *Reichswasserleiche* (the Reich's drowned corpse). To women the film's message, at a time when many were not content to remain on the farm, was unmistakable: stay at home and do as father says.[83] Given the heroine's tainted origins, audiences should not have expected a happy end. But since Söderbaum was very popular, some may have felt she deserved better. *Die goldene Stadt* won a prize at the Venice Film Festival for its colour cinematography; Söderbaum also won an award for her acting. The film prize may have been for the novelty of a European colour film; the acting prize may have been an act of kindness towards the wife of the leading film director of Italy's wartime ally.

To cut costs, the next two Harlan colour films were made as a double production, one following the other in a colour-adapted studio. Both starred Söderbaum but the premières were almost a year apart (late 1943 and 1944). *Immensee*, Harlan's literary adaptation of a Theodor Storm novella, faced a number of problems including bad weather which affected outdoor filming.[84] It therefore took longer to make than the melodrama, *Opfergang*, another of Harlan's literary adaptations. But *Opfergang* took longer to come to the screen because it was subject to script changes due to the Söderbaum character having an affair with a married man.[85] In 1944 adultery could not be seen to be rewarded.[86] Goebbels informed Harlan that many soldiers had deserted because they believed their wives were deceiving them.[87] Thus the Söderbaum character is subjected to a lingering death though displays moral qualities in wanting her lover to be reunited with his wife. The film was also billed as an achievement for managing to appear in the sixth year of the war.[88]

Harlan's last colour film was the Agfacolor blockbuster costume drama, and Third Reich swansong, *Kolberg*, a response to Goebbels's call for total war and total sacrifice by the German people. As usual, the titles announced that the film was based on history, and as usual it was history in the service of the Nazis. It also included an unusual piece of information, namely the date on which the film *began*: 'this film was written and begun in the year 1942'. That was to disguise the fact that the film was a response to the worsening military situation: Stalingrad, the defeat of the *Afrikakorps* and the failure of the Luftwaffe to protect German cities.[89] And worse was soon to come, for that summer the RAF firebombed Hamburg, causing the loss of 50,000 lives.

Despite these events, the belief that the war was being lost had not yet taken hold. That took place later, nearer to the film's première than to its launch. Two-thirds of the German population lived outside the heavily bombed cities; rationing was only introduced in the autumn and winter of 1944, after the D-Day landings and the attempt on Hitler's life. Allied bombing increased: three weeks before *Kolberg* opened, Nuremberg's medieval old town was destroyed; two weeks after it opened, Dresden was bombed with the loss of more than 30,000 lives. Victor Klemperer, a Dresden resident and avid cinema-goer, makes clear that *Kolberg* would have had difficulty reaching the audience for which it was intended. On 6 February 1945, one week before the Dresden bombing, he recorded:

> Since yesterday all cinemas have been shut. Officially, and it's very likely, because of lack of coal. Frau Stühler thinks, to avoid people gathering. But I don't know: cinema is a distraction: reflection and anger grow where distraction and gathering together are absent.[90]

By the time the extravaganza was ready, many German cinemas had been destroyed, including Ufa's flagship Berlin cinema since 1919, the Ufa-Palast am Zoo. In a directive dated 29 May 1940, Goebbels had managed to set up a system of air-raid shelters in the cinemas themselves, but now few cinemas were in use or even in existence.[91] According to the Stockholm correspondent for the *Daily Telegraph and Morning Post* in early January 1945, a recently arrived German from Berlin reported that all but thirty-one of Berlin's four hundred cinemas had been put out of action. In the summer of 1944 ninety-six cinemas were still open and in the summer of 1943 two hundred. 'Schools now closed for the duration are being converted into film theatres,' as were theatres. 'Cinema is the only amusement left ... and cinemas the only warm places above ground,' despite not having heating. Though cinemas had their own shelters, generally they were not as safe as the public shelters and the performance stopped immediately the siren went off inside the cinema. Queues formed from early in the day.[92] Given these problems, *Kolberg* had a potential rather than actual audience, though its subject matter hardly counted as distraction.

Historic Kolberg was a Baltic fortress town whose Prussian inhabitants had held out against a French siege during the Napoleonic wars.[93] Though a minor incident during the war, its story was now intended by way of a parable to rally German audiences. Goebbels spelled out the message when commissioning Harlan: 'the film's purpose is to show that a people united at home and at the front will overcome any enemy.'[94] Film treatments had been presented prior to the outbreak of the war.[95] A play on the subject by Nobel Prize winner Paul Heyse had appeared on the eve of German unification in 1868 and was republished during the First World War. But since his mother had been Jewish, no reference was made to this possible source.[96] After Stalingrad, however, Goebbels's commission had an added urgency, though he was intent on obscuring the link. Discussions with the director took place in May 1943, by which time Harlan had in eight days produced a 'brilliant outline'; he would start filming at the end of June and optimistically hoped to have the film ready by Christmas 1943.[97] His contract was dated 1 June 1943, but another twenty months passed before the première on 30 January 1945, the twelfth anniversary of the Nazi takeover.

It starred yet again Söderbaum as Maria, and Heinrich George in familiar role as paterfamilias, though in this case more *in loco parentis*. He plays Joachim Nettelbeck, the town's spokesman (*Bürgerrepresentant*) who rallies the town (and the audience) and opposes the collaborationist town commander, Loucadou (Paul Wegener). 'Better to die in the rubble than capitulate!', Nettelbeck declares. He sends Maria on a secret mission to the Prussian Queen Luise (played by the cool and lovely Irene Meyerhoff – the betrayed wife in *Opfergang*) to request a dynamic commander for Kolberg. Nettelbeck praises Maria for her bravery. She has given her all, he tells her, which has not been in vain, for 'that which is great is always born in pain: You are great, Maria! ... you have done your duty, have not been afraid of death. You have also triumphed ... Maria! You also.'

Not only were audiences being instructed about appropriate behaviour now that Germany was no longer victorious, but they were also being encouraged to believe that Germany could repeat Prussia's eventual triumph over the French. Moreover, there was emphasis on women's wartime role since it is Maria who acts as messenger, and the Prussian Queen who acts as intermediary. Unfortunately, there was a downside: Maria may be the heroine, but at the expense of her personal life. In contrast to *Die grosse Liebe*, renunciation is now the order of the day: her romance with her headstrong officer, Lieutenant Ferdinand von Schill, is doomed. Declaring his love for Maria, he announces that he will never marry a woman, as he is married to war. The historic Schill character had appeared on the screen before in both silent and sound versions. In the latter, *Die elf Schill'schen Offiziere* (*The eleven Schillish Officers*) (1932), a late Weimar nationalist film, Harlan had played one of the doomed officers shot by the French. Indeed Harlan had acted in other late Weimar nationalist films, *Yorck* and *Der Choral von Leuthen*.

Aside from having a heroine and an elderly civilian hero, *Kolberg* also has a military hero, the future Prussian general Gneisenau, then only a major (played by stage actor Horst Caspar, a *Mischling* second degree). He is the commander sent to Kolberg to prepare for the siege. The historic Gneisenau was subsequently instrumental in reforming the Prussian army, which ensured victory over the French seven years later. In the film's framing device, set in 1813 on the eve of the Wars of Liberation, it is he who relates the story of Kolberg to the Prussian king to persuade him of the marvels of patriotism, and in particular how the right attitude can save a hopeless situation, after which the story unfolds. The script makes Gneisenau younger than the king, though in fact, at fifty-three, he was ten years his senior. But the leader of the national uprising, the wave of the future, must, by definition, be seen to be younger than the hereditary ruler. By 1944 Hitler was already a year older than the historic Gneisenau; accuracy here was not Goebbels's concern.[98]

The Germans are depicted as heroic with the exception of the coward, a farmer's son, an artistic, gallicized type who once studied music in Strasbourg. His hysterical outbursts were, on Goebbels's order, truncated.[99] Goebbels also thought it prudent to order Harlan to delete long shelling sequences for fear they might demoralize viewers; finding them more suited to a film advocating pacifism.[100]

The cast of thousands, according to Harlan, included 187,000 Wehrmacht soldiers. At most, they would have been used for only a few days at a time. It is unlikely, however, that such numbers were actually used over the ten-month filming period; such numbers are also not evident in the completed film.[101] One might think that in 1943–44 German soldiers would have been better deployed fighting real rather than mock battles. Contrary to the mythology that has grown up around this film, however, the soldier extras were not taken from real battles.[102] By the autumn of 1944, by which time the filming of the battle scenes had been completed, the military had become so overstretched that the *Volkssturm* was formed to mobilize a civilian defence force of over-age or under-age males (under sixteen or over sixty).

Shooting began in October 1943; some scenes were being re-shot as late as July 1944.[103] A rough cut was ready for viewing by 30 November 1944 and seen by Goebbels the following day.[104] He wanted further cuts and even discussed this with Hitler. The latter was 'moved … almost to the point of tears', Goebbels recorded, and wanted the film released 'as quickly as possible'.[105] Harlan was forced to make changes to the script, which required additional filming, and was still incorporating Goebbels's changes, even to the dialogue, as late as 7 December when he agreed to do two to three days' additional filming.[106] Still Goebbels was dissatisfied with the final version screened on 23 December. In his view Harlan, had made matters worse, and he wanted the film recut, this time by director Wolfgang Liebeneiner, now head of Ufa, a task which Liebeneiner accomplished by 3 January 1945.[107]

Ensuring that copies of the completed film were available within five weeks posed another problem: colour film copies normally took three months. The Ministry insisted that work be done during the Christmas period and at weekends so as to enable the première to take place on 30 January.[108] Parallel viewings were to be coordinated in two Berlin cinemas as well as in a cut-off Atlantic base to make certain of a 'psychologically outstanding impact'.[109]

Twelve days before the première it was noted that only two copies of the film would definitely be available by 30 January, though every effort was being made to produce a third copy by 29 January.[110] Aside from Goebbels, Hitler and Reichsmarschall Hermann Goering were also involved in the decision to airlift a copy in a race against time. Six days later, another problem became apparent. The Luftwaffe made clear that they could not guarantee a specific delivery date unless an extra plane was made available. This was dependent on a personal order from Goering, which was thought unlikely to be forthcoming.[111] However, approval was granted, as revealed by the comments pencilled in on the letter's margins: 'We have spoken with the Führer. Yes, the plane must fly'.[112]

By 26 January no decision had been taken as to which base it would be to: either Saint-Nazaire or La Rochelle, depending on the weather and enemy flights. Two couriers were to be despatched with the film reels (they weighed eighty pounds) for take-off from western Germany (the Hanau area) to fly over enemy territory. Success, came the warning, was by no means assured.[113]

A successful drop was made, however, over the Atlantic fortress of La Rochelle, a submarine haven and the so-called 'Western Wall', now behind enemy lines and under British bombardment. The fortress commander, Vice-Admiral Schirwitz, gave his thanks on radio. Greatly impressed by the heroic stand at Kolberg, he declared his commitment to repeating the feat.[114] La Rochelle held out to the end of the war, though more due to geography than any inspiration from the film.

Five weeks after *Kolberg*'s première, Kolberg itself was surrounded by Soviet troops. In just over two weeks they took Kolberg, achieving what the French in the previous century had failed to do. The Red Army soon reached the Oder; the Americans were closing in from the west. Those cinema-goers able to view *Kolberg* were unlikely, or unwilling, to take comfort from the words of Nettelbeck to Gneisenau: 'We will sooner be buried under the ruins, than surrender,' nor from Gneisenau's reply: 'Now we can all die together.'

13

Film and the 'Final Solution'

If feature film offered audiences the opportunity to escape the war, newsreels did not. Feature films were only part of the cinema programme, and from late 1938 onwards were always screened in conjunction with a newsreel, indeed were always preceded by a newsreel and a *Kulturfilm* (educational short), the latter compulsory since 1934. Goebbels had shown little interest in newsreels and had been unwilling to introduce state- or party-produced newsreels, though that policy had the advantage of concealing the extent of his control. Newsreels continued to be produced by the various film companies.[1]

Things changed at the time of the Munich agreement. In preparation for war, PK units (*Propagandakompanie*) were up set within the Wehrmacht and integrated into the military, the men receiving some military training. Many, in previous civilian life, had been cameramen, journalists or editors. Their brief was to send back footage for the exclusive use of the Propaganda Ministry. Newsreels now helped prepare the German public for war.[2]

Once war began, there was an organizational shake-up. Goebbels assumed full control, and the four existing German newsreel companies were merged into the *Deutsche Wochenschau* (German Newsreel). The number of prints in circulation was also increased from about 400 in 1939 to 2,400 by 1943.[3] Earlier in the 1930s it had taken up to sixteen weeks for newsreels to reach rural areas, hardly making them topical.[4]

Extended to forty minutes in May 1940, the newsreels began to occupy significant space in the cinema programme. Feature films were just over double that length, though doubtless remaining the main attraction which drew in audiences. Even when escapist, they were still a part of a cinema programme, in which the newsreels prevented audiences from escaping the war. On occasion, the newsreel even reinforced a message in the feature film.

Newsreels helped sustain enthusiasm for the war. Audiences were attracted by the dynamic, often spectacular footage, shot from tanks or planes with advanced camera equipment. In contrast to British or American newsreels, direct combat was often shown, shot by daredevil cameramen, many of whom lost their lives. Their names appeared in the credits and, on occasion, when killed on duty, marked with a cross. By October 1943 sixty-two cameramen had either been killed in combat or were missing, and fifty-seven had been wounded.[5] Despite this reference to death, it has been claimed that a peculiarity of Nazi propaganda was the abolition from all newsreels of images of death.[6] A Goebbels directive dated 10 June 1940 stipulated that realistic representations likely to arouse a horror of war were to be avoided.[7] Images of death, however, were not totally abolished: though German corpses were unacceptable, enemy corpses were not. German deaths could be alluded to indirectly: soldiers' funerals were shown, though obviously most German soldiers did not have funerals.[8]

German newsreels also differed from British and American newsreels in that the word counted for less. They were far more cinematic, for which they received (albeit reluctant) praise from Siegfried Kracauer, caught between aesthetics and politics. Having recently arrived in the US from France, he was involved in a project at the Museum of Modern Art which examined the early German wartime newsreels. In his estimate, words accompanied only a third of the shots, in contrast to American newsreels where they accompanied roughly 80 to 90 per cent.[9] Graham Greene, the film critic for the *Spectator*, also had nothing but praise for the German newsreels which he viewed shortly after the outbreak of war, finding them, in contrast to the British newsreel, 'beautifully shot and well-staged'.[10] As in the Riefenstahl documentaries, music was very important (folk song, classical music, military marches) and could be considered another voice. Closely matched to the image, music also ensured that the message was delivered in a non-verbal manner. Live sound, of equipment, explosions or the tramp of marching feet, was also significant. Often at key points the music stopped to allow for the sounds of battle.[11] In purely cinematic terms, the *Deutsche Wochenschau* was state-of-the-art, which *cinéastes* on the Allied side acknowledged.

Fritz Hippler, who had been involved with newsreels since 1935, was made head of *Deutsche Wochenschau* in 1940. Given the minor role played by the narrator in the German newsreel, in contrast to the hectoring voice in *Der ewige Jude* which Hippler had directed, he should not be credited with the newsreel's cinematic achievements. In Kracauer's view, the different parts of the newsreel belonged to an organic whole: the same message, namely that of a victorious Germany under Nazi rule, being repeated in the different items.[12] Cinematic quality and the careful calibration of the message could not, however, be divorced from context. The medium was not the message. The newsreels worked as long as Germany was winning.

Goebbels was closely involved with newsreel production, viewing all the films: the footage first without sound, and then the rough cut.[13] But he did not have a completely free hand. Hitler demanded that victories be proclaimed when they had not occurred, as in the Battle of Moscow in December 1941.[14] He also had the final cut, which he exercised personally until 1942, after which he left it to his military advisers at his headquarters.[15] He also did not want to be filmed with original sound, nor with sufficient light at his headquarters, which resulted in dark images.[16] Much to Goebbels's annoyance, the Führer was even reluctant to be filmed. Finally, as the war went badly wrong, he was rarely seen, though he managed to put in an appearance after the 20 July plot on his life.

In the spring of 1943 the Germans discovered in the Katyn forest over 40,000 bodies of Polish soldiers and officers executed by the Soviet army in April 1940. This provided an opportunity to sow discord amongst the allies with anti-Bolshevik propaganda.[17] Goebbels was keen to screen the footage showing the bodies being dug up. He also blamed the Jews, giving more emphasis to Jewish 'blood guilt' than to Bolshevik.[18] But he was stopped by Hitler, or to be precise by staff at his headquarters, on the grounds that this would upset German audiences.[19] This footage, however, was screened in a newsreel version compiled for the occupied countries, the *Auslandstonwoche* (*Foreign Weekly Newsreel*), evidence that newsreels intended for German audiences could differ from those intended for occupied and neutral countries.[20] This was not the only example of Hitler's interventions: he prevented Goebbels from screening the destruction of German cities by Allied bombing.[21]

Once it became apparent that the war would not result in a rapid German victory, the newsreels began to lose their appeal. This first became evident in late October 1941 with an item on the building of winter quarters on the Eastern Front.[22] In January 1942, Goebbels noted the decline in applause for the *Wochenschau*.[23] People also began hovering outside cinemas, waiting for the feature to begin before entering. From the time of Stalingrad, and on Goebbels's orders, cinema-goers were refused entry to cinemas once the programme had begun. Doors were often locked.[24] By the spring of 1943, Goebbels mentioned that problems with the newsreels were increasing the longer the war continued.[25]

The deportation of German Jews began as early as January 1940 (from Stettin (Szczecin) and Schneidemühl (now Pila on the Baltic) but were discontinued a few months later. In October 1940 in a single night all the Jews of western Germany (Baden, the Saar and the Palatinate) were deported to Camp Gers in western France, and later to the East. From September 1941 German Jews were required to wear the yellow star, and from that autumn Jewish emigration from Germany was stopped. After that the deportation of all German Jews began on a systematic basis. The majority were sent to ghettos in the East (to Łódź, Warsaw, Riga, Kovno and Minsk) where the *Einsatzgruppen* were already at work; many were liquidated on arrival. Those who were not were later sent to Auschwitz or, if 'privileged', to the Theresienstadt camp 'ghetto'. Preparations for extermination camps in Poland were well underway when Pearl Harbor was bombed in December. That brought the US into the war: after the US declared war on Japan, Germany's ally, Germany was forced to declare war on the US. Extermination camps were intended to replace on-the-spot killings by mobile units on the

Eastern Front after the attack on the Soviet Union. The Wannsee Conference of January 1942, chaired by Reinhard Heydrich, coordinated these efforts.

After the decision was taken to exterminate the Jews – which despite disagreement about the dating certainly occurred by the end of 1941 and was implemented on a systematic basis shortly thereafter – the Jews disappeared completely from the newsreels. Hitherto they had only featured marginally. Early in the war a few newsreels contained items showing Jews being forced to work: in Łódź (1939), in Belgrade and in Riga (1941) and work brigades of Soviet Jews at a location not specified.[26] A special newsreel report included an item showing the capture of a Yugoslav officer of Jewish origin, doubtless intended to illustrate the racial failings of the Yugoslav army, similar to attacks on the French and British for employing colonial troops.[27] The war with the Soviet Union made possible once again the linking of Jews with Bolshevism. As a consequence, in the summer of 1941, Jews appeared in several newsreel items;[28] one newsreel even contained two items on Jews (the Jewish inhabitants marching to a collection camp and a labour brigade of Jews).[29] Given the wealth of material, there were still surprisingly few items. After 1941 there were no further newsreel items either for German audiences or for non-German audiences, aside from one reference in a Polish newsreel of 1942.[30] From 1942 onwards German audiences saw no references to Jews in any newsreels.

A sequel to *Der ewige Jude* had been planned, based on the enormous amount of footage shot in the Warsaw ghetto in 1940, 1941 and even 1942. Probably a completely edited film was made of which some sequences survive though no soundtrack. The film was never distributed. Sections were used in newsreels and other films. The horrors of ghetto life were contrasted with lavish Jewish living also inside the ghetto, which was not dissimilar to photographs used to contrast rich with poor Jews (some staged), to show that Jews did not take care of their own people. Why this film was never completed is not known. Goebbels may have opposed its completion, on the grounds that it was too graphic and might arouse sympathy. In a German newsreel prepared for Poles, Polish labour battalions are shown demolishing buildings in the Lublin ghetto 'for hygienic reasons', while off camera the Jews were being marched away to the Belzec extermination camp.[31]

Germans could not plead ignorance of the Nazi persecution of the Jews, of the boycotts, the racial laws, the aryanization of property, arrests, concentration camps, emigration and deportation. Persecution was never secret; nor was deportation, though that might lead to the Jews being 'resettled', 'evacuated', 'removed' or even given 'special treatment'; Hitler's preferred term was 'transport of Jews'.[32] The 'Final Solution' of the so-called Jewish problem, however, was not made public.[33] The Nazi leadership intended the murder of European Jewry to be secret, in effect a 'state secret'. Though news did reach the Allies, details were not known, only reports that the Jews had disappeared.[34] Inside the Third Reich the 'Jewish Question' continued to be mentioned, though not its 'solution': extermination was the 'terrible secret'. And by late December 1942, Goebbels was even keen to 'get away from the embarrassing subject of the Jews'; it had become 'a delicate question' and was best not touched on at all.[35]

Given that the persecution of the Jews was not concealed from the public, indeed was widely publicized as part of a propaganda onslaught, the rarity of images of Jews in the newsreels is striking. One possible explanation is that sympathy might have been elicited were the enemy given a human face. In a feature film the director or the actor had greater control over the image, whereas in the newsreel, on occasion, the victim was even seen to smile, doubtless assuming this to be the correct response to the enemy cameraman.[36]

Yet conjuring up the Jewish enemy via the written or spoken word still remained acceptable. The 'Final Solution' may have been kept secret, but Nazi leaders did not desist from attacking Jews. To the very end Hitler, Goebbels, Goering and others, in their well-publicized speeches, kept blaming the Jews. Thus Hitler in a speech read out by Goebbels at the Berlin Sportpalast on 30 January 1942, the ninth anniversary of the Nazi takeover:

> I already stated on 1 September 1939 in the German Reichstag – and I refrain from over-hasty prophecies – that this war will not come to an end as the Jews imagine, with the extermination of the European-Aryan peoples, but that the result of this will be the annihilation of Jewry. For the first time the old Jewish law will now be applied: an eye for an eye, a tooth for a tooth.[37]

And again at the Sportpalast, this time Goering in early October 1942:

> This is not the Second World War, this is the Great Racial War. The meaning of this war, and the reason we are fighting out there, is to decide whether the German and Aryan will prevail or if the Jew will rule the world.[38]

Goebbels's 'Total War' speech also at the Sportpalast on 18 February 1943 proclaimed that only the Wehrmacht protected Germans from 'racial chaos'.[39] 'The goal of Bolshevism is the world revolution of the Jews,' which would bring chaos to the Reich and to Europe, for behind international Bolshevism lay their 'capitalist tyranny'.[40] He then played on the fears of a German defeat and rallied his audience:

> The Bolshevization of the Reich would bring the liquidation of our entire intelligentsia and leadership class ... and the working masses ... [would be forced to become] Bolshevik-Jewish slaves ... Behind the flooding Soviet divisions we already see the Jewish liquidation squads, and behind them the terror, the ghost of hungering millions, and European anarchy. Here international Jewry again shows itself to be the devilish ferment of decomposition enjoying a cynical satisfaction at dissolving the world into deepest

disorder and causing the disintegration of a culture thousands of years old, to which it
has never contributed. Thus we know the historical task which lies before us.[41]

A few days after the 'Total War' speech, on the anniversary of the founding of the
Nazi Party, Hitler's proclamation was read out and broadcast, another antisemitic
tirade against the 'Jewish Bolsheviks' of Moscow, supported by the Jewish bankers
of London and New York. The Reich would destroy the 'world Israelite coalition',
with Hitler repeating his threat that the war would not result in the annihilation
of the 'Aryan race, but will end with the destruction of European Jewry'.[42]

Two years later, at the time of Yalta (February 1945), Goebbels warned that
'every Russian, English, and American soldier is a mercenary of this race of
parasites and their world conspiracy, and in this war, not Europe but the Jews
will go to their destruction.'[43] The 'entire propaganda campaign following
Stalingrad', it has rightly been observed, 'was as much an anti-Jewish as an anti-
Bolshevik crusade'.[44] Victor Klemperer, who remained in Germany throughout
the war years as a Jew with 'privileged' status because he was married to an
'Aryan', felt this to be a 'Jewish War' rather than a war against Britain, France or
the US.[45]

Little of this was reflected in cinema, which is revealing about the Nazis' regard
for the medium. The Jews had not disappeared as a target, but had disappeared
from the screen. Feature film, to some extent, was the circus. Aside from a few
films which simultaneously entertained and had a definite propaganda target,
such as *Jud Süss*, it was not necessarily an appropriate vehicle for getting the Nazi
message across. It could never replace a political speech by the Nazi leadership.
Were it to attempt to do so, it would lose its audience. And keeping audiences was
paramount. Cinema had instead a less direct function: avoiding issues that might
raise (from the Nazi perspective) dangerous questions; providing distraction;
promoting Nazi values and role models. Spelling things out, even ad nauseam,
was best left to Nazi orators, cheered on by their diehard followers.

The image of the Jew was mostly absent in German feature film. Exceptions were
the *Kampfzeit* films and fleeting appearances during the thirties in a few other
films. In 1939 Jewish characters were more central in the two comedies. In 1940
they were central in two feature films. Minor Jewish characters appeared in other
films released in the same year as *Jud Süss*, and also in films released in 1941 and
1942 as well as in one in 1943, but that had been conceived during an earlier stage
of the war, its opening being delayed by a year. With this one exception, Jewish
characters disappeared from the screen after 1943. Moreover, given the length
of time involved in filmmaking, it is likely that those films opening in 1942 had
been in the pipeline at least since the previous year. After 1941, Jews disappeared
from German newsreels; we can assume that ideas for feature films with Jewish

characters also stopped at the same time. No Jewish characters, no matter how marginal, appeared in any film released in 1944 or 1945.

Great historical figures remained important as subject matter; self-sacrifice was also highly recommended. Since all Germans quickly became closely involved in the war effort – either at the front or through a close relative serving at the front, or later in finding their homes and places of work destroyed – keeping up morale also became important, and especially so from 1943 onwards.

Taking the films in chronological order, according to the date of the première, we find more Jewish characters in films in the first two years of the war than in the pre-war years. In 1940, the year that *Jud Süss* opened, three other films featured minor Jewish characters. Opening at the beginning of the year, *Der ewige Quell* (*The Eternal Source*), a Bavaria Filmkunst production, belonged to the *Heimat* genre and was intended for a provincial audience. Its première took place in the provincial town of Goslar on 19 January 1940; it only opened in Berlin seven months later on 23 August 1940.[46] Set in a remote village, with an 'Aryan' villain, it also included a minor Jewish character, given a Slavic name, Dr Ivan Wollinsky, a crooked lawyer from the city, who makes a brief appearance towards the film's end. Another character detects his 'racial' origins, but the sequence was so insignificant that the Allied censor did not notice and passed the film.[47]

The second film was *Ein Robinson* (*A Robinson Crusoe*), which opened in April 1940. The director was Arnold Fanck, who during the Weimar period had directed Leni Riefenstahl in mountain films. There were also mountains in this film, but in Chile, where the Robinson Crusoe-like character chooses to retreat. Earlier, as a sailor during the First World War, he had been taken prisoner in Chile after his ship, the *Dresden*, was sunk by the British, and interned on an island. He escapes to Germany in time to witness the German revolution, for which he has great distate. After discovering that his bride, the mother of his small son, has left him for someone else, he decides to return to his island to sit out the Republic. Many years later, a new *Dresden* sails into view, built by the new Reich; he goes on board where he discovers his long-lost sailor son. Now he can return to the new National Socialist Germany. An antisemitic sequence apparently occurs early in the film when the Robinson character decides to leave Germany. As he leaves, Eastern Jews arrive.[48]

The third and more significant film for that year was *Bismarck*, produced by Tobis, directed by Wolfgang Liebeneiner and starring Paul Hartmann. In early March 1940 Goebbels had mentioned the need for a film on the Iron Chancellor. By the end of the year it had opened in Berlin, three months after *Jud Süss*.[49] Subsequently banned by the Allies, the film focuses on Bismarck during the 1860s, prior to German unification, and concludes symbolically with the Kaiser proclaiming German unification at Versailles in 1871. Bismarck battles with his political enemies, who include short-sighted parliamentarians. His main opponent is the leader of the left liberals, the eminent pathologist Rudolf Virchow, who works closely with a Jewish deputy, Wilhelm Loewe (there was in fact a Jewish deputy allied to Virchow's group named Ludwig Loewe). With dark, curly hair, a sharp nose and exaggerated gestures, Loewe is played by the typecast Karl Meixner (Wilde in *Hitlerjunge Quex* and the Bolshevik in *Pour le mérite*). Virchow prefers liberty to national unification and happily works with Jews. Declaring that 'Not through speeches and majority resolutions will the great goals be reached but through blood and iron,' Bismarck dissolves the *Landtag*, builds up the army, makes the right decisions and triumphs for Germany.

The film is less antisemitic than the script: Loewe's part was reduced and he is not shown conspiring with Jewish colleagues.[50] Other sequences with Jewish characters are fleeting: audiences, for example, will not necessarily have been aware that the journalist from the Cologne newspaper was intended to be a Jew. The attempt on Bismarck's life by a dark-haired man is also fleeting, though later that character is referred to as an 'English Jew', Cohen-Blind. (Ferdinand Cohen-Blind was, in fact, not English but a student at Tübingen and the step-son of Karl Blind, a Baden revolutionary who, after the revolutions of 1848–49, was forced to live in exile in London.) In the script the sequence had been expanded, with Cohen-Blind's actions being linked to Jewish machinations.[51] The parliamentary deputies' unruly behaviour reflected the Nazis' contempt for parliamentary democracy, for which read the failure of Weimar democracy, which they closely associated with Jews.

Two years later on 6 October 1942 a second Bismarck film opened. *Die Entlassung* (*The Dismissal*) focused on Bismarck's dismissal in 1890 by the young Kaiser Wilhelm II. Again directed by Liebeneiner for Tobis with music by Herbert Windt, this time the elderly Bismarck was played by Emil Jannings. This film was rewarded with even more *Prädikate*.[52] Once the need for a sequel was recognized, even Bismarck's dismissal proved an acceptable subject. Kaiser Wilhelm II had died in Dutch exile in June 1941 shortly before the invasion of the Soviet Union and thus between the premières of the two Bismarck films. Press coverage was low-key for a man and a period which the Nazis were convinced had been superseded. They conceded that the Kaiser had wanted the best for Germany, but he represented a system which had fallen short 'at the threshold of destiny'. According to an article in *Das Reich*, he was not a Führer type, but rather a symbol of an 'unfulfilled' epoch.[53] That is also the line taken in *Die Entlassung*.

The Kaiser's disagreement with Bismarck on foreign policy, in particular the Chancellor's view that Germany should avoid a war on two fronts, is glossed over. After Bismarck's dismissal, the Kaiser did not renew the treaty of friendship with Russia, thus ensuring a war on two fronts which twenty-four years later Germany then lost. That same mistake was now being repeated. Goebbels, however, probably intended the film to be an 'indirect attack on the state bureaucracy'.

Doubtless he also expected the Soviet Union to have been defeated by the time of the film's release.[54] Now worried as to whether the film should even be released, he consulted Hitler, who consulted Martin Bormann. Hitler mentioned the problem in his table talk. A trial run was permitted, which accounts for its opening in the provincial Baltic town of Stettin. Alfred Rosenberg was against the film's release, but Goebbels, who considered the Stettin trial a success, prevailed.[55] It was intended that audiences leave the cinema with the thought that Bismarck's work remained unfinished, not that the present government was repeating the Kaiser's mistake.

A parliamentary sequence in *Die Entlassung* was not dissimilar to one in *Bismarck*, though the enemy was no longer the left liberals but the Social Democrats who by 1890 had replaced liberals of various persuasions as the main opposition to Bismarck. Their leader, August Bebel, was not Jewish, but his deputy, Paul Singer, was. The actor playing Bebel, Friedrich Maurer, did such a brilliant screen-test when delivering a Reichstag speech against war, that it drew applause on the film set. Word got back to Goebbels about an 'anti-national socialist demonstration'. Jannings and Liebeneiner were forced to play down the seriousness of the incident, with Goebbels finally being persuaded that it was just Jannings making trouble.[56]

The unruly Social Democrats were portrayed as traitors to the Fatherland, a charge levelled at them during the Bismarck era and subsequently, and not just by the Nazis, while the Jews, as always, were the enemy of the Reich. But the film also targets the bureaucrats opposing Bismarck, above all Privy Councillor Friedrich von Holstein, played by Werner Krauss in a manner not too dissimilar to his portrayal of Süss's secretary, Levi, two years earlier. Script and lighting as well as Krauss's performance, make him seem the Jewish villain of Nazi propaganda, though obviously the Prussian aristocrat Holstein could not have been a Jew.[57]

During 1941 seven films in all had Jewish characters. The first, which opened in Posen in March 1941 and two days later in Berlin, was particularly significant because it was set in the opening months of the war. *Über alles in der Welt* (*Over All in the World*), directed for Ufa by Karl Ritter, was based on his own idea; he also co-wrote the script (with Felix Lützkendorf). Herbert Windt provided the music. It was another episodic Ritter *Zeitfilm* with simultaneous plots and a great deal of action, which also incorporated newsreel aerial shots of swooping German war planes. It began with the outbreak of war in September 1939 and ended with the conquest of France. Carl Raddatz played an honourable German journalist caught up in the fighting in France, his only wish being to return to Germany to enlist. The Jews are shown working for the enemy: for 'Radio London', and for Austrian Free Radio, the latter encouraging Austrians to abandon the Reich. They also head the League of Human Rights which has links to the British Secret Service, 'human' here being a nasty word as distinct from 'German'. Jews are easily identifiable through a combination of physiognomy, language, gesture and behaviour, and are revealed as cowards. Germans living outside the Reich at the outbreak of war are shown as eager to return to Germany; anyone not so inclined is suspect and probably 'non-Aryan'.

On the same day that *Über alles in der Welt* had its Berlin première, *Carl Peters*, made by Bavaria Studios, had its première in Hamburg where Peters had once lived. The following day the formation of the *Afrikakorps* was announced, with Erwin Rommel as its commander. Two months later *Carl Peters* opened in Berlin, by which time the public was suitably impressed with reports coming in from the African campaign.[58] The colonialist and explorer Peters was depicted as a hero before his time. But the real Peters, who helped found Germany's East Africa colony, was an imperialist adventurer who secured treaties with native chiefs to bring their land under German control.[59] Later recalled, he was forced to stand trial, not for the numerous atrocities he had committed but for the execution of his African mistress and her lover. Hannah Arendt has suggested that Peters was a possible model for Joseph Conrad's character Kurtz in *Heart of Darkness*.[60] Though the Nazis would hardly have raised objections to his brutality, or his attempt to find Germany a place in the sun by hook or by crook, they would not have approved of miscegenation. This aspect of Peters's life was no secret. Audiences will have been well aware of this, yet the film chose to sanitize him and exclude all his relations with women – white as well as, understandably, black – aside from his mother, the only female to whom he is seen to have an attachment.[61]

Directed by Herbert Selpin, the popular and highly paid film actor Hans Albers played Peters. Set in the period 1882 to 1896, the film was anti-British and focused on Germany's rivalry with Britain in Africa. A man of action and a visionary, Peters despises Britain; he had lived in London for several years, where he spurned offers to work for the British in Africa, but he also went back to live in Britain after his trial, an inconvenient fact which the film neglects to mention. Like many others, this film was also anti-parliamentary in that it is parliamentarians who thwart Peters. It is also antisemitic in that Peters's anticolonial enemies within Germany are depicted as Jews. Peters was in fact antisemitic, so in this respect the film does not stray far from the truth.[62] The villains are two brothers: a baptized Jew who is a high-ranking civil servant in the colonial office with an ambitious non-Jewish wife, and his uncouth journalist brother who retains his Jewish mode of speech and behaviour. The cowardly and dissimulating civil servant is pro-British and opposes Peters's colonial projects. Played by Herbert Hübner – Ipelmeyer in *Robert und Bertram*, in another instance of typecasting – he is the 'Jew in disguise', keen to keep secret his link to his unsavoury brother (played by Justus Paris). Journalism, in Nazi eyes, was never an honourable profession and, to make matters worse, this particular journalist writes for the Social Democratic paper *Vorwärts*. The Social Democrats had strongly opposed Germany's quest for colonies, though it was only in 1907 that they took a principled stand, when Germany crushed the Herero Uprising in German South-West Africa. The film contrasts two Jewish stereotypes, from two different social strata, yet linked by blood, since they are in fact brothers. As in *Der ewige Jude* or in *Jud Süss*, the assimilated Jew, the Jew in disguise, posed one danger, with assimilation being a form of camouflage. His crude and repellent brother, however, posed another danger since his exposure of Peters's activities weakened Germany internationally. Both men, in their different ways, prevented Germany from taking its place on the world stage.

Ohm Krüger (*Uncle Krüger*) (Tobis) was the major anti-British film. It too was set in Africa, though during the period of the Boer War. A total of RM5.5 million was spent on the film which, one month before its opening on 4 April 1941, was declared 'important for the Reich' (*Reichswichtig*). It received the new classification of *Film der Nation* (Film of the Nation).[63] One of the two scriptwriters was Harold Bratt, the scriptwriter for *Leinen aus Irland*. The director was Hans Steinhoff who earlier had directed *Hitlerjunge Quex*, though Emil Jannings, who played Krüger, was also credited with 'overall direction'. Ferdinand Marian played Cecil Rhodes. Advance publicity suggested that Jews would be more prominent in the film, since according to Nazi beliefs Jews controlled England and financed war for their greater profit.[64] That some Jews also lived amongst the Boers is not alluded to.

In a brief opening sequence a journalist forces his way into a Swiss hotel room to obtain an exclusive interview with the elderly, partially blind Krüger (Jannings), now in exile. He works for the *Berliner Tageblatt*, the popular left liberal Berlin newspaper which in Nazi shorthand was a Jewish paper (it was owned by the Jewish Mosse family). Short, fat, dark-haired, pushy and obtuse, the journalist is obviously intended to be a Jew; he bribes the hotel porter using a Yiddish word, *Tacheles*, meaning to have a talk with. Played by Hans Stiebner, who three years earlier took the role of the Levantine villain in *Mit versiegelter Order* and the previous years as Rothechild's agent, he gets into Krüger's room where in order to get a better photograph, he insists on opening the blinds which destroys Krüger's limited eyesight. This sequence is brief. After that, Jewish characters do not appear again. More significant are the sequences exposing British brutality whereby British soldiers behave like German soldiers at this time: occupying a country; breaking into homes; rounding people up; putting them in camps; and executing them arbitrarily. There are also striking differences, in particular the absence of the racial aspect of Nazi behaviour. Still, the Boer camp inmates in this film get off lightly if compared to the experiences of the inmates of German concentration camps, though audiences were not to know this.

Arthur Maria Rabenalt's … *reitet für Deutschland* (*Riding for Germany*), an Ufa production, had its première the following month (11 April 1941). Based on the story of Carl Friedrich Freiherr von Langen, a cavalry officer and First World War hero, whose biography had appeared in 1936, the script was greatly fictionalized. The hero, played by Willy Birgel, is renamed Ernst von Brenken. Injured at the battle of Langemark, a heroic battle from the German perspective, he is saved by his horse. He later makes an astonishing physical recovery, though not a financial one. His estate is in difficulties, thanks to unscrupulous businessmen who are not actually Jews but are described as 'white Jews', a term not greatly in use but applied to 'Aryans' who behave like Jews.[65] His horse has been auctioned and is bought by Jewish horse traders; even the auctioneer is appalled that such a noble horse has gone to a Jew. Hübner (Ipelmeyer in *Robert und Bertram*) played the Jewish horse dealer. Other Jews are also involved in the horse sale. Though the sequence is brief, the characters would have been readily identifiable to a German audience as Jews (this sequence has been heavily cut in the post-war version).[66] But there is a happy end for Brenken, who finds his beloved horse and triumphs against adversity. He rides him to victory in an international tournament, winning first prize. Not only does he triumph for Germany, but the prize money enables him to get back his estate.[67]

One of the three scriptwriters was Fritz Reck von Malleczewen (1884–1945), who was arrested at the end of 1944 and died shortly thereafter in Dachau. His secret diary, which reveals his distaste for the Nazi regime, was posthumously published to much acclaim.[68] Much of Malleczewen's life, however, has been revealed as pure invention, including his aristocratic origins: he was in fact born Friedrich Reck in Malleczewen in Prussia but chose to live not in Prussia but outside Munich. Though an advocate of manly virtue and drawn to adventure, he did not fight in the First World War.[69] His diary, which he began in 1936 and covers the period when he was working on this film, makes no reference to his scriptwriting activities.

A costume drama, *Der Weg ins Freie* (*The Way to Freedom*), starring Zarah Leander, had its première on 7 May 1941 in Berlin. Produced by the (Carl) Froelich-Studio for Ufa, and directed by Rolf Hansen who directed other Leander vehicles, the script was by Harald Braun, Jacob Geis and Rolf Hansen. Leander plays a married opera singer who prefers a free life in Vienna to living with her husband on his Prussian estate in Pomerania. She of course pays for this when, after falling on hard times, she dies at the film's end. An early sequence provides a very small role for a Jewish character, a man with dark curly hair, a swollen nose and lorgnette, one of several unsavoury types at a decadent Viennese soirée given by the opera singer. This character makes a later appearance, along with another Jewish character: both men are responsible for denouncing the opera singer's friend, a Polish count. Though neither is actually described as a Jew, their Jewishness would have been apparent to contemporary audiences through voice and gesture. This, however, slipped the notice of the Allied Censor, who cleared the film.[70]

Venus vor Gericht (*Venus on Trial*) (1941) was directed and scripted by Hans Zerlett for Bavaria-Filmkunst with music by Leo Leux, who had provided the music for *Robert und Bertram* which Zerlett had also directed. Opening on 4 June 1941, it was later banned by the Allies. Set in 1930 in the bad old days of the Weimar Republic, it tells the story of a sculptor, Peter Brake, whose name is not far removed from Arno Breker, Hitler's favourite sculptor, known for his gigantic male nudes in classical style. Doubtless Zerlett was trying to ingratiate himself with the authorities, but his light touch proved too light for them, though not for audiences.

Since Brake is unable to produce what the Weimar art market now wants, namely primitive and ugly sculptures (otherwise known as 'Jewish art'), he plans a hoax to make a statement about contemporary art. After sculpting a Venus as though made by an ancient Greek, he buries it. When subsequently discovered, it is heralded as an authentic piece of antiquity. An art dealer, Benjamin Hecht, a polished and assimilated Jew, played by Siegfried Breuer (Dr Kuhn in *Leinen aus Irland*), gets involved in the authentication and sale. He has direct links to a high-ranking civil servant, also an assimilated Jew, who works in the ministry responsible for cultural matters. When Brake admits to the hoax, he is in trouble: the experts insist on the sculpture's authenticity, which means that Brake will be taken to court unless he can prove that he is the sculptor. At this point, in steps the model for Venus, now married to the mayor of a small town. Brake is saved; the art world is exposed; the model leaves her husband for the sculptor; and the Nazis are shown to have broad support from civil servants who reveal themselves to be secret party members. The joke is on the Weimar Republic and its supporters. Any remaining doubts about Zerlett's intentions in his earlier film, *Robert und Bertram*, are dispelled by this one. His light touch may not have gained him the accolades he craved from critics, or from high-ranking Nazis, but audiences were pleased.[71]

In the anti-Polish *Heimkehr* (*Homecoming*), which opened in October 1941, Poles were also attacked for being unable to control the Jews. In an opening sequence Jews participate in the persecution of the ethnic Germans. The Poles drag German children from their school. One Jewish boy, encouraged by other Jews, pours petrol on the school furniture and books; we know he is Jewish because he has side-locks. Shortly after this incident the heroine tells a Jewish shopkeeper who asks for her custom: 'No, Salomonsson, you know that we do not buy from Jews.' Nevertheless, Salomonsson (a Fagin lookalike, not dissimilar to Alec Guinness's 1947 impersonation in *Oliver Twist*, banned in the American sector in Germany) is not put off: he praises Hitler as a brilliant and great man, and expresses disappointment that he wants nothing to do with 'us poor Jews'. She dryly remarks that she will write to Hitler about this, after which Salomonsson berates her for making fun of 'poor Jews' and shouts curses to the amusement of her friend played by Berta Drews.

In 1942 only two films with Jewish characters appeared. But the reappearance of the Jew as Bolshevik is significant, made possible by the end of the Stalin–Hitler pact and the invasion of the Soviet Union. Hitler's proclamation announcing that invasion, read by Goebbels on the radio, confirmed the link: 'The hour has come in which it becomes necessary to move against this plot of the Jewish Anglo-Saxon warmongers and of the Jewish rulers of the Soviet Union.'[72]

Ritter, whose filmmaking activities had been thwarted by the pact, could now return to a favourite theme, the 'world Jewish conspiracy'. Having shown the Jew, in *Über alles in der Welt*, spreading anarchy and chaos in the West, he could now extend this to the East in *GPU* (1942). Ritter was one of the few known antisemitic directors, yet Jewish characters hardly appear in any of his films, and significantly only in two wartime films, if we exclude the fleeting appearance of the Jew as Bolshevik in *Pour le Mérite*.[73]

GPU is the German for OGPU, an earlier Russian acronym for the KGB, the Soviet Secret Police. In the opening titles the letters are made to be a play-on-words in German. Dripping in blood, they are linked to German words: G for the German word for horror, *Grauen*; P for panic, *Panik*; and U for ruin, *Untergang*. The GPU's crimes outside the Soviet Union are soon to be exposed.

Ritter co-scripted this Ufa film, Windt provided the music, but the idea for it came from the actor playing the Bolshevik villain and who, towards the end, seeks redemption, Andrews Engelmann. (Engelmann had a role as a villain in the classic Weimar film starring Louise Brooks, *Tagebuch einer Verlorenen* (*Diary of a Lost Soul*) (1929).) As in *Über alles in der Welt*, GPU mainly covers the plight of Germans abroad. The episodic plot, as in other Ritter films, is highly complicated. Jews pop up everywhere and are always easily identifiable: Bolshevik agents (excluding the Engelmann character); journalists; Communist Front organization members; and even an elderly Jew recruited to commit murder. The heroine, who comes from the Baltic where the Bolsheviks murdered her family when she was a child, seeks revenge by working as a Bolshevik agent but is in reality a double agent. She is, however, doomed: her motives may be noble, but she has (according to Nazi thinking) been seriously compromised by working for the Bolsheviks. The future lies with a young German couple attempting to escape the Bolsheviks who are eventually caught and imprisoned in the Soviet Trade Delegation in Rotterdam. In a scene reminiscent of the final sequence in *Heimkehr*, German planes bomb the building in which they are held: *Wochenschau* clips of Stukas dive-bombing Rotterdam have been used.[74] The couple are saved and the invasion of the Low Countries is justified. *GPU* also includes a night-club sequence in which Lale Anderson sings, her voice closely associated with the wartime hit, 'Lili Marlene'. This was her first movie role.[75]

Filming began in December 1941; the première was on 14 August 1942, but the Ministry of Propaganda was displeased by the heavy-handed anti-Bolshevik propaganda and *GPU* was not awarded any classification.[76] Ritter was now not popular, for both personal and political reasons, having built his reputation with the *Zeitfilm*, an episode of propaganda film. He fell on hard times. In 1940, already in debt and near to bankruptcy, he had appealed to Goebbels for help. Despite handouts and a tax-free payment of RM100,000 authorized by Hitler personally, his finances did not improve. After 1943 his services as a director were no longer in demand, since he could no longer deliver the kind of films then wanted.[77]

Rembrandt, directed by Hans Steinhoff and filmed in occupied studios in Amsterdam and The Hague, opened in June 1942. It belonged to the genre of 'genius films', a distinctly Nazi variant on the Hollywood biopic, in which famous men (usually German) acted as historical role models and contemporary object lessons.[78] That Rembrandt painted sympathetic portraits of elderly Amsterdam Jews had no place in this film. Instead, an antisemitic sequence is included, so fleeting – it lasts for only one minute – that it has usually been missed. The genius Rembrandt struggles against the narrow-minded, materialistic burghers of Amsterdam, who show themselves incapable of either recognizing or understanding his genius. Heavily in debt and now widowed, his wife's cousin, who holds a number of his IOUs, does a deal with three Jews. Their large black hats and coats, pointed beards, speech, gestures and acting style make their identity unmistakable and the sequence is filmed in dark shadow. They offer to take on the IOUs since Rembrandt's house, they explain, is full of valuable items and times are bad, which reminds audiences of the behaviour of speculators during the Weimar hyperinflation. Their business maxim is to buy cheap and sell dear. This is no ordinary business deal but one which is underhand, duplicitous and conspiratorial. Sharp practice was synonymous with Jews. The Jewish characters border on caricature, in stark contrast to Rembrandt's 'Aryan' broker.

The only film with Jewish characters to appear in 1943 had been intended for a much earlier release but was plagued with political problems. It passed the censor on 21 August 1942, but, unusually, another year passed before it opened in the late summer of 1943. As early as 17 March 1940 a film on the subject had been mentioned.[79] By the summer of 1941 Goebbels found the script to be both 'extremely interesting' and 'psychologically sophisticated'.[80]

Wien 1910 (Vienna 1910) focused on the death in 1910 of the demagogic antisemitic mayor of Vienna, Karl Lueger. It was he who coined the phrase occasionally attributed to others: 'I will determine who is a Jew' ('*Wer Jude ist, bestimme ich*'), a strong indication that his antisemitism was opportunistic.[81]

The drama centres on Lueger's conflict and imagined deathbed reconciliation with another antisemitic rabble-rouser, the more ruthless, but politically less successful, anticlerical leader of the Austrian Pan-German movement, Georg von Schönerer, who promoted Austrian unification with Germany.

When the young Hitler first came to Vienna in 1908 the populist Lueger, a Catholic lawyer, first elected in 1897, was still mayor. His popular touch and ability to draw large crowds impressed Hitler, but since he belonged to the Christian-Social Party he was ideologically unacceptable. Hitler supported the anticlerical Pan Germans, who were opposed to Habsburg rule, which was closely identified with Catholicism. In their view, the disintegrating Habsburg empire was enabling the Slavs to triumph at the expense of Germans. Thus Pan Germans supported the unification of German-speaking Austrians with predominantly Protestant Germany, a *Grossdeutsch* solution. The anticlerical Pan German Schönerer was more to Hitler's political taste but unfortunately lacked both Lueger's popular touch and electoral success. Heir to both men, Hitler combined the populist demagoguery and mass appeal of Lueger while realizing Schönerer's Pan German dream.

In the film, Lueger summons Schönerer to his deathbed. A reconciliation is necessary since both men want only the best for the people. Both recognize that a *judenfrei* future depends on the unity of their two movements. Towards the end of the film, as Schönerer watches Lueger's funeral cortège pass, he takes off his hat. Such a reconciliation was pure wish fulfilment on the part of some Nazis (including Goebbels), but not for all Nazis, which accounts for the film's delayed release. Lueger was hardly a suitable subject for an antisemitic film made in Vienna.

Austrian Nazis opposed this rewriting of history. In 1934 in a failed coup, they nevertheless succeeded in assassinating the Austrian Chancellor, Engelbert Dollfuss, a member of Lueger's Christian-Social Party. In 1938 Dollfuss's successor, Kurt Schuschnigg, held out unsuccessfully against *Anschluss* and then went into exile. Catholic loyalties had made members of the Christian-Social Party hostile to union with predominantly Protestant Germany. Nevertheless, by 1938 support for *Anschluss* was widespread in Austria, even among those who had voted Christian-Social. This doubtless encouraged support for the film from outside Austria.

In the autumn of 1940 Wien-Film announced that they would be making *Wien 1910 (Vienna 1910)* as well as *Heimkehr*. Both met the requirement to produce antisemitic films, though the Jewish Question was less prominent in *Heimkehr*, which opened one year later in October 1941. Filming on *Wien 1910* finally began in September 1941, partly in Berlin-Babelsberg and partly in Vienna; the following month the Propaganda Ministry instructed newspaper editors to prepare to discuss the film. Several months later, in February 1942, two film journals,

Filmwoche and *Filmwelt*, provided detailed reports about the filming as well as biographical information for those, especially outside the *Ostmark* (Austria), who might have forgotten who Schönerer and Lueger actually were.[82]

Since August 1940 Baldur von Schirach, previously head of the Hitler Youth, had been Gauleiter and Reichsstatthalter of Vienna. He had few friends in high places: Martin Bormann intrigued against him and Goebbels accused him of showing insufficient interest in Wien-Film, and later attempted to portray him in a bad light.[83] Schirach was not keen to make trouble in his new posting. But in March 1942 Goebbels complained to him about a 'radical political clique' trying to stop the film and noted in his diary:

> The film needs to be filmed, and then one can say whether corrections still need to be made or if it is to be completely altered. Doubtless Lueger is made out as heroic. But that is not so damaging since the events are already so far in the past that – apart from a small circle of interested people – they are completely unknown.[84]

Committed to a film about a man Hitler had admired – though with reservations – Goebbels, as usual, was not too bothered about getting the historical details right, unlike certain Austrian Nazis ('the radical clique'). One objector was the leader of the Austrian Nazis, Ernst Kaltenbrunner. A member of the Higher SS and police leader, responsible for the *Entjudung* of Vienna, he was later executed at Nuremberg. As a concession, it was announced in November 1942 that *Wien 1910* would open in Frankfurt and not be screened in Austria.[85]

In January 1943 Heinrich Himmler appointed Kaltenbrunner to head the Reichssicherheitshauptamt (RSHA), replacing Reinhard Heydrich, who had been assassinated seven months earlier. As a consequence, Kaltenbrunner was called to Berlin, which enabled the anti-Austrian Goebbels to triumph with this film. By the spring of 1943 Goebbels had successfully persuaded Hitler to let him have control of Viennese cultural politics.[86] After numerous delays, intimately connected with political infighting, the Lueger film was finally released, three years after it had first been announced.

Lueger was played by Rudolf Forster. He had played Mackie Messer (Mack the Knife) in the 1931 Georg Pabst-directed film of Bertolt Brecht's *Die Dreigroschenoper* (*The Threepenny Opera*) and the lead in *Morgenrot*. Forster had recently returned to Germany from the US, to which he had emigrated in 1937, after finding little work there and divorcing his Jewish wife.[87] Goebbels was keen that he take this role.[88] Heinrich George played Schönerer.

Jewish characters feature in minor parts. The film opens with a sequence set in the poor Jewish quarter of Vienna, the Leopoldstadt. A shabbily dressed young man in thick glasses enters a shop with the 'good' news that Lueger is dying. A Jewish apprentice wearing side-locks and skullcap then races off to Dr Viktor Adler (the typecast Herbert Hübner, Ipelmeyer in *Robert und Bertram*). Adler, the moderate leader of the Austrian Social Democrats, one of the outstanding leaders of European Social Democracy in the pre-1914 period, was of Jewish origin. In this film he is almost unrecognizable, since he is depicted as a lowly journalist: he contributed to the Socialist newspaper. That Schönerer happily worked with Adler in the early 1880s (in his pre-antisemitic period and when Adler himself was something of a German nationalist) is of course not alluded to.[89] In a later sequence the kindly Lueger visits an orphanage. Surrounded by children, he holds out his mayoral gold chain and tells them that each link represents a Viennese district. In the Second District (the Leopoldstadt) there was much money, 'Jewish money', and that is linked to two of the seven deadly sins: envy and avarice.

Lueger also has enemies who are non-Jews: the head of the state chancellery, a Habsburg civil servant, is one. The Austrian Emperor had refused to ratify Lueger's appointment three times, and the radical Lueger had few friends amongst the nobility or the civil service. Lueger's greatest hostility, however, was reserved for the Liberals, who represented the wealthy bourgeoisie which included Jews. In the film, Lerchner is Lueger's other non-Jewish enemy. An art connoisseur and speculator who supports the Liberals, he is played by Karl Kuhlmann (Nathan Rothschild in *Die Rothschilds*) as though a Jew. Lueger takes defensive action against Lerchner's financial manoeuvring; Lerchner is ruined and kills himself. The future, however, lies with his student son, the film's *de rigueur* proto-Nazi. At a meeting of the city council, Lueger delivers his last speech to great applause; Adler makes a sardonic comment and is physically assaulted by Lerchner, who tells him that Jews have no business there. When Adler calls for the police, Lerchner junior shouts: 'I am the police.'

A political debate between two antisemites of different persuasions was hardly a recipe for box office success. Undramatic, with too much talk and cardboard characters, it is not surprising that the film proved unpopular. A film that depicted an antisemite who was not a Nazi (Lueger) can hardly, however, be construed as anti-fascist, as it has erroneously been described.[90] *Wien 1910* was the last film to appear with minor Jewish characters.

As the Jews of Europe disappeared into extermination camps, they disappeared from the screen. That a film with Jewish characters opened as late as August 1943 was an aberration, the consequence of Nazi infighting. Minor Jewish characters had ceased to serve any purpose; with major characters this occurred even earlier, though *Jud Süss* still continued to be screened. By the time the machinery was in place for implementing the 'Final Solution' of the Jewish Question, the need for Jewish characters had disappeared. Only in 1944 did the image of the Jew return to the screen, but that was in a documentary not a feature film. Planned by the SS and not by the Propaganda Ministry, it had an altogether different purpose for an altogether different audience.

14

Theresienstadt

Not all films about Jews were made under the auspices of the Ministry of Propaganda. As its name implies, this ministry had control of film propaganda, but its control was not always complete. Under Heinrich Himmler the SS is better known for its role in running the Security Service (*Sicherheitsdienst*), the Secret Police (Gestapo), the concentration camps and, when 'armed' as the Waffen-SS, fighting on the Eastern Front, providing the killing squads which initiated the 'Final Solution' in the summer of 1941. It is less well known that they too on occasion ventured into filmmaking. Their subject was the model ghetto and concentration camp of Theresienstadt. Not one but two films were made. We know why they made the better-known film of 1944, but the reasons for making the earlier 1942 film are less clear.

Theresienstadt (Terezín in Czech) was built as a fortress by the Austrian Emperor, Josef II, in the late eighteenth century. A century later it became a garrison town. Forty miles to the north-west of Prague, since Munich and the German annexation of the predominantly German-speaking Sudetenland, now it was at the northernmost frontier of the Czech Protectorate. Consisting of a military garrison town and a prison, to become known respectively as the *Grosse Festung* (Large Fortress) and the *Kleine Festung* (Small Fortress), the latter during the First World War held Gavrilo Princip, the assassin of Archduke Franz Ferdinand, and under the Czechoslovak Republic hardened criminals. Geographically and administratively separate, the *Kleine Festung* served as a Gestapo prison for enemies of the Third Reich, and included some transfers from the Large Fortress, namely those who had incurred the wrath of the SS. Here thousands of prisoners, many not Jewish, were completely cut off, treated with great brutality and often left to die.

In October 1941, as part of the Nazi policy of ghettoization, the inhabitants of the *Grosse Festung* were made to leave to make way for the Jews of the Protectorate of Bohemia and Moravia, though many remained until as late as June 1942, continuing to live side by side with the new Jewish arrivals. Initially, the Czech Jews experienced some relief in being allowed to remain on Czech soil and were not being sent to Poland. This decision had been taken by the newly appointed Protector, Reinhard Heydrich, who considered Prague (unlike the Polish towns) unsuitable for the siting of a ghetto. Any illusions Czech Jews may have harboured were shattered on arrival. Measuring 700 yards long by 500 wide, its 219 houses had been built to house at most 7,000 and at that point only contained 3,700 inhabitants. During the course of the war, Jewish inmates numbered on average 35,000 and on occasion (September 1942) as many as 53,000. Overcrowding was only relieved by sudden massive deportations, including those of September and October 1944 when over 18,000 people were deported to Auschwitz.[1]

Initially described as a ghetto camp, Theresienstadt also became a transit camp for the majority of its inhabitants, a first stop on the journey to the extermination camps further east, especially Auschwitz. Officially designated an 'autonomous ghetto' under Jewish 'self-government', it was part of the Nazis' programme to concentrate Jews into particular areas, to facilitate the 'Final Solution'. Administered by a Council of Jewish Elders – hand-picked by the SS –who themselves could be deported further east at short notice or sent to the *Kleine Festung* as in the case of one chairman, it was ruled by the SS with an iron fist. It was not a model ghetto, as the Nazis hoped would be believed, or as the vigour of ghetto cultural life might suggest. Theresienstadt inmates may have had a rich cultural life, many of the highly assimilated Czech Jews having been active in the arts, but a cause for concern was that, in contrast to ghettos such as Łódź, it lacked an economic base (not that this ultimately helped the inhabitants of Łódź).

Within a few months of its creation in January 1942 (at the time of the Wannsee Conference, chaired by Heydrich) its status was changed from a ghetto for Czech Jews to a place for elderly Jews, war veterans and prominent or wealthy Jews (the *Prominente*) from Germany, Austria and other areas of occupied Western Europe. Like Belsen, Theresienstadt had the dubious honour of being designated a camp for privileged Jews: privileged being a rather relative term. The *Prominente* began arriving in June 1942. This was at a time when the original non-Jewish inhabitants were finally removed but also when some of the original Czech inmates were being deported. In April 1943, Jews from the Netherlands, mainly German refugees, began to arrive, followed by 456 Danish Jews six months later. This new designation might suggest that the Nazis, or rather the SS under Himmler, were wavering in their plan to exterminate all Jews. But the change was mainly cosmetic. In reality, Theresienstadt did not change its function as a transit camp for most of the new categories of Jewish inmates, though a small number, including Rabbi Leo Baeck, head of German reform Jewry, were never deported. Of the approximately 140,000 Jews sent to Theresienstadt, just over a quarter (34,000) died there, while under half (87,000) were deported to the east, of whom some 3,500 survived.[2]

Only fragments exist of the two Theresienstadt films made by the SS: there is no complete copy of either film. Of the earlier film very little remains apart from a script and some stills. Film fragments (ninety-five metres or eight minutes of 16 mm film on one reel) were only discovered in 1994 in a Warsaw archive. Donated by a private individual, though how he or she obtained them is unknown, they had been there since 1972 without anyone realizing their significance. It is possible that the entire film (or parts of the film) and the stills had once been smuggled out of Theresienstadt.[3]

The film from 1942 differed from the film from 1944 in a number of respects, aside from the propaganda purpose of the later film being more apparent. There is even some disagreement as to why the earlier film was made, and it is not known who gave the order to make the film. Some argue that it was made for Heinrich Himmler's 'private use', though there is no evidence of this in the Himmler papers. If this was the case, did Himmler want it as a documentary record to be kept in a vault, or was it to be screened? And if the latter, to what kind of audience and for what purpose? Or, could it have been part of a larger plan to document the deportation of the Jews from Germany for use in domestic propaganda? In an April 1942 diary entry, Goebbels refers to ordering extensive film documentation of deportations to the ghettos in the east, which suggests that this film could have been made with the connivance of the Propaganda Ministry. Or was the film intended for the Jews themselves, to assuage their fears and persuade them to go quietly? Unfortunately (in contrast to the later film) there is no conclusive proof one way or the other as to why this earlier film was made. In some respects, however, it was not dissimilar to the later film, insofar as it was made by the Jewish inmates with the SS camp leadership appointing a Jewish prisoner to head the film team. The initial scenarios were also written by the Jewish inmates, but it was filmed by professional non-Jewish cameramen.[4]

What has survived are some eight minutes of film fragments which contain sequences from the actual film with more than one take, along with shots of the camera crew in the act of filming or of camera equipment being hauled on trolleys or train wagons. One draft script (entitled 'Ghetto Theresienstadt: Rough Draft of a Film Report') has also survived. This charts the history of Theresienstadt as a ghetto from the autumn of 1941, just before the arrival of the first transports of Czech Jews, to the late summer of 1942, when the ghetto organization was breaking down under the pressure of overcrowding, hunger and disease. It was in September 1942 that the population peaked at 53,000, a population far from stable with 18,000 new arrivals and 13,000 deportees. It was also at this time that the first news of the extermination of the Jews reached the Allies.

The draft script, the only one to have survived, could not have been the one selected, for its tone was far too pessimistic and it also contradicted the official Nazi view that Theresienstadt was a 'model ghetto'. It made no attempt, either advertently or inadvertently, to hide the grim conditions. It even alluded to deportations at a time when officially Theresienstadt was not a designated transit camp.[5]

Statistics in pictures: as one train after another roars in, a schedule appears of arriving transports. Montage of cities from which they originate. Statistics on the development of the ghetto above endless rows of people. Trains disappear into the distance: transports to the east.[6]

The unknown author is believed to have been a German-speaking Czech, likely to have been one of the early arrivals who, with some kind of technical background, was a member of a team sent ahead to adapt the fortress town to the needs of its new inhabitants. This description fits Peter Kien who contributed to the final script. Kien had arrived on one of the very first transports, before his wife and parents.[7]

The SS deputy commander of the ghetto, First Lieutenant Otto (his first name is not known) was in charge of the film project. Apparently he ordered Irena Dodalová to have ready within eight days a draft for a *Kulturfilm* (a short documentary). Then aged forty-two, Dodalová claims her scenario was the one selected. She was probably given the task because of her film background. Before the war, she had with her husband, Karel Dodal, owned a Prague film company. Regarded as the 'father' of Czech animation film, he had the good fortune to be in the US at the outbreak of war, where he soon found work. But her claim that she wrote the final script on which the film was based has been discounted in favour of one of her collaborators, the gifted twenty-three-year-old Kien. A graphic artist and poet, he also wrote libretti for two (of the four) major Theresienstadt composers: for Viktor Ullmann, *Der Kaiser von Atlantis oder die Todverweigerung* (*The Kaiser of Atlantis or The Refusal of Death*), an absurdist short opera; and for Gideon Klein, a twenty-two-year-old music student turned composer, a poem cycle, *Peststadt* (*Plague Town*), for his song cycle, *Die Pest* (*The Plague*). (Ullmann, Klein and Kien perished, the last-mentioned as a volunteer accompanying his parents when they were deported in 1944.) Kien's script dealt with its subject 'vigorously and realistically', with 'very little staged', according to the poet and historian of the camp, the former inmate, H.G. Adler. (H.G. stood for Hans Gunther, but as that was the name of the chief of the Gestapo Office in Prague, he preferred to use his initials.)[8]

The 1942 film begins in Prague and then documents a transport of Jews to Theresienstadt, focusing on one individual family from their time of 'call-up' to their arrival at Theresienstadt. The family receive their deportation notice; they call in at the Jewish Community Centre; they pack; they go to the railway station and finally arrive at Theresienstadt, where they are observed being processed to begin a new life under very different conditions. Berlin (the Propaganda Ministry) approved the scenario, making minor changes such as providing the family with a name, Holländer.[9]

The Prague scenes were shot separately, without involving the Jewish members of the team, for this would have meant their leaving Theresienstadt. It is possible that these scenes were shot by the Prague newsreel company, Aktualitá, who also shot the second Theresienstadt film. For the camp scenes a few inmates assisted the cameramen as technicians and script girls, which we can observe in the film fragments. We even have a three-second shot of Dodalová smiling prettily to camera. Survivors who witnessed the filming, or who recall being filmed, believed the cameramen belonged to the Waffen-SS propaganda unit, fresh from the Eastern Front. The recently discovered footage contradicts this since it includes shots of cameramen in the act of filming: the insignia on their sleeves, clearly indicate that they belonged to the SS Security Service, the SD (*Sicherheitsdienst*).[10]

Shooting continued over a period of four weeks through October and November 1942, after which Dodalová was ordered to edit the 50,000 feet of film, consisting of more than twenty-five reels and 1,200 scenes, in the Commandant's office behind locked doors. On completion she was then sent back to farm work and survived the war by being part of the rescue train which left Theresienstadt for Switzerland with Himmler's approval in late January 1945, a Nazi 'humanitarian' gesture.[11]

Clumsily shot and put together, the film reveals confusion and congestion. At the same time, and probably inadvertently, the newly built crematorium appears in the background of a shot where camera equipment is being carried.[12] It is believed that the film was taken to Berlin and finally scrapped.[13] Made at a low point in the history of the ghetto, and well before its beautification for the Red Cross inspection, this first film did contain sequences that would reappear in the 1944 film: a soccer match, though not in the barracks but on an open field, and a cabaret. The latter included a barbershop act with the comic Karel Švenk and a mimed dance with the dancer Kamila Rosenbaumová. Shots of the audience include the face of one of the SS men, who after some hesitation smiles to camera. (Old habits die hard.) The images in this 1942 film, unlike those in the 1944 film, were of little use for an advertisement for the model ghetto, and precisely for this very reason, are of interest.

Within a few months of completing this first film, Germany's military fortunes declined. The need to impress neutral opinion became urgent, thus prompting another film about the model ghetto. Ten years to the month after Riefenstahl had filmed Nuremberg, extolling Hitler and National Socialism, the SS were making a film about the enemies of the Third Reich and extolling the benefits of life in a concentration camp. They hoped that the outside world would see how well they had solved the Jewish question, even to the satisfaction of the Jews themselves. The change in subject matter reflects National Socialism's reversal of fortune.

Made for external and not for internal consumption, the 1944 film in contrast to earlier films on the 'Jewish Question' such as *Jud Süss* or the documentary

Der ewige Jude, attempted to persuade non-German audiences that the Jews, despite having been hounded and removed, were being well treated. If intended for German audiences, it would only have served to confuse them: why reassure them about the deported Jews? With extermination in full swing, and the Jewish problem in the process of solution, there was no need to expose German audiences to additional films on the subject. Given the course of the war and the sacrifices Germans were now being called on to make, why remind cinema audiences that solving the Jewish problem had come with a price? The Jews may have disappeared, but Germany was by no means invincible and it was especially on the Eastern Front that a high price was being paid. Keeping up morale was more important for German audiences. This was best achieved through escapist froth even though elsewhere German propaganda did not let up on the Jewish Question.

By late 1942, there was some awareness that Jews were being exterminated in concentration camps. Even in Theresienstadt itself, some inmates with illicit access to radios knew from BBC broadcasts that gas was being used.[14] As early as December 1942 the name Auschwitz was mentioned in a Foreign Office document, part of the growing evidence that the Allies knew rather more than previously believed.[15] But knowing is not the same as comprehending what some deemed rumours. And whether the Allies could have acted on this knowledge is a cause for debate. Nevertheless, during 1943 as the German army was in retreat on the Eastern Front, in North Africa and in Italy, information about the fate of the Jews was being disseminated. With an eye on neutral opinion, Germany turned to propaganda to dispel rumours. A film would be made about a ghetto concentration camp. Having been designated 'privileged', Theresienstadt was the obvious choice.

Shot during the summer of 1944, shortly after an inspection by the International Red Cross, the privileged camp had been transformed for the occasion into a Potemkin village. The origins of this inspection go back to the previous October, when the Danish government resisted efforts to round up its Jews. Forewarned, it was able to help most Danish Jews escape to Sweden, but a small number were captured and sent to Theresienstadt. Both the Danish government and the International Red Cross put pressure on the Germans to allow them access to the camp. The remit of the Red Cross had been to oversee the treatment of military rather than civilian internees, though by the 1930s they had tentatively begun to extend that remit to inmates of concentration camps within the Reich. During the war they had become involved in channelling parcels to inmates and in inspections.[16]

The Danish role in the Holocaust has come in for high praise; in contrast that of the Red Cross has not. The inspection lasted only one day (23 June 1944) and included one representative of the International Red Cross and two

Danish officials. They visited the Large Fortress with its 35,000 inhabitants, now bedecked with flower-beds, and spoke to well-coached members of the Council of Elders, including its leader. They did not see the Small Fortress. The Red Cross representative accepted the SS explanation that Theresienstadt was not a transit camp but an *Endlager* or terminus camp, while the Danes were more cautious. Claude Lanzmann's interview with the Red Cross Representative, Dr Maurice Rossel, in an outtake from *Shoah*, which now exists as a separate documentary, leaves little doubt that he was antisemitic.[17] Rossel believed that rich Jews had bought their way into the camp and, in response to Lanzmann's questions about '*les Juifs*', persisted in referring to them as '*les israélites*', a pejorative term in French. After this visit the Red Cross made no further request to visit any camps further east, including the Auschwitz 'labour camp' where many Theresienstadt deportees were being held in the Czech 'family camp'.[18] Their fate was now sealed. Moreover, in the months following the Theresienstadt inspection a further 18,000 Jews were deported eastwards.

Seven weeks after this June visit, shooting began on a film. We now know that this film was made in the aftermath of the visit, and took advantage of the beautification campaign, which was mounted in preparation for the visit rather than for the film. But the decision to make the film had been taken earlier, probably in December 1943 when the beautification campaign was being planned. Filming, however, did not begin before August 1944. The decision to make the film was therefore not influenced by the events of 1944: it was neither a consequence of the success of the Red Cross visit, nor a part of the negotiations to rescue Hungarian Jewry, such as the Brand negotiations involving Himmler, which tried to 'sell' Jews for trucks for use on the Eastern Front.[19] (Joel Brand, a Hungarian Jew, was released to travel to Istanbul in the spring of 1944 to negotiate with the Allies at a time when Hungarian Jewry, hitherto untouched, was threatened with deportation to Auschwitz. Deportations began even before Brand had left Budapest and took place at an extraordinarily rapid rate.)[20]

Only fragments exist from this second Theresienstadt film, although rather more than from the first, a total of twenty-five minutes from a film originally, it is believed, to have been approximately ninety minutes in length. A Dutch painter, Jo (Josef) Spier, made sketches of scenes during shooting. They functioned as a 'visual log' of the scenes as they are being shot rather than merely illustrating those scenes before they have been shot. These sketches remain an important source for understanding what appears in the completed film and for revealing the order of the sequences.[21]

Often referred to by the title *Der Führer schenkt den Juden eine Stadt*, or *The Führer Grants the Jews a City*, this was only the film's 'working title', as used by the Jewish inmates, and first surfaced in survivor accounts. It was never the film's official title, but instead was a grim Jewish joke, a form of black humour, since the Jews well knew that the Führer had never given them anything. Nor would Hitler himself have wanted his name linked to the Jews in a film title. A recently discovered fragment from the film's opening confirms the title as *Theresienstadt: Ein Dokumentarfilm aus dem jüdischen Siedlungsgebiet*, or *Theresienstadt: A Documentary Film from the Jewish Settlement Area*. This official title accorded with Nazi objectives: a documentary film or report implied that it was 'objective'; a Jewish settlement was a more neutral term than ghetto, the Nazi designation; and an 'area' of settlement suggested that there were others, perhaps even a whole region devoted to them.[22]

The idea for this film came from SS Major Hans Günther, the head of the Gestapo Central Jewish Office in Prague (originally *Zentralstelle für jüdische Emigration* or Central Office for Jewish Emigration, when set up by Adolf Eichmann in Prague in June 1939, but later renamed *Zentralstelle zur Regelung der Judenfrage* or Central Office for the Regulation of the Jewish Question). It is likely that Günther did not even bother to contact his immediate superior, Eichmann, about the plan; at this time the right hand did not necessarily know what the left hand was doing. Film finance came from the Central Office, whose resources were derived from confiscated Jewish property. Ultimately, this second film whose purpose was to deny the existence of the 'Final Solution' was not only made by Jews but also financed by them.[23]

Theresienstadt inmates helped make the film, although they were not responsible for filming. This was done by Aktualitá, the Prague newsreel company. The film's director, if this term is even appropriate, was the German actor and director, Kurt Gerron. (Had he gone to the US no doubt he would have had a successful Hollywood career, as did his one-time film partner, Siegfried (Sig) Arno, but he is now conspicuous by his absence from English-language film encyclopedias and, when mentioned elsewhere, often and unjustly as the director of this film.) In March 1933 Gerron was expelled from the Berlin-Babelsberg film set where he had been directing a film. He left Germany immediately, initially for France, where he directed two films with scripts by Emeric Pressburger, one starring Pierre Brasseur. He eventually settled in the Netherlands where he also directed films, one of which became a landmark in Dutch filmmaking, *Merijntje Gijzen's Jeugd* (*Merijntje Gijzen's Youth*) (1936). Based on a best-selling novel, it was an artistic and commercial success, his direction of the children being singled out for praise. Though he had mastered Dutch, his Dutch directing career soon ended when foreign-born directors suddenly became unwanted. His last film job was synchronizing the Dutch-dubbed version of *Snow White and the Seven Dwarfs*.

Born in Berlin in 1897, Gerron had been a popular star of cabaret, stage and film during the Weimar period. He appeared in the first stage productions of three Bertolt Brecht plays: *Baal* (1926), *The Threepenny Opera* (1928) and *Happy*

End (1929), though he and Brecht were not on good terms since Gerron saw himself as an entertainer and was not political. Cast as Tiger Brown, the London police chief, in the popular *Threepenny Opera* and singing 'Mack the Knife' he gained a wide following.[24] Altogether he appeared in seventy-four films, many of which were highly successful such as E.A. Dupont's *Variété* (1925), *The Blue Angel* (1930) (where he played the magician) and *Die Drei von der Tankstelle*, a sunny musical about unemployment (1930). Large, dark, bald and rotund, he was quickly singled out by the Nazis, in a campaign of vilification, as a distinctly Jewish comedian embodying the evils of Weimar culture. It has been argued that even in Weimar his physiognomy and acting signified, despite assimilation, some-thing distinctly Jewish and hence dangerous.[25] In *Der ewige Jude* he is mentioned in conjunction with the 'disastrous' Jewish domination of German cinema during the pre-Hitler period. A clip of Gerron in *Flucht vor der Liebe* (*Flight from Love*) is accompanied by the comment: 'For the Jew an especially fruitful area for comic effect is the representation of the disreputable and the unsavoury.'[26]

In September 1943 Gerron was deported with his wife to Westerbork, the Dutch transit camp, where he again appeared in cabaret, but only with German stars of stage and screen of Jewish origin. On the evening after the deportations, the cabaret and musicians were to perform, though this did not save them from eventual deportation, as some – in particular the director of the cabaret, the comedian, Max Ehrlich – had hoped.[27] In late February 1944 Gerron was sent with his wife to Theresienstadt, at a time when initial work on the film had been suspended. As he had fought during the First World War (twice wounded) and had been an Ufa director, he was designated a *Prominente*, even being allowed to live with his wife, though he was roughed up on arrival. Appearing again in cabaret, he soon received permission to form his own cabaret group, which he called *Karussell*. A great success (in the circumstances), it took the minds of both performers and audiences off their daily conditions, as one member of the jazz band, the Ghettoswingers, recalled, a view repeated by other survivors.[28]

A Czech inmate, Jindrich Weill, a former scriptwriter in the Czech film industry, had initially been ordered by the SS to work on a script. Between December 1943 and March 1944 he produced a synopsis and two different scripts. On 20 January 1944 Aktualitá filmed transports arriving from the Netherlands being welcomed by the leader of the Council of Elders, but filming then stopped as beautification took precedence. The plan to make a film was revived after the one-day Red Cross visit. Karl Rahm, now camp commander, handed the task to Gerron. Weil was not involved in this new effort, nor was he likely to have even been a member of Gerron's Film Department.[29] Friction between German and Czech Jews has been noted: both often kept their distance, and not merely for the obvious reason that they spoke different languages. Many Czechs resented the Germans because they spoke the language of the conqueror, and before 1918 the language of Habsburg domination. Now also they often enjoyed privileged status. Furthermore, the Czechs regarded Theresienstadt as their camp: it was on Czech soil, and they had been actively involved in setting it up. Finally, and most importantly, many Czechs had been deported to make room for the new arrivals. That it was no longer their camp was driven home when the popular Czech leader of the Jewish Council, Jacob Edelstein, was demoted to deputy to the recently arrived German Jewish academic, Philip Eppstein. (Both men later perished, the latter in the Small Fortress shortly after filming had ended.)

In July 1944 Gerron was summoned to the Camp Commandant and charged with directing the film, a script having been approved in Berlin. It is assumed that Gerron used Weil's script as a basis, given the similarities between the latter and the finished film.[30] Notes for Gerron's film have survived.[31] Shooting began on 16 August and lasted eleven working days, finishing on 11 September. Describing Gerron as the film's 'director' is misleading, for he was under close guard. Strictly supervised by the SS, he could not be directly asked any questions by the Czech cameramen, they then had to go first via the SS and then through an interpreter. He was never allowed to view any rushes. Sometimes Rahm himself or Günther from Prague appeared on the 'set', mainly to ensure that there was footage of the ghetto's *Prominente*, though a celluloid image did not necessarily interfere with deportation – many disappeared shortly thereafter.

Gerron did not direct the film to the very end; he was removed halfway through filming. A Czech non-Jew, Karel Pečený, Aktualitá's managing director, was ordered to take over. Demoted to assistant director or technical adviser, Gerron was still present as the cameras continued to roll, but dealt only with the production side, such as calling up actors – he experienced increasing difficulty in finding willing extras – and reporting to the SS. On 28 October 1944 he was deported to Auschwitz along with his wife and died there on 15 November 1944.[32]

Some survivors have not been kind to Gerron. He has been accused of taking the SS at their word, of accepting this assignment in the hope that he would avoid deportation, of letting his vanity get the better of him, of being only too pleased to make the film, and of behaving as though he were in an Ufa studio.[33] The Czech cameraman, Ivan Fric, is kinder:

> I had the impression that Gerron throughout was in a state of shock. His eyes were always restless, he was always afraid. Like most of the people taking part in the film, he was also driven by the hope that he would be able to survive … I had the feeling that he relied on his fame and on his past, that he believed what the SS people had promised him.

He cautions that it is difficult for anyone who has not experienced a concentration camp to understand how it was possible to grasp at anything that offered the slightest glimmer of hope.[34]

In Gerron's defence one might point out that old habits die hard. An experienced director, a star in fact, he may have given the impression of confidence. But what career was there to further? The circumstances were hardly propitious. That composers produced their work in Theresienstadt under the most adverse conditions (Klein or Ullmann) is marvelled at. Why should other performers be viewed differently, including a film director? Admittedly, there are significant differences in that Ullmann's opera composed in Theresienstadt, *Der Kaiser von Atlantis*, satirized the Third Reich and its leader, while Gerron was engaged in a propaganda exercise on behalf of the Nazis. Like members of the Jewish Council, he could be perceived as a collaborator, though he has been treated less generously than members of the Council, especially by historian survivor Adler.[35] Accusations of collaboration have been rife amongst some survivors. Gerron, it must be emphasized, had little choice in helping to make this film and, as should be evident, absolutely no power.

The film was cut and edited by one of the two Actualitá cameramen, the twenty-two-year-old Fric, who ignored Gerron's editing instructions, cutting the film as he would a weekly newsreel, improvising and using rough notes while viewing the rushes.[36] Fric admits that they came from two different film traditions – he from documentary and Gerron from feature films.[37] Closely supervised by the Gestapo, Fric was forced to redo the final sequence three times to meet Günther's approval.[38]

Gerron was neither the director in any mundane sense and certainly not the *auteur*. The completed film differed not only in structure but also in other ways from what he had planned: it bore little resemblance to his original script or editing proposal and was by no means a Gerron creation.[39] This was also true of the soundtrack, though some of the music had been recorded live under Gerron's direction or in his presence. It was Peter Deutsch, a German-born conductor and film composer who had fled to Denmark in 1933, was deported in 1943 and survived to return to Denmark, who provided some of the music, made the selections, all of which were by Jewish composers, and conducted the orchestra.

The film shows a number of musical events: an orchestra conducted by the well-known Czech conductor, Karel Ančerl (who survived to become conductor of the Czech Philharmonic); the 'Ghettoswingers', a jazz band formed in Theresienstadt; and the children's opera *Brundibár* composed in 1938 by Hans Krása, now also an inmate. *Brundibár*, a fairy tale in which children defeat an evil organ-grinder, was directed by another well-known conductor, Rafael Schaechter, and who performed in Theresienstadt on more than fifty-five occasions. It proved not only for its musical qualities and its message of hope, but also because it provided an activity for the children and delighted audiences, especially the children's audiences that we see in the film. Once Gerron was deported, other musical pieces were not recorded, the soundtrack only being completed on 28 March 1945 with the arrival of an Aktualitá sound team from Prague.

Despite the missing footage, it has been possible to reconstruct the film and the order of sequences. The film begins with a choir singing Mendelssohn's *Elijah* followed by drawings depicting Theresienstadt in the eighteenth century, followed by photographs of the town. After this come three sequences (now lost) which included a jazz band on a bandstand playing to an audience seated on benches, waitresses serving lemonade on a terrace shaded by umbrellas while others (including many *Prominente*) stroll through an adjoining garden, followed by an evening café scene with music and dancing. More leisure activities appear in the next sequences: inmates strolling on the ramparts and enjoying the view; girls sunbathing; old men playing chess; men's athletics and women's handball; followed by a theatre sequence (now lost). Next came sequences (all lost) showing inmates at work: men and women shouldering spades leaving from the central square for work; a session of the Jewish Council; a trial; a bank; shops; a post office at which a Red Cross parcel is collected. The next sequences have survived: a hospital with an operation in progress, followed by patients enjoying the sun on the hospital grounds; a children's nursing home where children eat bread and fruit; children on a playground where a paddling pool is visible, and a nursery school with children drinking lemonade and milk; a performance of *Brundibár* before a large audience of children with close-ups of rapt faces. The next sequences are missing: the fire brigade putting out a fire, and railway construction. Some agricultural scenes showing the fields outside the fortress town have survived. Sequences that have not survived included preparing food in the kitchens and eating in the communal dining hall, which was followed by more leisure scenes: an open-air variety show with *Prominente* in the audience. The next sequence – swimming in the River Eger – has survived. After this came some labour sequences (now lost): the central laundry, and craftsmen working in woodwork. The next sequences showing blacksmiths, metalworkers, a ceramics workshop, repair shops, tailors and shoemakers at work, craftsmen making handbags have survived. More leisure activities follow: a soccer match played by sturdy males, the central bathhouse, the library again with elderly *Prominente* in discussion holding books to camera. This is followed by a lecture given by the Prague University philosophy professor Emil Utitz, previously a Rector of the University of Rostock, who survived to write a psychological account of life in a concentration camp.[40] Rabbi Leo Baeck, one of the *Prominente*, likened Theresienstadt to a university where one could attend lectures on anything from Nietzsche to food chemistry, to the history of the Roman Catholic Church; he himself initiated a series of lectures on philosophical thinkers from Plato to Kant.[41] *Prominente* are visible in the audiences. At a concert with Ančerl conducting, we see in the audience two composers, Pavel Haas (a Janáček pupil) and Krása. Next we see a family allotment in a moat below the ramparts: a woman wearing shorts smiles to camera while displaying the radish she has just dug up; a couple stroll along an irrigation channel, beside which boys play leapfrog. People relax outside the barracks, women sew or knit while inside some chat by bunk beds, with only two tiers in evidence. The film concludes with a family evening meal, consisting of three generations: incongruously, the eldest generation is a Dutch couple (*Prominente*) Professor David Cohen and his wife, who dine with a Berlin couple, the Kozowers and their two children. Philipp Kozower had been a lawyer and Zionist and was deported shortly thereafter.[42] After this a closing montage.[43]

The camera does not lie. But the camera selects and frames. In Theresienstadt not everything was filmed: in this sense it did lie. Though the inmates play themselves, and the set is Theresienstadt, we do not see the deportations. In preparation for the Red Cross visit in May (just prior to filming) to make the ghetto look less overcrowded, 7,503 – including the elderly – were deported. That was to make the ghetto look less crowded. Nor do we see emaciated figures, or despairing faces, the images we have learned to associate with concentration camp inmates. Much of what we know about the camps comes from written or oral but not visual testimony. There are some photographs of Theresienstadt, including ones taken secretly by Fric in April 1944.[44] Many were new arrivals who appear well fed and warmly dressed. Their faces show concern. Only a few smile, though that may have been a response to the photographer. The streets are very crowded in contrast to the film.

The photographs are very different from the film. The latter shows cafés, concerts, sport, playgrounds and other amenities – and this in wartime. Some inmates smile, though others look anxious. Little girls in shorts, if not wearing a top, display the Jewish star prominently on their shorts. It was a serious offence not to wear the star, yet many children wearing playsuits or shorts without tops appear without stars, especially obvious when the camera scans the children's chorus in *Brundibár*. The children appear clean, well fed, well dressed and smile to camera. We also know that for the football matches which had been taking place regularly for over a year, only young players were wanted. Inmates were requested to fill up a barracks courtyard where the match was to be played.

One deceptive scene shows young children on a sunny afternoon smiling to camera while eating bread and margarine. The cameramen were forced to film this sequence on three separate occasions because the hungry children had devoured the bread so rapidly that filming could not be completed. On each occasion they had been forced to wait an hour and a half for the arrival of another batch of bread from the bakery.[45]

The shots of Ančerl conducting the string orchestra he had founded in the autumn of the previous year obscure his feet since despite wearing a suit, his feet were in clogs. Survivors mention that in the sleeping quarters the top tier of beds had been removed to create a sense of space. We also do not see that children slept two to a bed. The children's 'nursing home' is a former SS villa, temporarily vacated for the Red Cross inspection and for filming. The library had been recently transferred to a larger building. Allotments had only recently been made available to some inmates; costumes and musical instruments were suddenly delivered; benches, signs, rose beds, sandpits were put in place. The shrubs look like stage props, they too were new arrivals. The ramparts were an area normally off limits as was the river where some (a few naked) swim, the dive being performed by a champion swimmer.[46] It is a summer idyll – almost.

We see illness, of which there was a great deal, but the ill seem well cared for both by doctors and nurses in clean, crisp uniforms. The patients look comfortable, even contented, as they rest in their beds. It has been noted that in the operation sequence the patient is actually missing.[47] Smiles are everywhere in evidence. Is this an advertisement for Theresienstadt, a ghetto paradise? People are well turned out: some even fashionably attired. No one appears underfed; Gerron saw to this since only the well fed were wanted for film work, which usually meant recent arrivals. There is an occasional awkwardness which at times creates a staged effect, though not when the camera picks out from the concert or lecture audiences the faces of *Prominente* or physically attractive individuals. But when individuals are called on to perform before the camera, when for example sitting on a bench reading or on a bed chatting, one can almost hear the stage directions.

Interestingly, there does not seem to have been a concerted effort to film only those with what was deemed a distinctive Jewish physiognomy. Though blondes were not wanted, as evident in a request from Gerron himself, they are not absent from the film.[48] Cameramen were instructed to remove blonde girls and boys, yet a number of fair-haired children still appear. One survivor, an actor who assisted Gerron, recalled:

> It was quite a task to find ... those who looked like typical Jews from the point of view of Rosenberg's racial theories ... I have not found so many Nordic-looking people even in SS barracks as in this Jewish ghetto. Blondes were automatically excluded from the film, and a champion woman high jumper could not take part because she was blonde.[49]

One almost gets the impression of a balance being struck. Yes, we will give you examples of the physiognomy you require, but not every time. And the instructions were contradictory, for amongst the *Prominente* it was not always possible to find 'non-Aryan' types. Members of the SS, not particularly known for their intelligence, could be fooled at times, according to some survivor testimony. Was this why the camera moves from the faces of *Prominente* in the audience to close in on a young, attractive woman in 1940s-style upswept hairdo, listening intently, her Jewish star prominently displayed, brooch-like? Is this why the camera lingers on physically attractive children who would not be out of place in a Nazi-produced film about *Lebensborn*, where perfect Aryan children were bred, or closes in on a fair-haired maternal type who would not have been out of place on the streets of Nuremberg in 1934, though she was probably a *Prominente* and thus merited a ten-second shot?

What we see are people leading active, purposeful lives, working hard, and engaged in sensible leisure activities such as reading, knitting, sport or enjoying themselves on sunny days, giving 'an impression of a completely normal life'. This 'hymn to work' and play is not dissimilar to Ruttmann's city film, *Berlin, die Symphonie der Grossstadt* (*Berlin: Symphony of a Large City*) (1926) which established the genre.[50] *Theresienstadt: Symphony of a Concentration Camp* could be an alternative title. The football reportage, it has also been noted, was not dissimilar to *Wochenshau* reportage.[51]

Riefenstahl referred to sunny days as '*Hitlerwetter*', once again sunny weather is exploited by the camera, and not merely because it made filming easier. But life, as we know, was not sunny in Theresienstadt. This is the lie. This is not to say that *Brundibár* was not performed, or that concerts were not given, or that football matches did not take place, or that lectures were not organized, enhancing the ghetto's image as 'privileged', as well as offering a form of distraction to the inmates. But, as we now know, something significant was missing. The camera does not lie but does not film everything; in this sense it lies. Viewing the film today we can supply some missing elements. Did audiences then?

By the time of its first viewing, the film served no real purpose, as Germany faced defeat. Completed by late March 1945, after most of the Jewish participants were dead, the film had only a few showings: the first took place in late March or April 1945 at the Czernin Palace in Prague in the presence of its SS 'producers', Günther and Rahm, and the *Reichsprotektor*, Karl Hermann Frank. The other documented screenings were in Theresienstadt itself in April 1945 (probably on 6 April) to representatives of foreign organizations, such as the Red Cross, who were then present to try and negotiate the release of the inmates.[52] It was also shown to Swiss citizens and to a Swiss diplomat, as well as to Reszö Kasztner of the Hungarian-Jewish Rescue Committee. He had been involved in the Jews for sale proposals, and had organized a rescue train of 1,684 Jews from Hungary in the summer of 1944 to Bergen-Belsen and eventually to Switzerland. Kasztner was now there at Eichmann's invitation to observe the workings of a model ghetto. Also present on this occasion was the then head of the Jewish Council of Elders, Benjamin Murmelstein.

The film never achieved the purpose for which it was intended. By the time a viewing copy was ready, the foreign observers in the audience had some knowledge of the extermination camps: just before filming had begun in July 1944 the Russians had reached Majdánek. By April 1945 as Germany faced defeat the film served no real purpose; it was a matter of weeks before the war ended. The Americans were already waiting on the western Czech borders for Soviet forces to arrive from the East.

15

Liberation

Western Allied cameramen accompanied the victorious troops, entering the concentration camps and filming as they became liberated. That was in April 1945, by which time the war was almost over, but filming also continued for a short time after Germany surrendered. Films and photographs would provide visual evidence of German atrocities. Earlier, in the summer of 1944, Soviet forces had swept into Poland, the location of the extermination camps, but little filming was done. In July and August 1944 Majdánek, with its abandoned gas chambers, mass graves and a warehouse with 800,000 shoes, was discovered, marking the beginning of systematic photographic coverage. With film and equipment in short supply, the coverage was quite meagre and had little international distribution since in the West it was perceived as tainted.[1] A few Western journalists were invited to inspect the site but what they found was not on the same scale as what later confronted the media in the West. For this reason it would be misleading to describe it as a 'dress rehearsal' for the spring liberation.[2]

By the summer of 1944 some extermination camps had already been closed down and dismantled, while Sobibor, after a revolt in the autumn of 1943, had been completely razed to the ground. When these camps, or sites of these camps, were overrun, they were quickly passed by and went unmentioned in the Soviet press.[3] In January 1945, in the course of the Soviet advance, Auschwitz was discovered but given far less publicity than Majdánek; again there was a 'dearth of photographs'.[4] Indeed, the Soviet government took two months to reply to a Foreign Office enquiry about Auschwitz, eventually admitting that four million European citizens had died there.[5] What they had found at Auschwitz were a few thousand ill survivors, since the other inmates had either died or been 'evacuated', often on forced marches ('death marches') to other camps.

On 4 April 1945 the Americans entered Ohrdruf, a sub-camp of Buchenwald, where the US Army Signal Corps cameramen began filming. Eleven days later the British liberated Bergen-Belsen, a concentration camp near Hanover which had undergone several transformations since its creation in 1943 from a POW camp. The British Army Film and Photographic Unit (AFPU) filmed there, only stopping when the camp was burnt in late May 1945. Two newsreel men (from British Movietone News) were also present in April for a short period and recorded sound interviews. No other camp was filmed so extensively or over such a long period.[6]

The images of emaciated survivors or piles of corpses have become synonymous with the Holocaust but represent only a small minority of Nazi victims. As Hannah Arendt has emphasized:

> all pictures of concentration camps are misleading insofar as they show the camps in their last stages, at the moment the Allied troops marched in. There were no death camps in Germany proper, and at that point all extermination equipment had already been dismantled.[7]

Camps located in Germany, such as Belsen, had never been involved in extermination: death there was a result of abuse. What exists on film comes from the final months of the war and is of concentration camps not involved in extermination.

Aside from documentaries made with the help of Jewish inmates – where the Jew as 'other' was called on to film fellow Jews, subject to the approval of the overseer, as in the two Theresienstadt films – we have almost no footage of the camps *before* liberation, nothing to reveal how they functioned as their creators intended. This in itself is a reason why some filmmakers, such as Claude Lanzmann, have rejected archive footage since it cannot show mass murder.[8] Despite their enthusiasm for film and photography, the Nazis chose not to film the internal workings of concentration camps, except for Theresienstadt which, in any case, was technically a ghetto.

Official and unofficial still and moving footage exists of mass executions during the invasion of the Soviet Union and the Balkans. German soldiers, unlike Allied soldiers, were allowed to carry their own photographic equipment to the front – usually high quality – but were often forbidden to film executions, a ban which was frequently disregarded even by the SS. Soldiers usually retained the photographs as souvenirs.[9] There are even photographs of soldiers gazing at photographs which they hold in their hands of executions, the reason for which is not wholly clear.[10] Ghettos were also filmed or photographed, in particular Warsaw and Łódź,[11] and not always by Germans. There is also still or moving footage of some deportations.[12] But what went on in concentration camps, and especially in extermination camps, was a secret, which explains the absence of film footage, aside from photographs which were part of the administrative records used to identify inmates or were for the purpose of recording medical experiments.[13] There was almost no moving film.[14]

In April 1945 Western Allied cameramen began filming the camps: the AFPU Belsen, and the US Army Signal Corps others beginning with Ohrdruf, the first to be liberated. Eisenhower, as head of Supreme Headquarters Allied Expeditionary

Forces (SHAEF), had visited Ohrdruf eight days after its liberation, on 12 April; he was filmed entering the camp, his face and demeanour reflecting his shock.[15] After this visit he ordered a mass witnessing of the atrocities. Film was to play its part since audiences were to see what he had seen.[16] At his suggestion, arrangements were made for parliamentary and congressional delegations to visit Buchenwald. German dignitaries, such as mayors of the nearby towns, also visited.[17] Mayors in other regions visited other camps. These visits were captured on film to be used later in newsreels, on the assumption that the presence of such visitors would serve to authenticate the footage. The cameraman's task was not just to record but also to ensure that there could be no suggestion of anything being faked. Instinctively, cameramen, in particular the British, knew how to do this, either by panning or by moving from long to medium shots to close-ups of the individual or the corpse. That made it possible to establish without cuts or interruptions the geographic location of the camp with its precise place in the landscape.[18]

Prior to April 1945 some footage had been staged. The Auschwitz children of varying ages who, in the familiar striped uniform, stare back at the camera through barbed wire, while revealing the numbers tattooed on their arms, are unlikely to have been filmed at the moment of liberation.[19] Another example is the earlier 'picturesque liberation' of the Italian concentration camp, Cosenza, where the inmates twice re-enacted the event for the camera.[20]

Black-and-white footage of the camps is now familiar, even over-familiar. Colour footage, on the other hand, has been less widely shown, some never at all. US cameramen, in addition to shooting in black and white, also filmed in colour: for example, the 2,000 residents of nearby Weimar who were brought to Buchenwald to inspect the bodies were filmed both in black and white and in colour. Some, caught on film, were visibly shocked and distressed, a few fainted, but others displayed anger, perhaps at being filmed.[21] Colour took longer to process and, in losing its immediacy, lost its news value. It also required three-track projectors which were not available in every cinema. Rarely seen, either at the time or since, this colour footage has an altogether different resonance, especially when contrasted with black-and-white footage of the same subject. Colour softened and dissipated the impact. After decades of exposure to black-and-white footage of the concentration camps, colour appears less authentic. Film drained of colour may also seem more appropriate to the subject.

Filming the camps had several purposes, one of which was to justify both the reasons for fighting and the costs of the war. In this sense, it too belonged to a propaganda offensive. Allied expectations were high. Widely shown to British, French, American and Soviet audiences, the footage appeared either in newsreels or at special showings. In Britain the length of the newsreel was extended and the item was repeated in the second issue of the bi-weekly newsreel.[22] Almost three weeks earlier, however, prior to Eisenhower's visit to Ohrdruf, one British newsreel company (British Movietone) had been reluctant to use such film.[23]

The victims' identity was played down; rarely were they identified as Jews. Of course not all camp inmates at, for example, Belsen were Jews. But the reluctance to identify those who were has been attributed to a latent antisemitism on the part of the editors, when in fact it was the Ministry of Information which vetted everything. (An infamous British Ministry of Information directive of 1941 relating to atrocity propaganda had stipulated that 'horror stuff' should be avoided; the emphasis should be on the treatment of 'indisputably innocent people' which excluded 'violent opponents' and Jews.)[24] Conversely, it may have been that it was too obvious to bear reiteration, or that it reflected the liberal tradition that religion is a private matter, hardly relevant since the Nazi persecution of the Jews was on racial grounds, regardless of the religion they did or did not practise.[25] Certainly the Belsen cameramen were fully well aware of the inmates' identity and this comes across in the dope sheets (the cameraman's notes which described the accompanying newsreel).[26]

German audiences saw the material, though usually in altered form and with more graphic images.[27] According to one dope sheet from late May 1945, the German people should be 'equally well acquainted with' the 'terrible deeds' which had been 'committed in their name' and which were 'only too well known to the British public'.[28] As early as May 1945, newsreel-type compilations were being screened to Germans.[29] German POWs were also shown films.[30] On grounds of practicality, cinema rather than visits to concentration camps soon became the preferred means of reaching Germans.

Documenting on film the criminal character of the Nazi regime also had a juridical purpose and was used in evidence at the Nuremberg Tribunal. Hollywood director George Stevens was part of the team which made a compilation film under the title, *The Nazi Plan*, intended as a documentary history of the Third Reich. Another film screened was the sixty-minute *Nazi Concentration Camps* which used footage shot by the US Signal Corps and British AFPU.[31] Earlier some of this footage had been used in the Belsen trial, which took place in nearby Lüneberg from September to November 1945. There the prosecutor invited the camp commandant 'to watch the degradation to which the human mind can descend'.[32] Nevertheless, film alone was never accepted as proof of the actual occurrence, but was used solely to authenticate witness testimony.[33]

Not only was concentration camp footage screened at Nuremberg, but the reactions of those standing trial who were forced to view that footage, was, unbeknownst to them, also filmed. Stuart Schulberg, son of Hollywood producer B. P. S. Schulberg and brother of the better-known screenwriter Budd, was a member of the Documentary Evidence Section of the American prosecution at Nuremberg. The night before the screening it became apparent that with the lights off 'it would be impossible to capture the defendants' reactions.' They then managed to devise a means of filming the defendants while keeping them unaware. Schulberg helped set up the camera and later commented that some like Rudolf Hess smiled, but within half an hour others had their smiles 'wiped off their faces as they went to the movies in Nuremberg'.[34]

Not everyone considered newsreels adequate for the purpose of exposing Nazi crimes. For this reason Britain and the US decided on a joint project to produce a documentary about the concentration and extermination camps. What eventually emerged, however, were two separate documentaries. The American-made two-reel *Die Todesmühlen* (*Death Mills*) was shown in the US Zone of Military Occupation in Germany in January 1946.[35] The British six-reel film (with one reel missing) was never completed and did not have a public screening until 1984. For a long time it was known only under its Ministry of Information file number, F3080, until allocated an archive title, *Memory of the Camps*.[36]

The British film was made on the instructions of Sidney Bernstein, head of the Film Section of the Psychological Warfare Division or PWD (Rear) of SHAEF. Bernstein also played an important role at the Ministry of Information as well as having responsibility for planning film production and exhibition in western occupied Germany. With a background in film production and distribution on both sides of the Atlantic and as one of the founders of the London Film Society twenty years previously, he had helped persuade the War Office to expand the Army Film Unit. In February 1945 Bernstein told the head of PWD, Brigadier General Robert McClure, that he had learned that the Soviets were preparing to show war films in Germany, 'particularly those which show the German atrocities, the damage done by Germans to Russian towns, and the general bestial attitude of the Germans'.[37] McClure was not impressed since he preferred films which emphasized 'the way of living in democratic countries' rather than war films which could drive audiences away.[38] He shared neither Bernstein's enthusiasm for film nor his belief in the power of film.[39]

Undeterred, Bernstein tried to collect as much German atrocity footage as possible, from the US Army Pictorial Service, the War Office, the RAF, British newsreel companies and Russian newsreels. After receiving some of the Belsen footage, he decided on making a film specifically for British audiences. On 22 April 1945, seven days after the camp had been liberated and eight days before Hitler's suicide, he visited Belsen. That visit transformed the project. What had begun as a retrospective compilation film project became a mission to produce a definitive full-length documentary, not only with archived material but also with new, specially shot sequences. It was also planned to show the film to German audiences to make them aware of Nazi crimes, remind them of their 'acquiescence' and force them to accept 'the justice of Allied occupation measures'.[40] Three separate versions were planned: for Germans in Germany; for German POWs; and for 'audiences, perhaps specialized, in neutral, liberated and allied territories'.[41]

Determined to build up a quasi-legal case on film, Bernstein gave meticulous instructions to the Belsen cameramen, such as asking them to photograph any material which revealed links between German industry and the concentration camps. For sanitary and humanitarian reasons the camps were in the process of quickly being cleared. There were also delays: the US Army Pictorial Service, for example, failed to supply duplicates of footage as originally agreed. And there was more material than originally envisaged.[42] Cutting could only commence once all the material was in.

In May, efforts were made to find a director. Alfred Hitchcock's name surfaced. Hitchcock was a friend of Bernstein, who had used him the previous year to make two short films for liberated France. Bernstein also approached the film director Sidney Gilliat and the producer and writer Colonel Eric Ambler, but neither was free.[43] Hitchcock did not arrive in London until late June, staying only one month. It would be more accurate to describe him as an adviser rather than a director, since he was never present at any of the filming.[44] His major concern was to avoid a charge of faking a film: he advised the editors to avoid tricky editing and, where possible, use long shots and panning shots without any cuts: for example, panning from a guard to a corpse to make apparent the relationship.[45]

The film incorporated footage from eleven camps. After a general preface came three reels from Belsen followed by other camps which included Dachau, Buchenwald and Ebensee with its dying inmates, but set in a beautiful Alpine landscape. After that, other camps, each with smaller and smaller numbers, including Mauthausen, Ludwigslust, Ohrdruf, Thekla, Gardelegen, and concluding with an extended sequence of two camps without inmates, the two extermination camps, Majdánek and Auschwitz.[46] It was Hitchcock who suggested the sequence in the final reel (now lost): the possessions of those who had died at Auschwitz, including wedding rings, toothbrushes, spectacles, as well as gold extracted from teeth and the mounds of hair.[47]

Cinemas remained closed in Germany until late July, except for some screenings of concentration camp material.[48] To test the waters, a trial screening of a two-reel film entitled *KZ*, short for *Konzentrationslager* (*Concentration Camp*),[49] took place in Erlangen in the American sector; a series of short films was screened and it came last.[50] It also appeared in a similarly entitled newsreel for *Welt im Film*, the Anglo-American newsreel for Occupied Germany, in its fifth issue shown in June 1945.[51] After this the Americans concluded that there was a need for a slightly longer atrocity film to be screened immediately rather than at a later date. Frustrated by the delays in Britain, they had decided, it seems, already in June to make their own film.[52] By the time Bernstein had finally managed to assemble his team, the Americans had backed out of the joint venture but he remained undetered.

In July SHAEF was also dissolved, and with it the PWD. Bernstein learned that the project now came under the auspices of the Foreign Office which believed the more pressing concern was to shake the Germans out of their apathy. Though press and radio had now become the preferred means of reaching them, the need for 'a first-class documentary record of these atrocities' was recognized but 'not the rather crude and un-thought out newsreel so far shown'. (That was a reference to the American-made *KZ*.) Such a film could be screened in nine months' time once the difficulties of the winter had been dealt with.[53] In September 1945 Bernstein left the MOI, leaving behind a fine cut of five of the six reels without sound, credits or titles. By then the Americans were producing their two-reel (twenty-two-minute) film *Todesmühlen* on which Hollywood émigré director Billy Wilder had briefly advised in August 1945. Earlier, in May, Bernstein had also consulted Wilder during his short visit to London.[54]

Eventually, *Todesmühlen* was screened in Germany in January 1946 as part of the denazification programme which was compulsory viewing in some areas. In some places theatre staff even stamped the food ration cards of members of the audience.[55] Sequences from *Triumph of the Will* were included to emphasize German complicity. Riefenstahl had captured on film the visible bond between Führer and people. As the crowds welcome Hitler, footage is superimposed of Germans, mainly female, walking towards Buchenwald in 1945 on their forced visit. On the soundtrack a narrator intones: as for the Germans who plead for sympathy, 'remember if they bear heavy crosses now they are the crosses of the millions crucified in Nazi death mills.'[56]

Sequences from *Triumph of the Will* also appeared at the beginning of *Memory of the Camps*.[57] That was no mere coincidence, since for filmmakers that was where the story began. *The Nazi Plan*, the title of the compilation film screened at Nuremberg, also incorporated sequences from *Triumph of the Will*, as well as from *Tag der Freiheit*.[58] And *Todesmühlen* incorporated the sequence showing Hitler on a balcony with the crowds below, their arms raised in the Hitler greeting.

Todesmühlen failed in its purpose, partly because by the time of its screening the Americans had abandoned the policy of collective guilt. But its failure can also be attributed to its makers' fervent belief in the transformative power of film.[59] Bernstein's better-crafted film, on the other hand, was deprived of the opportunity to fail in its purpose since it did not reach an audience for another thirty-nine years, and when it did it was in the atmosphere of a Berlin film festival, an altogether different context from what he had envisaged.[60]

If *Triumph of the Will* is shorthand for the triumph of Hitler, then images of the concentration camps twelve years later are shorthand for the cost of that triumph: human degradation on a colossal scale. Such images have come to signify the end of the Third Reich. They show the Nazis not as they wished to be seen but as seen by their enemies. It is their victims, both present and absent, who are the subject of these films. When fit to do so, camp inmates stare back at the camera, now held in the hands of their liberator rather than their incarcerator. Some, usually the more recent arrivals, attempt a smile. Six years earlier in Poland, young orthodox Jewish males before and after the cutting of their side-locks and beards stared, and occasionally even smiled, at the camera held by the enemy. That sequence appears in *Der ewige Jude*. In Theresienstadt, inmates, obviously recent arrivals, also smiled for the camera. It is, however, the better known footage from the concentration camps liberated by the Allies which now has the iconic status.

We know that the camera is not neutral. It can lie either through selection or omission, or by coaching the subject to elicit a particular response, or through framing, lighting, camera angle, editing. Concentration camps had been in existence for eighteen months when *Triumph of the Will* was filmed. For obvious reasons, they are absent from a film whose purpose was to show consent not terror. The images of ecstatic crowds greeting Hitler at Nuremberg were used after the war to suggest German complicity. At Nuremberg where, appropriately, the trial of the major war criminals was held, other sequences were offered as supporting evidence.[61] On these occasions, however, it was assumed that the camera had not lied.

Notes

Notes to Chapter 1: Hitler: Image-Building

1   Adolf Hitler, *Mein Kampf*, trans. R. Manheim (London, 1969), p. 427.
2   R.G. Reuth, *Goebbels*, trans. K. Winston (London, 1993), p. 81.
3   M.S. Phillips, 'The Nazi Control of the German Film Industry', *Journal of European Studies*, 1, (1971), p. 44. Freud also discussed Le Bon's theory of crowds in *Group Psychology and the Ego* (1921).
4   Ibid., p. 80.
5   Hitler, *Mein Kampf*, pp. 451–2.
6   Ibid., p. 440.
7   Ibid., p. 452.
8   H. Hoffmann, *The Triumph of Propaganda, Film and National Socialism 1933–1945*, trans. J. Broadwin (Providence, RI, and Oxford, 1996), p. 21.
9   Ibid., pp. 11–22.
10 I. Kershaw, *The 'Hitler Myth': Image and Reality in the Third Reich* (Oxford, 1987), pp. 21–4.
11 Ibid., p. 67.
12 I. Kershaw, *Hitler*, i, *1889–1936: Hubris* (London, 1998), p. 280.
13 R. Herz, *Hoffmann und Hitler* (Munich, 1994), pp. 103–6.
14 Ibid., p. 101.
15 Ibid., pp. 110–11.
16 Ibid., p. 108.
17 Herz, *Hoffmann und Hitler*, pp. 112, 113.
18 Kershaw, *Hitler*, i, p. 282.
19 Herz, *Hoffmann und Hitler*, p. 17.
20 Ibid., p. 119.
21 Ibid., p. 120.
22 Ibid., p. 122.
23 Ibid., pp. 242–51.
24 Ibid., p. 253.
25 Kershaw, *The 'Hitler Myth'*, p. 4.
26 Ibid., pp. 80–2.
27 Ibid., p. 93.
28 Ibid., p. 168.

29   Ibid., pp. 157–60.

30   Ibid., pp. 199, 210.

31   Ibid., pp. 211, 219.

32   Reuth, *Goebbels*, p. 211.

33   Susan Tegel, '"The Demonic Effect": Veit Harlan's Use of Jewish Extras in *Jud Süss* (1940)', *Holocaust and Genocide Studies*, 14 (2000), p. 215.

34   Kershaw, *Hitler*, i, p. 485.

35   I. Kershaw, *Hitler*, ii, *Nemesis: 1936–1945* (London, 2000), p. 33.

36   E. Fröhlich, ed., *Die Tagebücher von Joseph Goebbels* (Munich, 2000), pt 1, vol. v, p. 64 (22 December 1937).

37   Kershaw, *Hitler*, p. 105.

38   Ibid., p. 211; Fröhlich, *Die Tagebücher von Joseph Goebbels* (Munich, 1998), pt 1, vol. vii, p. 75 (24 August 1939).

39   M. Balfour, *Propaganda in War* (London, 1979), p. 19.

40   Kershaw, *Hitler*, i, p. 440.

41   Heinz Pohle, *Der Rundfunk als Instrument der Politik*, cited in Balfour, *Propaganda in War*, p. 19; Z.A.B. Zeman, *Nazi Propaganda* (London, 1964), p. 51.

42   Balfour, *Propaganda in War*, p. 19.

43   Zeman, *Nazi Propaganda*, p. 51.

44   Ibid. He was spurred on by the rhythmic chant of '*Sieg Heil*' which formed an 'acoustic backdrop'.

45   Hitler, *Mein Kampf*, p. 427.

46   Balfour, *Propaganda in War*, pp. 123, 308, 309.

47   D. Welch, *Propaganda and the German Cinema*, 2nd edn (London, 2001), p. 5.

48   Eric Rentschler, *The Ministry of Illusion* (Cambridge, MA, 1999), p. 172.

49   K. Hoffmann, 'Propagandistic Problems of German Newsreels in World War II', *Historical Journal of Film, Radio and Television*, 24 (2004), p. 137.

50   F. Moeller, *The Film Minister: Goebbels and the Cinema in the 'Third Reich'*, trans. M. Robinson (Stuttgart and London, 2000), p. 151.

51   Ibid., p. 156.

52   Fröhlich, *Die Tagebücher von Joseph Goebbels* (Munich, 1996), pt 2, vol. viii, p. 81 (6 October 1942).

53   Ibid., p. 156 (20 October 1942).

54   Moeller, *The Film Minister*, p. 151.

55   A. Bullock, *Hitler, a Study in Tyranny*, 2nd edn (London, 1962), p. 722.

56   Hoffmann, 'Propagandistic Problems of German Newsreels in World War II', p. 137; Moeller, *The Film Minister*, p. 157.

57   *Deutsche Wochenschau*, no. 725 (27 July 1944).

58   *Deutsche Wochenschau*, no. 755 (22 March 1945). See the *Independent*, 26 April 2005, for an interview with the Hitler Youth who was awarded the Iron Cross, where the occasion is wrongly dated to 20 April 1945, Hitler's birthday. Number 755 was the last issue of *Wochenschau*. See P. Bucher, *Wochenschauen und Dokumentarfilme 1895–1950 im Bundesarchiv-Filmarchiv* (Koblenz, 1984), p. 152.

Notes to Chapter 2: Nazi Propaganda

1   A. Bullock, *Hitler, a Study in Tyranny*, 2nd edn (London, 1964), p. 57; N. Ferguson, *The Pity of War* (London, 1998), pp. 313–14.

2   Lord Beaverbrook, *Men and Power, 1917–1918* (New York, 1956), p. 303, cited in A.G. Marquis, 'Words as Weapons: Propaganda in Germany during the First World War', *Journal of Contemporary History*, 13 (1978), p. 493.

3   Quoted in P. Taylor, 'Psychological Warfare', in N. Cull, D. Culbert and D. Welch, eds, *Propaganda and Mass Persuasion: A Historical Encyclopedia, 1500 to the Present* (Santa Barbara, CA, Denver, CO, and Cambridge, 2003), p. 325.

4   D. Welch, *Germany, Propaganda and Total War 1914–1918: The Sins of Omission* (London, 2000), pp. 7, 237–9, 247, 252–6.

5   P. Taylor, *Munitions of the Mind: A History of Propaganda from the Ancient World to the Present Era* (Manchester, 1995), p. 191.

6   E. Hadamovsky, *Propaganda und nationale Macht: Die Organisation der öffentlichen Meinung für die nationale Politik* (Oldenburg, 1933), pp. 14–15.

7   Adolf Hitler, *Mein Kampf*, trans. R. Manheim (London, 1969), p. 528.

8   Ibid., p. 161.

9   Ibid.

10   Ibid., p. 169.

11   Ibid., pp. 167–8.

12   Ibid., p. 165.

13   Ibid., p. 169.

14   Ibid., p. 163.

15   Ibid., p. 167.

16   Ibid., p. 168.

17   Ibid., p. 169.

18   Étienne Cabet, *Voyage en Icarie*, 2nd edn, (Paris, 1842). Chapter 15 is entitled 'Association et propagande pour la communauté'. For the use of propaganda in political discourse see Christopher Johnson, *Utopian Communism in France: Cabet and the Icarians, 1839–1851* (Ithaca, NY, 1974), pp. 82–8.

19   Taylor, *Munitions of the Mind*, p. 197.

20   Ibid., passim, pp. 21–4, 29–32.

21   R. Herzstein, *The War that Hitler Won: The Most Infamous Propaganda Campaign in History* (New York, 1978), pp. 22, 431.

22   I. Kershaw, 'How Effective was Nazi Propaganda?', in D. Welch, ed., *Nazi Propaganda* (Totowa, NJ, 1983), pp. 184, 188.

23   Aldous Huxley, 'Notes on Propaganda', *Harper's Monthly Magazine*, 174 (December 1936), p. 39.

24   Kershaw, 'How Effective was Nazi Propaganda?', pp. 189–90; D. Welch, 'Nazi Propaganda and the *Volksgemeinschaft*', *Journal of Contemporary History*, 39 (April 2004), p. 236.

25   D. Welch, *The Third Reich: Politics and Propaganda* (London, 1993), p. 23.

26   R.G. Reuth, *Goebbels*, trans. Krishna Winston (London, 1993), pp. 37, 50, 52.

27   Ibid., pp. 52, 76, 77.

28 Ibid., p. 93.

29 Ibid., p. 53.

30 Ibid., pp. 62–4.

31 Ibid., p. 71.

32 Goebbels, 'Mein Kampf um Berlin', cited in Reuth, *Goebbels*, p. 81.

33 M. Ecksteins, 'War, Memory and Politics: The Fate of the Film *All Quiet on the Western Front*', *Central European History*, 13 (1980), p. 71; J.W. Chambers, II, '*All Quiet on the Western Front* (US, 1930): The Antiwar Film and the Image of the Modern War', in J.W. Chambers, II and D. Culbert, eds, *World War II: Film and History* (New York, 1996), pp. 22–3.

34 Ibid., p. 65.

35 Reuth, *Goebbels*, p. 124.

36 G. Stahr, *Volksgemeinschaft vor der Leinwand? Der nationalsozialistische Film und sein Publicum* (Berlin, 2001), p. 118.

37 Ibid., p. 118; Ecksteins, 'War, Memory and Politics', pp. 77, 82.

38 J. Garncarz, 'Hollywood in Germany: The Role of American Films in Germany', in D. Ellwood and R. Kroes, eds, *Hollywood in Europe: Experiences of a Cultural Hegemony* (Amsterdam, 1994), p. 123.

39 Ibid., p. 73.

40 H. Korte, *Der Spielfilm und das Ende der Weimarer Republik* (Göttingen, 1998), p. 423.

41 Ibid., p. 75.

42 E. Fröhlich, ed., *Die Tagebücher von Joseph Goebbels* (Munich, 2005), pt 1, 2/i, p. 300 (9 December 1930).

43 Reuth, *Goebbels*, pp. 172–3.

44 Ibid., p. 172.

45 *Presse in Fesseln*, cited in Reuth, *Goebbels*, p. 172; Balfour, *Propaganda in War* (London, 1979), p. 12.

46 Ibid., p. 180.

47 Balfour, *Propaganda in War*, p. 104.

48 Reuth, *Goebbels*, p. 184.

49 Ibid., p. 176.

50 D. Peukert, *Inside Nazi Germany: Conformity, Opposition, and Racism in Everyday Life*, trans. R. Deveson (New Haven, CT, 1987), p. 78.

51 Z.A.B. Zeman, *Nazi Propaganda*, 2nd edn (London, Oxford and New York, 1973), p. 49; C. Zimmermann, 'From Propaganda to Modernization: Media Policy and Media Audiences under National Socialism', *German History*, 24 (2006), p. 446.

52 Balfour, *Propaganda in War*, p. 15.

53 Zeman, *Nazi Propaganda*, p. 49.

54 Peukert, *Inside Nazi Germany*, p. 78.

55 Zimmermann, 'The Media under National Socialism', p. 442.

56 R. Taylor, *Film Propaganda: Soviet Russia and Nazi Germany*, 2nd edn (London, 1998), p. 30.

57 Goebbels's speech, 9 February 1934, in E. Leiser, *Nazi Cinema*, trans. G. Mander and D. Wilson (London, 1974), p. 47.

58   F. Moeller, *The Film Minister: Goebbels and the Cinema in the 'Third Reich'*, trans. M. Robinson (Stuttgart and London, 2000), p. 10.

59   H. Heiber, ed., *Goebbels-Reden 1932–1939* (Düsseldorf, 1971), p. 94.

60   Taylor, *Film Propaganda*, p. 10. G. Albrecht, *Der Film im 3. Reich* (Karlsruhe, 1979), pp. 76, 77.

61   Moeller, *The Film Minister*, p. 10.

Notes to Chapter 3: The German Film Industry to 1918

1   J. Garncarz, 'The Origins of Film Exhibition in Germany', in T. Bergfelder, E. Carter and D. Göktürk, eds, *The German Cinema Book* (London, 2002), p. 113.

2   O. Kalbus, *Vom Werden deutscher Filmkunst* (Altona, 1935), i, p. 11; F. Zglinicki, *Der Weg des Film* (Frankfurt, 1956)), pp. 241–53; S. Hake, *German National Cinema* (London and New York, 2002), p. 10; Garncarz, 'The Origins of Film Exhibition in Germany', p. 113.

3   M. Hansen, 'Early Silent Cinema: Whose Public Sphere?', *New German Critique*, 29 (1983), p. 162.

4   Neil Gabler, *An Empire of their Own: How the Jews Invented Hollywood* (New York, 1988), p. 24.

5   K. Kreimeier, *The Ufa Story: A History of Germany's Greatest Film Company*, trans. R. and R. Kimber (Berkeley, CA, Los Angeles and London, 1999), p. 35.

6   K. Thompson, *Exporting Entertainment: America in the World Film Market, 1907–1934* (London 1985), p. 37.

7   W. Jacobsen, 'Frühgeschichte des deutschen Films', in W. Jacobsen, A. Kaes and H.H. Prinzler, eds, *Geschichte des deutschen Films* (Stuttgart, 1993), p. 20; D. Welch, *Germany, Propaganda and Total War: The Sins of Omission* (London 2000), p. 41.

8   E. Altenloh, *Zur Soziologie des Kinos* (Jena, 1914), p. 55. Part of this study has been translated into English: see *Screen* 42 (2001), pp. 249–93.

9   G. Stark, 'Cinema, Society and the State: Policing the Film Industry in Imperial Germany', in G. Stark and B.H. Lackner, eds, *Essays on Culture and Society in Modern Germany History* (Arlington, TX, 1982), p. 133.

10   J. Robertson, *The British Board of Film Censors* (London, 1985), pp. 2–5.

11   Kalbus, *Vom Werden deutscher Filmkunst*, p. 13; Zglinicki, *Der Weg des Films*, pp. 370–1.

12   Stark, 'Cinema, Society and the State', pp. 149–52; H.H. Wollenberg, *Fifty Years of German Film* (London, 1947), p. 9.

13   Welch, *Germany, Propaganda and Total War*, pp. 43–4; Stark, 'Cinema, Society and the State', pp. 136–48.

14   Hake, *German National Cinema*, p. 10.

15   Welch, *Germany, Propaganda and Total War*, pp. 49–50.

16   Ibid., p. 45.

17   Ibid., p. 57.

18   Ibid., p. 54.

19   Zglinicki, *Der Weg des Films*, pp. 394–5.

20   Hake, *German National Cinema*, pp. 24–5.

21   Welch, *Germany, Propaganda and Total War*, p. 56; Zglienicki, *Der Weg des Films*, p. 328.

22   Kreimeier, *The Ufa Story*, p. 36.

23   Ibid., pp. 36, 44.

24   Hake, *German National Cinema*, p. 14.

Notes to Chapter 4: Weimar Cinema

 1   N. Ferguson, *The Pity of War* (London, 1998), p. 295.

 2   K. Thompson, 'Dr Caligari at the Folies-Bergère or the Success of an Avant-Garde Film', in M. Budd, ed., *The Cabinet of Dr Caligari* (New Brunswick, NJ, and London, 1990), pp. 124–5.

 3   K. Thompson and D. Bordwell, *Film History: An Introduction* (New York, 1994), pp. 106–7.

 4   A. Kaes, 'Film in der Weimarer Republik', in W. Jacobsen, A. Kaes and H.H. Prinzler, eds, *Geschichte des deutschen Films* (Stuttgart, 1993), p. 72; P. Monaco, *Cinema and Society: France and Germany during the Twenties* (New York and Amsterdam, 1976), p. 31; H.H. Wollenberg, *Fifty Years of German Film* (London, 1948), p. 32.

 5   D. Peukert, *The Weimar Republic*, trans. R. Deveson (New York, 1989), pp. 275–6.

 6   Ibid., p. 164.

 7   K. Gough-Yates, 'The British Feature Film as a European Concern: Britain and the Emigré Film-Maker', in G. Berghaus, ed., *Theatre and Film in Exile: German Artists in Britain, 1933–1945* (Oxford, 1989), p. 152.

 8   L. Eisner, *The Haunted Screen*, trans. R. Greaves (Berkeley, CA, and Los Angeles, 1973), p. 19.

 9   Thompson, 'Dr Caligari at the Folies-Bergère or the Success of an Avant-Garde Film', esp. pp. 123–24.

10   Ibid., pp. 138–9.

11   S. Hake, *German National Cinema* (London and New York, 2002), p. 31.

12   N. Gabler, *An Empire of their Own: How the Jews Invented Hollywood* (New York, 1988), pp. 24, 207.

13   K. Thompson, *Exporting Entertainment: America in the World Film Market, 1907–1934* (London, 1985), p. 168.

14   Quoted in A. Kaes, 'The Debate about Cinema: Charting a Controversy, 1909–1929', *New German Critique*, 40 (1987), p. 21.

15   Monaco, *Cinema and Society*, esp. ch. 3.

16   J. Garncarz, 'Hollywood in Germany: The Role of American Films in Germany', in D. Ellwood and R. Kroes, eds, *Hollywood in Europe: Experiences of a Cultural Hegemony* (Amsterdam, 1994), pp. 94–9, 116–17, 122–4.

17   B. Murray, *Film and The German Left in the Weimar Republic: From Caligari to Kuhle Wampe* (Austin, TE, 1990) p. 121; J.C. Robertson, *The Hidden Cinema: British Censorship in Action, 1913–1975* (London and New York, 1989), p. 31; Wollenberg, *Fifty Years of German Film*, pp. 32–3.

18   Gough-Yates, 'The British Feature Film as a European Concern', pp. 135–6, 142–46.

19   Ibid., p. 150.

20   S. Kracauer, *From Caligari to Hitler: A Psychological History of the German Film* (Princeton, NJ, 1947), p. 11.

21   L. Quaresima, 'Introduction', *From Caligari to Hitler: A Psychological History of the German Film* (Princeton, NJ, 2004), pp. xxvi–xxix.

22   K. Witte, 'Introduction to Siegfried Kracauer's "The Mass Ornament"', *New German Critique*, 5 (1975), p. 61.

23   Gerhard Stahr, *Volksgemeinschaft vor der Leinwand? Der nationalsozialistische Film und sein Publicum* (Berlin, 2001), p. 100.

24   S.S. Prawer, *Caligari's Children: The Film as Tale of Terror* (Oxford, 1980), pp. 168–9; T.E. Isaesser, *Weimar Cinema and after: Germany's Historical Imaginary* (London and New York, 2000), pp. 162–74.

25   Wollenberg, *Fifty Years of German Film*, p. 19.

26   Kaes, 'Film in der Weimarer Republik', p. 46.

27   Monaco, *Cinema and Society*, pp. 148–9.

28   C. Usborne, 'Reblious Girls and Pitiable Women: Abortion Narratives in Weimar Popular Culture', *Germany History*, 23 (2005), pp. 323–6.

29   Kaes, 'Film in der Weimarer Republik', p. 61; Petro, P. *Joyless Streets: Women and Melodramatic Representation in Weimar Germany* (Princeton, NJ, 1989), pp. 160–74.

30   Wollenberg, *Fifty Years of German Film*, pp. 13–14.

31   Kaes, 'Film in der Weimarer Republik', p. 54.

32   Kreimeier, *The Ufa Story*, pp. 144–45.

33   H. Loewy, *Béla Balázs: Märchen, Ritual und Film* (Berlin, 2003), p. 360.

34   Garncarz, 'Hollywood in Germany', p. 123.

35   Ibid.

36   Kracauer, *From Caligari to Hitler*, pp. 115–19; Kreimeier, *The Ufa Story*, pp. 93–6; D. Welch, *Propaganda and the German Cinema*, 2nd edn (London, 2001), pp. 147–55.

37   Kracauer, *From Caligari to Hitler*, pp. 115–19.

38   Harlan, *Im Schatten meiner Filme* (Gütersloh, 1966), pp. 133–4.

39   Script at Stiftung Deutsche Kinemathek, Schriftgut Archiv, Berlin.

40   Helmut Korte, *Der Spielfilm und das Ende der Weimarer Republik* (Göttingen, 1998), pp. 126ff. and 422–8.

Notes to Chapter 5: The Nazi Film Industry

1   M. Balfour, *Propaganda in War* (London, 1979), p. 38.

2   Ibid.

3   Ibid.; J. Wulf, *Theater und Film im dritten Reich: eine Dokumentation* (Frankfurt am Main, 1983), pp. 324–6; W. Becker, *Film und Herrschaft: Organisationsprinzipien und Organisationsstrukturen der nationalsozialistischen Filmpropaganda* (Berlin, 1973), p. 54.

4   Becker, *Film und Herrschaft*, p. 55.

5   M.S. Phillips, 'The Nazi Control of the German Film Industry', *Journal of European Studies*, 1 (1971), p. 41.

6   Arnold Raether to Hans Hinkel, 8 September 1933, Berlin Document Centre, in D. Culbert, ed., Leni Riefenstahl's *Triumph of the Will* (University Publications of America, 1986), microform.

7   J. Petley, 'Film Policy in the Third Reich', in T. Bergfelder, E. Carter and D. Göktürk, eds, *The German Cinema Book* (London, 2002), pp. 174–5; Becker, *Film und Herrschaft*, pp. 131, 161.

8   M. Loiperdinger, 'State Legislation, Censorship and Funding', in Bergfelder, Carter and Göktürk, eds, *The German Cinema Book*, p. 151; Becker, *Film und Herrschaft*, p. 70.

9   L. Kopenick, *The Dark Mirror: German Cinema between Hitler and Hollywood* (Berkeley, CA, Los Angeles and London, 2002), pp. 52, 282 n.8.

10 S. Tegel, 'Veit Harlan and the Origins of *Jud Süss*, 1938–1939: Opportunism in the Creation of Nazi Anti-Semitic Film Propaganda', *Historical Journal of Film, Radio and Television*, 16 (1996), pp. 517–18.

11 Veit Harlan, *Im Schatten meiner Filme* (Gütersloh, 1966), pp. 89–90.

12 Bundesarchiv Berlin (hereafter BArch), Berlin Document Centre, RKK 2100 (0453, 3), Adolf Teichs file; see also Tegel, 'Veit Harlan and the Origins of *Jud Süss*', p. 528 n.25.

13 G. Albrecht, *Nationalsozialistische Filmpolitik: eine soziologische Untersuchung über die Spielfilme des dritten Reiches* (Stuttgart, 1969), pp. 208–9.

14 B. Panse, 'Der Reichspropagandaminister über seine besten Helfer: "Diese Künstler sind wie Kinder"', *Theater Heute*, 9 (1989), 7, 21 n.1.

15 K. Witte, *Lachende Erben, Toller Tag: Film Kömodie im Dritten Reich* (Berlin, 1995), pp. 88ff.

16 P. McGilligan, *Fritz Lang: The Nature of the Beast* (New York, 1997), pp. 11, 111, 184.

17 Wulf, *Theater und Film im dritten Reich*, p. 94.

18 BArch, Sammlung Brammer, ZSg. 101/15, 3 January 1940.

19 E. Fröhlich, ed., *Die Tagebücher von Joseph Goebbels* (Munich, 1996), pt 2, vol. vi, p. 155 (20 October 1942).

20 K. Gough-Yates, 'The British Feature Film as a European Concern: Britain and the Emigré Film-Maker, 1933–1945', in G. Berghaus, ed., *Theatre and Film in Exile: German Artists in Britain, 1933–1945* (Oxford, 1989), p. 136.

21 *Filmwoche*, 10 (7 March 1934), p. 291.

22 B. Felsmann, and K. Prümm, *Kurt Gerron — Gefeiert und Gejagt, 1897–1944* (Berlin, 1992), p. 63.

23 Carl Zuckmayer, *Geheimreport* (Göttingen, 2002), p. 12.

24 Becker, *Film und Herrschaft*, p. 63; Balfour, *Propaganda in War*, p. 40.

25 *Filmwoche*, 1 (3 January 1934), p. 10; 2 (10 January 1934), p. 62; 3 (17 January 1934), p. 94; 4 (24 January 1934). The biography, by Paul Ickes, was advertised during the month of January.

26 S. Tegel, 'The Politics of Censorship: Britain's *Jew Süss* (1934) in London, New York and Vienna', *Historical Journal of Film, Radio and Television*, 15 (1995), pp. 223–4.

27 Loiperdinger, 'State Legislation, Censorship and Funding', p. 155.

28 Fröhlich, *Die Tagebücher von Joseph Goebbels* (Munich, 1998), pt 1, vol. viii, p. 98 (7 May 1940), p. 317 (10 September 1940).

29 E. Rentschler, *The Ministry of Illusion: Nazi Cinema and its Afterlife* (Cambridge, MA, 1996), pp. 176–90.

30   H.-M. Bock, 'Georg Wilhelm Pabst: Documenting a Life and a Career', in E. Rentschler, ed., *The Films of G.W. Pabst: An Extraterritorial Cinema* (New Brunswick, NJ, 1990), pp. 231–3.

31   Loiperdinger, 'State Legislation, Censorship and Funding', pp. 149, 151.

32   Phillips, 'The Nazi Control of the German Film Industry', p. 43; Balfour, *Propaganda in War*, p. 38.

33   Petley, 'Film Policy in the Third Reich', p. 177.

34   Loiperdinger, 'State Legislation, Censorship and Funding', pp. 149–50.

35   Ibid., p. 152.

36   Phillips, 'The Nazi Control of the German Film Industry', p. 49.

37   R.G. Reuth, *Goebbels*, trans. K. Winston (London, 1993), p. 219; F. Moeller, *The Film Minister: Goebbels and the Cinema in the 'Third Reich'*, trans. M. Robinson (Stuttgart and London, 2000), pp. 148–50.

38   D. Welch, *The Third Reich: Politics and Propaganda* (London and New York, 1993), p. 45.

39   Balfour, *Propaganda in War*, p. 45.

40   D. Welch, *Propaganda and the German Cinema*, 2nd edn (London, 2001), p. 14.

41   Balfour, *Propaganda in War*, p. 39; Becker, *Film und Herrschaft*, pp. 79, 84; Philips, 'The Nazi Control of the German Film Industry', p. 51.

42   Welch, *Propaganda and the German Cinema*, p. 16.

43   K. Wetzel and P. Hagemann, *Zensur: Verbotene deutsche Filme, 1933–1945* (Berlin, 1978), pp. 7, 44 n.4.

44   Welch, *The Third Reich: Politics and Propaganda*, p. 45; Welch, *Propaganda and the German Cinema*, p. 20.

45   Ibid.

46   Ibid., p. 3; Balfour, *Propaganda in War*, p. 39; Albrecht, *Nationalsozialistische Filmpolitik*, pp. 503ff.; Welch, *The Third Reich: Politics and Propaganda*, pp. 46–7.

47   *Deutsche Presse*, no. 51/52, 21 December 1935, cited in E. Leiser, *Nazi Cinema*, trans. G. Mander and D. Wilson (London 1974), pp. 47–8.

48   *Völkischer Beobachter*, 29 November 1936, cited in Leiser, *Nazi Cinema*, p. 49; Welch, *The Third Reich: Politics and Propaganda*, p. 28.

49   Welch, *The Third Reich: Politics and Propaganda*, p. 179 n.25.

50   Balfour, *Propaganda in War*, p. 37.

51   Phillips, 'Nazi Control of the German Film Industry', p. 46; Welch, *The Third Reich: Politics and Propaganda*, p. 41; Welch, *Propaganda and the German Cinema*, pp. 8–9.

52   Ibid., pp. 45, 46; Balfour, *Propaganda in War*, p. 39.

53   Petley, 'Film Policy in the Third Reich', p. 175; Balfour, *Propaganda in War*, p. 38.

54   Ibid., pp. 174, 175.

55   Julian Petley, *Capital and Culture: German Cinema, 1933–45* (London, 1979), p. 52.

56   Balfour, *Propaganda in War*, p. 40.

57   Petley, 'Film Policy in the Third Reich', p. 175; Petley, *Capital and Culture*, p. 53; Becker, *Film und Herrschaft*, pp. 36, 161.

58   Petley, 'Film Policy in the Third Reich', p. 175.

59   Balfour, *Propaganda in War*, p. 40–1.

60   Phillips, 'Nazi Control of the German Film Industry', p. 55; Welch, *The Third Reich: Politics and Propaganda*, p. 42; Welch, *Propaganda and the German Cinema*, pp. 26, 27; Petley, *Capital and Culture*, p. 75.
61   Welch, *Propaganda and the German Cinema*, p. 256.
62   Ibid., p. 23–4; Phillips, 'Nazi Control of the German Film Industry', pp. 53–4.
63   Balfour, *Propaganda in War*, p. 23; Becker, *Film und Herrschaft*, pp. 133–9.
64   The *New York Times*, 6 May 1937.
65   H. Barkhausen, 'Footnote to the History of Riefenstahl's "Olympia"', *Film Quarterly*, 28 (Fall 1974), pp. 8–12.
66   Welch, *Propaganda and the German Cinema*, pp. 25–7.
67   Balfour, *Propaganda in War*, p. 111.
68   Petley, *Capital and Culture*, p. 77.
69   Ibid., p. 79; Phillips, 'Nazi Control of the German Film Industry', p. 47.
70   Becker, *Film und Herrschaft*, p. 161.
71   BArch, R055/000879, 2.

Notes to Chapter 6: The Kampfzeit *Films*

1   E. Fröhlich, ed., *Die Tagebücher von Joseph Goebbels* (Munich, 2006) pt 1, vol. 2/iii, p. 142 (8 March 1933).
2   M. Loiperdinger and D. Culbert, 'Leni Riefenstahl, the SA, and the Nazi Party Rally Films, Nuremberg 1933–1934: "Sieg des Glaubens" and "Triumph des Willens"', *Historical Journal of Film, Radio and Television*, 8 (1988), p. 8.
3   H. Korte, *Der Spielfilm und das Ende der Weimarer Republik* (Göttingen, 1998), p. 392. See pp. 392–441 for a detailed examination of the film.
4   I. Kershaw, *Hitler*, i, *1889–1936* (London, 1998), p. 461, is wrong in describing the 'Choral von Leuthen' as the 'Niederländische Gedenkgebet'. These are two different hymns; the latter, based on a sixteenth-century Dutch melody, was put into Latin for male choir by the Viennese Choir Master, Eduard Kremser, in 1877. An English version, 'We Gather Together to ask the Lord's Blessing', appeared seventeen years later. I am grateful to David Culbert for the information about the Niederländische Gedankgebet.
5   Bundesarchiv, Berlin (cited hereafter as BArch), Berlin Document Centre (ehem. BDC), RKK file on Froelich.
6   K.R.M. Short, ed., *Catalogue of Forbidden German Feature and Short Film Production* (Trowbridge, 1995), p. xxxv n.10. Günther Dahlke and Karl Günter, eds, *Deutsche Spielfilme von den Anfängen bis 1933* (Berlin 1993), p. 313; *Variety*, 28 February 1933; Fröhlich, ed., *Die Tagebücher von Joseph Goebbels* (Munich, 2006) pt 1, vol. 2/iii, p. 142 (8 March 1933).
7   S. Kracauer, *From Caligari to Hitler: A Psychological History of the German Film* (Princeton, NJ, 1947), p. 270.
8   M. Truppner, '"Zeitgemässe Neu-Aufführungen" eine Text genetische Untersuchung zum U-Boot-Drama *Morgenrot*', in M. Schaudig, ed., *Positionen deutscher Filmgeschichte: 100 Jahren Kinematographie: Strukturen, Diskurse, Kontexte* (Munich, 1996), esp. pp. 155–78.

9   R. Volker, 'Vom Thingspiel zur filmeigenen Musik: Herbert Windt und seine Zusammenarbeit mit Leni Riefenstahl', *Filmblatt*, 8, 21 (2003), p. 29.

10   Klimt never officially acknowledged Ucicky but left him a legacy. See G. Dörfler, 'Gustav Ucicky', *Anthologie du Cinéma*, XI (1983), pp. 243–4.

11   RKK, Berlin Document Centre microfilm, Wiener Library. See also O. Rathkolb, *Führertreu und gottbegnadet: Künstlereliten im dritten Reich* (Vienna, 1991), pp. 232–5.

12   Dörfler, 'Gustav Ucicky', pp. 244–5

13   F. Moeller, *The Film Minister: Goebbels and the Cinema in the 'Third Reich'*, trans. M. Robinson (Stuttgart and London, 2000), p. 74.

14   H. Hoffmann, *The Triumph of Propaganda: Film and National Socialism*, trans. J. Broadwin and V.R. Berghahn (Providence, RI, and Oxford, 1996), p. 26. This dedication does not appear in the 1939 version held by the Imperial War Museum, London. For a discussion of the different versions and the extent to which those commenting on the film seem unaware of their existence see Truppner, '"Zeitgemässe Neu-Aufführungen" eine Text genetische Untersuchung zum U-Boot-Drama *Morgenrot*', esp. pp. 156–7.

15   *Völkischer Beobachter*, 2 February 1933. Two other actors disappeared from the credits of later versions, one on racial grounds and the other on grounds of political unreliability.

16   *Monthly Film Bulletin*, 1934, p. 23.

17   J. Baird, *To Die for Germany: Heroes in the Nazi Pantheon* (Bloomington, IN, and Indianapolis, 1990), p. xi; Truppner, '"Zeitgemässe Neu-Aufführungen" eine Text genetische Untersuchung zum U-Boot-Drama *Morgenrot*', pp. 155–7. See also Kracauer, *From Caligari to Hitler*, pp. 269–70.

18   *From Caligari to Hitler*, p. 270.

19   J. Robertson, *The Hidden Cinema* (London, 1989), pp. 162–3, 170–1.

20   M. Loiperdinger, 'Goebbels' Filmpolitik überwältigt die Schatten der Kampfzeit: Zur Bewältigung nationalsozialistischer Vergangenheit im Jahr 1933', in M. Loiperdinger, ed., *Märtyrer-Legenden im NS-Film* (Opladen, 1991), p. 30.

21   *Völkischer Beobachter*, 16 June 1933.

22   D. Welch, *Propaganda and the German Cinema*, 2nd edn (London, 2001), p. 272.

23   Loiperdinger, 'Goebbels' Filmpolitik', pp. 31–2.

24   His last words are: 'I go to my father in heaven', as first correctly noted by Heidi Faletti, 'Reflections of Weimar Cinema in Nazi Propaganda Film', in R. Reimer, ed., *Cultural History through a National Socialist Lens* (Rochester, NY, and Woodbridge, 2000), p. 19. Others such as Hilmar Hoffmann and David Welch have claimed, wrongly, that his dying words were: 'I go to the Führer in heaven.' Aside from the actual words on the soundtrack (*Ich gehe zum Vater im Himmel*), this would not make sense. The father is his own father and he knows now that he will be joining him, another hero who has died for the Fatherland. A *Völkischer Beobachter* critic also apparently heard Führer rather than father. *Völkischer Beobachter*, 16 June 1933.

25   *Variety*, 29 May 1934. I am grateful to Tom Doherty for drawing my attention to this review. However, the phrase 'Jude Verrecke' cannot now be heard on the soundtrack of the Bundesarchiv or history of Congress. It is likely that both copies are the later version made for the US.

26   *Variety*, 11 July 1933. The scriptwriter was Curt Braun. The other two scriptwriters who got credit were Joe Stöckl and Joseph Dalman: Loiperdinger, 'Goebbels' Filmpolitik', p. 31.

27   Ibid. For information on Fraenkel see E. Betts, Introduction to *Jew Süss* (London, 1935), p. xiv. Fraenkel later wrote *Unsterblicher Film* (Munich, 1957) and with Roger Manvell, *Goebbels: eine Biographie* (Cologne, 1960) and again with Manvell, *German Cinema* (London, 1971).

28   *Variety*, 11 July 1933.

29   *The New York Times*, 28 May 1934.

30   *Der Angriff*, 14 June 1933, cited in Welch, *Propaganda and the German Cinema*, p. 44.

31   Welch, *Propaganda and the German Cinema*, p. 44.

32   Tennis Hall speech, 19 May 1933 in G. Albrecht, *Nationalsozialistische Filmpolitik: eine soziologische Untersuchung über die Spielfilme des dritten Reich* (Stuttgart, 1969), p. 442. Again on 13 October 1933 he declared 'The SA's rightful place is on the streets and not on the … screen.' *Lichtbildbühne*, 13 October 1933, cited in Welch, *Propaganda and the German Cinema*, p. 63.

33   *Variety*, 11 July 1933; *Völkischer Beobachter*, 16 June 1933.

34   *Frankfurter Zeitung*, 17 June 1933 (second morning edn) and 20 June 1933 (first edn). Welch, *Propaganda and the German Cinema*, p. 44, cites J. Wulf, *Theater und Film im dritten Reich: eine Dokumentation* (Frankfurt, 1983), pp. 390–1, who gives the incorrect date of 16 June 1933. Welch is in error in thinking that the Gloria-Palast is in Berlin and hence that this incident occurred at the Berlin première.

35   Kershaw, *Hitler*, i, pp. 509–10, points out that in June 1934 the paper was 'still able to avoid the tightening Nazi straitjacket on the press' when it reported a speech by the non-Nazi Vice-Chancellor, Franz von Papen, who criticized the new Nazi state. This speech ensured the death of his close associates a few weeks later in the Röhm purge.

36   Welch, *Propaganda and the German Cinema*, p. 50; R. Rother, '"Hier erhielt der Gedanke eine fest Form": Karl Ritters Regie-Karriere im Nationalsozialismus', in H.-M. Bock and M. Töteberg, eds, *Das Ufa-Buch* (Hamburg, 1992), pp. 422.

37   For details about Herbert Norkus see J. Baird, 'From Berlin to Neu Babelsberg; Nazi Film Propaganda and *Hitler Youth Quex*', *Journal of Contemporary History*, 18 (1983), esp. pp. 596–602.

38   Baird, *To Die for Germany*, p. 277, n.52; 'Wie der Hitlerjunge Quex gefunden wurde', *Die Filmwoche*, 37 (13 September 1933), cited in Baird, 'From Berlin to Neu Babelsberg', p. 514, n.31.

39   U. Klaus, *Deutsche Ton Filme*, iv (1933) (Berlin, 1993), p. 71. Two films in which Ohlsen had leads were *Das ist die Liebe der Matrosen* (*That is the Sailor's Love*) (1934) and *Wunder des Fliegens* (*The Marvel of Flying*) (1935). (Klaus, *Deutsche Ton Filme*, vi (Berlin, 1994), p. 209; Witte, 'Der Apfel under der Stamm', p. 307.)

40   *Völkischer Beobachter*, 16 June 1933.

41   Kracauer, *From Caligari to Hitler*, p. 225.

42   Rentschler, *The Ministry of Illusion*, p. 62; Kracauer, *From Caligari to Hitler*, p. 73.

43   *Völkischer Beobachter*, 3 November 1933.

44   Bertolt Brecht, 'Offener Brief an den Schauspieler Heinrich George', *Gesammelte Werke*, 15 (Frankfurt, 1967), pp. 229ff.

45   E. Rosenhaft, 'Working-Class Life and Working-Class Politics: Communists, Nazis and the State in the Battle for the Streets, Berlin 1928–1932', in R. Bessel and E. Feuchtwanger, eds, *Social Change and Political Development in Weimar Germany* (London, 1981), p. 133.

46 D. Culbert, 'The Rockefeller Foundation, The Museum of Modern Art Film Library and Siegfried Kracauer, 1941', *Historical Journal of Film, Radio and Television*, 13 (1993), pp. 508–9. Baird also, almost in passing, describes him as 'the incarnation of the Jewish Bolshevik will to destruction' ('From Berlin to Neu Babelsberg', p. 504, and *To Die for Germany*, p. 121).

47 Hoffmann, *The Triumph of Propaganda*, p. 52. The book's title was more descriptive of the contents: *Und die Fahne führt uns in die Ewigkeit: Propaganda im NS-Film* (Frankfurt/Main, 1988) which translated into English is 'And the Flag Leads us into Eternity: Propaganda in Nationalist Socialist Film'.

48 K.A. Schenzinger, *Der Hitlerjunge Quex* (Berlin and Leipzig, 1932), p. 261; Baird, *To Die for Germany*, pp. 115–16, 275 n.30.

49 E. Rentschler, The *Ministry of Illusion: Nazi Cinema and its Afterlife* (Cambridge, MA, 1996), pp. 65–6; see also K. Witte, 'Der Apfel und der Stamm: Jugend und Propaganda, am Beispiel *Hitler-Junge Quex* (1933)', in W. Bucher and K. Pohl, eds, *Schock und Schöpfung: Jugendästhetik im 20. Jahrhundert* (Darmstadt, 1986), pp. 302–7.

50 Baird, *To Die for Germany*, p. 111.

51 G. Bateson, 'An Analysis of the Nazi Film', in M. Mead and R. Métraux, eds, *The Study of Culture at a Distance* (New York, 1953), pp. 302–14.

52 There are several in which the theme of Nazi male foster-parenting is apparent. They include *Kopf Hoch, Johannes! (Head Up, Johannes)* (1941) and *Junge Adler (Young Eagles)* (1944).

53 *Lichtbildbühne*, 12 September 1933, p. 1.

54 K. Witte, 'Der Apfel und der Stamm', in W. Bucher and K. Pohl, eds, *Schock und Schöpfung: Jugendästhetik im 20. Jahrhundert* (Stuttgart, 1986), p. 302. Witte cites Harry Graf Kessler (1961, p. 741) reporting on a conversation he had in Paris with ousted Chancellor Heinrich Brüning.

55 Welch, *Propaganda and the German Cinema*, p. 51.

56 Baird, 'From Berlin to Neu Babelsberg', p. 510.

57 *Kinematograph*, 176, 12 September 1933, cited in Baird, 'From Berlin to Neu Babelsberg', p. 511.

58 Baird, *To Die for Germany*, p. 127. See also Goebbels's comments in *Der Angriff*, 9 August, 25 September and 10 October 1933.

59 According to Albrecht, *Nationalsozialistische Film*, p. 370, Wenzler made only three films.

60 Leni Riefenstahl, *The Sieve of Time* (London 1992), p. 137.

61 H.H. Ewers, *Horst Wessel: ein deutsches Schicksal* (Stuttgart, 1932).

62 E. Hanfstaengl, *The Missing Years* (London, 1957), p. 232.

63 T. Oertel, *Horst Wessel Untersuchung einer Legende* (Cologne, 1987), p. 132.

64 Ibid., pp. 292–9.

65 Oertel, *Horst Wessel*, pp. 135–6.

66 Ibid., p. 233.

67 Hanfstaengl, *The Missing Years*, pp. 188, 292–9.

68 *Lichtbildbühne*, 12 September 1933.

69 Wulf, *Theater und Film*, p. 389.

70 H. Barkhausen, 'Die NSDAP als Filmproduzentin, mit kurz Übersicht: Filme der NSDAP, 1927–1945' in G. Moltmann and K.F. Reimers, eds, *Zeitgeschichte in Film- und Tondokument* (Göttingen, 1970), pp. 155–6.

71   *Lichtbildbühne*, 11 October 1933.

72   Baird, *To Die for Germany*, p. 73.

73   Oertel, *Horst Wessel*, pp. 106–13.

74   D. Culbert, 'Horst Wessel' in N. Cull, D. Culbert and D. Welch, eds, *Propaganda and Mass Persuasion: A Historical Encyclopedia, 1500 to Present* (Santa Barbara, CA, Denver, CO, and Cambridge, 2003), p. 69.

75   Hoffmann, *The Triumph of Propaganda*, p. 55.

76   J. Winter, *Sites of Memory, Sites of Mourning: The Great War in European Cultural History* (Cambridge, 1995), pp. 15–17.

77   Baird, *To Die for Germany*, pp. 75–80.

78   Ibid., p. 80.

79   I. Lazar, *Der Fall Horst Wessel* (Stuttgart and Zurich, 1980), p. 126; Oertel, *Horst Wessel*, p. 86.

80   Oertel, *Horst Wessel*, p. 103.

81   Kershaw, *Hitler*, i, p. 133.

82   Baird, *To Die for Germany*, pp. 74–5.

83   Fröhlich, *Die Tagebücher von Joseph Goebbels* (Munich, 2005), pt 1, vol. 2/iii, p. 203 (10 June 1933).

84   Ibid., pp. 75–88; Lazar, *Der Fall Horst Wessel*, pp. 186–7.

85   Rudolf Diels, *Lucifer ante Portas* (Zürich, n.d. [1949?]), p. 223. Diels, the founder and first chief of the Gestapo, was a non-Nazi opportunist civil servant. Oertel, *Horst Wessel*, p. 105 n.293, points out that, according to one witness, Diels was present at the murder.

86   *Lichtbildbühne*, 13 July 1933, cited in Oertel, *Horst Wessel*, p. 155.

87   Lazar, *Der Fall Horst Wessel*, pp. 138–9; Oertel, *Horst Wessel*, p. 90.

88   Ibid., pp. 143, 155.

89   See E. Leiser, *Nazi Cinema*, trans. G. Mander and D. Wilson (London, 1974), p. 35, where she is also identified as a Jew.

90   Ruth Fischer, *Inside German Communism* (London, 1977), pp. 65–7 and passim. For an unflattering portrait of Fischer by a contemporary see R. Leviné-Meyer, *Inside German Communism: Memoirs of Party Life in the Weimar Republic* (London, 1977), pp. 65–6, 84–5.

91   O. Flechtheim, *Die KPD in der Weimarer Republik* (Frankfurt, 1969), pp. 178–9.

92   Lazar, *Der Fall Horst Wessel*, pp. 125, 139.

93   Ibid., pp. 125, 133.

94   Ibid., pp. 214–18.

95   Ewers, *Horst Wessel*, p. 214.

96   Oertel, *Horst Wessel*, p. 151.

97   Welch, *Propaganda and the German Cinema*, describes him as a 'Jewish-looking lecturer', p. 64; D. Hollstein, *Jud Süss und die Deutschen: Antisemitische Vorurteile im nationalsozialistischen Spielfilm* (Berlin, 1983), p. 34, describes him as a 'Jewish-looking professor'.

98   Loiperdinger, 'Goebbels' Filmpolitik', p. 72.

99   Loiperdinger gives him the name of Kütemeyer (p. 72), while Oertel gives him the name of Meier (p. 152), but neither name is mentioned in the film, unless the soundtrack of the copy at the Imperial War Museum, London is flawed.

100   Ewers, *Horst Wessel*, p. 119.

101   Oertel, *Horst Wessel*, p. 146, n.118.

102   Ibid., p. 149; *Lichtbildbühne*, 13 July 1933, mentions the difficulties with casting for the role of Erna, not Agnes.

103   Ewers, *Horst Wessel*, pp. 89–91.

104   Oertel, *Horst Wessel*, p. 105.

105   Ewers, *Horst Wessel*, pp. 225–9.

106   L. Hanlon, 'Film Document and the Myth of Horst Wessel', *Film and History*, September 1975, 5, 3, p. 16. The newsreel is used in a documentary about the national uprising, *Blutendes Deutschland* (*Bleeding Germany*) (1933), Bundesarchiv. Several reels are missing but the reel including the funeral is intact. The fragment containing the Wessel funeral begins: 'Loyal to the Führer, Horst Wessel, the poet and leader of the struggle, fell to a cowardly murder.'

107   Oertel, *Horst Wessel*, p. 157.

108   Ibid. Oertel states that this is the first time the song has been heard, but has overlooked the tune being hummed in an opening sequence.

109   Ibid., pp. 152–4.

110   Hoffmann, *The Triumph of Propaganda*, p. 54; Kershaw, *Hitler*, i, p. 433.

Notes to Chapter 7: Leni Riefenstahl's Triumph of the Will

1   E. Barnouw, *Documentary: A History of the Non-Fiction Film*, 2nd edn, (Oxford, 1983), p. 105.

2   E. Leiser, *Nazi Cinema*, trans. G. Mander and D. Wilson (London, 1974), pp. 25, 29.

3   R. Rother, *Leni Riefenstahl: The Seduction of Genius*, trans. M. Bott (New York and London, 2002), p. 20.

4   B. Winston, *Claiming the Real: The Documentary Film Revisited* (London, 1995), p. 75.

5   I. Kershaw, *The Hitler Myth: Image and Reality in Third Reich* (Oxford, 1989), esp. pp. 102–4; Nicholas Reeves, *The Power of Film Propaganda: Myth or Reality?* (London, 1999), pp. 107–11.

6   I. Kershaw, *Hitler*, i, *1889–1936: Hubris* (London, 1998), p. 542.

7   Albert Speer, *Inside the Third Reich*, trans. R. and C. Winston (London, 1971), pp. 58–9; G. Sereny, *Albert Speer: His Battle with Truth* (London, 1996), p. 132.

8   M. Delahaye, 'Leni et le Loup: entrétien avec Leni Riefenstahl par Michel Delahaye', *Cahiers du cinéma*, 170 (September 1965), pp. 46, 48.

9   Cited in Kershaw, *Hitler*, i, p. 566.

10   Ibid., p. 526.

11   C. Koonz, *Mothers in the Fatherland: Women, Family and Nazi Politics* (London, 1987), p. 145.

12   J. Trimborn, *Riefenstahl: eine deutsche Karriere. Biographie* (Berlin, 2002), pp. 276, 538 n.326; Lutz Kinkel, *Die Scheinwerferin: Leni Riefenstahl und das 'Dritte Reich'* (Hamburg and Vienna, 2002), p. 317 n.70.

13   Recent studies of Riefenstahl shed light on how she advanced her career. See Kinkel, *Die Scheinwerferin*, and Trimborn, *Riefenstahl*.

14 Trimborn, *Riefenstahl*, p. 363, and Kinkel, *Die Scheinwerferin*, pp. 38, 42.

15 Leni Riefenstahl, *The Sieve of Time* (London 1992), pp. 142–4.

16 D. Culbert, 'Leni Riefenstahl and the Diaries of Joseph Goebbels', *Historical Journal of Film, Radio and Television*, 13 (1993), pp. 85–93. Trimborn argues that Goebbels's opposition became a plank in her strategy to achieve rehabilitation. See *Riefenstahl*, pp. 385–8.

17 Elke Fröhlich, ed., *Die Tagebücher von Joseph Goebbels* (Munich, 2005), pt 1, vol. 2/ i, p. 29 (1 December 1929), pt 1, vol. 2/ iii, p. 188 (17 May 1933), p. 193 (26 May 1933), p. 205 (12 June 1933), p. 206 (14 June 1933), p. 208 (16 June 1933), p. 211 (20 June 1933), p. 224 (9 July 1933), p. 227 (14 July 1933), p. 246 (14 August 1933), p. 247 (16 August 1933), p. 248 (17 August 1933), p. 254 (27 August 1933), p. 265 (11 September, 1933), p. 271 (19 September 1933), p. 275 ((23 September 1933), p. 287 (9 October 1933), p. 292 (16 October 1933), p. 325 (29 November 1933), p. 328 (2 December 1933); (Munich 2005) pt 1, vol. 3/1, p. 43 (4 May 1934), p. 121 (17 October 1934), p. 140 (22 November 1934), p. 207 (28 March 1935), p. 225 (25 April 1935), p. 305 (5 October 1935).

18 Kershaw, *The Hitler Myth*, pp. 97ff., 199.

19 Riefenstahl, *The Sieve of Time*, p. 102.

20 Leni Riefenstahl, *Kampf im Schnee und Eis* (Leipzig, 1933). See Kinkel, *Die Scheinwerferin*, p. 42.

21 S. Kracauer, *From Caligari to Hitler: A Psychological History of the German Film* (Princeton, NJ, 1947), pp. 112, 257–8. Trimborn, *Riefenstahl*, pp. 99–103, 117–19.

22 Trimborn, *Riefenstahl*, p. 76.

23 Ibid., p. 132; H. Loewy, *Béla Balázs, Märchen, Ritual und Film* (Berlin, 2003), p. 366.

24 E. Rentschler, *The Ministry of Illusion: Nazi Cinema and its Afterlife* (Cambridge, MA, 1996), p. 32.

25 Trimborn, *Riefenstahl*, pp. 107–8.

26 S. Sontag, 'Fascinating Fascism', in *Under the Sign of Saturn* (London, 1983), p. 87.

27 Riefenstahl, *The Sieve of Time*, p. 98.

28 Loewy, *Béla Balázs*, p. 375.

29 Riefenstahl, *The Sieve of Time*, pp. 103, 136–8, 143–7.

30 Ibid., pp. 101–3.

31 J. Fox, *Filming Women in the Third Reich* (Oxford, 2000), p. 221.

32 *Filmwoche*, no. 34, 11 (23 August 1933), pp. 965–7.

33 Rother, *Leni Riefenstahl*, p. 45.

34 Trimborn, *Riefenstahl*, pp. 342–3, 546 nn.122 and 125.

35 Rother, *Leni Riefenstahl*, pp. 91–103.

36 Trimborn, *Riefenstahl*, pp. 292–313.

37 Ibid., p. 295.

38 Bundesarchiv, Berlin (hereafter cited as BArch) R43II/810b, Funk to Goebbels, 11 March 1942.

39 Ibid., Bormann to Lammers, 2 August 1942.

40 Ibid., Bormann to Lammers, 9 May 1943.

41 Fröhlich, ed, *Die Tagebücher von Joseph Goebbels* (Munich, 1996), pt 2, *Diktate 1941–1945*, vol. vi, p. 456 (16 December 1942).

42 E. Thurner, *National Socialism and Gypsies in Austria*, trans. G. Gerda Schmidt (Tuscaloosa, AL, and London, 1998), pp. 33–4; E. Thurner, 'Die Verfolgung der Zigeuner', in C.

Mitterrutzner and G. Ungar, eds, *Widerstand und Verfolgung in Salzburg 1934–1945* (Vienna and Salzburg, 1991), p. 476; R. Gilsenbach and O. Rosenberg, *Berliner Zeitung*, 17, 18 February 2001.

43 The *Independent*, 20 October 2000.

44 S. Tegel, 'Leni Riefenstahl's "Gypsy Question"', *Historical Journal of Film, Radio and Television*, 23, 1 (2003), pp. 3–10; S. Tegel, 'Leni Riefenstahl's "Gypsy Question" Revisited', *Historical Journal of Film, Radio and Television*, 26 (2006), pp. 21–43.

45 Delahaye, 'Leni et la Loup', p. 46; Riefenstahl, *The Sieve of Time*, p. 150.

46 M. Loiperdinger and D. Culbert, 'Leni Riefenstahl, the SA, and the Nazi Party Rally Films, Nuremberg 1933–1934: "Sieg des Glaubens" and "Triumph des Willens", *Historical Journal of Film, Radio and Television*, 8 (1988), p. 16.

47 Ibid., pp. 10, 17. The Bundesarchiv copy is fifty-one minutes.

48 Riefenstahl, *The Sieve of Time*, p. 158.

49 Riefenstahl gives the first figure, while others amend this. See Leni Riefenstahl, *Hinter den Kulissen des Reichsparteitags-Film* (Munich, 1935), pp. 8–9, 11–12; R.M. Barsam, *Filmguide to* Triumph of the Will (Bloomington, IN, 1975), pp. 1–3, 23. Barsam lists eighteen cameramen on pp. 1–2 but states sixteen on p. 23 and refers to a staff of 172; B. Winston, 'Reconsidering *Triumph of the Will*: Was Hitler There?', *Sight and Sound* (1981), pp. 102–9.

50 Riefenstahl, *Hinter den Kulissen*, pp. 16, 24.

51 Barsam, *Filmguide*, p. 23; Hinton, *The Films of Leni Riefenstahl*, p. 38.

52 Sereny, *Albert Speer*, p. 131; Speer, *Inside the Third Reich*, pp. 58–9; Hinton, *The Films of Leni Riefenstahl*, p. 31.

53 Barsam, *Filmguide*, p. 29; Riefenstahl, *The Sieve of Time*, p. 157; Hinton, *The Films of Leni Riefenstahl*, p. 22.

54 B. Winston, 'Was Leni There?', *Sight and Sound*, (1981), pp. 102–7; D. Culbert, in D. Culbert, ed., 'Leni Riefenstahl's *Triumph of the Will*', University Publications of America, 1986, microform, p. 3.

55 J. Goergen, 'Walter Ruttmann – Ein Porträt', in J. Goergen, ed., *Walter Ruttmann: Eine Dokumentation* (Berlin 1989), p. 41. See also Rother, *Leni Riefenstahl*, pp. 61–3.

56 Riefenstahl, *Hinter den Kulissen*, pp. 11, 12.

57 Martin Loiperdinger, *Der Parteitagsfilm* Triumph des Willens: *Rituale der Mobilmachung* (Opladen, 1987), pp. 59–63. However, Loiperdinger also points out (p. 60) that slightly different versions of the film have been in circulation, one of which shows the merging of two night scenes (the political leaders sequence and the SA evening sequence), and that some studies are based on this particular version, e.g. K. Fledelius, K. Rubner Jørgensen and P. Nørgart, 'Der Film *Triumph des Willens* als Geschichtsquelle' (Copenhagen, 1976), unpublished but reproduced in Culbert, *Triumph of the Will*; and P. Nowotny, *Leni Riefenstahls* Triumph des Willens (Dortmund, 1981). Loiperdinger considers the Bundesarchiv version the closest to the version shown in 1935.

58 R. Volker, 'Herbert Windt's film music to *Triumph of the Will*: Ersatz-Wagner or incidental music to the ultimate Nazi-Gesamtkunstwerk?', unpublished paper delivered at Southampton, April 2001. I am most grateful to Reimar Volker for letting me read this paper, an illuminating analysis of Windt's music which also identifies Windt's original

contribution. See also Volker, 'Vom Thingspiel zur filmeigenen Musik: Herbert Windt und seine Zusammenarbeit mit Leni Riefenstahl', *Filmblatt*, 8, 21 (2003), pp. 29–39; and Volker, *Herbert Windt 'Von oben sehr erwünscht': Die Filmmusik Herbert Windts im NS-Propagandafilm* (Trier, 2003).

59 Ibid.
60 Speer, *Inside the Third Reich*, pp. 60–1.
61 Volker, 'Herbert Windt's film music to *Triumph of the Will*'.
62 Volker, unpublished paper for Student Symposium prior to the international conference 'Music and Nazism', October, 2001, Toronto.
63 Hinton, *The Films of Leni Riefenstahl*, p. 22.
64 Winston, 'Reconsidering *Triumph of the Will*', p. 106.
65 Hinton, *The Films of Leni Riefenstahl*, p. 31.
66 Ibid., p. 33.
67 Barsam, *Filmguide*, p. 25; Riefenstahl, *The Sieve of Time*, pp. 572–4; Speer, *Inside the Third Reich*, p. 62.
68 Riefenstahl, *Hinter den Kulissen*, p. 21.
69 Rother, *Leni Riefenstahl*, p. 71.
70 Ibid., p. 26; Riefenstahl, *The Sieve of Time*, p. 162.
71 Hinton, *The Films of Leni Riefenstahl*, p. 37.
72 Sereny, *Albert Speer*, p. 131; Speer, *Inside the Third Reich*, p. 58.
73 Nowotny, *Leni Riefenstahls Triumph des Willens*, p. 131.
74 Barsam, *Filmguide*, p. 26; Volker, Herbert Windt *'Von oben sehr erwünscht'*, p. 220.
75 Nowotny, *Leni Riefenstahls* Triumph des Willens, p. 133.
76 Winston, 'Reconsidering *Triumph of the Will*', p. 103; Barsam, *Filmguide*, pp. 22–3.
77 Adolf Hitler, *Mein Kampf*, trans. R. Manheim (London, 1969), p. 435.
78 Loiperdinger, *Der Parteitagsfilm*, p. 112.
79 Winston, 'Reconsidering *Triumph of the Will*', p. 103.
80 Barsam, *Filmguide*, pp. 22–3.
81 Sontag, 'Fascinating Fascism', p. 91; Winston, 'Reconsidering *Triumph of the Will*', pp. 103–4.
82 *Film-Kurier*, 27 March 1935, cited in Nowotny, *Leni Riefenstahls* Triumph des Willens, p. 151.
83 D. Welch, *Propaganda and the German Cinema, 1933–1945*, 2nd edn (London, 2001), p. 134.
84 Barsam, *Film Guide*, p. 26.
85 *Observer*, 31 March 1935, cited in Loiperdinger, *Der Parteitagsfilm*, pp. 131–2.
86 Welch, cited in Reeves, *The Power of Film Propaganda*, pp. 107, 132 n.67; Culbert, *Triumph of the Will*, p. 3; in Loiperdinger, *Der Parteitagsfilm*, p. 50.
87 Riefenstahl, *Hinter den Kulissen*, p. 26.
88 The Bundesarchiv copy is twenty-eight minutes; the BFI copy nineteen minutes with reel two missing. See D. Culbert and M. Loiperdinger, 'Leni Riefenstahl's *Tag der Freiheit*: the 1935 Party Rally film', *Historical Journal of Film, Radio and Television*, 12 (1992), p. 3; D.B. Hinton, *The Films of Leni Riefenstahl* (Lanham, MD, and London, 2000), p. 44.

89   Riefenstahl, *The Sieve of Time*, pp. 162ff.
90   Kershaw, *Hitler*, i, pp. 567–9.
91   Trimborn, *Riefenstahl*, p. 236, cites reports in *Film Kurier*.
92   Culbert and Loiperdinger, 'Leni Riefenstahl's *Tag der Freiheit*', pp. 3–6, 12.
93   Ibid., p. 10.
94   Ibid., p. 4.
95   Ibid., p. 16.
96   Ibid.
97   Ibid., pp. 17–18.
98   L. Koepnick, *The Dark Mirror: German Cinema between Hitler and Hollywood* (Berkeley, CA, Los Angeles and London, 2002), p. 280, n.58.
99   Culbert and Loiperdinger, 'Leni Riefenstahl's *Tag der Freiheit*', pp. 17–18.
100 Hinton, *The Films of Leni Riefenstahl*, p. 44.
101 Daniel Wildmann, *Begehrte Körper: Konstruktion und Inszenierung des 'arische' Männnerkörpers im Dritten Reich* (Würzburg, 1998), p. 19.
102 Ibid., pp. 21–2.
103 H. Barkhausen, 'Footnote to the History of Riefenstahl's *Olympia*', *Film Quarterly*, 28, 1 (Fall 1974), pp. 8–12. Sontag, 'Fascinating Fascism', p. 79.
104 Sontag, 'Fascinating Fascism', p. 79.
105 C. Graham, '*Olympia* in America, 1938: Leni Riefenstahl, Hollywood, and the *Kristallnacht*', *Historical Journal of Film, Radio and Television*, 13 (1993), p. 444.
106 Ibid., p. 433.
107 Riefenstahl, *The Sieve of Time*, p. 154.

Notes to Chapter 8: A Judenfrei *Cinema: 1934–1938*

1   J.W. Baird, 'The Great War and Literary Reaction: Hans Zöberlein as Prophet of the Third Reich', in G. Kent, ed., *Historians and Archivists: Essays on Modern German History and Archival Policy* (Fairfax, VA, 1991), pp. 45–6.
2   Ibid., p. 57.
3   Berlin Document Centre, microfilm, Wiener Library.
4   A. Rose, *Werwolf 1944–45* (Stuttgart, 1980); F. Osterroth, *Biographische Lexikon der Sozialismus* (Hanover, 1960), p. 258. Baird, 'The Great War and Literary Reaction', pp. 59, 62 n.40, mentions only three victims, citing as his source the obituary in the right-wing *National Zeitung und Soldatenzeitung*, 6 March 1964.
5   K. Witte, *Lachende Erben, Toller Tag: Film Kömodie im Dritten Reich* (Berlin, 1995), p. 167.
6   *Völkischer Beobachter*, 23 December 1938.
7   R. Manvell and H. Frankel, *The German Cinema* (London 1971), p. 86.
8   Ibid., p. 46.
9   Ibid.; J. Altmann, 'The Technique and Content of Hitler's War Propaganda Films', *Hollywood Quarterly*, 4 (1950), p. 385.
10 Ibid.

11   R. Rother, "'Hier erhielt der Gedanke eine feste Form'": Karl Ritters Regie-Karriere im Nationalsozialismus', in H.-M. Bock and M. Töteberg, eds, *Das Ufa-Buch* (Hamburg, 1992), p. 423.

12   D. Welch, *Propaganda and the German Cinema* (Oxford, 1983), p. 189.

13   *Filmwelt*, no. 20, 13 May 1938, quoted in Welch, *Propaganda*, p. 189.

14   Rother, 'Karl Ritters Regie-Karriere im Nationalsozialismus', p. 423.

15   J. Baird, *To Die for Germany: Heroes in the Nazi Pantheon* (Bloomington, IN, 1990), p. 175; Welch, *Propaganda and the German Cinema*, p. 256.

16   H.-G. Seraphim, ed., *Das politische Tagebuch Alfred Rosenbergs, 1934/35 und 1939/40* (Munich, 1964), p. 111.

17   Baird, *To Die for Germany*, p. 175, describes him as a Jew, though other commentators do not suggest this: E. Leiser, *Nazi Cinema*, trans. G. Mander and D. Wilson (London, 1974), p. 96; Welch, *Propaganda and the German Cinema*, pp. 257–9; K. Kanzog, 'Staatspolitisch besonders wertvolle': Ein handbuch zu 30 deutschen Spielfilmen der Jahre 1934 bis 1945 (Munich, 1994), pp. 131–40; U. von der Osten, *NS-filme im Kontext sehen! 'Staatspolitisch besonders wertvolle' Filme der Jahre 1934–1938* (Munich, 1998), pp. 75–83. D. Hollstein, *Jud Süss und die Deutschen: antisemitische Vorurteile im nationalsozialistichen Spielfilm* (Berlin, 1983), whose focus is on antisemitism, discusses Ritter but does not even examine the film and makes only one brief reference to it on p. 320 n.49.

18   von der Osten, *NS-filme im Kontext sehen!*, p. 79.

19   V. Klemperer, *I Shall Bear Witness: The Diaries of Victor Klemperer 1933–41*, trans. M. Chalmers (London, 1998), p. 125.

20   Klaus, *Deutsche Ton Filme*, vi, (1935) (Berlin, 1995), p. 111.

21   Hollstein, *Jud Süss und die Deutschen*, p. 43. Hollstein expresses surprise that the two scriptwriters, Felix von Eckardt and Georg C. Klaren, as well as the director, Anton, made a one-off contribution to antisemitic film propaganda. But since the villain was not a Jew, the film was not antisemitic.

22   S. Friedländer, *Nazi Germany and the Jews: The Years of Persecution, 1933–1939* (London, 1997), p. 138; Kershaw, *Hitler*, i, p. 562.

23   I. Kershaw, *The Hitler Myth: Image and Reality in the Third Reich* (Oxford, 1989), i, p. 562.

24   *Völkischer Beobachter*, 14 July 1935, p. 5.

25   Ibid.

26   Ibid.

27   *Völkischer Beobachter*, 15 July 1935, p. 1.

28   Ernst Züchner, 'Petersson & Bendel', *Völkischer Beobachter*, 15 July 1935, p. 2.

29   *Völkischer Beobachter*, 15 July 1935, p. 2.

30   *Neue Züricher Zeitung*, 16 July 1935, p. 2.

31   *Zwölf Uhr Blatt* cited in *The New York Times*, 17 July 1935, p. 4.

32   *New York Times*, 16 July 1935, p. 6.

33   Ibid.

34   E. Fröhlich, ed., *Die Tagebücher von Joseph Goebbels* (Munich, 2005), pt 1, vol. 3/i, p. 262 (15 July 1935).

35   G. Stahr, *Volksgemeinschaft vor der Leinwand? Der nationalsozialistische Film und sein Publicum* (Berlin, 2001), p. 153.

36 Ibid., pp. 153, 156.

37 Joseph Wulf, *Theater und Film im Dritten Reich: eine Dokumentation* (Frankfurt, 1983), p. 460.

38 Stahr, *Volksgemeinschaft vor der Leinwand?*, p. 155.

39 Ibid., pp. 153–4.

40 P. Lesch, *Heim ins Ufa-Reich?: NS-Filmpolitk und die Rezeption deutscher Filme in Luxemburg 1933–1944* (Trier, 2002), p. 88. See also the special issue of *The Historical Journal of Film, Radio and Television*, 24 (2004), which is devoted to newsreels and refers to hostile cinema audience responses in occupied countries.

41 Stahr, *Volksgemeinschaft vor der Leinwand?*, pp. 156–7.

42 Ibid., p. 156.

43 M. Domarus, ed., *Hitler, Speeches and Proclamations, 1932–1945*, i, trans. Mary Gilbert (London, 1990), p. 706.

44 Hollstein, *Jud Süss und die Deutschen*, p. 42.

45 Ibid., pp. 39, 319 n.38; and J. Wulf, *Theater und Film im dritten Reich* (Gütersloh, 1964), p. 414.

46 Hollstein, *Jud Süss und die Deutschen*, p. 52.

47 R. Wright, *The Visible Wall: Jews and other Ethnic Outsiders in Swedish Film* (Carbondale and Edwardsville, IL, 1998), p. 52.

48 Ibid., p. 12.

49 Ibid., pp. 56–8; a view confirmed by Erwin Leiser, who lived in Sweden as a refugee, in a written communication to Hollstein. See Hollstein, *Jud Süss und die Deutschen*, p. 319 n.36.

50 *Socialdemokraten* (Stockholm) quoted in Ernst Züchner, 'Petersson & Bendel', *Völkischer Beobachter*, 15 July 1935, p. 2.

51 Wright, *The Visible Wall*, p. 49.

52 Ibid.

53 Ibid., p. 51.

54 Ibid., p. 54.

55 Ibid., p. 52.

56 J. Robertson, *The British Board of Film Censors: Film Censorship in Britain, 1896–1950* (Beckenham, 1985), pp. 132, 137.

Notes to Chapter 9: Two German Comedies (1939)

1 S. Friedländer, *Nazi Germany and the Jews* (London, 1997), pp. 241–4.

2 Ibid., p. 261.

3 *Filmwelt*, 1 April 1938, cited in D. Hollstein, *Jud Süss und die Deutschen: Antisemitische Vorurteile im nationalsozialistichen Spielfilm* (Berlin, 1983), p. 48.

4 G. Raeder, *Robert und Bertram: oder die lustigen Vagabunden: Posse mit Gesängen und Tänzen in vier Abtheilungen, in Gesammelte Komische Theaterstücke* (Leipzig, 1859).

5 I am grateful to Isa van Eeghen for this information. The video gives a copyright date of 1992.

6   That line, quoted in Hollstein, *Jud Süss und die Deutschen*, p. 49, appears truncated in the video version. According to Isa van Eeghen it was removed at the suggestion of the German censors, who requested that three cuts be made.

7   Those who find it relatively harmless include D. Welch, *Propaganda and the German Cinema*, 2nd edn (London, 2001), p. 238, and D.S. Hull, *Film in the Third Reich* (Berkeley, CA, and Los Angeles, 1969), pp. 156–9. Those who find it harmful include Hollstein, *Jud Süss und die Deutschen*, pp. 48–53, and L. Schulte-Sasse, *Entertaining the Third Reich* (Durham, NC, 1996), p. 235.

8   See I. van Eeghen, '"Lieux de Mémoire" Recycled: The Denazification of German Feature Films with a Historical Subject', *European Review of History*, 4 (1997), pp. 48–9.

9   Ibid., p. 48; M. Truppner, '"Zeitgemässe Neu-Aufführungen": eine Textgenetische Untersuchung zum U-Boot-Drama *Morgenrot*', in M. Schaudig, ed., *Positionen deutscher Filmgeschichte 100 Jahre Kinematographie: Strukturen, Diskurse, Kontexte* (Munich, 1996), pp. 155–7.

10 Hollstein refers to it as first being performed in 1865, but it is not clear how she has arrived at this date. As Raeder died three years later and the play had been published six years earlier, it is more likely that the play was published after it was first performed. Hollstein's mistake is repeated by Schulte-Sasse, *Entertaining the Third Reich*, p. 235, who claims that it is a farce of 1856 which was first performed in the theatre in 1865. Elisabeth Frenzel, who in the service of Nazi enlightenment provided an exhaustive survey of Jewish characters on the German stage, is unable to provide a date for the première, though she is able to do this for many other plays. E. Frenzel, *Judengestalten auf den deutschen Bühne: ein notwendiger Querschnitt durch 700 Jahre Rollengeschichte* (Munich, 1942).

11 L. Barnay, *Erinnerungen* (Berlin, 1903), i, p. 110. Frenzel, *Judengestalten auf den deutschen Bühne*, pp. 134, 170ff., because of her Nazi sympathies, quotes Barnay selectively. She omits the information that Barnay had taken the part as a wager with his director, doubtless because she was loath to accept that a Jewish actor could be on friendly terms with a non-Jew, and comments sardonically: 'One cannot but smile when the Jew Barnay speaks so proudly about his success in a Jewish role, for which he did not need to transform his face.'

12 Ibid.

13 Raeder, *Robert und Bertram*, p. 67.

14 It is thought that Wilhelm Marr first coined this term in his book, *Der Sieg des Judenthums über das Germanenthum* (Bern, 1874), which can be crudely translated as 'The Victory of Jewry over Germanness'. It was subtitled *vom nichtkonfessionellen Standpunkt ausbetracht* ('From a Non-Denominational Point of View'). See P.L. Rose, *German Question/Jewish Question: Revolutionary Antisemitism from Kant to Wagner* (Princeton, NJ, 1990), p. 288. Rose suggests that the term was actually first coined by a Jewish writer, M. Steinschneider, in a polemic with Ernst Renan in 1860. See also M. Zimmermann, *Wilhelm Marr: Patriarch of Anti-Semitism* (New York, 1986).

15 Richard Wagner, *Prose Works*, trans. W.A. Ellis (London, 1912), pp. 79–100.

16 Jean-Paul Sartre, 'Portrait of the Antisemite', trans. M. Guggenheim, in W. Kaufmann, ed., *Existentialism from Dostoevsky to Sartre* (New York, 1956), pp. 277–8.

17 'Judaism in Music', in *Richard Wagner's Prose Works*, trans. W.A. Ellis, ii, pt 3, pp. 84–5.

18 P.L. Rose, *Wagner, Race and Revolution* (London, 1992), pp. 74–5.

19 *Allgemeine deutsche Biographie* (Leipzig, 1888), xxvii, p. 120.

20 H.-P. Bayerdörfer, '"Lokalformel" und Bürgerpatent": Ausgrenzung und Zugehörigkeit in der Posse zwischen 1815 und 1860', in M. Porrmann and F. Vassen, eds, *Theaterverhältnisse im Vormärz*, Jahrbuch 7 (2001), pp. 139–40.

21 Ibid., p. 155.

22 Ibid., pp. 154–5.

23 Ibid., p. 168.

24 Ibid., p. 156.

25 Ibid., pp. 168–73.

26 F. Stern, 'Kluger Kommis oder Naiver Michel: Die Varianten von Robert und Bertram (1915, 1928, 1939)', in *Spass beiseite, Film ab: Jüdischer Humor und verdrängendes Lachen in der Filmkomödie bis 1945* (Hamburg, 2006) p. 59.

27 U. Klaus, *Deutsche Ton Filme*, x (Berlin, 1999), p. 160; Stern, 'Kluger Kommis oder Naiver Michel', p. 59.

28 Hollstein, *Jud Süss und die Deutschen*, p. 48.

29 Klaus, *Deutsche Ton Filme*, x, p. 160.

30 Hollstein, *Jud Süss und die Deutschen*, pp. 48–53, assumes that it is antisemitic, while Welch, *Propaganda and the German Cinema*, p. 238, disagrees. Schulte-Sasse, *Entertaining the Third Reich*, pp. 235, 243–5, also finds it antisemitic, though her argument is highly theoretical. Furthermore, she makes assertions which, had she been familiar with the play, she might have avoided which revealing an ignorance of the conditions of production, as when she states (p. 235 n.8) that none of the actors in the 1939 film were Jews, seemingly unaware that since 1933 Jews had been excluded from performing.

31 Raeder, *Robert und Bertram*, pp. 96ff.

32 Karsten Witte, *Lachende Erben, Toller Tag: Film Kömodie im Dritten Reich* (Berlin, 1995), p. 166.

33 See S. Gilman, *The Jew's Body* (New York, 1991), pp. 38–59.

34 Raeder, *Robert und Bertram*, p. 70.

35 The cast list describes him as Dr Cordvan, but in the film he is addressed as Dr Kaftan. See Klaus, *Deutsche Ton Filme*, x, p. 158.

36 'Ungeduld' (Impatience) from *Die schöne Müllerin* – 'my heart is yours and so shall it always be.'

37 Bayerdörfer, '"Lokalformel" und Bürgerpatent', p. 167.

38 W. Jacobsen, A. Kaes and J. Prinzler, eds, *Geschichte des deutschen Films* (Stuttgart, 1993), pp. 133, 134.

39 The script is at the Archiv der Stiftung Deutsche Kinemathek, Berlin.

40 Stern, 'Kluger Kommis oder Naiver Michel', p. 57.

41 *Der Deutsche Film*, 1939/40, p. 55.

42 Tobis-Presseheft, p. 17, Archiv der Stiftung Deutsche Kinemathek, Berlin.

43 Entry for 23 May 1939, cited in F. Moeller, *The Film Minister: Goebbels and the Cinema in the 'Third Reich'*, trans. M. Robinson (Stuttgart/London, 2000), p. 197 n.721.

44 Moeller, *The Film Minister*, pp. 59, 191 n.394.

45 Bundesarchiv, Berlin (cited hereafter as BArch) (ehem. Berlin Document Centre) MFOK Z0074. His card indicates he joined on 15 November 1937.

46 *Film-Kurier*, 14, 17 January 1939 cited in *Cinegraph*, p. 37.

47 Ibid.

48 BArch RK (ehem. BDC), JO 124.

49 H.G. Seraphim, ed., *Das politische Tagebuch Alfred Rosenbergs, 1934–39 und 1939–40* (Göttingen, 1955), pp. 110ff.

50 Hollstein, *Jud Süss und die Deutschen*, p. 52.

51 Ibid. Stern, 'Kluger Kommis oder Naiver Michel', p. 60, cites *Reklams deutsches Filmlexikon* (Stuttgart, 1984), p. 120, to the effect that this new version never reached audiences. However, U. Klaus, *Deutsche Ton Filme: 1929–45*, (Berlin 1999), p. 159, claims that it did.

52 Hollstein, *Jud Süss und die Deutschen*, p. 52.

53 *Das Programm von Heute*, no. 385, cited in Hollstein, *Jud Süss und die Deutschen*, p. 321 n.72.

54 Staatsarchiv Hamburg, Misc 6911, Veit Harlan, Marian's account, 20 September 1945; which also appears in *Filmpress* (22 July 1950), p. 2.

55 S. Kamare, Leinen aus Irland: *ein Lustspiel aus dem alten Österreich in vier Atken* (Berlin, 1928).

56 Frenzel, *Judengestalten auf den deutschen Bühne*, p. 246.

57 Welch, *Propaganda and the German Cinema*, p. 238, though Hollstein, *Jud Süss und die Deutschen*, p. 53, makes a distinction between the two, describing the former as comedy and the latter as the 'bitter satire of an *Untermensch*'.

58 Friedlander, *Nazi Germany and the Jews*, pp. 241–4.

59 Hollstein, *Jud Süss und die Deutschen*, p. 53.

60 Ibid., pp. 53, 321 nn.74, 75; *Mein Film*, 16 June 1939, p. 3.

61 Entry for 16 September 1939, cited in Moeller, *The Film Minister*, p. 97.

62 Kamare, Leinen aus Irland, pp. 40–1.

63 Ibid., pp. 40–2.

64 Bavaria-Filmkunst Wien Film/Styria Publicity, Archiv der Stiftung Deutsche Kinemathek, Berlin.

Notes to Chapter 10: *The Rothschilds and* Jud Süss

1 Based on witness testimony at Veit Harlan's 1949 trial for crimes against humanity and the judges' summing up: Bundesarchiv, Berlin (cited hereafter as BArch), Z38/392. See also *Filmpress* (Hamburg) 22 July 1950.

2 M. Domarus, ed., *Hitler, Reden und Proklamationen* (Munich, 1963), ii, p. 1064.

3 P. Burrin, *Hitler and the Jews: The Genesis of the Holocaust*, trans. P. Southgate (London, 1992), pp. 62, 68.

4 R. Cole, 'Anglo-American Anti-Fascist Film Propaganda in a Time of Neutrality: *The Great Dictator*, 1940', *Historical Journal of Film, Radio and Television*, 21 (2001), pp. 142–3.

5 R. Geehr, J. Heineman and G. Herman, '*Wien 1910*: An Example of Nazi Antisemitism', *Film and History*, 15 (1985), pp. 50–3.

6 D. Welch, *Propaganda and the German Cinema*, 2nd edn (London, 2001), pp. 222–3.

7 Ibid., p. 227.

8 J. Petley, *Capital and Culture: German Cinema, 1933–45* (London, 1979), p. 152.

9 Ibid., pp. 220–1, 226.

10 Ibid., pp. 219–29. Welch (p. 219) cites Milan Hauner's phrase 'Nordic similarity'. See M. Hauner, 'Did Hitler Want a World Dominion?', *Journal of Contemporary History*, 13 (1978), p. 26.

11 BArch, ZSg 102/62, fol.1, Sammlung Sänger, Kulturkonferenz 12 April 1940 and 3 May 1940.

12 Welch, *Propaganda and the German Cinema*, p. 227.

13 E. Frenzel, *Judengestalten auf den deutschen Bühne* (Munich 1942), pp. 79, 258; Dorothea Hollstein, *Jud Süss und die Deutschen: Antisemitische Vorurteile im nationalsozialistishen Spielfilm* (Berlin, 1983), p. 67; R.-M. Friedman, *L'image et son Juif* (Paris, 1983), p. 96.

14 N. Ferguson, *The World's Banker: The History of the House of Rothschild* (London, 1998), p. 27.

15 Ibid.

16 BBC Written Archives, Caversham, reveal that the Czech-born Julius Gellner, formerly head of the Munich Kammertheater, emigrated to Britain from Czechoslovakia in the summer of 1939 and joined the BBC German Service in January 1941; interview with Leonard Miall, Deputy Head of German Service, 1940–42, 7 June 2001; Friedrich Knilli, *Ich war Jud Süss* (Berlin 2000), p. 75.

17 See M. Landy, *British Genres: Cinema and Society, 1930–1960* (Princeton, NJ, 1991), pp. 53ff.

18 F.L. Carsten, 'The Court Jews: Prelude to Emancipation', *Leo Baeck Yearbook*, iii, pp. 140–56; S. Stern–Taeubler, *The Court Jew* (Philadelphia, PA, 1950).

19 S. Stern, *Jud Süss: Ein Beitrag zur deutschen und zur jüdischen Geschichte* (Berlin 1929), pp. 88, 105, 112. Heinrich Schnee opposed Stern. He had researched the Jewish Question during the Third Reich, but publication followed later: *Die Hoffinanz und der moderne Staat: Geschichte und System der Hoffaktoren an deutschen Fürstenhöfen im Zeitalter des Absolutismus* (Berlin 1963), iv, pp. 87–148; vi, pp. 57–70. For a more recent study see H. Haasis, *Joseph Süss Oppenheimer, Genannt Jud Süss, Finanzier, Freidenker, Justizopfer* (Hamburg, 1998), pp. 377, 390.

20 W. Hauff, *Jud Süss* (Stuttgart, 1827); A.E. Ellerman, *The Prince Minister of Württemberg* (London 1897).

21 S. Tegel, 'The Politics of Censorship: Britain's *Jew Süss* (1934) in London, New York and Vienna', *Historical Journal of Film, Radio and Television*, 15 (1995), pp. 219–44.

22 *Deutsche Filmzeitung*, 4 November 1934; *Deutsche Zeitung*, 19 and 24 October, 1934, Deutsches Institut für Filmkunde, Frankfurt.

23 J. Sedgwick, 'The Market for Feature Films in Britain in 1934: A Viable National Cinema', *Historical Journal of Film, Radio and Television*, 14 (1994), pp. 19, 34.

24 Tegel, 'Censorship', pp. 219–20, 240.

25 S. Tegel, 'Veit Harlan and the Origins of *Jud Süss*, 1938–1939: Opportunism in the Creation of Nazi Anti-Semitic Film Propaganda', *Historical Journal of Film, Radio and Television*, 16 (1966), pp. 515–31; L. Schmitt, 'Der Fall Veit Harlan', *Film und Mode Revue* (1952), p. 12;

Filmpress, 22 July 1950, p. 2; Veit Harlan, *Im Schatten meiner Filme* (Gütersloh, 1966), pp. 89 ff.; Staatsanwaltschaft bei dem Landgericht Hamburg, Strafverfahren gegen Veit Harlan, AZ 14JS/555/48, iv (Berthold Ebbecke deposition), p. 340; (Hans-Joachim Beyer deposition), p. 301.

26   *Film und Mode Revue* (1952), p. 12.

27   Letter to the author from Hauptstaatsarchiv, Stuttgart, 2 February 1995.

28   Terra Catalogue, Institut für Filmkunde, Frankfurt, also reprinted in *Filmpress* (22 July 1950), pp. 5–6.

29   Tegel, 'Veit Harlan and the Origins of *Jud Süss*', p. 521.

30   Ibid. A film treatment, as opposed to a script, is summarized by Friedrich Knilli (see Knilli, *Ich war Jud Süss*, p. 121), who was given it by Metzger's widow. It differs from the synopsis as publicized in the summer of 1939. Metzger denied that he had ever written a script, though it was in his interest after the war to say this, and it is unlikely that the film would have been publicized without some sort of script. One witness at Harlan's trial claims that he had advised Metzger to destroy it at the war's end. See Tegel, 'Veit Harlan and the Origins of *Jud Süss*', pp. 518–21.

31   Berlin Document Centre RKK 2703 0131 24 Kreisverlag. See also Tegel, 'Veit Harlan and the Origins of *Jud Süss*', pp. 521, 529 nn.47 and 48. In 1946 Metzger claimed to have received RM4,000 for the script, and an additional RM4,000 plus RM2,000 for a treatment. An average script fee was RM8,000–15,000, Thea von Harbou received RM80,000.

32   *Lichtbildbühne*, 25 October 1939.

33   Staatsarchiv Hamburg, Misc 6911, Veit Harlan, Marian's account 20 September 1945; *Filmpress* (22 July 1950), p. 2; Harlan, *Im Schatten meiner Filme*, p. 90; Hippler, *Die Verstrickung: Einstellungen und Rückblenden* (Düsseldorf, 1982), p. 197; Schmitt, 'Der Fall Veit Harlan', p. 13.

34   Harlan, *Im Schatten meiner Filme*, p. 103.

35   Ibid., p. 91.

36   Staatsarchiv, Hamburg Misc. 6911 Veit Harlan. Marian's account is dated 20 September 1945; *Filmpress*, p. 2.

37   Elke Fröhlich, ed., *Die Tagebücher von Joseph Goebbels* (Munich, 1998), pt 1, vol. vii, p. 177 (2 November 1939).

38   Staatsarchiv Hamburg, Misc. 6911, Veit Harlan, letter to Peter Paul Brauer, 22 November 1947; Harlan, 'My Attitude towards National Socialism'; Hippler, *Die Verstrickung*, p. 197.

39   Harlan, *Im Schatten meiner Filme*, pp. 91–4, 100; *Film und Mode Revue*, 14, p. 21; *Kölnische Rundschau*, 28 October 1948.

40   J. Wulf, *Theater und Film im dritten Reich: eine Dokumentation* (Frankfurt, 1983), p. 189.

41   Tegel, 'Veit Harlan and the Origins of *Jud Süss*', pp. 525–6, 530 n.86.

42   Fröhlich, *Die Tagebücher von Joseph Goebbels* (Munich, 2000), pt 1, vol. iv, p. 95 (15 April 1937); p. 111 (26 April 1937); p. 253 (6 August 1937); p. 364 (18 October 1937); pt 1, vol v, p. 61 (20 December 1937), p. 154 (14 February 1938), p. 206 (13 March 1938).

43   Fröhlich, *Die Tagebücher von Joseph Goebbels* (Munich, 1998), pt 1, vol. vii, p. 220 (5 December 1939).

44   Staatsanwaltschaft bei dem Landgericht Hamburg: Lehmann deposition, i, pp. 83–4; Carstennsen deposition, i, p. 70; Hippler deposition, iii, pp. 44–9.

45 BArch, Sammlung Brammer, 17 January 1940, ZSg. 101/15; Zeitschiften-Dienst, 40: 1705, 26 January 1940.

46 Staatsanwaltschaft bei dem Landgericht Hamburg, Carstennson deposition, i, pp. 72–3.

47 *Film und Mode Revue*, 18, p. 29.

48 I am grateful to Victor Tunkel for this information.

49 Veit Harlan, 'Wie es War ... Erlebnis eines Filmregisseurs unter seinem aller höchsten Chef, dem "Schirmherrn des deutschen Films", Dr Goebbels', typescript, *c.* 1960, Schriftliche Abteilung der Bayerischen Staatsbibliothek, Munich, p. 209.

50 'Bertolt Brecht, 'Offener Brief an den Schauspieler Heinrich George' (1933), *Gesammelte Werke* (Frankfurt am Main, 1967), xv, pp. 229ff.

51 W.Boelcke, ed., *Kriegspropaganda* (Stuttgart, 1966), p. 526; *Hamburger Tageblatt*, 18 November 1939.

52 W. Petzet, *Theater: Die Münchenerkammerspiele* (Munich 1973), Austrian Film Institute, Vienna; Fröhlich, *Die Tagebücher von Joseph Goebbels* (Munich, 1998), pt 1, vol. vii, p. 258 (5 January 1940), p. 276 (18 January, 1940); Harlan, *Im Schatten meiner Filme*, p. 225; Klaus Kanzog, *Staatspolitisch, besonders Wertvoll: Ein Handbuch zu 30 deutschen Spielfilmen der Jahre 1934 bis 1945* (Munich, 1994), p. 219 n.99.

53 Harlan, *Im Schatten meiner Filme*, pp. 103–6; W. Krauss, *Das Schauspiel meines Lebens* (Stuttgart, 1958), pp. 199–200. Both Harlan and Krauss mention five roles, rather than four, three of which are in the ghetto scene, but there are only two characters, not three, in this sequence.

54 Michael Billington, *Peggy Ashcroft* (London, 1989), pp. 68–71.

55 Letter of Shaw to Krauss, 9 December 1947, in reply to Krauss's letter of 25 November 1947, cited in Krauss, *Das Schauspiel meines Lebens*, p. 228.

56 BArch, R109I/1568, Ufa Bestände.

57 Harlan, *Im Schatten meiner Filme*, p. 117. Harlan believed that both these films were obtained from Poland, but in fact the last mentioned was already available in Germany, distributed by the Palestine Film Office which had paid Tobis RM3,500 for a production licence which the Polish production company had failed to obtain, RM1,000 for an export licence plus 7½% of the box office for an exhibition licence from which Tobis Klangfilm made a profit. See J.-C. Horak, 'Zionist Film Propaganda in Germany', *Historical Journal of Film, Radio and Television*, 4 (1984), pp. 55, 58 n.39.

58 For a more detailed analysis see S. Tegel, *Jew Süss, Jud Süss* (Trowbridge, 1996).

59 M. Ferro, 'Dissolves in *Jud Süss*,' in *Cinema and History*, trans. N. Greene (Detroit, MI, 1988), p. 140; E. Rentschler, *The Ministry of Illusion: Nazi Cinema and its Afterlife* (Cambridge, MA, 1996), pp. 160–1.

60 The composer was Yedidya (Gideon) Admon-Gorochov (1897–1973). Recorded in Paris, the song was included in a collection which Jakob Schönberg published in Berlin in 1935. See S. Tegel, '"The Demonic Effect": Veit Harlan's Use of Jewish Extras in *Jud Süss* (1940)', *Holocaust and Genocide Studies*, 14 (2000), pp. 215–41, esp. pp. 223–4.

61 F. Hippler, *Betrachtungen zum Filmschaffen* (Berlin, 1942), p. 107.

62 Harlan refers to the fan mail in an open letter (12 December 1947) to Lion Feuchtwanger presumably hoping that the letter would encourage Feuchtwanger to intercede and facilitate his denazification. It is published in H. Pardo and S. Schiffner, eds, Jud Süss:

Historisches und juristisches Material zum Fall Veit Harlan (Hamburg, 1949), p. 66. Those who do not question the existence of fan mail include: R.-M. Friedman, 'Male Gaze and Female Reaction: Veit Harlan's *Jew Süss* (1940)', in S. Frieden, R. McCormick *et al.*, eds, *Gender and German Cinema* (Providence, RI, and Oxford, 1993), pp. 132–3, and M. Klotz, 'Epistemological Ambiguity and the Fascist Text: *Jew Süss*, *Carl Peters* and *Ohm Krüger*', *New German Critique*, 74 (1998), p. 99.

63   Frenzel, *Judengestalten auf den deutschen Bühnen*, passim.

64   B. Gerber, *Jud Süss: Aufstieg und Fall im frühen 18. Jahrhundert* (Hamburg, 1990), p. 282.

65   Linda Schulte-Sasse, *Entertaining the Third Reich* (Durham, NC, and London, 1996), p. 52.

66   R. Proctor, *The Nazi War on Cancer* (Princeton, NJ, 1999), p. 221.

67   Harlan, *Im Schatten meiner Filme*, pp. 127–9; *Film und Mode Revue*, 13, p. 17; Knilli, *Ich war Jud Süss: Die Geschichte des Filmstars Ferdinand Marian* (Berlin, 2000), p. 179.

68   Friedman, on the other hand, argues that the film is misogynist, and that ultimately the repudiation of women is not less than that of the Jews: 'Male Gaze and Female Reaction: Veit Harlan's *Jew Süss* (1940)', p. 126.

69   Harlan, *Im Schatten meiner Filme*, pp. 112–13; Krauss, *Das Schauspiel*, p. 202; '*Jud Süss* ein historischer Film. Regie: Veit Harlan, Terra Filmkunst GmbH', Typescript in Archiv der Stiftung Deutsche Kinemathek, Berlin.

70   Rentschler, *The Ministry of Illusion*, pp. 154–5.

71   BArch, RA56/132. Also reproduced in Wulf, *Theater und Film im Dritten Reich*, pp. 450–1.

72   Knilli, *Ich war Jud Süss*, p. 143.

73   Ibid., p. 159.

74   BArch, R58/156 (Sicherheitsdienst reports, 28 November 1940).

75   *Film Kurier*, 26 May 1941.

76   Knilli, *Ich war Jud Süss*, pp. 177–8.

77   G. Albrecht, *Film im Dritten Reich: eine Dokumentation* (Karlsruhe, 1979), p. 251.

78   Knilli, *Ich war Jud Süss*, p. 159.

79   Ibid., p. 145.

80   BArch, R43II 389. Letter, 31 March 1941, from Hadamovsky in the Propaganda Ministry to Dr Lammers, Chef der Reichskanzlei.

81   F. Knillli, 'Die Gemeinsamkeit von Faschisten und Antifaschisten gegenüber dem NS-Film *Jud Süss*', in F. Knillli, T. Maurer, T. Radevagen and S. Zielinski, eds., *Jud Süss: Filmprotokoll, Programmheft und Einzelanalysen* (Berlin, 1983), p. 67. See also Schulte-Sasse, *Entertaining the Third Reich*, p. 81.

82   I. Kershaw, 'How Effective was Nazi Propaganda?', in D. Welch, ed., *Nazi Propaganda* (London, 1983), pp. 180–205; N. Reeves, *The Power of Film Propaganda: Myth or Reality?* (London, 1999), pp. 83–135.

83   Interview with Ralph Giordano, 16 August 2002.

84   BArch, Z38/392; *Frankfurter Allegemeine Zeitung*, 3 April 1950.

Notes to Chapter 11: Der ewige Jude *(1940)*

1 Bundesarchiv, Berlin (cited hereafter as BArch), R58/157, pp. 7–9 (20 January 1941), also in H. Boberach, *Meldungen aus dem Reich* (Berlin, 1965), vi, no. 155.

2 Ibid.

3 G.K. Anderson, *The Legend of the Wandering Jew* (Providence, RI, 1965), p. 11.

4 *Filmwelt*, 28 July 1939. See also L. Schulte-Sasse, *Entertaining the Third Reich* (Durham, NC, and London, 1996), pp. 64ff., for making literary rather than historical connections to the Dracula legend.

5 Script, Stiftung Deutsche Kinemathek, Berlin.

6 H. Diebow, *Der ewige Jude* (Munich, 1937).

7 V. Klemperer, *I Shall Bear Witness: The Diaries of Victor Klemperer 1933–41*, trans. M. Chalmers (London, 1998), p. 285.

8 S. Hornshøy-Møller, *Quellenkritische Analyse eines antisemitischen Propagandafilm* (Göttingen, 1995), p. 7.

9 S. Hornshøy-Møller and D. Culbert, '*Der ewige Jude* (1940): Joseph Goebbels' Unequaled Monument to Antisemitism', *Historical Journal of Film, Radio and Television*, 12 (1992), p. 42.

10 *Lichtbildbühne*, 25 October 1939.

11 *Hamburger Tageblatt*, 18 November 1939.

12 K. Himmel, *Lichtbildbühne*, 18 July 1939.

13 J. Trimborn, *Riefenstahl: eine deutsche Karriere. Biographie* (Berlin, 2002), pp. 307–12.

14 Hornshøy-Møller and Culbert, '*Der ewige Jude*', pp. 42–7.

15 Ibid., p. 43; Hippler, *Die Verstrickung: Einstellungen und Rückblenden* (Dusseldorf, 1982), pp. 253–5.

16 Ibid., p. 206.

17 Y. Ahren, S. Hornshøy-Møller and C. Melchers, '*Der ewige Jude*' *oder wie Goebbels hetzte, Untersuchungen zum nationalsozialistischen Propagandafilm* (Aachen, 1990), p. 19.

18 Das Reichsfilmarchiv, No. 5660, describes Taubert as the author of the manuscript, cited in D. Hollstein, *Jud Süss und die Deutschen: Antisemitische Vorurteile im nationalsozialistischen Spielfilm* (Berlin, 1983), p. 331, n.270.

19 Hornshøy-Møller and Culbert, '*Der ewige Jude*', p. 42.

20 Ibid., p. 41.

21 H. Hoffmann, *The Triumph of Propaganda: Film and National Socialism*, trans. J. Broadwin and V.R. Berghahn (Providence, RI, and Oxford, 1996), p. 161.

22 V. Petric, 'Esther Shub: Film as Historical Discourse', in T. Waugh, ed., *Show us Life* (Metuchen, NJ, and London, 1984), pp. 22, 27–9.

23 Hornshøy-Møller and Culbert, '*Der ewige Jude*', p. 55.

24 Ibid., pp. 43, 50. See also R. Vande Winkel, 'Nazi Germany's Fritz Hippler, 1909–2002', *Historical Journal of Film, Radio and Television*, 23 (2003), pp. 91–100.

25 Ibid., pp. 41, 53 n.5.

26 Hippler, *Die Verstrickung*, p. 187.

27 Hornshøy-Møller and Culbert, '*Der ewige Jude*', p. 42; E. Fröhlich, *Die Tagebücher von Joseph Goebbels* (Munich, 1998), pt 1, vol. viii, p. 157 (17 October 1939); Hippler, *Die Verstrickung*, p. 187.

28   Ahren, Hornshøy-Møller and Melchers, '*Der ewige Jude*', p. 19.

29   Ibid., pp. 16–18.

30   Hornshøy-Møller and Culbert, '*Der ewige Jude*', pp. 41–2.

31   Fröhlich, *Die Tagebücher von Joseph Goebbels*, pt. 1, vol. vii, p. 177 (2 November 1939).

32   Ahren, Hornshøy-Møller and Melchers, '*Der ewige Jude*', p. 20.

33   Ibid., p. 21.

34   Fröhlich, *Die Tagebücher von Joseph Goebbels* (Munich, 1998), pt 1, vol. viii, p. 304 (3 September 1940).

35   Ahren, Hornshøy-Møller and Melchers, '*Der ewige Jude*', pp. 28–9; Hornshøy-Møller, *Quellenkritische Analyse eines antisemitischen Propagandafilm*, pp. 305–7; Hollstein, *Jud Süss und die Deutschen*, p. 117.

36   Ahren, Hornshøy-Møller and Melchers, '*Der ewige Jude*', p. 24.

37   *Der Film*, 30 November 1940; see also Hollstein, *Jud Süss und die Deutschen*, p. 111.

38   Ahren, Hornshøy-Møller and Melchers, '*Der ewige Jude*'; Hornshøy-Møller, *Quellenkritische Analyse eines antisemitischen Propagandafilm*, p. 26; and P. Bucher, 'Die Bedeutung des Films als historische Quelle: "*Der ewige Jude*"', in H. Duchardt and M. Schlenke, eds., *Festschrift für Eberhard Kessel zum 75. Geburstag* (Munich, 1982), p. 318. Hornshøy-Møller and Culbert, '*Der ewige Jude*', pp. 48, 54 n.18.

39   *Deutsche Filmzeitung*, 1 December 1940, cited in Arens, Hornshøy-Møller and Melchers, '*Der ewige Jude*', p. 26.

40   R. Taylor, *Film Propaganda: Soviet Russia and Nazi Germany*, 2nd edn (London, 1998), p. 190.

41   D.S. Hull, *Film in the Third Reich* (Berkeley, CA, and Los Angeles, 1969), p. 175.

42   L. Furhammar and F. Isaksson, *Politics and Film*, trans. K. French (London 1971), p. 116.

43   Hornshøy-Møller and Culbert, '*Der ewige Jude*', p. 41.

44   E. Leiser, *Deutschland erwache* (Hamburg, 1968), p. 67.

45   Taylor, *Film Propaganda*, p. 190.

46   Hornshøy-Møller and Culbert, '*Der ewige Jude*', p. 45.

47   Hornshøy-Møller, '*Der ewige Jude*', pp.199–200.

48   Ibid., p. 204.

49   Ibid., pp. 78, 212. See also J.-C. Horak, 'Zionist Film Propaganda in Germany', *Historical Journal of Film, Radio and Television*, 4 (1984), pp. 49–58.

50   Hornshøy-Møller and Culbert, '*Der ewige Jude*', p. 43.

51   Ahren, Hornshøy-Møller and Melchers, '*Der ewige Jude*', p. 86.

52   J. Clinefelter, 'A Cinematic Construction of Nazi Anti-Semitism, the Documentary *Der ewige Jude*', in R. Reimer, ed., *Cultural History through a National Socialist Lens: Essays on the Cinema of the Third Reich* (Rochester, NY, and Woodbridge, 2000), p. 138.

53   Ibid., p. 223.

54   J. Baird, *The Mythical World of Nazi War Propaganda* (Minneapolis, 1974), p. 170.

55   B. Wasserstein, *Britain and the Jews of Europe 1939–1945*, 2nd edn (London and New York, 1999), p. 84.

56   Ahren, Hornshøy-Møller and Melchers, '*Der ewige Jude*', p. 102.

57   D. Wildmann, *Begehrte Körper- Konstruktion und Inszenierung des 'arischen' Männerkörpers im dritten Reich* (Würzburg, 1998), pp. 23–6.

58   See S. Tegel, '"The Demonic Effect": Veit Harlan's Use of Jewish Extras in *Jud Süss* (1940)', *Holocaust and Genocide Studies*, 14 (2000), pp. 224–6.

59   F. Maraun, 'Symphonies des Ekels: *Der ewige Jude* – ein abendfüllender Dokumentfilm', *Der deutsche Film*, 4 (1940), p. 157, cited in H.-J. Brandt, *NS-Filmtheorie und Dokumentarische Praxis: Hippler, Noldan, Junghans* (Tübingen, 1987), pp. 73–4, cited in Clinefelter, 'A Cinematic Construction of Nazi Antisemitism', pp. 146–7.

60   Ahren, Hornshøy-Møller and Melchers, '*Der ewige Jude*', pp. 160, 170.

61   Hornshøy-Møller and Culbert, '*Der ewige Jude*', p. 43.

62   Ibid., p. 45.

63   Ahren, Hornshøy-Møller and Melchers, '*Der ewige Jude*', p. 170.

64   *Die Tagebücher von Joseph Goebbels* (Munich, 1998), pt 1, vol. vii, p. 157 (17 October 1939). See also Hippler, *Die Verstrickung*, p.187.

65   *Die Tagebücher von Joseph Goebbels* (Munich, 1998), pt 1, vol. vii, p. 173 (29 October 1939).

66   Dubow, *Der ewige Jude*, p. 85.

67   Baird, *The Mythical World of Nazi War Propaganda*, p. 170.

68   *Das Reich*, 25 April 1941, cited in Baird, *The Mythical World of Nazi War Propaganda*, pp. 170–1.

69   Hornshøy-Møller and Culbert, '*Der ewige Jude*', p. 48.

70   N. Reeves, *The Power of Film Propaganda* (London, 1999), p. 115.

71   D. Welch, *Propaganda and the German Cinema, 1933–1945*, 2nd edn (London, 2001), pp. 11–12.

72   Hornshøy-Møller and Culbert, '*Der ewige Jude*', p. 49.

73   Ahren, Hornshøy-Møller and Melchers, '*Der ewige Jude*', p. 29, cites the statistics on Berlin provided by Peter Bucher.

74   Ibid., p. 49.

75   This is the argument of Daniel Goldhagen's controversial *Hitler's Willing Executioners* (New York and London, 1996).

76   For an alternative view, which links the genesis of the film and the inclusion of Hitler's prophetic speech to the decision, see '"*Der ewige Jude*": Legitimation und Auslöser eines Völkermordes', in K.F. Reimers, C. Hackel and B. Scherer, eds, *Unser Jahrhundert in Film und Fernsehen* (Munich, 1995), pp. 58–97.

77   The historians involved in these debates for more than thirty years are too numerous to list. An early 'Functionalist' contributor was Martin Broszat, 'Hitler and the Genesis of the "Final solution": An Assessment of David Irving's Theses', *Yad Vashem Studies*, 13 (1979), pp. 61–98. A later example of a modified 'Functionalist' is Christopher Browning. See 'Hitler and the Euphoria of Victory: The Path to the Final Solution', in D. Cesarani, ed., *The Final Solution* (London, 1994). With the opening of previously inaccessible archives, especially in Poland and the Soviet Union, rather more is now known about the year 1941.

78   See, for example, H. Mommsen, *From Weimar to Auschwitz* (Princeton, NJ, 1991). For a summary of the variety of historical positions see P. Burrin, *Hitler and the Jews: The Genesis of the Holocaust*, trans. P. Southgate (London, 1992), esp. pp. 114–48.

79   The best example of an 'Intentionalist' is Lucy Dawidowicz, *The War against the Jews, 1933–45* (London, 1975). The terms Functionalist and Intentionalist were first used by T.W.

Mason in 'Intention and Explanation: A Current Controversy about the Interpretation of National Socialism', in G. Hirschfeld and L. Kettenacker, eds, *Der Führerstaat: Mythos und Realität* (Stuttgart, 1981), pp. 21–40.

80   P. Longerich, *The Wannsee Conference in the Development of the 'Final Solution'* (London, 2000), p. 7.

81   E. Leiser, *Nazi Cinema*, trans. G. Mander and D. Wilson (London, 1974), p. 85.

Notes to Chapter 12: The Second World War

1   Ufa minutes cited in F. Moeller, *The Film Minister: Goebbels and the Cinema in the 'Third Reich'*, trans. M. Robinson (Stuttgart and London, 2000), p. 90.

2   The higher estimate can be found in A. Bauer, *Deutsche Spielfilmalmanach, 1929–1950* (Munich, 1950), passim; the lower estimate in G. Albrecht, *Nationalsozialistische Filmpolitik: eine soziologische Untersuchung über die Spielfilme des dritten Reiches* (Stuttgart, 1969), esp. pp. 90, 371–95, where the total adds up to 1,090, but on p. 123 the total appears as 1,094. More recently, E. Rentschler, *The Ministry of Illusion: Nazi Cinema and its Afterlife* (Cambridge, MA, 1996), p. 225, gives 1,086 as the number of German feature films that passed the censors and had their premières in the Reich's cinemas between 30 January 1933 and 8 May 1945. In this total, however, he too included a few late Weimar productions released after 30 January 1933.

3   I. van Eeghen, '"Lieux de mémoire" Recycled: The Denazification of German Feature Films with a Historical Subject', *European Review of History*, 4 (1997), pp. 48–9.

4   Albrecht, *Nationalsozialistische Filmpolitik*, p. 109.

5   K.R.M. Short, ed., *Catalogue of Forbidden German Feature and Short Film Productions* (Trowbridge, 1996), p. 30.

6   R. Peck, 'Misinformation, Missing Information, and Conjecture: *Titanic* and the Historiography of Third Reich Cinema', *Media History*, 6, 1 (2000), pp. 59–73; R. Peck, 'The Banning of *Titanic*: A Study of British Postwar Film Censorship in Germany', *Historical Journal of Film, Radio and Television*, 20 (2000), pp. 427–44.

7   K. Wetzel, 'Filmzensur im Dritten Reich: zu verbotenen deutschen Film, 1933–1945', in K. Wetzel and P. Hagemann, *Zensur: Verbotene deutsche Filme, 1933–1945* (Berlin, 1978), p. 7.

8   Ibid., pp. 33–4, 40–1.

9   Ibid., pp. 24–7; K. Kreimeier, *The Ufa Story: A History of Germany's Greatest Film Company*, trans. R. and R. Kimber (Berkeley, CA, Los Angeles and London, 1999), p. 301; Wetzel and Hagemann, *Zensur*, p. 90.

10   Peck, 'Misinformation, Missing Information and Conjecture', p. 60; Moeller, *The Film Minister*, pp. 171–2; J. Wulf, *Theater und Film im Dritten Reich: eine Dokumentation* (Frankfurt, 1983), p. 329.

11   Ibid., p. 170; Veit Harlan, *Im Schatten meiner Filme* (Gütersloh, 1966), pp. 127–9; F. Knilli, *Ich war Jud Süss: die Geschichte des Filmstars Ferdinand Marian* (Berlin, 2000), p. 179.

12   Harlan, *Im Schatten meiner Filme*, pp. 141–6.

13   Wetzel and Hagemann, *Zensur*, p. 73.

14 Ibid., pp. 143–5; Kreimeier, *The Ufa Story*, p. 329.

15 E. Leiser, *Nazi Cinema*, trans. Gertrud Mander and D. Wilson (London, 1974), pp. 16–17.

16 Rentschler, *The Ministry of Illusion*, p. 11.

17 Albrecht, *Nationalsozialistische Filmpolitik*, pp. 371–4, classifies 139 films as political; David Welch gives a larger number, 229 (one-third), as overtly propagandistic with direct political content. See D. Welch, 'Hitler's History Films', *History Today* (December 2002), p. 21.

18 Rentschler, *The Ministry of Illusion*, p. 4.

19 See above, Chapter 9.

20 Van Eeghen, '"Lieux de mémoire" Recycled', p. 46.

21 K. Witte, *Lachende Erben, Toller Tag: Film Kömodie im Dritten Reich* (Berlin, 1995), a chapter of which has been translated: 'How Fascist is the Punch Bowl?', *New German Critique*, 74 (1998), pp. 31–6. See also S. Lowry, *Pathos und Politik: Ideologie in Spielfilmen des Nationalsozialismus* (Tübingen, 1991), esp. pp. 4, 5, 236–7.

22 M. Truppner, '"Zeitgemässe Neu-Aufführungen": eine Textgenetische Untersuchung zum U-Boot-Drama *Morgenrot*', in M. Schaudig, ed., *Positionen deutscher Filmgeschichte 100 Jahre Kinematographie: Strukturen, Diskurse, Kontexte* (Munich, 1996), p. 166. The film was reissued twice (November 1939 and December 1940). The second wartime reissue had even more excisions.

23 Moeller, *The Film Minister*, p. 95.

24 Ibid.

25 Ibid., p. 93.

26 Ibid., p. 169.

27 Leiser, *Nazi Cinema*, p. 69.

28 Moeller, *The Film Minister*, p. 93.

29 O. Rathkolb, *Führertreu und gottbegnadet: Künstlereliten im Dritten Reich* (Vienna, 1991), pp. 242, 264.

30 G. Albrecht, *Film im dritten Reich: eine Dokumentation* (Karlsruhe, 1979), p. 480.

31 Albrecht, *Nationalsozialistische Filmpolitik*, p. 468.

32 D. Welch, *Propaganda and the German Cinema*, 2nd edn (London, 2001), p. 115.

33 E. Fröhlich, ed., *Die Tagebücher von Joseph Goebbels* (Munich, 1996), pt 2, vol i, p. 279 (20 August 1941).

34 Leiser, *Nazi Cinema*, pp. 71–2.

35 Ibid., p. 93.

36 Welch, *Propaganda and the German Cinema*, pp. 219–21.

37 Ibid., pp. 230–1.

38 Peck, 'Misinformation, Missing Information, and Conjecture', p. 60.

39 Ibid., pp. 69–70.

40 Moeller, *The Film Minister*, p. 93.

41 M.-E. O'Brien, *Nazi Cinema as Enchantment: The Politics of Entertainment in the Third Reich* (Rochester, NY, and Woodbridge, 2004), p. 127.

42 Albrecht, *Film im dritten Reich*, p. 251.

43 Stephen Lowry, 'Heinz Rühmann – The Archetypal German', in T. Bergfelder, E. Carter and D. Göktürk, eds, *The German Cinema Book* (London, 2002), p. 80.

44   Moeller, *The Film Minister*, p. 97.

45   Kreimeier, *The Ufa Story*, p. 304.

46   Ibid.

47   Moeller, *The Film Minister*, p. 93.

48   Harlan, *Im Schatten meiner Filme*, p. 137.

49   Hans Hinkel to Hans Zerlett, 21 December 1944, in which her name becomes a verb 'to zarahleandern', to sing in bass. Bundesarchiv, Berlin (cited hereafter as BArch), ehemalige BDC, Zerlett file, JO 124.

50   M. Loiperdinger and K. Schönekäs, '*Die grosse Liebe*: Propaganda im Unterhaltungsfilm', in R. Rother, ed., *Bilder Schreiben Geschichte: Der Historiker im Kino* (Berlin 1991), p. 143.

51   K. Wendtland, *Geliebter Kientop: Jahrgang 1941–42* (Berlin, n.d.), p. 103 cited in Kreimeier, *The Ufa Story*, p. 317.

52   Moeller, *The Film Minister*, p. 164.

53   Kreimeier, *The Ufa Story*, p. 301.

54   Moeller, *The Film Minister*, pp. 182–3.

55   Kreimeier, *The Ufa Story*, p. 302.

56   L. Kinkel, *Die Scheinwerferin: Leni Riefenstahl und das 'Dritte Reich'* (Hamburg and Vienna, 2002), p. 226.

57   B. Drewniak, *Der Deutsche Film 1938–1945: ein gesamt Überblick* (Dusseldorf, 1987), pp. 619, 625–7; Albrecht, *Nationalsozialistische Filmpolitik*, pp. 220–1.

58   G. Sadoul, *Le cinéma pendant la guerre, 1939–1945* (Paris, 1954), p. 31; F. Courtade and P. Cadars, *Histoire du cinéma nazi* (Toulouse, 1972), p. 300; Leiser, *Nazi Cinema*, pp. 15–16.

59   M. Silberman, *German Cinema: Texts in Context* (Detroit, MI, 1995), p. 82.

60   J. Fox, *Filming Women in the Third Reich* (Oxford, 2000), p. 94.

61   Ibid., p. 91; R. Reimer, 'Turning Inward: Helmut Käutner's Films', in R. Reimer, ed., *Cultural History through a National Socialist Lens* (Rochester, NY, and Woodbridge, 2000), p. 220; Leiser, *Nazi Cinema*, p. 65.

62   Ibid., pp. 222–6; Silberman, *German Cinema*, p. 95.

63   Silberman, *German Cinema*, p. 82.

64   Wetzel and Hagemann, *Zensur*, p. 72.

65   Reimer, 'Turning Inward: Helmut Käutner's Films', pp. 221, 238, n.4.

66   Wetzel and Hagemann, *Zensur*, p. 73.

67   Courtade and Cadars, *Histoire du cinéma nazi*, p. 299

68   Reimer, 'Turning Inward', pp. 233–4.

69   L.A. Bawden, ed., *Oxford Companion to Film* (New York and London, 1976), p. 149.

70   Fröhlich, *Goebbels Tagebücher* (Munich, 1998), pt 1, vol viii, p. 245 (30 July 1940).

71   M. Rökk, *Herz mit Paprika* (Berlin, 1974), p. 157.

72   Ibid., pp. 155–7.

73   Ibid., p. 158.

74   Kreimeier, *The Ufa Story*, pp. 303–4.

75   F. Hippler, *Die Verstrickung: Einstellungen und Rückblenden* (Dusseldorf, 1982), pp. 253–5. See also above, Chapter 11.

76   Bauer, *Deutsche Spielfilmalmanach*, pp. 645–76.

77 For a different view see S. Lowry, 'Ideology and Excess in Nazi Melodrama: The Golden City', *New German Critique*, 74 (1998), esp. p. 147.

78 U. von der Osten, *NS-filme im Kontext sehen! 'Staatspolitisch besonders wertvolle' Filme der Jahre 1934–1938* (Munich, 1998), p. 229.

79 C. Zuckmayer, *Geheimreport* (Göttingen, 2002), pp. 69–73.

80 For these ambiguities see J. Herf, *Reactionary Modernism: Technology, Culture and Politics in Weimar and the Third Reich* (Cambridge, 1984).

81 J. Fox, *Filming Women in the Third Reich* (Oxford and New York, 2000), p. 170.

82 Harlan, *Im Schatten meiner Filme*, pp.148–9.

83 Fox, *Filming Women in the Third Reich*, p. 176; T. Mason, 'Women in Germany, 1925–1940, Family, Welfare and Work, Conclusion', *History Workshop Journal* (1976), pp. 17, 18, also reproduced in J. Caplan, ed., *Nazism, Fascism and the Working Class: Essays by Tim Mason* (Cambridge, 1995) pp. 196–7.

84 R. Rother, 'Suggestion der Farben: die Doppelproduktion *Immensee* und *Opfergang*', in H.M. Bock and M. Töteberg, eds, *Das Ufa-Buch* (Hamburg, 1992), p. 453.

85 Harlan, *Im Schatten meiner Filme*, p. 164.

86 Fox, *Filming Women in the Third Reich*, pp. 201–5.

87 Harlan, *Im Schatten meiner Filme*, p. 164.

88 Rother, 'Suggestion der Farben', p. 454.

89 P. Paret, '*Kolberg* (Germany 1945) as Historical Film and Historical Document', in J.W. Chambers, II and D. Culbert, eds, *World War II: Film and History* (New York, 1996), p. 50; Harlan, *Im Schatten meiner Filme*, p. 183.

90 V. Klemperer, *I Shall Bear Witness: The Diaries of Victor Klemperer, 1942–45*, trans. M. Chalmers (London, 1999), pp. 400–1.

91 Welch, *Propaganda and the German Cinema*, p. 202 n.83.

92 *Daily Telegraph and Morning Post* 3 January 1945. I am grateful to Barbara Rogers for finding this information.

93 Paret, '*Kolberg*', p. 48.

94 Harlan, *Im Schatten meiner Filme*, p. 183.

95 One had been submitted in 1935, according to *Film Kurier*, 6 March 1935, no. 55, cited in K. Kanzog, '*Staatspolitisch besonders wertvolle*': ein handbuch zu 30 deutschen Spielfilmen der Jahre 1934 bis 1945 (Munich, 1994), p. 356 n.6.

96 Ibid., p. 362. *Colberg. Historisches Schauspiel in fünf Akten* (Berlin 1868) was also republished in 1917.

97 Fröhlich, *Goebbels Tagebücher* (Munich, 1993), pt 2, vol viii, p. 221 (7 May 1943).

98 Ibid., p. 51.

99 Hinkel to Goebbels, 6 December 1944 and 8 December 1944, RMVP T70, US National Archives at College Park.

100 Harlan, *Im Schatten meiner Filme*, pp. 192–3; Kanzog, '*Staatspolitisch besonders wertvolle*', p. 361 n.182, also cites BAR55/664, f.7 f., and OMGUS-Akten, Institut für Zeitgeschichte, Munich, 10/13–21.

101 Paret, '*Kolberg*', pp. 47, 64 n.1; R. Aurich, 'Film als Durchhalteration: *Kolberg* von Veit Harlan', in Bock and Töteberg, *Das Ufa-Buch*, p. 462.

102 Paret, '*Kolberg*', p. 64 n.1.

103 Paret, '*Kolberg*', p. 64 n.1, gives the period of filming as fourteen months, but this includes the additional changes required by Goebbels late in 1944. Shooting ended in the summer of 1944. Aurich, on the other hand, gives only ten months: 'Film als Durchhalteration: *Kolberg* von Veit Harlan', p. 462. See also D. Culbert, 'The Goebbels Diaries and Poland's Kotobrzeg Today', in Chambers and Culbert, *World War II*, p. 71.

104 Fröhlich, *Goebbels Tagebücher* (Munich 1996), pt 2, vol xiv, pp. 310–11 (1 December 1944).

105 Ibid., p. 331 (2 December 1944).

106 Hinkel to Goebbels, 8 December 1944, RMVP T70, US National Archives at College Park.

107 Fröhlich, *Goebbels Tagebücher*, pt 2, vol xiv (23 December 1944), pp. 469–70, and H.-C. Blumenberg, *Das Leben geht weiter*, p. 174, cited in Culbert, 'The Goebbels Diaries and Poland's Kotobrzeg Today', p. 72.

108 Hinkel to Goebbels, 26 December 1944, RMVP T70, National Archives at College Park.

109 Hinkel to Goebbels, 18 January 1945, ehemalige BDC, Harlan File.

110 Ibid.

111 Heinrichsdorff to Goebbels, 24 January 1945, ehemalige BDC, Harlan File.

112 Ibid.

113 Hinkel to Goebbels, 26 January 1945, RMVP T70, National Archives at College Park.

114 Aurich, 'Film als Durchhalteration', p. 464.

Notes to Chapter 13: Film and the 'Final Solution'

1 D. Welch, *Propaganda and the German Cinema*, 2nd edn (London, 2001), p. 166.

2 Ibid.

3 K. Hoffmann, 'Propagandistic Problems of German Newsreels in World War II', *Historical Journal of Film, Radio and Television*, 24 (2004), p. 133.

4 Ibid., p. 134.

5 H. von Wedel, *Die Propagandatruppen der Deutschen Wehrmacht* (Neckargemund, 1962), p. 70, cited in Hoffmann, 'Propagandistic Problems of German Newsreels in World War II', p. 134.

6 Welch, *Propaganda and the German Cinema*, p. 170.

7 Ibid., pp. 169–70.

8 F. Moeller, *The Film Minister: Goebbels and the Cinema in the 'Third Reich'*, trans. M. Robinson (Stuttgart and London, 2000), p. 156.

9 S. Kracauer, 'The Conquest of Europe on the Screen: The Nazi Newsreel, 1939–40', *Social Research*, 3 (1943), p. 339. His 'Propaganda and the Nazi War Film', 1942, originally issued by the Museum of Modern Art Film Library, is reproduced in *From Caligari to Hitler* (Princeton, NJ, 1947), pp. 275–331.

10 Graham Greene, 'The Cinema News Reels at Various Cinemas', *Spectator*, 29 September 1939. I am grateful to Susan Szczetnikowicz for drawing my attention to this review.

11 S. Tegel, 'Third Reich Newsreels: An Effective Tool of Propaganda?', *Historical Journal of Film, Radio and Television*, 24 (2004), p. 152.

12   Kracauer, 'The Conquest of Europe on the Screen', p. 339.

13   R. Herzstein, *The War that Hitler Won: The Most Infamous Propaganda Campaign in History* (London, 1978), p. 224.

14   J. Baird, *The Mythical World of Nazi Film Propaganda* (Minneapolis, 1974), pp. 166–8; P. Bucher, 'Goebbels und die Deutsche Wochenschau: Nationalsozialistische Filmpropaganda im Zweiten Weltkrieg, 1939–1945', *Militärgeschichtliche Mitteilungen*, 2 (1986), p. 57.

15   Herzstein, *The War that Hitler Won*, p. 231.

16   Hoffmann, 'Propagandistic Problems of German Newsreels in World War II', p. 137.

17   R. Vande Winkel, 'Nazi Newsreels in Europe, 1939–1945: The Many Faces of Ufa's Foreign Weekly Newsreel (*Auslandstonwoche*) versus German's Weekly Newsreel (*Deutsche Wochenschau*)', *Historical Journal of Film, Radio and Television*, 24 (2004), p. 10.

18   Baird, *The Mythical World of Nazi War Propaganda*, p. 196.

19   Herzstein, *The War that Hitler Won*, p. 231.

20   Vande Winkel, 'Nazi Newsreels in Europe, 1939–1945', pp. 9–10.

21   Hoffmann, 'Propagandistic Problems of German Newsreels in World War II', p. 140.

22   Bucher, 'Goebbels und die Deutsche Wochenschau', p. 58.

23   E. Fröhlich, ed., *Die Tagebücher von Joseph Goebbels* (Munich, 1996), pt 2, vol iii, p. 92 (11 January 1942).

24   Welch, *Propaganda and the German Cinema*, p. 170.

25   Fröhlich, *Goebbels Tagebücher* (Munich, 1993), pt 2, vol. viii, p. 366 (25 May 1943); (Munich, 1998), pt 1, vol. viii, p. 304 (3 September 1940).

26   *Ufa Tonwoche*, no. 472 (censor 20 September 1939); *Deutsche Wochenschau*, no. 558 (censor 14 May 1941); *Deutsche Wochenschau*, no. 567 (censor 16 July 1941); *Deutsche Wochenschau*, no. 570 (censor 6 August 1941).

27   *Sonderbericht der Wochenschau* (6 April 1941).

28   *Deutsche Wochenschau*, no. 566 (censor 10 July 1941); *Deutsche Wochenschau*, no. 567 (censor 16 July 1941).

29   *Deutsche Wochenschau*, no. 570 (censor 6 August 1941).

30   R.C. Raack, 'Nazi Film Propaganda and the Horrors of War', *Historical Journal of Film, Radio and Television* 6 (1986), p. 194 n.9. The Polish archive had originally dated it to 1941.

31   Ibid., p. 191.

32   Ibid., pp. 17–18.

33   R. Gellately, *Backing Hitler: Consent and Coercion in Nazi Germany* (Oxford, 2001), pp. 121–50, 261.

34   W. Laqueur, *The Terrible Secret* (London, 1980), pp. 12, 13.

35   Ibid., pp. 13, 27–28, 110. These comments were made on 18 and 26 December 1942.

36   *Wochenschau*, no. 558 (14 May 1941), had an item on the Jews of Belgrade involved in clearing rubble.

37   I. Kershaw, *Hitler*, ii, *Nemesis: 1936–1945* (London, 2000), p. 459.

38   Quoted in Baird, *The Mythical World of Nazi War Propaganda*, p. 6.

39   Ibid., p. 192.

40   Helmut Heiber, ed., *Goebbels Reden, 1939–45*, ii (Düsseldorf, 1972), p. 177.

41   Ibid., pp. 178–9.

42   Cited in Baird, *The Mythical World of Nazi War Propaganda*, pp. 195–6.

43   Goebbels, 'Das Jahr 2000', in *Das Reich*, 25 February 1946, cited in Baird, *The Mythical World of Nazi War Propaganda*, p. 245.

44   Ibid., p. 196.

45   V. Klemperer, *The Language of the Third Reich: LTI – Lingua Tertii Imperii: a Philologist's Notebook*, trans. M. Brady (London and New Brunswick, NJ, 2000), pp. 172–81. The chapter entitled 'The Jewish War' takes its title from a Lion Feuchtwanger novel, *The Jewish War* (1931), which was translated into English as *Josephus*.

46   D. Hollstein, *Jud Süss und die Deutschen: Antisemitische Vorurteile im nationalsozialistichen Spielfilm* (Berlin, 1983), pp. 58–61.

47   Rentschler, *The Ministry of Illusion*, p. 361.

48   Hollstein, *Jud Süss und die Deutschen*, p. 61. This sequence however, does not appear in the Imperial War Museum copy. Either the copy has been cut though John Kelson, *Catalogue of Forbidden Films* (Trowbridge, 1996) does not mention such a sequence. Kelson examined all the feature films, many of which were denied exhibition in The British zone of control and compiled a catalogue in 1981 (subsequently reprinted). The conclusion is that Hollstein may have confused it with a sequence in *Um das Menschenrecht*.

49   Moeller, *The Film Minister*, p. 93.

50   Hollstein, *Jud Süss und die Deutschen*, p. 121.

51   Ibid.

52   Film der Nation, Staatspolitisch und künstlerisch besonders wertvoll, kulturell wertvoll, volkstümlich wertvoll, anerkennenswert, volksbildend, jugendwert.

53   Goebbels, in *Das Reich*, 15 June 1941, cited in Baird, *The Mythical World of Nazi War Propaganda*, p. 146.

54   Welch, *Propaganda and the German Cinema*, p. 145.

55   Ibid., 173; K. Kanzog, *'Staatspolitisch besonders wertvolle': ein handbuch zu 30 deutschen Spielfilmen der Jahre 1934 bis 1945* (Munich, 1994), p. 320 n.158; B. Drewniak, *Der deutsche Film, 1938–1945: ein gesamt Überblick* (Düsseldorf, 1987), pp. 198ff.

56   Kanzog, 'Staatspolitisch besonders wertvolle', p. 316 n.156; Fröhlich, *Tagebücher* (Munich 1994), pt 2, vol iii, p. 412 (4 March 1942); F. Hippler, *Die Verstrickung* (Düsseldorf, 1982), p. 235–36.

57   Hollstein, *Jud Süss und die Deutschen*, p. 163.

58   Ibid., p. 127.

59   G. Craig, *Germany, 1866–1945* (New York and Oxford 1980), p. 122.

60   H. Arendt, *The Origins of Totalitarianism* (London, 1986), p. 189; M. Klotz, 'Epistemological Ambiguity and the Fascist Text', *New German Critique*, 74 (1998), p. 103 refers to the Conrad reference.

61   Klotz, 'Epistemological Ambiguity and the Fascist Text', p. 103.

62   Craig, *Germany, 1866–1945*, p. 119.

63   Hollstein, *Jud Süss und die Deutschen*, p. 132.

64   Ibid., p. 133.

65   Ibid., pp. 139, 336 n.371.

66   Initially, the Allied Military Government forbade its viewing, but the West German censors (the FSK no. 4416) passed it on 30 June 1952 subject to cuts. It was cut from 2,513 metres

to 2,169 with the antisemitic sequences removed. See also Hollstein, *Jud Süss und die Deutschen*, p. 336 n.372.

67 Ibid., pp. 261–2; E. Leiser, *Nazi Cinema*, trans. G. Mander and D. Wilson (London 1974), pp. 16–18.

68 His diary, *Tagebuch eines Verzweifelten*, first published in 1947, was later translated into English as *Diary of a Man in Despair*, trans. P. Rubens. A recent edition (London, 2000) includes an introduction by Norman Stone on the Prussian aristocracy. Stone is not the only historian to assume that Reck von Malleczewen was a Prussian aristocrat; the same mistake is made by Michael Burleigh, *The Third Reich, A New History* (London, 2000), pp. 689–91.

69 A. Kappeler, *Ein Fall von 'Pseudologia phantastica' in der deutschen Literatur; Fritz Reck-Malleczewen, Göppingen Arbeit zur Germanistik* (Göppingen, 1975), i, esp. pp. 5–12, 33–43.

70 Hollstein, *Jud Süss und die Deutschen*, pp. 142, 336 n.378.

71 Ibid., p. 149.

72 A.-I. Berndt and H. von Wedel, eds, *Deutschland im Kampf* (Berlin, 1939–44, xliii, 4 June 1941, pp. 73–9), cited in Baird, *The Mythical World of Nazi War Propaganda*, p. 152.

73 Hollstein, *Jud Süss und die Deutschen*, p. 47.

74 Ibid., p. 159.

75 U. Klaus, *Deutsche Ton Filme*, xi, 1942 (Berlin, 2002), p. 50.

76 Welch, *Propaganda and the German Cinema*, p. 253; Hollstein, *Jud Süss und die Deutschen*, p. 217.

77 Moeller, *The Film Minister*, p. 174.

78 E. Rentschler, *The Ministry of Illusion: Nazi Cinema and its Afterlife* (Cambridge, MA, 1996), p. 181. I am grateful to Horst Klaus for help in viewing *Rembrandt*.

79 Moeller, *The Film Minister*, p. 93.

80 Fröhlich, *Goebbels Tagebücher* (Munich, 1996), pt 2, vol ii, p. 196 (8 August 1941).

81 C. Schorske, *Fin-de-Siècle Vienna: Politics and Culture* (New York, 1981), p.145

82 Hollstein, *Jud Süss und die Deutschen*, p. 165.

83 Ibid., pp. 165–6.

84 Fröhlich, *Goebbels Tagebücher* (Munich, 1998), pt 1, vol. iv, p. 306 (3 September 1940).

85 Hollstein, *Jud Süss und die Deutschen*, p. 166.

86 Fröhlich, *Goebbels Tagebücher* (Munich, 1996), pt 2, vol vii, p. 580 (18 March 1943).

87 C. Zuckmayer, *Geheimreport* (Göttingen, 2000), pp. 50–1.

88 Forster, see O. Rathkolb, *Führertreu und gottbegnade: Künstlereliten im Dritten Reich* (Vienna, 1991), p. 240; Fröhlich, *Goebbels Tagebücher* (Munich, 1998), pt 1, vol. viii, pp. 98, 317, (7 May 1940, 10 September 1940).

89 P. Pulzer, *The Rise of Political Anti-Semitism in Germany and Austria* (London, 1988), p. 146.

90 T. Elsaesser with M. Wedel, eds, *The BFI Companion to German Cinema* (London, 1999), p. 105.

Notes to Chapter 14: Theresienstadt

1   Z. Lederer, *Ghetto Theresienstadt* (London, 1953), pp. 247–8.

2   Ibid., p. 258. The most recent precise figures are given by Terezin historian Vojtech Blodig in L. Becker, 'Film Documents of Theresienstadt', in T. Haggith and J. Newman, eds, *Holocaust and the Moving Image: Representations in Film and Television since 1933* (London 2005), p. 100 n.2.

3   The ninety-five metres of 16 mm film on one reel have now been transferred to 35 mm at Wytórnia Filmow Dokumentalnych I Fabularnych, Warsaw, a copy of which is now available for viewing in the Film Department at the Imperial War Museum, London. Unless otherwise stated, information pertaining to this film comes from the extensive research undertaken by Karel Margry, 'The First Theresienstadt Film (1942)', *Historical Journal of Film, Radio and Television*, 19 (1999), pp. 309–38.

4   Margry, 'The First Theresienstadt Film', pp. 309, 324.

5   Ibid., p. 314.

6   The script is at the YIVO Institute, New York, Terr. Coll. RG116 – Czechoslovakia folder 1.22.

7   Margry, 'The First Theresienstadt Film', pp. 314, 335 n.10. The former inmate and historian H.G. Adler mentions that Kien wrote two scripts: H.G. Adler, *Die verheimlichte Wahrheit: Theresienstadter Dokumente* (Tübingen, 1958), p. 275.

8   H.G. Adler, *Theresienstadt, 1941–1945, Das Antlitz einer Zwangsgemeinschaft*, 2nd edn (Tübingen: 1955), p. 178. See also Lederer, *Ghetto Theresienstadt*, pp. 128–31

9   Margry, 'The First Theresienstadt Film', p. 317. See also H. Hofer, 'The Film about Theresienstadt: A Late Report', in R. Iltis, F. Ehrmann and O. Heitlinger, eds, *Theresienstadt* (Prague, 1965), p. 195.

10 Margry, 'The First Theresienstadt Film', p. 318.

11 Dodalová's account appears anonymously in *The Black Book: The Nazi Crime against the Jewish People* (New York, 1946), pp. 292–7, 535. Yehuda Bauer, *Jews for Sale: Nazi–Jewish Negotiations 1933–1945* (New Haven, CT, 1994), p. 230.

12 Margry, 'The First Theresienstadt Film', p. 333.

13 G. Berkley, *Theresienstadt* (Boston, MA, 1993), p. 77.

14 Ibid., p. 77.

15 B. Rogers, 'British Intelligence and the Holocaust: Auschwitz and the Allies Reexamined', *The Journal of Holocaust Education*, 8 (1999), pp. 89–106.

16 J.-C. Favez, *The Red Cross and the Holocaust*, ed. and trans. J. and B. Fletcher (Cambridge, 1999), p. 274.

17 *Shoah: Un Vivant qui passé: Auschwitz 1943, Theresienstadt 1944 (A Visitor from the Living)* (1997), director Claude Lanzmann, based on an interview in 1979, and screened at the Imperial War Museum conference, 'Holocaust, Genocide and the Moving Image: Film and Television Representations since 1933', April 2001; R. Farr, 'Some reflections on Claude Lanzmann's Approach to the Examination of the Holocaust', in Haggith and Newman, *Holocaust and the Moving Image*, pp. 161, 165.

18 Ibid., pp. 44, 73–4.

19 K. Margry, '"Theresienstadt" 1944–1945: The Nazi Propaganda Film Depicting the

Concentration Camp as Paradise', *Historical Journal of Film, Radio and Television*, 12 (1992), p. 149.

20 Bauer, *Jews for Sale*, pp. 145–95, esp. p. 170.

21 Margry, 'Theresienstadt (1944–1945)', p. 153. The fragments have been restored to the correct order by Margry, and a video copy is available from the Center for Jewish Film, Brandeis University, Waltham, Massachusetts.

22 Margry, 'Theresienstadt, 1944–1945', pp. 149–50.

23 Ibid., pp. 148–9.

24 B. Felsmann and K. Prümm, *Kurt Gerron – Gefeiert und Gejagt 1897–1944* (Berlin, 1992), pp. 18–26.

25 Ibid., p. 206.

26 Ibid., p. 80.

27 Ibid., pp. 79–80.

28 An interview appears in the film documentary *Kurt Gerrons Karussell* (1999), directed by Ilona Ziok.

29 Margry, 'Theresienstadt, 1944–1945', pp. 149–50.

30 Ibid., p. 152.

31 The Gerron film notes can be found in the Rijksinstituut voor Oorlogsdokumentatie, Amsterdam, Adler Collection, folder 12F, most of which is reproduced in Adler, *Die verheimlichte Wahrheit: Theresienstadter Dokumente*.

32 Some accounts refer to Gerron as being deported in September, but Margry, the most reliable source, gives October. See Margry, 'Theresienstadt, 1944–1945', p. 153. Felsmann reports that the Berlin Landeswohneramt, in a communication to her dated 26 November 1991, gives his date of death as 15 November 1944. See Felsmann and Prümm, *Kurt Gerron*, pp. 112, 236c n.235.

33 As recounted in *Kurt Gerrons Karussell*. See also the comment by the Czech actress Vera Schönova (later in Israel known as Nava Shan) quoted in F. Gehl, 'Zwischen Kabarett und KZ', in H.-M. Bock and M. Töteberg, eds, *Das Ufa-Buch* (Hamburg, 1992), p. 313.

34 Felsmann interview with Fric, summer 1991, in Felsmann and Prümm, *Kurt Gerron*, p. 141.

35 H.G. Adler has been more sympathetic to the members of the Council than to Gerron.

36 Margry, 'Theresienstadt 1944–1945', pp. 152–3.

37 Felsmann interview with Fric, in Felsmann and Prümm, *Kurt Gerron*, p. 142.

38 Margry, 'Theresienstadt 1944–1945', pp. 152–3.

39 Ibid., p. 152.

40 E. Makarova, S. Makarov and V. Kuperman, *University over the Abyss: The Story behind 489 Lecturers and 2309 Lectures in KZ Theresienstadt 1942–1944* (Jerusalem, 2000), pp. 457–8.

41 Berkley, *Theresienstadt*, p. 135.

42 Makarova, Makarov and Kuperman, *University over the Abyss*, p. 416.

43 Ibid., pp. 156–8, for the order of the sequences, based on stills, the Spier drawings, film fragments and other evidence.

44 Reproduced in Felsmann and Prümm, *Kurt Gerron*, pp. 123–39.

45 As recounted in *Kurt Gerrons Karussell* (1997), directed by Ilona Ziok.

46 Adler, *Die verheimlichte Wahrheit*, p. 336.

47 R.M. Friedman, 'Theresienstadt: The Film about "The Town which the Führer Donated to the Jews"', in *Remembering for the Future: The Impact of the Holocaust on the Contemporary World* (Oxford, 1988), ii, p. 1701.
48 Adler, *Die verheimlichte Wahrheit*, p. 344.
49 H. Hofer, 'The Film about Terezin: A Belated Report', in R. Iltis *et al.*, *Terezin* (Prague, 1965), p. 183.
50 Prümm, *Kurt Gerron*, p. 231.
51 Ibid.
52 Favez, *Red Cross*, p. 268.

Notes to Chapter 15: Liberation

1 J. Struk, *Photographing the Holocaust: Interpretations of the Evidence* (London, 2004), pp. 140–2, 148–9; D. Bloxham, *Genocide on Trial: War Crimes Trials and the Formation of Holocaust History and Memory* (Oxford, 2001), p. 82. See also S. Milton, 'Photography as Evidence of the Holocaust', *History of Photography*, 23 (1999), p. 309.
2 B. Zelizer, *Remembering to Forget: Holocaust Memory through the Camera's Eye* (Chicago, 1998), pp. 51–2, 61. *Life* provided photographic coverage, 28 August 1944, followed by *Illustrated London News*, 14 October 1944.
3 J. Bridgman, *The Liberation of the Camps* (London, 1990), p. 17.
4 Bloxham, *Genocide on Trial*, p. 82.
5 Ibid., p. 26.
6 T. Haggith, 'Filming the Liberation of Bergen-Belsen', in T. Haggith and J. Newman, eds, *Holocaust and the Moving Image: Representations in Film and Television since 1933* (London, 2005), p. 33; S. Szczetnikowicz, 'British Newsreels and the Plight of European Jews: 1933–1945', PhD thesis, University of Hertfordshire (2006), p. 243.
7 H. Arendt, *The Origins of Totalitarianism* (London, 1986), p. 446.
8 Raye Farr, 'Some Reflections on Claude Lanzmann's Approach to the Examination of the Holocaust', in Haggith and Newman, *Holocaust and the Moving Image* (London, 2005), p. 164; C. Lanzmann, in 'Le Lieu et la Parole', *Cahiers du cinéma*, no. 374 (July/August, 1985), republished in B. Cuau, M. Deguy, R. Ertel and C. Lanzmann, *Au sujet de Shoah, le film de Claude Lanzmann* (Paris, 1990), p. 295.
9 D. Reifarth and V. Schmidt Linsesen, 'Die Kamera der Täter, Text aus Fotogeschichte', 3, in H. Heer and K. Naumann, eds, *Vernichtungskrieg: Verbrechen der Wehrmacht, 1941–1944* (Hamburg, 1995), p. 485; G. Schoenberner, *The Yellow Star: The Persecution of the Jews in Europe, 1933–1945*, trans. S. Sweet (London, 1969), pp. 7, 221; Milton, 'Photography as Evidence of the Holocaust', p. 306; Struk, *Photographing the Holocaust*, pp. 70–3.
10 M. Hirsch, 'Surviving Images', in B. Zelizer, ed., *Visual Culture and the Holocaust* (London, 2001), pp. 233–5; A. Rossino, 'Eastern Europe through German Eyes: German Soldiers' Photographs, 1939–1944', *History of Photography*, 23 (1999), p. 313.
11 Rossino, 'Eastern Europe through German Eyes', p. 313; Struk, *Photographing the Holocaust*, pp. 74–99.

12 Milton, 'Photography as Evidence of the Holocaust', p. 303; Zelizer, *Remembering to Forget*, p. 44.

13 Ibid., pp. 303, 306, 307; Struk, *Photographing the Holocaust*, pp. 102–16

14 Ibid., p. 105.

15 B. Chamberlin, '*Death Mills*: An Early Attempt at Mass "Re-education" in Occupied Germany', in G. Kent, ed., *Historians and Archivists: Essays on Modern German History and Archival Policy* (Fairfax, VA, 1991), p. 246 n.17; Elizabeth Sussex, 'The Fate of F3080', *Sight and Sound* (1984), p. 92.

16 Zelizer, *Remembering to Forget*, p. 64.

17 Ibid.

18 Haggith, 'Filming the Liberation of Bergen-Belsen', pp. 39–40.

19 Struk, *Photographing the Holocaust*, p. 146.

20 Haggith, 'Filming the Liberation of Bergen-Belsen', p. 39.

21 I am grateful to the US Holocaust Museum for screening this colour footage at a 'Film and the Holocaust' workshop in summer 2000; L. Douglas, 'Film as Witness: Screening Nazi Concentration Camps before the Nuremberg Tribunal', 105 *Yale Law Journal*, (1995), pp. 468–9.

22 H. Caven, 'Horror in our Time', *Historical Journal of Film, Radio and Television*, 21 (2001), p. 239.

23 Ibid., pp. 228, 243; TNA (PRO) INF 1/636, Jack Beddington to E.T. Adams, 11 April 1945. I am grateful to Susan Szczetnikowicz for the last-mentioned reference.

24 Caven, 'Horror in our Time', p. 229.

25 Joanne Reilly, *Belsen: The Liberation of a Concentration Camp* (New York and London, 1998), pp. 75–7; Haggith, 'Filming the Liberation of Bergen-Belsen', p. 34; Tony Kushner, *The Holocaust and the Liberal Imagination* (Oxford, 1994) pp. 213–16; Caven, 'Horror in our Time', p. 229.

26 Caven, 'Horror in our Time', p. 209–10; PRO INF 1/6/36, E.T. Adams to Beddington, 11 April 1945.

27 Caven, 'Horror in our Time', p. 243.

28 Comment in 'Dope Sheet', *British Paramount News*, issue 1487, 31 May 1945, 2/4 cited in Szczetnikowicz, 'British Newsreels and the Plight of European Jews', p. 251.

29 Sussex, 'The Fate of F3080', p. 95.

30 S.L. Carruthers, 'Compulsory Viewing: Concentration Camp Film and German Re-Education', *Millennium, Journal of International Studies*, 30 (2001), pp. 747–53.

31 Ibid., p. 737; Telford Taylor, *The Anatomy of the Nuremberg Trials* (London, 1993), pp. 186–7.

32 *The Times*, 18 September 1945, p. 4.

33 Douglas, 'Film as Witness', p. 466.

34 Stuart Schulberg, 'Notes and Communications', *Hollywood Quarterly*, 2 (1947), p. 414.

35 Gladstone, 'Separate Intentions', p. 50.

36 Ibid., pp. 50, 62 n.2.

37 Ibid., p. 51.

38 Ibid.

39 Ibid.

40   Ibid., p. 56.

41   Sussex, 'The Fate of F3080', p. 92.

42   Gladstone, 'Separate Intentions', p. 54; Chamberlin, 'Death Mills', p. 234.

43   Ibid.; Sussex, 'The Fate of F3080', pp. 94–5.

44   Sussex, 'The Fate of F3080', p. 95; Gladstone, 'Separate Intentions', p. 56.

45   Sussex, 'The Fate of F3080', p. 95; Gladstone, 'Separate Intentions', pp. 56–7.

46   Sussex, 'The Fate of F3080', p. 97.

47   Ibid.; Gladstone, 'Separate Intentions', p. 56.

48   Gladstone, 'Separate Intentions', p. 57.

49   *KZ* is, according to Gladstone, *Welt im Film*, No. 5, the German newsreel, a copy of which is at the Imperial War Museum, London.

50   Gladstone, 'Separate Intentions', pp. 60, 64 n.39.

51   David Culbert, 'American Film Policy in the Re-education of Germany after 1945', in Nicholas Pronay and Keith Wilson, eds, *The Political Re-Education of Germany and the Allies after World War II* (Totowa, NJ, 1985), p. 177; Bloxham, *Genocide on Trial*, p. 82.

52   Chamberlin, 'Death Mills', pp. 234–6.

53   Gladstone, 'Separate Intentions', p. 60; Sussex, 'The Fate of F3080', p. 97.

54   Chamberlin, 'Death Mills', pp. 234, 238.

55   Ibid., p. 239.

56   See also Culbert, 'American Film Policy in the Re-education of Germany after 1945', p. 179.

57   See also Sussex, 'The Fate of F3080', p. 96.

58   See also Taylor, *The Anatomy of the Nuremberg Trials*, p. 200.

59   Chamberlin, 'Death Mills', p. 245.

60   It was screened under the German title, *Erinnerungen an die Lager (Memories of the Camps)*.

61   Telford Taylor, *The Anatomy of the Nuremberg Trials*, p. 200; *Trial of the Major War Criminals before the International Military Tribunal* (Nuremberg, 1948), xxx, pp. 459–62.

Filmography

BISMARCK

Producer: Tobis
Director: Wolfgang Liebeneiner; assistants: Peter Pewas, Sieg Krügler
Script: Rolf Lauckner and Wolfgang Liebeneiner
Camera: Bruno Mondi
Music: Norbert Schulze
Censor: 19 November 1940   Première: 6 December 1940
Actors: Paul Hartmann, Werner Hinz, Lil Dagover
Category: politically and artistically especially valuable; valuable for youth.

CARL PETERS

Producer: Bavaria
Director: Herbert Selpin
Script: Ernst von Salomon, Walter Zerlett-Olfenius, Herbert Selpin
Camera: Franz Koch
Music: Franz Doelle
Censor: 20 March 1941   Première: 21 March 1941
Actors: Hans Albers, Herbert Hübner, Fritz Odemar, Friedrich Otto, Karl Dannemann
Category: politically and artistically valuable, artistically valuable, educational, valuable
   for youth.

DER CHORAL VON LEUTHEN (THE CHORALE OF LEUTHEN)

Producer: Carl Froelich-Film
Director: Carl Froelich
Script: Johannes Brandt and Isle Spath-Baron based on motifs from Walter von Mole's
   novel, *Fridericus*
Camera: Hugo von Kaweczinski and Franz Planer
Music: Marc Roland
Censor: 30 January 1933   Première: 3 February 1933
Actors: Otto Gebühr, Olga Tschechowa, Veit Harlan, Wolfgang Staudte
Category: educational.

DER WEG INS FREIE (THE WAY TO FREEDOM)

Producer: Carl Froelich Studio for Ufa
Director: Rolf Hansen
Script: Harald Braun, Jacob Geis
Camera: Franz Weihmayr
Music: Theo Mackeben
Censor: 25 April 1941   Première: 25 April 1941 (unsuitable for children)
Actors: Zarah Leander, Hans Stüwe, Albert Florath, Viktor Jansen, Hilde von Stolz, Jakob
    Tiedtke Herbert Hübner, Siegfried Breuer
Category: of artistic value.

DIE DEGENHARDTS (THE DEGENHARDTS)

Producer: Tobis
Director: Werner Klingler
Script: Wilhelm Krug, Georg Zoch
Camera: Georg Bruck Bauer
Music: Herbert Windt
Censor: 28 June 1944   Première: 6 July 1944
Actors: Heinrich Georg, Erich Ziegel,Wolfgang Lukschy
Category: politically valuable, artistically valuable.

DIE ENTLASSUNG (THE DISMISSAL)

Producer: Tobis
Director: Wolfgang Liebeneiner
Script: Curt Johannes Braun, Felix von Eckhardt
Camera: Fritz Arno Wagner
Music: Herbert Windt
Censor: 28 August 1942   Première: 6 October 1942 (Berlin); (unofficial,
    15 September 1942, Stettin)
Actors: Emil Jannings, Werner Krauss, Werner Hinz, Theodor Loos, Herbert Hübner
Category: Film of the Nation, artistically and politically of value to the state.

DIE EWIGE QUELL (THE ETERNAL SOURCE)

Producer: Bavaria
Director: Fritz Kirchoff
Script: Felix Lützkendorf and Hans Joachim Beyer (after a story told by Joannes Linke)
Camera: Franz Koch, Josef Illig
Music: Anton Profes
Censor: 14 December 1939   Première: 19 January 1940 (Goslar); 23 August 1940
    (Berlin)
Actors: Eugen Klöpfer, Lina Carstens, Bernhard Minetti, Alexander Keppler, Käte Merk,
    Albert Hörrmann
Category: none.

FEINDE (ENEMIES)

Producer: Bavaria
Director: Viktor Tourjansky
Script: Emil Burri, Arthur Luethy, Viktor Tourjansky
Camera: Fritz Arno Wagner
Music: Lothar Brühne
Censor: 11 November 1940   Première: 13 November 1940
Actors: Willy Birgel, Brigitte Horney, Ludwig Schmid-Wildy, Hedwig Wangel
Category: politically valuable, artistically valuable, valuable for youth.

FLÜCHTLINGE (REFUGEES)

Producer: Ufa
Director: Gustav Ucicky
Script: Gerhard Menzel (after his own novel)
Camera: Fritz Arno Wagner
Music: Herbert Windt
Censor: 1 December 1933   Première: 8 December 1933
Actors: Hans Albers, Eugen Klöpfer, Andrews Engelmann, Käthe von Nagy
Category: of special artistic value.

DIE GOLDENE STADT (THE GOLDEN CITY)

Producer: Ufa
Director: Veit Harlan
Script: Alfred Braun, Veit Harlan after Richard Billinger's play, *Der Gigant* (*The Giant*)
Camera: Bruno Mondi (in colour)
Music: Hans-Otto Borgmann
Censor: 7 August 1942   Première: 24 November 1942
Actors: Kristina Söderbaum, Eugen Klöpfer
Category: artistically valuable; Venice Film Festival (1942) prize for colour
  cinematography and for Söderbaum's acting.

GPU (OGPU)

Producer: Ufa
Director: Karl Ritter
Script: Karl Ritter, Felix Lützenkendorf, Andrews Engelmann based on an idea from
  Engelmann
Camera: Igor Oberberg
Music: Herbert Windt
Censor: 17 July 1942   Première: 14 August 1942
Actors: Andrews Engelmann, Laura Solari, Will Quadflieg
Category: none.

GROSSE FREIHEIT NR. 7 (GREAT FREEDOM, NUMBER 7)

Producer: Ufa
Director: Helmut Käutner
Script: Helmut Käutner, Richard Nicolas
Camera: Werner Krien
Music: Werner Eisbrenner
Censor: 20 September 1944   Première: Prague 15 December 1944
Actors: Hans Albers, Ilse Werner, Hans Söhnker
Category: March 1945 further cuts required for German screening.

DER GROSSE KÖNIG (THE GREAT KING)

Producer: Tobis
Director: Veit Harlan
Script: Veit Harlan
Camera: Bruno Mondi
Music: Hans-Otto Borgmann
Censor: 28 February 1942   Première: 3 March 1942
Actors: Otto Gebühr, Kristina Söderbaum, Gustav Fröhlich, Paul Wegener, Kurt Meisel,
    Hilde Körber, Herbert Hübner, Claus Detlef Sierck
Category: Film of the Nation, politically and artistically especially valuable, culturally
    valuable, nationally valuable, educational, valuable for youth.

DIE GROSSE LIEBE (THE GREAT LOVE)

Producer: Ufa
Director: Peter Groll, Rolf Hansen
Script: Peter Groll, Rolf Hansen, based on an idea from Alexander Lernet-Holenia
Camera: Franz Weihmayr
Music: Michael Jary
Censor: 6 June 1942   Première: 12 June 1942
Actors: Zarah Leander, Viktor Staal, Paul Hörbiger
Category: politically and artistically valuable; nationally valuable.

HANS WESTMAR (1933)

Producer: Volksdeutsche Film
Director: Franz Wenzler
Script: Hanns Heinz Ewers (based on his book)
Camera: Franz Weihmayr
Music: Giuseppe Becce, Ernst Hanfstaengoel
Censor: 13 November 1933   Première: 13 December 1933
Actors: Emil Lohkamp, Carla Bartheel, Paul Wegener, Carl Auen
Category: none.

HEIMKEHR (HOMECOMING)

Producer: Wien-Film
Director: Gustav Ucicky
Script: Gerhard Menzel
Camera: Günther Anders
Music: Willy Schmidt-Gentner
Censor: 26 August 1941   Première: 10 October 1941
Actors: Paula Wessely, Carl Raddatz, Attila Hörbiger, Otto Wernicke
Category: Film of the Nation, of special political and artistic value, valuable for youth.

HITLERJUNGE QUEX (HITLER YOUTH QUEX)

Producer: Ufa
Director: Hans Steinhoff
Script: K.A. Schenzinger, B.E. Luthge
Camera: Konstantin Irmen-Tschet
Music: Hans Otto Borgmann
Censor: 7 September 1933   Première: 19 September 1933
Actors: Heinrich George, Berta Drews, Claus Clausen, Hermann Speelmans, Karl Meixner
Category: of special political and artistic value (valuable for youth added at a later date).

IMMENSEE

Producer: Ufa
Director: Veit Harlan
Script: Alfred Braun, Veit Harlan
Camera: Bruno Mondi (colour)
Music: Wolfgang Zeller
Censor: 28 September 1943   Première: 17 December 1943
Actors: Kristina Söderbaum, Carl Raddatz, Paul Klinger
Category: artistically valuable, culturally valuable, nationally valuable.

JUD SÜSS

Producer: Terra
Director: Veit Harlan
Script: Veit Harlan, Eberhard Wolfgang Möller and Ludwig Metzger
Camera: Bruno Mondi
Music: Wolfgang Zeller
Censor: 6 September 1940   Première: 24 September 1940
Actors: Ferdinand Marian, Werner Krauss, Heinrich George, Eugen Klöpfer, Kristina
    Soderbaum
Category: of special political and artistic value, valuable for youth.

KOLBERG

Producer: Ufa
Director: Veit Harlan
Script: Veit Harlan, Alfred Braun
Camera: Bruno Mondi (colour)
Music: Norbert Schultze
Censor: 26 January 1945   Première: 30 January 1945
Actors: Heinrich George, Kristina Söderbaum, Paul Wegener, Horst Caspar, Claus
    Clausen, Irene von Meyendorff, Otto Wernicke
Category: Film of the Nation, of special political and artistic value, culturally valuable,
    nationally valuable, commendable, educational, valuable for youth.

LEINEN AUS IRLAND (LINEN FROM IRELAND)

Producer: Styria Film for Wien-Film
Director: Heinz Helbig
Script: Harald Bratt from the play by Stefan von Kamare
Camera: Hans Schneeberger
Music: Anton Profes
Censor: 22 September 1939   Première: 16 October 1939
Actors: Irene von Meyendorff, Siegfried Breuer, Rolf Wanke, Oskar Sima, Fritz Imkof
Category: politically valuable, artistically valuable.

MIT VERSIEGELTER ORDER (WITH SEALED ORDERS)

Producer: Tobis
Director: Karl Anton
Script: Felix von Eckardt
Camera: Herbert Körner
Music: Fritz Wenneis, Willy Engel-Berger
Censor: 7 January 1938   Première: 14 January 1938
Actors: Victor de Kowa, Paul Harmann, Suse Graf, Tatjana Sais, Hans Stiebner
Category: artistically valuable.

MORGENROT (DAWN)

Producer: Ufa
Director: Gustav Ucicky
Script: Gerhard Menzel, based on his novel
Camera: Carl Hoffmann
Music: Herbert Windt
Censor: 26 January 1933   Première: 31 January 1933
Actors: Rudolf Forster, Adele Sandrock, Camilla Spiro
Category: artistically valuable.

MÜNCHHAUSEN

Producer: Ufa
Director: Josef von Baky
Script: Berthold Bürger (Erich Kästner)
Camera: Werner Krien, Konstantin Irmen-Tschet (trick shots)
Music: Georg Jaentzschel
Censor: 3 March 1943, 17 June 1943, 29 June 1943   Première: 5 March 1943
Actors: Hans Albers, Käte Haack, Herbert Speelmans, Brigitte Horney, Ilse Werner,
    Ferdinand Marian, Hilde von Stolz, Andrews Engelmann, Viktor Janson
Category: of special artistic value, nationally valuable.

OHM KRÜGER (UNCLE KRÜGER)

Producer: Tobis
Director: Hans Steinhoff
Script: Harald Bratt, Kurt Henser based on motifs from Arnold Krieger's novel, *Mann
    ohne Volk* (*Man without a People*)
Camera: Fritz Arno Wagner
Music: Theo Mackeben
Censor: 2 April 1941   Première: 4 April 1941
Actors: Emil Jannings, Gustaf Gründgens, Ferdinand Marian, Otto Wernicke, Werner
    Hinz, Eduard von Winterstein
Category: Film of the Nation, of special political and artistic value, culturally valuable,
    nationally valuable, valuable for youth.

OPFERGANG (SELF-SACRIFICE)

Producer: Ufa
Director: Veit Harlan
Script: Veit Harlan, Alfred Braun
Camera: Bruno Mondi (in colour)
Music: Hans-Otto Borgmann
Censor: 14 February 1944   Première: 8 December 1944
Actors: Carl Raddatz, Kristina Söderbaum, Irene von Meyendorff
Category: artistically of special value.

PETTERSON UND BENDEL (PETTERSON & BENDEL
[SWEDISH TITLE])

Producer: A.B. Wive-Film, Stockholm
Director: Per Axel Branner
Script: Gunnar Skoglund, Per Axel Branner after Waldemar Hammenhög's novel
Camera: Ake Dahlquisk
Music: Eric Bengdson
Première: Berlin, 12 July 1935 Dubbed version: 2 December 1938 (Berlin)
Actors: Adolf Jahr, Semmy Friedmann, Birgit Sergelius

German actors for dubbed version: Siegfried Schürenberg, Rudolf Schündler, Johanna
  Bassermann, Alexa von Porembsky, Wolfgang Staudte
Category: politically valuable for both the subtitled version and the dubbed version.

POUR LE MÉRITE

Producer: Ufa
Director: Karl Ritter
Script: Fred Hildenbrand and Karl Ritter
Camera: Günter Anders, Heinz Jaworsky (aerial shots)
Music: Herbert Windt
Censor: 7 December 1938   Première: 22 December 1938
Actors: Paul Hartmann, Herbert A.E. Böhme, Paul Otto, Fritz Kampers, Albert Hehn,
  Carsta Löck, Wolfgang Staudte
Category: of special political and artistic value, valuable for youth.

… REITET FÜR DEUTSCHLAND (RIDING FOR GERMANY)

Producer: Ufa
Director: Arthur Maria Rabenalt
Script: Fritz Reck von Malleczewen, Richard Riedel, Josef Maria Frank
Camera: Werner Krien
Music: Alois Melichar
Censor: 4 April 1941   Première: 11 April 1941 (Hanover); 30 May 1941
  (Berlin)
Actors: Willy Birgel, Herbert A.E. Böhme, Walter Werner, Gerhild Weber, Herbert Hübner,
  Wolfgang Staudte
Category: politically valuable, valuable for youth.

REMBRANDT

Producer: Terra
Director: Hans Steinhoff
Script: Kurt Heuser and Hans Steinhoff after Valerian Tornius's novel, *Between Darkness
  and Light*
Camera: Richard Angst
Music: Alois Melichar
Censor: 17 June 1942   Première: 19 June 1942
Actors: Ewald Balser, Hertha Feiler, Elisabeth Flickenschildt, Theodor Loos
Category: artistically valuable.

ROBERT UND BERTRAM

Producer: Tobis
Director: Hans Heinz Zerlett
Script: Hans Heinz Zerlett based on the farce by Gustav Raeder

Camera: Friedl Behn-Grund, Ernst Kunstmann (trick shots)
Music: Leo Leux
Censor: 20 June 1939   Première: 7 July 1939 (Hamburg); 14 July 1939
    (Berlin)
Actors: Ruddi Godden, Kurt Seiffert, Herbert Hübner, Fritz Kampers, Carla Rust, Inge
    von Straaten, Tatjana Sais, Ursula Deinert, Robert Dorsay, Hans Stiebner
Category: none.

EIN ROBINSON (A ROBINSON CRUSOE)

Producer: Bavaria
Director: Arnold Fanck
Script: Arnold Fanck
Camera: Albert Benitz, Hans Ertl, Sepp Allgeier
Music: Werner Bochmann
Censor: 23 April 1940   Première: 25 April 1940
Actors: Herbert A.E. Böhme, Claus Clausen, Malte Jaeger, Wolf Dietrich, Ludwig Schmid-
    Wildy
Category: of special artistic value.

ROMANZE IN MOLL (ROMANCE IN A MINOR KEY)

Producer: Tobis
Director: Helmut Käutner
Script: Willy Clever, Helmut Käutner
Camera: Georg Bruckbauer
Music: Lothar Brühne, Werner Eisbrenner
Censor: 28 January 1943   Première: 25 June 1943
Actors: Marianne Hoppe, Paul Dahlke, Ferdinand Marian, Siegfried Breuer
Category: of special artistic value.

DIE ROTHSCHILDS (THE ROTHSCHILDS)

Producer: Ufa
Director: Erich Waschneck
Script: C.M. Köhn and T. Bucholz from an idea from Mirko Jelusich
Camera: Robert Baberske
Music: Johannes Müller
Censor: 16 July 1940   Première: 17 July 1940
Actors: Carl Kuhlmann, Hilde Weissner, Herbert Hübner, Albert Florath, Erich Ponto,
    Hans Stiebner
Category: none.

SA-MANN BRANDT

Producer: Bavaria
Director: Franz Seitz
Script: Joseph Dalman and Joe Stöckel
Camera: Franz Koch
Music: Toni Thoms
Censor: 9 June 1933   Première: 14 June 1933
Actors: Otto Wernicke, Elise Aulinger, Joe Stöckel
Category: of special artistic value, educational.

ÜBER ALLES IN DER WELT (ABOVE ALL IN THE WORLD)

Producer: Ufa
Director: Karl Ritter
Script: Karl Ritter, Felix Lützkendorf
Camera: Werner Krien, Gerhard Huttala (trick shots)
Music: Herbert Windt
Censor: 14 March 1941   Première: 19 March 1941
Actors: Carl Raddatz, Fritz Kampers, Paul Hartmann, Carsta Löck
Category: politically valuable, valuable for youth.

UM DAS MENSCHENRECHT (FOR HUMAN RIGHTS)

Producer: Arya Film
Director: Hans Zöberlein and Ludwig Schmid-Wildy
Script: Hans Zöberlein
Camera: Ludwig Zahn Bartle Seyr
Music: not known
Censor: 22 December 1934   Première: 28 December 1934
Actors: Hans Sclenck, Kurt Holm Ernst Matens, Beppo Brem
Category: artistically valuable, banned [???]for youth.

UNTER DEN BRÜCKEN (UNDER THE BRIDGES)

Producer: Ufa
Director: Helmut Käutner
Script: Helmut Käutner
Camera: Igor Oberberg
Music: Bernhard Eichhorn
Censor: March 1945
Première: 12 November 1945 (Stockholm); 15 September 1950 (Göttingen); 22 March
    1951 (West Berlin)
Actors: Carl Raddatz, Gustav Knuth, Hannelore Schroth, Hildegard Knef
Category: too late for decision.

VENUS VOR GERICHT (VENUS ON TRIAL)

Producer: Bavaria
Director: Hans Heinz Zerlett
Script: Hans Heinz Zerlett
Camera: Oskar Schnirch
Music: Leo Leux
Censor: 27 May 1941   Première: 4 June 1941
Actors: Siegfried Breuer, Paul Dahlke, Hansi Knoteck, Hannes Stelzer
Category: nationally valuable.

VERRÄTER (TRAITORS)

Producer: Ufa
Director: Karl Ritter
Script: Hans Fritz Beckmann
Camera: Günther Anders, Heinz von Jaworsky (aerial shots)
Music: Harold M. Kirchstein
Censor: 19 August 1936   Première: 9 September 1936 (Nuremberg);
                               15 September 1936 (Berlin)
Actors: Lida Baarova, Willy Birgel, Theodor Loos
Category: of special political and artistic value, educational.

WIEN 1910 (VIENNA 1910)

Producer: Wien-Film
Director: E.W. Emo
Script: Gerhard Menzel
Camera: Hans Schneeberger
Music: Willy Schmidt-Gentner
Censor: 21 August 1942
Première: 26 August 1943 (Frankfurt am Main); 2 September 1943 (Berlin)
Actors: Heinrich George, Rudolf Forster, Lil Dagover, Herbert Hübner, Karl Kuhlmann,
    O.W. Fischer
Category: politically and artistically valuable.

WUNSCHKONZERT (REQUEST CONCERT)

Producer: Cine-Allianz
Director: Eduard von Borsody
Script: Felix Lützkendorf, Eduard von Borsody
Camera: Franz Weihmayr, Günther Anders, Carl Drews
Music: Werner Bochmann
Censor: 12 December 1940   Première: 30 December 1940
Actors: Ilse Werner, Carl Raddatz, Ida Wüst, Malte Jäger
Category: politically valuable, artistically valuable, nationally valuable, valuable for youth.

Bibliography

PRIMARY SOURCES (UNPUBLISHED)

BAYERISCHE HAUPTSTAATSARCHIV, MUNICH

Sammlung Rehse, 7008 Eberhard Wolfgang Möller.

BAYERISCHEN STAATSBIBLIOTHEK, HANDSCHRIFTENABTEILUNG, MUNICH

Veit Harlan, 'Wie es War … Erlebnis eines Filmregisseurs unter seinem aller höchsten Chef, dem "Schirmherrn des deutschen Films", Dr Goebbels', typescript, *c.* 1960.

BBC WRITTEN ARCHIVES, CAVENSHAM

Julius Gellner.

BUNDESARCHIV, BERLIN

R43II/389; R43II/810b
R109/ I, R109/II, R109III/16Ufa Bestände
R43II
R55
R56
R58
Z38/392, Sammlung Sänger
ZSg 102/62, Sammlung Brammer
ZSg. 101/15
Zeitschriften-Dienst
Berlin Document Center/RKK.

DEUTSCHES INSTITUT FÜR FILMKUNDE, FRANKFURT/MAIN

Jud Süss cuttings file.

STAATSANWALTSCHAFT BEI DEM LANDGERICHT HAMBURG

Strafverfahren gegen Veit Harlan, AZ 14JS.

STAATSARCHIV HAMBURG

Misc 6911, Veit Harlan.

STIFTUNG DEUTSCHE KINEMATHEK, SCHRIFTGUTARCHIV, BERLIN

Tobis-Presseheft.
Unpublished scripts:
    '*Jud Süss* ein historischer Film'. Regie: Veit Harlan, Terra Filmkunst GmbH,
       Typescript
    '*Jud Süss* ein historischer Film' (Endgültige Fassung). Eberhard Wolfgamg
       Möller and Ludwig Metzger, Rige: Dr. Peter Paul Brauer, Terra Filmkunst
       GmbH, Typescript
    'Robert und Bertram'
    'Der Feuerteufel'.

US NATIONAL ARCHIVES AT COLLEGE PARK

RG 260/OMGUS.
RMVP T70

YIVO INSTITUTE FOR JEWISH RESEARCH, NEW YORK

Terr. Coll. RG116 – Czechoslovakia folder 1.22.

INTERVIEWS

Interview with Ralph Giordano, 16 August 2002.
Interview with Leonard Miall, 7 June 2001.

PRIMARY SOURCES (PUBLISHED)

NEWSPAPERS, MAGAZINES

Der Deutsche Film
Deutsche Filmzeitung

Film-Kurier
Filmpress
Film und Mode Revue
Filmwelt
Filmwoche
Frankfurter Allegemeine Zeitung
Frankfurter Zeitung
Hamburger Tageblatt
Independent
Lichtbildbühne
Monthly Film Bulletin
Neue Zürcher Zeitung
New York Times
The Times
Variety
Völkische Beobachter

BOOKS AND ARTICLES

Barnay, L., *Erinnerungen* (Berlin, 1903).

The Black Book: The Nazi Crime against the Jewish People (New York, 1946).

Boberach, H., *Meldungen aus dem Reich* (Berlin, 1965).

Boelcke, W., ed., *Kriegspropaganda* (Stuttgart, 1966).

Brecht, B., 'Offener Brief an den Schauspieler Heinrich George (1933)', *Gesammelte Werke*, 15 (Frankfurt am Main, 1967).

Cabet, É., *Voyage en Icarie*, 2nd edn (Paris, 1842).

Culbert, D., Leni Riefenstahl's *Triumph of the Will* (Frederick, MD, 1986).

Diebow, H., *Der ewige Jude* (Munich, 1937).

Diels, R., *Lucifer ante Portas* (Zurich, n.d. [1949?]).

Domarus, M., ed., *Hitler, Reden und Proklamationen*, 2 vols in 5 parts (Munich 1963).

—, *Hitler, Speeches and Proclamations, 1932–1945*, 4 vols, trans. M. Gilbert (London, 1990).

Ellerman, A.E., *The Prince Minster of Württemberg* (London, 1897).

Ewers, H.H., *Horst Wessel: ein deutsches Schicksal* (Stuttgart, 1932).

Frenzel, E., *Judengestalten auf den deutschen Bühne: ein notwendiger Querschnitt durch 700 Jahre Rollengeschichte* (Munich, 1942).

Fröhlich, E., ed, *Die Tagebücher von Joseph Goebbels*, 25 vols. (Munich, 1987–2005).

Greene, G., 'The Cinema News Reels at Various Cinemas', *Spectator*, 29 (September, 1939).

Hadamovsky, E., *Propaganda und nationale Macht: Die Organisation der öffentlichen Meinung für die nationale Politik* (Oldenburg, 1933).

Hanfstaengl, E., *The Missing Years* (London, 1957).

Harlan, V., *Im Schatten meiner Filme* (Gütersloh, 1966).

Hauff, W., *Jud Süss* (Stuttgart, 1827).

Heiber, H., ed., *Goebbels-Reden 1932–1939* (Düsseldorf, 1971).

Hippler, F., *Betrachtungen zum Filmschaffen* (Berlin, 1942).

—, *Die Verstrickung: Einstellungen und Rückblenden* (Düsseldorf, 1982).

Hitler, A., *Mein Kampf*, trans. R. Manheim (London, 1969).

Hofer, H., 'The Film about Terezin: A Belated Report', in R. Iltis *et al.*, *Terezin* (Prague, 1965).

Klemperer, V., *I Shall Bear Witness: The Diaries of Victor Klemperer 1933–41*, trans. M. Chalmers (London, 1998).

—, *I Shall Bear Witness: The Diaries of Victor Klemperer 1942–45*, trans. M. Chalmers (London, 1999).

Kamare, S., *Leinen aus Irland: ein Lustspiel aus dem alten Österreich in vier Akten* (Berlin, 1928).

Krauss, W., *Das Schauspiel meines Lebens* (Stuttgart, 1958).

Leviné-Meyer, R., *Inside German Communism: Memoirs of Party Life in the Weimar Republic* (London, 1977).

Pardo H., and S. Schiffner, eds, *Jud Süss: Historisches und juristisches Material zum Fall Veit Harlan* (Hamburg, 1949).

Raeder, G., *Robert und Bertram: oder die lustigen Vagabunden: Posse mit Gesängen und Tänzen in vier Abtheilungen*, in *Gesammelte Komische Theaterstücke* (Leipzig, 1859).

Riefenstahl, L., *Hinter den Kulissen des Reichsparteitags-Film* (Munich, 1935).

—, *Kampf im Schnee und Eis* (Leipzig, 1933).

—, *The Sieve of Time* (London, 1992).

Rökk, M., *Herz mit Paprika* (Berlin, 1974).

Schenzinger, K.A., *Der Hitlerjunge Quex* (Berlin and Leipzig, 1932).

Schulberg, S., 'Notes and Communications', *Hollywood Quarterly*, 2 (1947), pp. 412–14.

Seraphim, H.G., ed., *Das politische Tagebuch Alfred Rosenbergs, 1934–39 und 1939–40* (Göttingen, 1955).

Short, K.R.M., ed., *Catalogue of Forbidden German Feature and Short Film Production* (Trowbridge, 1995).

Söderbaum, Kristina, *Nichts bleibt immer so: Rückblenden auf ein Leben vor und hinter der Kamera* (Bayreuth, 1983).

Speer, A., *Inside the Third Reich*, trans. R. and C. Winston (London, 1971).

Stahr, G., *Volksgemeinschaft vor der Leinwand? Der nationalsozialistische Film und sein Publicum* (Berlin, 2001).

Trial of the Major War Criminals before the International Military Tribunal, 14 November 1945–1 October 1946, vol. xxx (Nuremberg, 1948).

Wagner, R., *Prose Works*, trans. W.A. Ellis (London, 1912).

Wulf, J., *Theater und Film im dritten Reich: eine Dokumentation* (Frankfurt, 1983).

Zuckmayer, C., *Geheimreport* (Göttingen, 2002).

SECONDARY SOURCES

UNPUBLISHED THESES

Szczetnikowicz, S., 'British Newsreels and the Plight of European Jews: 1933–1945', PhD thesis, University of Hertfordshire (2006).

DOCUMENTARIES

Das Ghetto Theresienstadt: Täuschung und Wirklichkeit (1997), dir. Irmgard von zur Mühlen.

Kurt Gerrons Karussell (1999), dir. Ilona Ziok.

Zeit des Schweigen und der Dunkelheit (1982), dir. Nina Gladitz.

BOOKS

Adler, H.G., *Theresienstadt: 1941–5: Das Antlitz einer Zwangsgemeinschaft*, 2nd edn (Tübingen, 1955).

—, *Die verheimlichte Wahrheit: Theresienstadter Dokumente* (Tübingen, 1958).

Ahren, Y., S. Hornshøy-Møller and C. Melchers, *'Der ewige Jude' oder wie Goebbels hetzte, Untersuchungen zum nationalsozialistischen Propagandafilm* (Aachen, 1990).

Albrecht, G., *Der Film im 3. Reich: eine Dokumentation* (Karlsruhe, 1979).

—, *Nationalsozialistische Filmpolitik: eine soziologische Untersuchung über die Spielfilme des dritten Reich* (Stuttgart, 1969).

Altenloh, E., *Zur Soziologie des Kinos* (Jena, 1914).

Anderson, G.K., *The Legend of the Wandering Jew* (Providence, RI, 1965).

Arendt, H., *The Origins of Totalitarianism* (London, 1986).

Baird, J., *The Mythical World of Nazi War Propaganda* (Minneapolis, 1974).

—, *To Die for Germany: Heroes in the Nazi Pantheon* (Bloomington, IN, and Indianapolis, 1990).

Balfour, M., *Propaganda in War* (London, 1979).

Bardèche, M. and R. Brasillach, *Histoire du cinéma*, édition définitive (Paris, 1943).

Barnouw, E., *Documentary: A History of the Non-Fiction Film*, 2nd edn (Oxford, 1983).

Barsam, R.M., *Filmguide to* Triumph of the Will (Bloomington, IN, 1975).

Bauer, A., *Deutsche Spielfilmalmanach, 1929–1950* (Munich, 1950).

Bauer, Y., *Jews for Sale: Nazi–Jewish Negotiations 1933–1945* (New Haven, CT, 1994).

Bawden, L.A., ed., *Oxford Companion to Film* (New York and London, 1976).

Becker, W., *Film und Herrschaft: Organisationsprinzipien und Organisationsstrukturen der nationalsozialistischen Filmpropaganda* (Berlin, 1973).

Bergfelder, T., E. Carter and D. Göktürk, eds, *The German Cinema Book* (London, 2002).

Berkley, G., *Theresienstadt* (Boston, MA, 1993).

Billington, M., *Peggy Ashcroft* (London, 1989).

Bloxham, D., *Genocide on Trial: War Crimes Trials and the Formation of Holocaust History and Memory* (Oxford, 2001).

Bridgman, J., *The Liberation of the Camps* (London, 1990).

Bucher, P., *Wochenschauen und Dokumentarfilme 1895–1950 im Bundesarchiv-Filmarchiv* (Koblenz, 1984).

Bullock, A., *Hitler, a Study in Tyranny*, 2nd edn (London, 1962).

Burleigh, M., *The Third Reich, A New History* (London, 2000).

Burrin, P., *Hitler and the Jews: The Genesis of the Holocaust*, trans. P. Southgate (London, 1992).

Cadars, P. and F. Courtade, *Histoire du cinéma nazi* (Toulouse, 1972).

—, *Veit Harlan. Anthologie du cinéma* 72 (Paris, 1973).

Carter, E., *Dietrich's Ghosts: The Sublime and the Beautiful in Third Reich Film* (London, 2004).

Chambers, J.W. and D. Culbert, eds, *World War II: Film and History* (New York, 1996).

Chapman, J., *Cinemas of the World* (London, 2003).

Craig, G., *Germany, 1866–1945* (New York and Oxford, 1980).

Cull, N., D. Culbert and D. Welch, eds, *Propaganda and Mass Persuasion: A Historical Encyclopedia, 1500 to the Present* (Santa Barbara, CA, Denver, CO, and Cambridge, 2003).

Dahlke, G. and K. Günter, eds, *Deutsche Spielfilme von den Anfängen bis 1933* (Berlin, 1993).

Dawidowicz, L., *The War against the Jews, 1933–45* (London, 1975).

Drewniak, B., *Der Deutsche Film 1938–1945: ein gesamt Überblick* (Dusseldorf, 1987).

Eisner, L., *The Haunted Screen*, trans. R. Greaves (Berkeley, CA, and Los Angeles, 1973).

Elsaesser T., *Weimar Cinema and After: Germany's Historical Imaginary* (London and New York, 2000).

—, with M. Wedel, eds, *The BFI Companion to German Cinema* (London, 1999).

Favez, J.-C., *The Red Cross and the Holocaust*, ed. and trans. John and Beryl Fletcher (Cambridge, 1999).

Felsmann, B. and Prümm, K., *Kurt Gerron—Gefeiert und Gejagt 1897–1944* (Berlin, 1992).

Ferguson, N., *The Pity of War* (London, 1998)

—, *The World's Banker: The History of the House of Rothschild* (London, 1998).

Flechtheim, O., *Die KPD in der Weimarer Republik* (Frankfurt, 1969).

Fox, J., *Filming Women in the Third Reich* (Oxford, 2000).

Fraenkel, E., *Goebbels: eine Biographie* (Cologne, 1960).

—, *Unsterblicher Film* (Munich, 1957).

Fraenkel, E. and R. Manvell, *German Cinema* (London, 1971).

Friedländer, S., *Nazi Germany and the Jews: The Years of Persecution, 1933–1939* (London, 1997).

Friedman, R.-M., *L'Image et son Juif* (Paris, 1983).

Furhammar L., and F. Isaksson, *Politics and Film*, trans. K. French (London, 1971).

Gabler, N., *An Empire of their Own: How the Jews Invented Hollywood* (New York, 1988).

Gellately, R., *Backing Hitler: Consent and Coercion in Nazi Germany* (Oxford, 2001).

Gerber, B., *Jud Süss: Aufstieg und Fall im frühen 18. Jahrhundert* (Hamburg, 1990).

Gilman, S., *The Jew's Body* (New York, 1991).

Haasis, H., *Joseph Süss Oppenheimer, genannt Jud Süss, Finanzier, Freidenker, Justizopfer* (Hamburg, 1998).

Hake, S., *German National Cinema* (London and New York, 2002).

—, *Popular Cinema of the Third Reich* (Austin, TX, 2001).

Hamann, B., *Vienna, a Dictatorship's Apprenticeship*, trans. T. Thornton (New York and Oxford, 1999).

Herf, J., *Reactionary Modernism: Technology, Culture and Politics in Weimar and the Third Reich* (Cambridge, 1984).

Herz, R., *Hoffmann und Hitler* (Munich, 1994).

Herzstein, R., *The War that Hitler Won: The Most Infamous Propaganda Campaign in History* (New York, 1978).

Hinton, D.B., *The Films of Leni Riefenstahl*, 3rd edn (Lanham, MD, and London, 2000).

Hoffmann, H., *The Triumph of Propaganda: Film and National Socialism*, trans. J. Broadwin and V.R. Berghahn (Providence, RI, and Oxford, 1996).

Hollstein, D., *Jud Süss und die Deutschen: antisemitische Vorurteile im nationalsozialistischen Spielfilm* (Berlin, 1983).

Hornshøy-Møller, S., *Quellenkritische Analyse eines antisemitischen Propagandafilm* (Göttingen, 1995).

Hull, D.S., *Film in the Third Reich* (Berkeley, CA, and Los Angeles, 1969).

Jacobsen, W., A. Kaes and J. Prinzler, eds, *Geschichte des deutschen Films* (Stuttgart, 1993).

Johnson, C., *Utopian Communism in France: Cabet and the Icarians, 1839–1851* (Ithaca, NY, 1974).

Kalbus, O., *Vom Werden deutscher Filmkunst*, 2 vols (Altona, 1935).

Kanzog, K., *'Staatspolitisch besonders wertvolle': Ein handbuch zu 30 deutschen Spielfilmen der Jahre 1934 bis 1945* (Munich, 1994).

Kappeler, A., *Ein Fall von 'Pseudologia phantastica' in der deutschen Literatur; Fritz Reck-Malleczewen, Göppingen Arbeit zur Germanistik*, 2 vols (Göppingen, 1975).

Kelso, J., *Catalogue of Forbidden German Feature and Short Film Production*, ed. K.R.M. Short (Trowbridge, 1995).

Kershaw, I., *Hitler*, i, *1889–1936: Hubris* (London, 1998).

—, *Hitler*, ii, *1936–1945: Nemesis* (London, 2000).

—, *The Hitler Myth: Image and Reality in the Third Reich* (Oxford, 1987).

Kinkel, L., *Die Scheinwerferin: Leni Riefenstahl und das 'Dritte Reich'* (Hamburg and Vienna, 2002).

Klaus, U., *Deutsche Tonfilme*, (1929/30–1944/45). 13 vols (Berlin, 1993 ff).

Klemperer, V., *The Language of the Third Reich: LTI – Lingua Tertii Imperii: A Philologist's Notebook*, trans. M. Brady (London and New Brunswick, NJ, 2000).

Knilli, F., *Ich war Jud Süss: Die Geschichte des Filmstars Ferdinand Marian* (Berlin, 2000).

Knilli, F., T. Maurer, T. Radevagen and S. Zielinski, eds, Jud Süss: *Filmprotokoll, Programmheft und Einzelanalysen* (Berlin, 1983).

Koonz, C., *Mothers in the Fatherland: Women, Family and Nazi Politics* (London, 1987).

Kopenick, L., *The Dark Mirror: German Cinema between Hitler and Hollywood* (Berkeley, CA, Los Angeles and London, 2002).

Korte, H., *Der Spielfilm und das Ende der Weimarer Republik* (Göttingen, 1998).

Kracauer, S., *From Caligari to Hitler: A Psychological History of the German Film* (Princeton, NJ, 1947).

Kreimeier, K., *The Ufa Story: A History of Germany's Greatest Film Company*, trans. R. and R. Kimber (Berkeley, CA, Los Angeles and London, 1999).

Kushner, T., *The Holocaust and the Liberal Imagination* (Oxford, 1994).

Landy, M., *British Genres: Cinema and Society, 1930–1960* (Princeton, NJ, 1991).

Laqueur, W., *The Terrible Secret* (London, 1980).

Lazar, I., *Der Fall Horst Wessel* (Stuttgart and Zurich, 1980).

Lederer, Z., *Ghetto Theresienstadt* (London, 1953).

Leiser, E., *Nazi Cinema*, trans. G. Mander and D. Wilson (London, 1974).

Lesch, P., *Heim ins Ufa-Reich?: NS-Filmpolitk und die Rezeption deutscher Filme in Luxemburg 1933–1944* (Trier, 2002).

Loewy, H., *Béla Balázs, Märchen, Ritual und Film* (Berlin, 2003).

Loiperdinger, M., *Der Parteitagsfilm* Triumph des Willens: *Rituale der Mobilmachung* (Opladen, 1987).

—, ed., *Märtyrer-Legenden im NS-Film* (Opladen, 1991).

Longerich, P., *The Wannsee Conference in the Development of the 'Final Solution'* (London, 2000).

Lowry, S., *Pathos und Politik: Ideologie in Spielfilmen des Nationalsozialismus* (Tübingen, 1991).

Makarova, E., S. Makarov and V. Kuperman, *University over the Abyss: The Story behind 489 Lecturers and 2309 Lectures in KZ Theresienstadt 1942–1944* (Jerusalem, 2000).

Manvell, R. and H. Frankel, *The German Cinema* (London, 1971).

McGilligan, P., *Fritz Lang: The Nature of the Beast* (New York, 1997).

Moeller, F., *The Film Minister: Goebbels and the Cinema in the 'Third Reich'*, trans. M. Robinson (Stuttgart and London, 2000).

Monaco, P., *France and Germany during the Twenties* (New York and Amsterdam, 1976).

Murray, B., *Film and the German Left in the Weimar Republic: from Calgari to Kuhle Wampe* (Austin, TE, 1990).

Noack, Frank, *Veit Harlan* (Munich, 2000).

Nowotny, P., *Leni Riefenstahls 'Triumph des Willens'* (Dortmund, 1981).

O'Brien, M.-E., *Nazi Cinema as Enchantment: the Politics of Entertainment in the Third Reich* (Rochester, NY, and Woodbridge, 2004).

Oertel, T., *Horst Wessel, Untersuchung einer Legende* (Cologne, 1987).

Osterroth, F., *Biographische Lexikon der Sozialismus* (Hanover, 1960).

Pardo, H. and S. Schiffner, eds, *Jud Süss: Historisches und juristisches Material zum Fall Veit Harlan* (Hamburg, 1949).

Petley, J., *Capital and Culture: German Cinema, 1933–45* (London, 1979).

Petro, P., *Joyless Streets: Women and Melodramatic Representation in Weimar Germany* (Princeton, NJ, 1989).

Petzet, W., *Theater: Die Münchenerkammerspiel* (Munich, 1973).

Peukert, D., *Inside Nazi Germany: Conformity, Opposition, and Racism in Everyday Life*, trans. R. Deveson (New Haven, CT, 1987).

—, *The Weimar Republic*, trans. R. Deveson (New York, 1989).

Prawer, S.S., *Caligari's Children: The Film as Tale of Terror* (Oxford, 1980).

Proctor, R., *The Nazi War on Cancer* (Princeton, NJ, 1999).

Pulzer, P., *The Rise of Political Anti-Semitism in Germany and Austria*, 2nd edn (London, 1988).

Rathkolb, O., *Führertreu und gottbegnadet: Künstlereliten im Dritten Reich* (Vienna, 1991).

Reeves, N., *The Power of Film Propaganda: Myth or Reality?* (London, 1999).

Reilly, J., *Belsen: The Liberation of a Concentration Camp* (New York and London, 1998).

Rentschler, E., *The Ministry of Illusion: Nazi Cinema and its Afterlife* (Cambridge, MA, 1999).

Reuth, R.G., *Goebbels*, trans. K. Winston (London, 1993).

Robertson, J., *The British Board of Film Censors: Film Censorship in Britain, 1896–1950* (Beckenham, 1985).

—, *The Hidden Cinema* (London, 1989).

Rose, A., *Werwolf 1944–45* (Stuttgart, 1980).

Rose, P. L., *German Question/Jewish Question: Revolutionary Antisemitism from Kant to Wagner* (Princeton, NJ, 1990).

—, *Wagner, Race and Revolution* (London, 1992).

Rother, R., *Leni Riefenstahl: The Seduction of Genius*, trans. M. Bott (New York and London, 2002).

Sadoul, G., *Le cinéma pendant la guerre, 1939–1945* (Paris, 1954).

Saunders, *Hollywood in Berlin: American Cinema and Weimar Germany* (Berkeley, CA, Los Angeles and London, 1994).

Schnee, H., *Die Hoffinanz und der moderne Staat: Geschichte und System der Hoffaktoren an deutschen Fürstenhöfen im Zeitalter des Absolutismus* (Berlin, 1963).

Schoenberner, G., *The Yellow Star: The Persecution of the Jews in Europe, 1933–1945*, trans. S. Sweet (London, 1969).

Schorske, C., *Fin-de-Siècle Vienna: Politics and Culture* (New York, 1981).

Schulte-Sasse, L., *Entertaining the Third Reich* (Durham, NC, and London, 1996).

Sereny, G., *Albert Speer: His Battle with Truth* (London, 1996).

Silberman, M., *German Cinema: Texts in Context* (Detroit, MI, 1995).

Singer, Claude, *Le Juif Süss et la propagande nazie: l'histoire confisquée* (Paris, 2003).

Spiker, J., *Film und Kapital* (Berlin, 1975).

Stahr, G., *Volksgemeinschaft vor der Leinwand? Der nationalsozialistische Film und sein Publicum* (Berlin, 2001).

Stern, S., *Jud Süss: Ein Beitrag zur deutschen und zur jüdischen Geschichte* (Berlin, 1929).

Stern-Taeubler, S., *The Court Jew* (Philadelphia, PA, 1950).

Struk, Janina, *Photographing the Holocaust: Interpretations of the Evidence* (London, 2005).

Stutterheim, Kerstin, *Okkulte Weltvorstellungen im Hintergrund dokumentarischer Filme des 'dritten Reichs'* (Berlin, 2000).

Taylor, P., *Munitions of the Mind: A History of Propaganda from the Ancient World to the Present Era* (Manchester, 1995).

Taylor, R., *Film Propaganda: Soviet Russia and Nazi Germany*, 2nd edn (London, 1998).

Taylor, T., *The Anatomy of the Nuremberg Trials* (London, 1993).

Tegel, S., *Jew Süss, Jud Süss* (Trowbridge, 1996).

Thompson, K., *Exporting Entertainment: America in the World Film Market, 1907–1934* (London, 1985).

Thompson, K. and D. Bordwell, *Film History: An Introduction* (New York, 1994).

Thurner, E., *National Socialism and Gypsies in Austria*, trans. G.G. Schmidt (Tuscaloosa, AL, and London, 1998).

Trimborn, J., *Riefenstahl: eine deutsche Karriere. Biographie* (Berlin, 2002).

Volker, R., *"Von oben sehr erwünscht": die Filmmusik Herbert Windts im NS-Propagandafilm* (Trier, 2003).

von der Osten, U., *NS-filme im Kontext sehen! 'Staatspolitisch besonders wertvolle' Filme der Jahre 1934–1938* (Munich, 1998).

Wasserstein, B., *Britain and the Jews of Europe 1939–1945*, 2nd edn (London and New York, 1999).

Welch, D., *Germany, Propaganda and Total War 1914–1918: The Sins of Omission* (London, 2000).

—, *Propaganda and the German Cinema, 1933–1945*, 2nd edn (London, 2001).

—, *The Third Reich: Politics and Propaganda* (London, 1993).

—, ed., *Nazi Propaganda* (Beckenham, 1983).

Wetzel, K. and P. Hagemann, *Zensur: Verbotene deutsche Filme, 1933–1945* (Berlin, 1978).

Wildmann, D., *Begehrte Körper: Konstruktion und Inszenierung des 'arischen' Männnerkörpers im dritten Reich* (Würzburg, 1998).

Winston, B., *Claiming the Real: The Documentary Film Revisited* (London, 1995).

Winter, J., *Sites of Memory, Sites of Mourning: The Great War in European Cultural History* (Cambridge, 1995).

Witte, K., *Lachende Erben, Toller Tag: Film Kömodie im dritten Reich* (Berlin, 1995).

Wollenberg, H.H., *Fifty Years of German Film* (London, 1947).

Wright, R., *The Visible Wall: Jews and other Ethnic Outsiders in Swedish Film* (Carbondale and Edwardsville, IL, 1998).

Wulf, J., *Theater und Film im dritten Reich: eine Dokumentation* (Frankfurt, 1983).

Zelizer, B., *Remembering to Forget: Holocaust Memory through the Camera's Eye* (Chicago, 1998).

Zeman, Z.A.B., *Nazi Propaganda*, 2nd edn (London, 1973).

Zglinicki, F., *Der Weg des Film* (Frankfurt, 1956).

Zielinski, S., *Veit Harlan: Analysen und Materialien zur Auseinandersetzung mit einem Film-Regisseur des deutschen Faschismus* (Frankfurt, 1981).

Zimmermann, M., *Wilhelm Marr: Patriarch of Anti-semitism* (New York, 1986).

ARTICLES

Altmann, J., 'Karl Ritter's "Soldiers Films"', *Hollywood Quarterly*, 5 (1950), pp. 61–72.

—, 'Movies' Role in Hitler's Conquest of German Youth', *Hollywood Quarterly*, 3 (1949), pp. 379–86.

—, 'The Technique and Content of Hitler's War Propaganda Films: Karl Ritter and his Early Films', *Hollywood Quarterly*, 4 (1949), pp. 385–91.

Aurich, R., 'Film als Durchhalteration: *Kolberg* von Veit Harlan', in H.-M. Bock and M. Töteberg, eds, *Das Ufa-Buch* (Berlin, 1992).

Baird, J., 'From Berlin to Neu Babelsberg; Nazi Film Propaganda and *Hitler Youth Quex*', *Journal of Contemporary History*, 18 (1983), pp. 495–515.

—, 'The Great War and Literary Reaction: Hans Zöberlein as Prophet of the Third Reich', in G. Kent, ed., *Historians and Archivists: Essays on Modern German History and Archival Policy* (Fairfax, VA, 1991).

Barkhausen, B., 'Footnote to the History of Riefenstahl's "Olympia"', *Film Quarterly*, 28 (1974), pp. 8–12.

—, 'Die NSDAP als Filmproduzentin, mit Kurzübersicht: Filme der NSDAP, 1927–1945', in G. Moltmann and K.F. Reimers, eds, *Zeitgeschichte in Film- und Tondokument* (Göttingen, 1970).

Bateson, G., 'An Analysis of the Nazi Film', in M. Mead and R. Métraux, eds, *The Study of Culture at a Distance* (New York, 1953).

Bayerdörfer, H.P., '"Lokalformel" und "Bürgerpatent": Ausgrenzung und Zugehörigkeit in der Posse zwischen 1815 und 1860', in M. Porrmann and F. Vassen, eds, *Theaterverhältnisse im Vormärz*, 7 (2001).

Becker, L., 'Film Documents of Theresienstadt', in T. Haggith and J. Newman, eds, *Holocaust and the Moving Image: Representations in Film and Television since 1933* (London, 2005).

Betts, E.M., Introduction, *Jew Süss* (London, 1935).

Bock, H.-M., 'Georg Wilhelm Pabst: Documenting a Life and a Career', in E. Rentschler, ed., *The Films of G.W. Pabst: An Extraterritorial Cinema* (New Brunswick, NJ, 1990).

Bucher, P., 'Die Bedeutung des Films als historische Quelle: *"Der ewige Jude"*', in H. Duchardt and M. Schlenke, eds, *Festschrift für Eberhard Kessel zum 75. Geburtstag* (Munich, 1982).

—, 'Goebbels und die Deutsche Wochenschau: Nationalsozialistische Filmpropaganda im Zweiten Weltkrieg, 1939–1945', *Militärgeschichtliche Mitteilungen*, 2 (1986), pp. 205–53.

Carruthers, S.L., 'Compulsory Viewing: Concentration Camp Film and German Re-Education', *Millennium, Journal of International Studies*, 30 (2001), pp. 747–53.

Carsten, F.L., 'The Court Jews: Prelude to Emancipation', *Leo Baeck Yearbook*, 3 (1958), pp. 140–56.

Caven, H., 'Horror in our Time', *Historical Journal of Film, Radio and Television*, 21 (2001), pp. 205–53.

Chamberlin, B., '*Death Mills*: An Early Attempt at Mass "Re-education" in Occupied Germany', in G. Kent, ed., *Historians and Archivists: Essays on Modern German History and Archival Policy* (Fairfax, VA, 1991).

Chambers, J.W., '*All Quiet on the Western Front* (US, 1930): The Antiwar Film and the Image of the Modern War', in J.W. Chambers and D. Culbert, eds, *World War II: Film and History* (New York, 1996).

Clinefelter, J., 'A Cinematic Construction of Nazi Anti-Semitism, the Documentary *Der ewige Jude*', in R. Reimer, ed., *Cultural History through a National Socialist Lens: Essays on the Cinema of the Third Reich* (Rochester, NY, and Woodbridge, 2000).

Cole, R., 'Anglo-American Anti-Fascist Film Propaganda in a Time of Neutrality: *The Great Dictator*, 1940', *Historical Journal of Film, Radio and Television*, 21 (2001), pp. 137–52.

Culbert, D., 'American Film Policy in the Re-education of Germany after 1945', in N. Pronay and K. Wilson, eds, *The Political Re-Education of Germany and the Allies after World War II* (Totowa, NJ, 1985).

—, 'The Goebbels Diaries and Poland's Kolobrzeg Today', in J.W. Chambers and D. Culbert, eds, *World War II: Film and History* (New York, 1996).

—, 'Leni Riefenstahl and the Diaries of Joseph Goebbels', *Historical Journal of Film, Radio and Television*, 13 (1993), pp. 85–93.

—, 'The Rockefeller Foundation, The Museum of Modern Art Film Library and Siegfried Kracauer, 1941', 13 (1993), pp. 495–522.

Culbert D. and M. Loiperdinger, 'Leni Riefenstahl's *Tag der Freiheit*': the 1935 Nazi Party Rally film', *Historical Journal of Film, Radio and Television*, 12, 1 (1992), pp. 3–40.

—, 'Leni Riefenstahl, the SA, and the Nazi Party Rally Films', *Historical Journal of Film, Radio and Television*, 8 (1988), pp. 3–38.

—, 'Nuremberg 1933–1934: *Sieg des Glaubens* and *Triumph des Willens*', *Historical Journal of Film, Radio and Television*, 12, 1 (1992), pp. 3–40.

Delahaye, M., 'Leni et le Loup: entrétien avec Leni Riefenstahl par Michel Delahaye', *Cahiers du Cinéma*, 170 (September 1965), pp. 42–51, 62–3.

Dörfler, G., 'Gustav Ucicky', *Anthologie du Cinéma*, XI (1983), pp. 243–4.

Douglas, L., 'Film as Witness: Screening Nazi Concentration Camps before the Nuremberg Tribunal', 105 *Yale Law Journal* (1995), pp. 449–81.

Ecksteins, M., 'War, Memory and Politics: The Fate of the Film *All Quiet on the Western Front*', *Central European History*, 13 (1980), pp. 60–82.

Faletti, H., 'Reflections of Weimar Cinema in Nazi Propaganda Film', in R. Reimer, ed., *Cultural History through a National Socialist Lens* (Rochester, NY, and Woodbridge, 2000).

Farr, R., 'Some Reflections on Claude Lanzmann's Approach to the Examination of the Holocaust', in T. Haggith and J. Newman, eds, *Holocaust and the Moving Image: Representations in Film and Television since 1933* (London 2005).

Ferro, M., 'Dissolves in *Jud Süss*', in *Cinema and History*, trans. N. Greene (Detroit, MI, 1988).

Fischer, H.H., '"Was gestrichen ist, kann nicht durchfallen". Trauerarbeit, Vergangenheitsverdrängung oder sentimentalische Glorifizierung? Wie sich Schauspieler an ihre Arbeit im Dritten Reich erinnern', *Theater Heute*, 9 (1989), pp. 1–5.

Friedman, R.-M., 'Male Gaze and Female Reaction: Veit Harlan's *Jew Süss* (1940)', in S. Frieden, R. McCormick *et al.*, eds, *Gender and German Cinema* (Providence, RI, and Oxford, 1993).

—, 'Theresienstadt: The Film about "The Town which the Fuhrer Donated to the Jews"', in *Remembering for the Future: The Impact of the Holocaust on the Contemporary World*, ii (Oxford, 1988).

Garçon, F., 'Cinéma et histoire, Les trois discours du Juif Süss', *Annales* (1979), pp. 694–720.

Garncarz, J., 'Hollywood in Germany: The Role of American Films in Germany', in D. Ellwood and R. Kroes, eds, *Hollywood in Europe: Experiences of a Cultural Hegemony* (Amsterdam, 1994).

—, 'The Origins of Film Exhibition in Germany', in T. Bergfelder, E. Carter and D. Göktürk, eds, *The German Cinema Book* (London, 2002).

Geehr, R., J. Heineman and G. Herman, '*Wien 1910*: An Example of Nazi Antisemitism', *Film and History*, 15 (1985), pp. 50–63.

Gehl, F., 'Zwischen Kabarett und KZ', in H.-M. Bock and M. Töteberg, eds, *Das Ufa-Buch* (Hamburg, 1992).

Gilsenbach, R. and O. Rosenberg, *Berliner Zeitung*, 17, 18 February 2001.

Gladstone, K., 'Separate Intentions: The Allied Screening of Concentration Camp Documentaries in Defeated Germany in 1945–46: *Death Mills* and *Memory of the Camps*', in T. Haggith and J. Newman, eds, *Holocaust and the Moving Image: Representations in Film and Television since 1933* (London, 2005).

Goergen, J., 'Walter Ruttmann – Ein Porträt', in J. Goergen, ed., *Walter Ruttmann: Eine Dokumentation* (Berlin 1989).

Gough-Yates, K., 'The British Feature Film as a European Concern: Britain and the Emigré Film-Maker', in G. Berghaus, ed., *Theatre and Film in Exile: German Artists in Britain, 1933–1945* (Oxford, 1989).

Graham, C., '*Olympia* in America, 1938: Leni Riefenstahl, Hollywood, and the Kristallnacht', *Historical Journal of Film, Radio and Television*, 13 (1993), pp. 433–50.

Haggith, T., 'Filming the Liberation of Bergen-Belsen', in T. Haggith and J. Newman, eds, *Holocaust and the Moving Image: Representations in Film and Television since 1933* (London, 2005).

Hanlon, L., 'Film Document and the Myth of Horst Wessel', *Film and History*, 5 (1975), pp. 16–18.

Hansen, M., 'Early Silent Cinema: Whose Public Sphere?', *New German Critique*, 29 (1983), pp. 147–84.

Hirsch, M., 'Surviving Images', in B. Zelizer, ed., *Visual Culture and the Holocaust* (London, 2001).

Hofer, H., 'The Film about Terezin: A Belated Report', in R. Iltis et al., *Terezin* (Prague, 1965).

Hoffmann, K., 'Propagandistic Problems of German Newsreels in World War II', *Historical Journal of Film, Radio and Television*, 24 (2004), pp. 133–42.

Horak, J.-C., 'Zionist Film Propaganda in Germany', *Historical Journal of Film, Radio and Television*, 4, 1 (1984), pp. 49–58.

Hornshøy-Møller, S. and Culbert, D., '*Der ewige Jude* (1940): Joseph Goebbels' Unequaled Monument to Antisemitism', *Historical Journal of Film, Radio and Television*, 12 (1992), pp. 41–67.

Hull, D., '"Forbidden Fruit": The Harvest of the German Cinema 1933–1945', *Film Quarterly*, 14 (1961), pp. 16–30.

Huxley, A., 'Notes on Propaganda', *Harper's Monthly Magazine*, 174 (December 1936), pp. 32–41.

Kaes, A., 'The Debate about Cinema: Charting a Controversy, 1909–1929', *New German Critique*, 40 (1987), pp. 7–33.

—, 'Film in der Weimarer Republik', in W. Jacobsen, A. Kaes and H.H. Prinzler, eds, *Geschichte des deutschen Films* (Stuttgart, 1993).

Kershaw, I., 'How Effective was Nazi Propaganda?', in D. Welch, ed., *Nazi Propaganda* (Totowa, NJ, 1983).

Klotz, M., 'Epistemological Ambiguity and the Fascist Text: *Jew Süss, Carl Peters* and *Ohm Krüger*', *New German Critique*, 74 (1998), pp. 91–124.

Kracauer, S., 'The Conquest of Europe on the Screen: The Nazi Newsreel, 1939–40', *Social Research*, 3 (1943), pp. 337–57.

Lanzmann, C., in 'Le lieu et la parole', *Cahiers du cinéma*, no. 374 (July/August, 1985), republished in B. Cuau, M. Deguy, R. Ertel and C. Lanzmann, eds, *Au sujet de Shoah, le film de Claude Lanzmann* (Paris, 1990).

Loiperdinger, M., 'Goebbels' Filmpolitik überwältigt die Schatten der Kampfzeit: Zur Bewältigung nationalsozialistischer Vergangenheit im Jahr 1933', in M. Loiperdinger, ed., *Märtyrer-Legenden im NS-Film* (Opladen, 1991).

—, 'State Legislation, Censorship and Funding', in T. Bergfelder, E. Carter and D. Göktürk, eds, *The German Cinema Book* (London, 2002).

Loiperdinger, M. and D. Culbert, 'Leni Riefenstahl, the SA, and the Nazi Party Rally Films, Nuremberg 1933–1934: "Sieg des Glaubens" and "Triumph des Willens"', *Historical Journal of Film, Radio and Television*, 8 (1988), pp. 3–38.

Loiperdinger, M. and K. Schönekäs, '*Die Grosse Liebe* – Propaganda im Unterhaltungsfilm', in R. Rother, ed., *Bilder schreiben Geschichte: Der Historiker im Kino* (Berlin, 1991).

Lowry, S., 'Heinz Rühmann – The Archetypal German', in T. Bergfelder, E. Carter and D. Göktürk, eds, *The German Cinema Book* (London, 2002).

—, 'Ideology and Excess in Nazi Melodrama: The Golden City', *New German Critique*, 74 (1998), pp. 125–49.

Margry, K., 'The First Theresienstadt Film (1942)', *Historical Journal of Film, Radio and Television*, 19 (1999), pp. 309–38.

—, '"Theresienstadt" 1944–1945: The Nazi Propaganda Film Depicting the Concentration Camp as Paradise', *Historical Journal of Film, Radio and Television*, 12 (1992), pp. 145–62.

Marquis, A.G., 'Words as Weapons', *Journal of Contemporary History*, 13 (1978), pp. 467–98.

Mason, T., 'Women in Germany, 1925–1940: Family, Welfare and Work', Conclusion', *History Workshop Journal* (1976), pp. 5–32.

Milton, S., 'Photography as Evidence of the Holocaust', *History of Photography*, 23 (1999), pp. 303–12.

Neale, S., 'Propaganda', *Screen* (1977), pp. 9–41.

Panse, B., 'Der Reichspropagandaminister über seine besten Helfer: "Diese Künstler sind wie Kinder"', *Theater Heute*, 9 (1989), pp. 4–21.

Paret, P., 'Kolberg (Germany 1945) as Historical Film and Historical Document', in J.W. Chambers, II and D. Culbert, eds, World War II: Film and History (New York, 1996).

Peck, R., 'The Banning of Titanic: A Study of British Postwar Film Censorship in Germany', Historical Journal of Film, Radio and Television, 20 (2000), pp. 427–44.

—, 'Misinformation, Missing Information, and Conjecture: Titanic and the Historiography of Third Reich Cinema', Media History, 6, 1 (2000), pp. 59–73.

Petley, J., 'Film Policy in the Third Reich', in T. Bergfelder, E. Carter and D. Göktürk, eds, The German Cinema Book (London, 2002).

Petric, V., 'Esther Shub: Film as Historical Discourse', in T. Waugh, ed., Show us Life (Metuchen, NJ, and London, 1984).

Phillips, M.S., 'The Nazi Control of the German Film Industry', Journal of European Studies, 1 (1971).

Quaresima, L., 'Introduction', in S. Kracauer, From Caligari to Hitler: A Psychological History of the German Film, ed. L. Quaresima (Princeton, NJ, 2004).

Raack, R.C., 'Nazi Film Propaganda and the Horrors of War', Historical Journal of Film, Radio and Television, 6 (1986), pp. 189–95.

Reifarth, D. and V. Schmidt Linsesen, 'Die Kamera der Täter, Text aus Fotogeschichte', 3, in H. Heer and K. Naumann, eds, Vernichtungskrieg: Verbrechen der Wehrmacht, 1941–1944 (Hamburg, 1995).

Reimer, R., 'Turning Inward: Helmut Käutner's Films', in R. Reimer, ed., Cultural History through a National Socialist Lens (Rochester, NY, and Woodbridge, 2000).

Rogers, B., 'British Intelligence and the Holocaust: Auschwitz and the Allies Reexamined', The Journal of Holocaust Education, 8 (1999), pp. 89–106.

Rosenhaft, E., 'Working-Class Life and Working-Class Politics: Communists, Nazis and the State in the Battle for the Streets, Berlin 1928–1932', in R. Bessel and E. Feuchtwanger, eds, Social Change and Political Development in Weimar Germany (London, 1981).

Rossino, A., 'Eastern Europe through German Eyes: German Soldiers' Photographs, 1939–1944', History of Photography, 23 (1999), pp. 313–21.

Rother, R., '"Hier erhielt der Gedanke eine fest Form": Karl Ritters Regie-Karriere im Nationalsozialismus', in H.-M. Bock and M. Töteberg, eds, Das Ufa-Buch (Hamburg, 1992).

—, 'Suggestion der Farben, Die Doppelproduktion: Immensee und Opfergang', in H.-M. Bock and M. Töteberg, eds, Das Ufa-Buch (Hamburg, 1992).

Sartre, J.-P., 'Portrait of the Antisemite', trans. M. Guggenheim, in W. Kaufmann, ed., Existentialism from Dostoevsky to Sartre (New York, 1956).

Schmitt, L., 'Der Fall Veit Harlan', *Film und Mode Revue* (1952).

Sedgwick, J., 'The Market for Feature Films in Britain in 1934: A Viable National Cinema', *Historical Journal of Film, Radio and Television*, 14 (1994), pp. 15–36.

Sontag, S., 'Fascinating Fascism', in *Under the Sign of Saturn* (London, 1983).

Spector, S., 'Was the Third Reich Movie-Made? Interdisciplinarity and the Reframing of "Ideology"', *American Historical Review*, 106 (2001), pp. 460–84.

Stark, G., 'Cinema, Society and the State: Policing the Film Industry in Imperial Germany', in G. Stark and B.H. Lackner, eds, *Essays on Culture and Society in Modern Germany History* (Arlington, TX, 1982).

Stern, F., 'Kluger Kommis oder Naiver Michel: Die Varianten von *Robert und Bertram* (1915, 1928, 1939)', in J. Distelmeyer, ed., *Spass beiseite, Film ab: Jüdischer Humor und verdrängendes Lachen in der Filmkomödie bis 1945* (Hamburg, 2006).

Sussex, E., 'The Fate of F3080', *Sight and Sound*, 53 (1984), pp. 92–7.

Tegel, S., '"The Demonic Effect": Veit Harlan's Use of Jewish Extras in *Jud Süss* (1940)', *Holocaust and Genocide Studies*, 14 (2000), pp. 215–41.

—, 'Leni Riefenstahl's "Gypsy Question"', *Historical Journal of Film, Radio and Television*, 23, 1 (2003), pp. 3–10.

—, 'Leni Riefenstahl's "Gypsy Question" Revisited', *Historical Journal of Film, Radio and Television*, 26 (2006), pp. 21–43.

—, 'The Politics of Censorship: Britain's *Jew Süss* (1934) in London, New York and Vienna', *Historical Journal of Film, Radio and Television*, 15 (1995), pp. 219–44.

—, 'Third Reich Newsreels: An Effective Tool of Propaganda?', *Historical Journal of Film, Radio and Television*, 24 (2004), pp. 143–54.

—, 'Veit Harlan and the Origins of *Jud Süss*, 1938–1939: Opportunism in the Creation of Nazi Anti-Semitic Film Propaganda', *Historical Journal of Film, Radio and Television*, 16 (1996), pp. 515–31.

Thompson, K., 'Dr Caligari at the Folies-Bergère or the Success of an Avant-Garde Film', in M. Budd, ed., *The Cabinet of Dr Caligari* (New Brunswick, NJ, and London, 1990).

Thurner, E., 'Die Verfolgung der Zigeuner', in C. Mitterrutzner and G. Ungar, eds, *Widerstand und Verfolgung in Salzburg 1934–1945* (Vienna and Salzburg, 1991).

Truppner, M., '"Zeitgemässe Neu-Aufführungen" eine Text genetische Untersuchung zum U-Boot-Drama *Morgenrot*', in M. Schaudig, ed., *Positionen deutscher Filmgeschichte 100 Jahren Kinematographie: Strukturen, Diskurse, Kontexte* (Munich, 1996).

Usborne, C., 'Rebellious Girls and Pitiable Women: Abortion Narratives in Weimar Popular Culture', *German History* 23 (2005), pp. 321–38.

van Eeghen, I., '"Lieux de Mémoire" Recycled: The Denazification of German Feature Films with a Historical Subject', *European Review of History*, 4 (1997), pp. 45–71.

Vande Winkel, R., 'Nazi Germany's Fritz Hippler, 1909–2002', *Historical Journal of Film, Radio and Television*, 23 (2003), pp. 91–100.

—, 'Nazi Newsreels in Europe, 1939–1945: The Many Faces of Ufa's Foreign Weekly Newsreel (*Auslandstonwoche*) versus German's Weekly Newsreel (*Deutsche Wochenschau*)', *Historical Journal of Film, Radio and Television*, 24 (2004), pp. 5–34.

Volker, R., 'Vom Thingspiel zur filmeigenen Musik: Herbert Windt und seine Zusammenarbeit mit Leni Riefenstahl', *Filmblatt*, 21 (2003), pp. 29–37.

Welch, D., 'Nazi Propaganda and the *Volksgemeinschaft*', *Journal of Contemporary History*, 39 (April 2004), pp. 213–38.

—, 'Nazi Wartime Newsreel Propaganda', in K.R.M. Short, ed., *Film and Radio Propaganda* (London and Canberra, 1983).

Wetzel, K., 'Filmzensur im Dritten Reich: zu verbotenen deutschen Film, 1933–1945', in K. Wetzel and P. Hagemann, *Zensur: Verbotene deutsche Filme, 1933–1945* (Berlin, 1978).

Winston, B., 'Reconsidering *Triumph of the Will*: Was Hitler There?', *Sight and Sound* (1981), pp. 102–9.

Witte, K., 'Der Apfel und der Stamm: Jugend und Propaganda am Beispiel *Hitlerjunge Quex* (1933)', in W. Bucher and K. Pohl, eds, *Schock und Schöpfung: Jugendaesthetik im 20. Jahrhundert* (Stuttgart, 1986).

—, 'Der barocke Faschist:Veit Harlan und seine Filme', in K. Corino, ed., *Intellektuelle im Bann des Nationalsozialismus* (Hamburg, 1980).

—, 'How Fascist is the Punch Bowl?', *New German Critique*, 74 (1998) pp. 31–6.

—, 'The Individual Legacy of Nazi Cinema', *New German Critique*, 74 (1998), pp. 23–30.

—, 'Introduction to Siegfried Kracauer's "The Mass Ornament"', *New German Critique*, 5 (1975), pp. 59–66.

Zimmermann, C., 'From Propaganda to Modernization: Media Policy and Media Audiences under National Socialism', *German History*, 24 (2006), pp. 431–54.

Index